Real Options

Real Options

Managerial Flexibility
and Strategy
in Resource Allocation

Lenos Trigeorgis

The MIT Press
Cambridge, Massachusetts
London, England

Set in Palatino by Asco Trade Typesetting Ltd., Hong Kong.
Printed and bound in the United States of America.

Library of Congress Cataloging-in-Publication Data

Real options: managerial flexibility and strategy in resource allocation / Lenos Trigeorgis.
 p. cm.
Includes bibliographical references and index.
ISBN 0-262-20102-X
1. Capital budget. 2. Resource allocation. I. Title.
HG4028.C4T73 1996
658.15′4—dc20   95-17410
                                                             CIP

to Maria, George, Christina, my parents, and my teachers and colleagues who offered me growth options and s(t)imulation

Contents

Foreword by Scott P. Mason   ix

Preface   xi

1   **Introduction and Overview**   1

2   **Traditional Capital Budgeting**   23

3   **Option-Pricing Theory and Financial-Options Applications**   69

4   **A Conceptual Options Framework for Capital Budgeting**   121

5   **Quantifying Flexibility in Capital Budgeting: Discrete-Time Analysis**   151

6   **Quantifying Flexibility: Some Continuous-Time Analytic Models**   203

7   **Interactions among Multiple Real Options**   227

8   **Strategic Planning and Control**   257

9   **Competition and Strategy**   273

10   **Numerical Analysis**   305

11   **Applications**   341

12 Conclusions and Implications   367

Appendix   379

Notes   389
Bibliography   411
Index   421

Foreword

Flexibility has value. While this statement is obvious at the conceptual level, it is surprisingly subtle at the applied level. Professional managers have long intuited that both operating flexibility and strategic flexibility (that is, the option to alter a planned course of action in the future, given then-available information) are important elements in valuation and planning decisions. But precisely how valuable is flexibility, and how can its value be quantified? Are there various types of flexibility? If there are, how do they interact? How does the presence of competition affect the value of flexibility? Isn't the presence of flexibility fully reflected in the proper application of traditional valuation techniques like discounted cash flow, Monte Carlo simulation, or decision-tree analysis?

Thanks to the path-breaking contributions of Louis Bachelier, Paul Samuelson, Fischer Black, Myron Scholes, and Robert Merton, researchers over the last ten years have made great progress in capturing in option-based models the impact of flexibility on resource-allocation decisions. In *Real Options* Lenos Trigeorgis has brought together, and meaningfully added to, the options-based research into the value of flexibility. In this comprehensive book one will find the development of the pricing of both financial and real options, discrete-time and continuous-time formulations, full coverage of both theoretical and numerical research, and many examples of applications.

The application of the options-based framework to the valuation of flexibility is both beautiful and complex. Its beauty is in its unification of strong economic and mathematical principals in dealing with the full ramifications of uncertainty in resource-allocation and planning decisions. This comprehensive benefit comes at the cost of the complexity of actually applying option-based techniques to everyday situations, but the merits of this insight are so significant that we cannot permit them be lost to decision makers solely because of complexity. Someone must begin the long education process, moving us all toward the day when option-based approaches to capital budgeting and to strategic decisions will be as much a part of a decision maker's tool kit as discounted cash flow is today.

We are all fortunate that Lenos Trigeorgis has taken up this challenge. His command of and his love for this body of knowledge assure us that this first step will be a significant one. So do not delay; expand your mind by reading *Real Options*, after which you will surely abandon your old ways of thinking and switch (always with the option of switching back, of course) to this exciting view of real resource-allocation decisions.

Scott P. Mason
Edmund Cogswell Converse Professor of Finance and Banking
Harvard University

Preface

This book deals with the classical subject of resource allocation or project appraisal under uncertainty, particularly with the valuation of managerial operating flexibility and strategic interactions as corporate *real options*. Similar to options on financial securities, real options involve discretionary decisions or rights, with no obligation, to acquire or exchange an asset for a specified alternative price. The ability to value real options (e.g., to defer, expand, contract, abandon, switch use, or otherwise alter a capital investment) has brought a revolution to modern corporate resource allocation.

Corporate value creation and competitive position are critically determined by corporate resource allocation and by the proper evaluation of investment alternatives. American companies have been steadily losing their competitive position relative to their Japanese and German counterparts in recent decades, despite their use of more "powerful" quantitative techniques such as discounted-cash-flow (DCF) analysis. An increasing number of academics and practicing managers are now convinced that the standard approaches to corporate resource allocation have failed. They have failed because they cannot properly capture managerial flexibility to adapt and revise later decisions in response to unexpected market developments and because they cannot capture the strategic value resulting from proving a technology or capture the impact of project interdependencies and competitive interaction. In a constantly changing and uncertain world marketplace, managerial operating flexibility and strategic adaptability have become crucial to capitalizing successfully on favorable future investment opportunities and to limiting losses from adverse market developments or competitive moves. Corporate capabilities that enhance adaptability and strategic positioning provide the infrastructure for the creation, preservation, and exercise of corporate real options.

The field of capital budgeting remained stagnant for several decades. Recent developments in real options, however, have provided the tools for a revolution in this field. The insights and techniques derived from option pricing are capable of quantifying the elusive elements of managerial operating flexibility and strategic interactions thus far ignored or underestimated by the conventional net-present-value approach and by other quantitative approaches.

Interest in these developments is unusually high among academics and practitioners. This book is intended to make a scholarly contribution, advancing knowledge about the use of option theory in capital budgeting, and to offer insights into and have implications for a wide range of practical applications. The book can serve as a text or as supplementary material for the academic audience (e.g., in advanced finance courses in capital budgeting, valuation, or in option pricing), in doctoral seminars, and as a library resource. The book may also be of interest to the professional audience, including corporate planners and finance executives concerned with capital budgeting or strategic planning, particularly in industries facing a lot of uncertainty and long investment horizons. Some indirect practitioners, such as valuation experts and management and strategy consultants, may also find this a helpful reference. It may also interest academics and professionals from related areas, such as general economists and decision analysts. The book is written in such a way as to be accessible to a wider audience. Mathematical sections that can be omitted without loss of continuity are asterisked.

I owe an intellectual debt to the many scholars who have made significant contributions to this literature and to many individuals for their stimulus and generosity. The early stages of much of this work were conceived in my doctoral dissertation days at Harvard University. I am particularly grateful to Professor Scott P. Mason, chairman of my dissertation committee at Harvard, for frequent, stimulating, fruitful, and enlightening discussions, and for enthusiastic support and guidance, and to Professor Stewart C. Myers of MIT, who, amidst the tightest of schedules, always found the time over many years to stimulate and to challenge. Professor Myers read every sentence with utmost care and attention, letting no question go unasked and always offering the most insightful of comments. I could not have known better scholars to work so closely with. For their valued contributions and support, I would also like to thank Professors W. Carl Kester and Carliss Y. Baldwin at Harvard (whose early work and our initial discussions attracted me to this research), Professor George M. Constantinides of the University of Chicago (for reading my work with enthusiasm on a regular basis over the years and offering many insightful comments and encouragement), Han Smit of Erasmus University, and my colleague at Boston University Nalin Kulatilaka. I am also thankful to Gordon Sick of the University of Calgary (visiting Yale), to Michael Edleson of Harvard University, and to five anonymous MIT Press reviewers whose comments and suggestions were helpful in improving many parts of the book. At The MIT Press, acquisitions editor Terry Vaughn, manuscript editor Paul Bethge, and the other members of the staff were always very enthusiastic and supportive. Last, but not least, my family deserve special appreciation for their patience and unfailing support, despite my frequent neglect of their needs, during the long development of this work. I hope that, by systematically collecting my thoughts and those of many other important individuals, this book may spark further interest and subsequent developments in the vital and growing area of real options.

Τά πάντα ρεί
(Everything is in a state of flux.)

—Heracleitus, pre-Socratic Greek philosopher

Do I dare?
Disturb the Universe?
In a minute there is time
For decisions and revisions
Which a minute can reverse

—T. S. Eliot, "The Love Song of J. Alfred Prufrock"

Financial theory, properly applied, is critical to managing in an increasingly complex and risky business climate.... Option analysis provides a more flexible approach to valuing our [research] investments.... To me all kinds of business decisions are options.

—Judy Lewent, chief financial officer, Merck & Co., quoted in *Harvard Business Review* (January–February 1994)

Real Options

1 Introduction and Overview

An increasing number of academics and corporate practitioners have been dissatisfied with the existing methods of resource allocation. Studies of corporate practices by Donaldson and Lorsch (1983), among others, reveal a continuing discrepancy between traditional finance theory and corporate reality, suggesting that managers have often been willing to overrule traditional investment criteria in order to accommodate operating flexibility and other strategic considerations they consider just as valuable as direct cash flows. It is now widely recognized, for example, that traditional discounted-cash-flow (DCF) approaches to the appraisal of capital-investment projects, such as the standard net-present-value (NPV) rule, cannot properly capture management's flexibility to adapt and revise later decisions in response to unexpected market developments. Traditional DCF approaches make implicit assumptions concerning an "expected scenario" of cash flows and presume management's passive commitment to a certain static "operating strategy" (e.g., to initiate a capital project immediately, and to operate it continuously at base scale until the end of its prespecified expected useful life).

However, in the actual marketplace, which is characterized by change, uncertainty and competitive interactions, the realization of cash flows will probably differ from what management expected at the outset. As new information arrives and uncertainty about market conditions and future cash flows is gradually resolved, management may have valuable flexibility to alter its initial operating strategy in order to capitalize on favorable future opportunities or to react so as to mitigate losses. For example, management may be able to defer, expand, contract, abandon, or otherwise alter a project at various stages of its useful operating life.

This managerial operating flexibility is likened to financial options. A *call option* on an asset (with current value V) gives the right, with no obligation, to acquire the underlying asset by paying a prespecified price (the

Table 1.1
Common real options.

Category	Description	Important in	References
Option to defer	Management holds a lease on (or an option to buy) valuable land or resources. It can wait x years to see if output prices justify constructing a building or a plant or developing a field.	All natural-resource-extraction industries; real-estate development; farming; paper products.	McDonald and Siegel 1986; Paddock et al. 1988; Tourinho 1979; Titman 1985; Ingersoll and Ross 1992
Time-to-build option (staged investment)	Staging investment as a series of outlays creates the option to abandon the enterprise in midstream if new information is unfavorable. Each stage can be viewed as an option on the value of subsequent stages and valued as a compound option.	All R&D-intensive industries, especially pharmaceuticals; long-development capital-intensive projects (e.g. large-scale construction or energy-generating plants); startup ventures.	Majd and Pindyck 1987; Carr 1988; Trigeorgis 1993
Option to alter operating scale (e.g. to expand; to contract; to shut down and restart)	If market conditions are more favorable than expected, the firm can expand the scale of production or accelerate resource utilization. Conversely, if conditions are less favorable than expected, it can reduce the scale of operations. In extreme cases, production may be halted and restarted.	Natural-resource industries (e.g. mining); facilities planning and construction in cyclical industries; fashion apparel; consumer goods; commercial real estate.	Trigeorgis and Mason 1987; Pindyck 1988; McDonald and Siegel 1985; Brennan and Schwartz 1985
Option to abandon	If market conditions decline severely, management can abandon current operations permanently and realize the resale value of capital equipment and other assets on secondhand markets.	Capital-intensive industries (e.g. airlines, railroads); financial services; new-product introductions in uncertain markets.	Myers and Majd 1990

Category	Description	Examples	References
Option to switch (e.g. outputs or inputs)	If prices or demand change, management can change the output mix of the facility (product flexibility). Alternatively, the same outputs can be produced using different types of inputs (process flexibility).	*Output shifts:* Any good sought in small batches or subject to volatile demand (e.g. consumer electronics); toys; specialty paper; machine parts; autos. *Input shifts:* All feedstock-dependent facilities; electric power; chemicals; crop switching; sourcing.	Margrabe 1978; Kensinger 1987; Kulatilaka 1988; Kulatilaka and Trigeorgis 1994
Growth options	An early investment (e.g. R&D, lease on undeveloped land or oil reserves, strategic acquisition, information network) is a prerequisite or a link in a chain of interrelated projects, opening up future growth opportunities (e.g. new product or process, oil reserves, access to new market, strengthening of core capabilities). Like interproject compound options.	All infrastructure-based or strategic industries—esp. high tech, R&D, and industries with multiple product generations or applications (e.g. computers, pharmaceuticals); multinational operations; strategic acquisitions.	Myers 1977; Brealey and Myers 1991; Kester 1984, 1993; Trigeorgis 1988; Pindyck 1988; Chung and Charoenwong 1991
Multiple interacting options	Real-life projects often involve a collection of various options. Upward-potential-enhancing and downward-protection options are present in combination. Their combined value may differ from the sum of their separate values; i.e., they interact. They may also interact with financial flexibility options.	Real-life projects in most industries listed above.	Trigeorgis 1993; Brennan and Schwartz 1985; Kulatilaka 1994

exercise price, I) on or before a given maturity. Similarly, a *put option* gives the right to sell (or exchange) the underlying asset and receive the exercise price.[1] The asymmetry deriving from having the right but not the obligation to exercise the option lies at the heart of the option's value.

As with options on financial securities, management's flexibility to adapt its future actions in response to altered future market conditions and competitive reactions expands a capital-investment opportunity's value by improving its upside potential while limiting downside losses relative to the initial expectations of a passive management. I will argue that the resulting asymmetry caused by managerial adaptability calls for an *expanded* or *strategic* investment criterion, reflecting both value components: the traditional (static or passive) NPV of direct cash flows and the option value of operating flexibility and strategic interactions.

An options approach to capital budgeting has the potential to conceptualize and quantify the value of options from active management and strategic interactions. This value is typically manifest as a collection of "real options" embedded in capital-investment opportunities, having as underlying asset the gross project value of discounted expected operating cash inflows. Many of these real options (e.g., to defer, contract, shut down, or abandon a capital investment) occur naturally; others may be planned and built in at some extra cost from the outset (e.g., to expand capacity or build growth options, to default when investment is staged sequentially, or to switch between alternative inputs or outputs). Table 1.1 introduces the most common categories of encountered real options, the industries in which they are important, and some representative authors who have analyzed them.

1.1 The Failure of Traditional Capital Budgeting[2]

Consider the following example of the risk-treatment difficulties of traditional DCF in the presence of an option: A company wishes to value an opportunity to invest in a project (such as a research and development effort to discover a new drug) that one year later will generate an expected value of subsequent cash flows of $180 million under good conditions ($V^+ = 180$) or $60 million under bad conditions ($V^- = 60$). There is an equal probability ($q = 0.5$) of each outcome. The government, wishing to support this project, offers a guarantee (or insurance policy) to buy the entire output for $180 million if the bad conditions occur. Without the government's guarantee, the project's cash flows have an expected rate of return (or risk-adjusted discount rate) of $k = 20\%$, while the risk-free in-

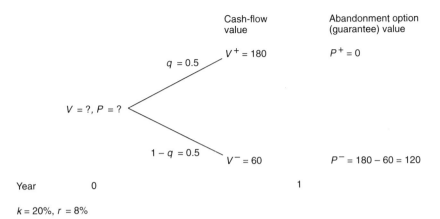

Figure 1.1
A generic project with an abandonment put option (government guarantee). V: Present value of subsequent expected cash flows from the project. P: Value of abandonment put option via guarantee. k: Risk-adjusted discount rate (expected rate of return). r: Risk-free interest rate.

terest rate is $r = 8\%$ (figure 1.1.) What is the present value of this project (V), and of the abandonment put option provided by the guarantee (P)?

The government's guarantee (insurance policy) is like a put option giving the company the right to "sell" the project's value and receive the guaranteed amount (or exercise price) of $180 million. Under the good conditions, next year the guarantee would be worthless ($P^+ = 0$); under the bad conditions it would be worth $120 million ($P^- = 180 - 60 = 120$).

Using traditional DCF techniques, one would get for the present value of the project without the guarantee

$$V = \frac{E(C_1)}{1+k} = \frac{qV^+ + (1-q)V^-}{1+k} = \frac{0.5 \times 180 + 0.5 \times 60}{1+0.20} = 100$$

and for the value of the project with the guarantee

$$V^* = \frac{0.5 \times 180 + 0.5 \times (60 + 120)}{1.20} = 150,$$

so the value of the put option provided by the guarantee would be estimated as

Value of guarantee (abandonment option)

= Project's value with guarantee (V^*)

−Project's value without guarantee (V)

$$= 150 - 100$$

$$= 50.$$

This traditional valuation assumes that the payoff of the put option (guarantee) has the same risk and can be discounted at the same rate as that for the naked project (without the guarantee), i.e.,

$$\text{Value of guarantee (put option)} = \frac{0.5 \times 0 + 0.5 \times 120}{1.20} = 50.$$

This traditional DCF calculation, however, is clearly wrong, since the flexibility to abandon the project for a guaranteed price would alter the project's risk and its discount rate. In fact, in this case (where the exercise price is the same as $V^+ = 180$) the government guarantee eliminates the project's risk entirely, since the firm will receive \$180 million under any conditions. Since the project is completely riskless, the sure \$180 million cash flow should be discounted at the 8% risk-free rate (r) rather than the standard 20% risk-adjusted rate (k). Thus, done correctly, $V^* = 180/1.08 = 166.7$, so that the correct value of the guarantee is

Value of guarantee (abandonment put option) $= 166.7 - 100 = 66.7$.

Note that this value is consistent with a negative *ad hoc* discount rate for the put option of -10% (since the guarantee acts as a hedge), as is confirmed by the following equation:

$$\text{Value of guarantee (put option)} = \frac{0.5 \times 0 + 0.5 \times 120}{1 + (-0.10)} = 66.7.$$

The traditional DCF estimate of the guarantee (50) therefore underestimates its true value as a put option (66.7) if the discount rate is not adjusted downward to reflect the change in risk brought about by active management. Although the correct discount rate for the project with the guarantee is clear (it is equal to the risk-free rate) in this special case where risk is eliminated completely, finding the correct risk-adjusted discount rate via standard DCF analysis is practically infeasible in most actual situations involving real options. Even in the simple example above, if the put exercise price were different from $V^+ = 180$ (say, 100) the correct discount rate could not be readily determined.

Employing the risk-free discount rate would be inconsistent with use of the actual probabilities ($q = 0.5$) if risk were not completely eliminated. However, as we will see in later chapters, we could still discount at the riskless rate, r ($= 0.08$), provided the cash-flow expectations were formed using "certainty-equivalent" or "risk-neutral" probabilities (p). Using $p = 0.4$ (and $1 - p = 0.6$) in this case, we can value correctly both the naked project as well as the put option (guarantee)[3]:

$$V = \frac{0.4 \times 180 + 0.6 \times 60}{1.08} = 100,$$

$$\text{Put option (guarantee)} = \frac{0.4 \times 0 + 0.6 \times 120}{1.08} = 66.7$$

(and $V^* = 100 + 66.7 = 166.7$).

Even a guarantee with a different exercise price ($100 million) that does not eliminate risk completely can be valued readily:

$$\text{Put option (guarantee at 100)} = \frac{0.4 \times 0 + 0.6 \times 40}{1.08} = 22.2.$$

The above example provides a simple illustration of the difficulty of traditional DCF methods to determine the correct discount rate when a simple abandonment option is involved. The failures of traditional capital-budgeting systems, however, are broader. After the Second World War, *capital budgeting* and *strategic planning* emerged as two complementary but distinct systems for resource allocation.[4] Myers (1987) refers to the two systems as "two cultures looking at the same problem." Capital budgeting developed into a decentralized process organized around individual or stand-alone projects based on DCF techniques. Unlike strategic planning, it focused on measurable cash flows, rather than on intangible strategic benefits that may result from developing competitive advantage, and it sought to make appropriate adjustments for the timing and riskiness of these cash flows.

However, beyond well-known problems of managerial bias in forecasting cash flows, DCF techniques were likely to be biased against capital investments with operating and strategic adaptability. As conventionally applied, DCF techniques, which were originally developed to value passive investments in bonds and stocks, were predicated on the implicit assumption of passive management, and allowed no flexibility to defer, abandon, or otherwise alter a project. In view of the rather passive attitudes of lenders and stockholders, the application of passive DCF techniques seemed, for the most part, natural.

Because of these inherent limitations, DCF techniques have not gained as much acceptance in strategic planning, where competitive advantage, market leadership, and industry structure remain dominant concepts. Corporate planners have instead focused on trading long-term or strategic measures (such as a firm's growth rate and relative market share) against short-term profitability measures (such as return on assets). The Boston Consulting Group's simple growth matrix, developed in the 1970s, was intended to capture the tradeoff between a business's short-term need for funds (or its ability to generate cash) and its long-term growth potential and market leadership. Porter's (1980) industry and competitive analysis subsequently widened the focus of strategic analysis to include suppliers, customers, and competitors. However, his framework emphasized how to take advantage of existing resources within a given market structure more than how to create resources or change a market structure. Shapiro (1985), among others, sought to link competitive advantage to the existence of internal organizational capabilities.

As businesses grew in the 1970s and the 1980s, they saw a greater need for decentralization of decision making and compartmentalization into separate divisions. Along with the new decentralized organizational structures (such as strategic business units) came decentralized resource allocation, often favoring a piecemeal approach. Organizational capabilities and infrastructure investments would often "fall through the cracks." Individual divisions could easily see the immediate tangible costs affecting their own budget but could not always recognize the remote, intangible, or contingent benefits derived from such investments, especially when these were spread across the entire organization.

A good example of the failure to recognize managerial flexibility is given in Bower 1970. National Products was considering an opportunity to invest in a flexible plant, that would allow rapid switchovers in response to changing demand and production of small lots of new products in early stages of commercial development. Operating managers had a difficult time classifying the project into a standard category. Engineers could not readily translate promised efficiency and quality improvements into measurable cash flows. The value of flexibility in the form of a variable production scale and mix of products was similarly elusive. Although justifying the project became easier (on strategic grounds) at progressively higher levels in the organization, approvals were delayed unduly and the project never took off.

By the 1980s the failures of passive DCF analysis and traditional capital-budgeting systems were becoming increasingly apparent.[5] Many experts proposed alternate techniques of analysis, and some even called for abandoning quantitative criteria in evaluating major investments. Despite the failure of DCF analysis, these very same techniques continued to be used to value corporate acquisitions and spinoffs. At about the same time, while American companies focused on the status quo as reflected in a static scenario of cash flows, a number of Japanese firms managed to incorporate real options into their manufacturing systems and their strategic thinking. By systematically developing these options, these companies achieved continuous improvement in operating flexibility and strategic adaptability, thus gaining a substantial competitive advantage over their rivals. Their success vividly illustrates the added value of active, hands-on management. The failure of traditional DCF methods to channel resources appropriately derives mainly from their inability to properly recognize the value of active management in adapting to changing market conditions or to properly capture strategic value.

1.2 Examples of Real Options

Various examples of real options that can provide management with valuable operating flexibility and strategic adaptability are provided by the capital-investment opportunity illustrated in figure 1.2, which involves an oil extraction and refinery operation. Suppose that a large oil company has a one-year lease to start drilling on undeveloped land with potential

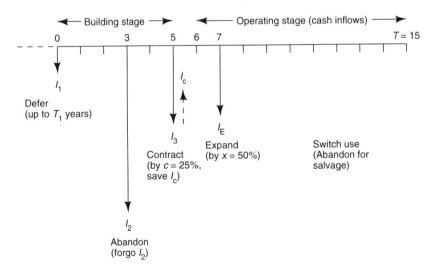

Figure 1.2
A generic project requiring a series of outlays (vertical arrows, I's), allowing management the flexibility (collection of real options) to defer, to abandon, to contract or expand investment, and to switch use.

oil reserves for up to a year ($T_1 = 1$). Initiating the project may require certain exploration costs, to be followed by outlays for roads and other infrastructure (I_1). This will be followed by outlays for the construction of a new processing facility (I_2). Extraction can begin only after construction is completed; i.e., cash flows are generated only during the "operating stage" that follows the last outlay. During construction, if market conditions deteriorate, management can choose to forgo any future planned outlays (e.g., I_2). Management may also choose to reduce the scale of operation by c%, saving a portion, I_C, of the last outlay (I_3) if the market is weak. The processing plant can be designed up front such that, if oil prices turn out higher than expected, the rate of production can be enhanced by x%, with a follow-on outlay of I_E. At any time, management may salvage a portion of its investment by selling the plant and equipment for their salvage value or switch them to an alternative-use value, A. An associated refinery—which may be designed to operate with alternative sources of energy inputs—can convert crude oil into a variety of refined products. This type of project presents a number of important real options.

Option to Defer Investment

The lease enables management to defer investment for up to a year and benefit from the resolution of uncertainty about oil prices during this period. Management will invest the outlay I_1 (i.e., exercise its option to extract oil) only if oil prices increase sufficiently, but will not commit to the project (thus saving the planned outlays) if prices decline. Just before the expiration of the lease, the investment opportunity's value will be max($V - I_1$, 0). The option to defer is thus analogous to an American call option on the gross present value of the completed project's expected operating cash flows, V, with an exercise price equal to the required outlay, I_1.[6] Since early investment implies sacrificing the value of the option to wait, this option-value loss is like an additional investment opportunity cost, justifying investment only if the value of cash benefits, V, actually exceeds the required outlay by a substantial premium. As noted in table 1.1, the option to wait is particularly valuable in resource extraction industries, farming, paper products, and real estate development, because of the high uncertainties and the long investment horizons.

Option to Default during Staged Construction (Time-to-Build Option)

In most real-life projects, the required investment is not incurred as a single up-front outlay. The actual staging of capital investment as a series of outlays over time creates valuable options to "default" at any given stage (e.g., after exploration if the reserves or oil prices turn out very low). Thus, each stage (e.g., building necessary infrastructure) can be viewed as an option on the value of subsequent stages by incurring the installment-cost outlay (e.g., I_1) required to proceed to the next stage, and can therefore be valued similar to options on options (or compound options). This option is valuable in all R&D-intensive industries (especially pharmaceuticals), in highly uncertain, long-development, capital-intensive industries (such as energy-generating plants or large-scale construction), and in venture-capital financing.

Option to Expand

If oil prices or other market conditions turn out more favorable than expected, management can accelerate the rate or expand the scale of production (by $x\%$) by incurring a follow-on cost (I_E). This is similar to a call option to acquire an additional part ($x\%$) of the base-scale project, paying I_E as exercise price. The investment opportunity with the option to expand can be viewed as the base-scale project plus a call option on future investment, i.e., $V + \max(xV - I_E, 0)$. Given an initial design choice, management may deliberately favor a more expensive technology for the built-in flexibility to expand production if and when it becomes desirable. The option to expand may also be of strategic importance, especially if it enables the firm to capitalize on future growth opportunities. When the firm buys vacant undeveloped land, or when it builds a small plant in a new geographic location (domestic or overseas) to position itself to take advantage of a developing large market, it essentially installs an option for future growth. This option, which will be exercised only if future market developments turn out favorable, can make a seemingly unprofitable (on the basis of static NPV) base-case investment worth undertaking.

Option to Contract

If market conditions turn weaker than originally expected, management can operate below capacity or even reduce the scale of operations (by $c\%$), thereby saving part of the planned investment outlays (I_C). This flexibility to mitigate loss is analogous to a put option on part ($c\%$) of the base-scale project, with exercise price equal to the potential cost savings (I_C), giving $\max(I_C - cV, 0)$. The option to contract, like the option to expand, may be particularly valuable in the case of new-product introductions in uncertain markets. The option to contract may also be important, for example, in choosing among technologies or plants with different ratios of construction cost to maintenance cost, where it may be preferable to build a plant with lower initial construction costs and higher maintenance expenditures in order to acquire the flexibility to contract operations by cutting down on maintenance if market conditions turn unfavorable.

Option to Shut Down and Restart Operations

In real life, the plant does not have to operate (i.e., extract oil) in each and every period. In fact, if oil prices are such that cash revenues are not sufficient to cover variable operating (e.g., maintenance) costs, it might be better not to operate temporarily (especially if the costs of switching between the operating and idle modes are relatively small). If prices rise sufficiently, operations can be restarted. Thus, operation in each year may be seen as a call option to acquire that year's cash revenues (C) by paying the variable costs of operating (I_V) as exercise price, i.e., $\max(C - I_V, 0)$. Options to alter the operating scale (i.e., expand, contract, or shut down) are typically found in natural-resource industries, such as mine operations, facilities planning and construction in cyclical industries, fashion apparel, consumer goods, and commercial real estate.

Option to Abandon for Salvage Value

If oil prices suffer a sustainable decline or the operation does poorly for some other reason, management does not have to continue incurring the fixed costs. Instead, management may have a valuable option to abandon the project permanently in exchange for its salvage value (i.e., the resale value of its capital equipment and other assets on the secondhand market). This option can be valued as an American put option on the project's current value (V) with an exercise price the salvage or best-alternative-use value (A), entitling management to receive $V + \max(A - V, 0)$ or $\max(V, A)$. Naturally, more general-purpose capital assets would have a higher salvage and abandonment option value than special-purpose assets. Valuable abandonment options are generally found in capital-intensive industries (such as airlines and railroads), in financial services, and in new-product introductions in uncertain markets. However, abandonment should not be exercised lightly (without fully accounting for all the costs) if it might lead to eventual loss or erosion of valuable expertise and other crucial organizational capabilities that could be applied elsewhere in the business or that could prevent the firm from participating in future technological developments (as happened with Ford and RCA).

Option to Switch Use (e.g., Inputs or Outputs)

Suppose the associated oil refinery can be designed to use alternative forms of energy (e.g., fuel oil, gas, or electricity) to convert crude oil into a variety of output products (e.g., gasoline, lubricants, or polyester). This would provide valuable built-in flexibility to switch from the current input to the cheapest future input, or from the current output to the most profitable future product mix, as the relative prices of the inputs or outputs fluctuate over time. In fact, the firm should be willing to pay a certain positive premium for such a flexible technology over the cost of a rigid alternative that confers no or less choice. Indeed, a firm that develops extra uses for its assets may have a significant advantage over its competitors. Generally, process flexibility can be achieved not only via technology (e.g., by building a flexible facility that can switch among alternative energy inputs), but also by maintaining relationships with a variety of suppliers and switching among them as their relative prices change. Subcontracting policies may allow further flexibility to contract the scale of future operations at a low cost in case of unfavorable market developments. Similarly, a multinational oil company may locate production facilities in various countries in order to acquire the flexibility to shift production to the lowest-cost producing facilities as relative costs, other local market conditions, or exchange rates change over time. Process flexibility is valuable in feedstock-dependent facilities, such as oil, electric power, chemicals, and crop switching. Product flexibility, enabling the firm to switch among alternative outputs, is more valuable in industries such as automobiles, consumer electronics, toys, and pharmaceuticals, where product differentiation and diversity are important and/or product demand is volatile. In such cases, it may be worthwhile to install a more costly flexible capacity to acquire the ability to alter product mix or production scale in response to changing market demands.

Corporate Growth Options

Corporate growth options that set the path of future opportunities are of considerable strategic importance. Suppose, in the above example, that the proposed refinery is based on a new and technologically superior process developed and tested in a pilot plant. Although in isolation the proposed facility may appear unattractive, it may be only the first in a series of similar facilities if the process is successfully developed and commercialized, and it may even lead to entirely new oil by-products. More generally, many early investments (e.g., in R&D or a pilot project, in a lease on undeveloped land or on a tract with potential oil reserves, in a strategic acquisition, or in an information-technology network) can be seen as prerequisites or links in a chain of interrelated projects. The value of these early projects derives not so much from their expected directly measurable cash flows as from the future growth opportunities they may unlock (e.g., a new-generation product or process, oil reserves, access to a new market, or strengthening of the firm's core capabilities and its strategic positioning). An opportunity to invest in a first-generation high-tech product, for example, is analogous to an option on options (an interproject compound option). Despite a seemingly negative NPV, the infrastructure, experience, and potential by-products generated during the development of the first-generation product may serve as springboards for developing lower-cost or higher-quality future generations of that product, or even for generating entirely new applications. But unless the firm makes that initial investment, subsequent generations or other applications will not even be feasible. The infrastructure and experience gained, if proprietary, can place the firm at a competitive advantage, which may even reinforce itself if learning-cost-curve effects are present. Growth options are found in all infrastructure-based or strategic industries—especially in high technology, in R&D, in industries with multiple product generations or applications (e.g., semiconductors, computers, pharmaceuticals), in multinational operations, and in strategic acquisitions.

In a more general context, such operating and strategic adaptability represented by corporate real options can be achieved at various stages during the value chain, from switching the factor input mix among various suppliers and subcontracting practices, to rapid product design (e.g., computer-aided design) and modularity in design, to shifting production among various products rapidly and cost-efficiently in a flexible manufacturing system.

1.3   Overview and Evolution of the Literature on Real Options

Early Criticisms and Remedies

The real-options revolution arose in part as a response to the dissatisfaction of corporate practitioners, strategists, and some academics with traditional techniques of capital budgeting. Well before the development of real options, corporate managers and strategists were grappling intuitively with the elusive elements of managerial operating flexibility and strategic interactions. Dean (1951), Hayes and Abernathy (1980), and Hayes and Garvin (1982) recognized early on that standard DCF criteria often undervalued investment opportunities, leading to myopic decisions, underinvestment, and eventual loss of competitive position, because they either ignored or did not properly value important strategic considerations. Decision scientists further maintained that the problem lied in the application of the wrong valuation techniques, proposing instead the use of simulation and decision-tree analysis (Hertz 1964; Magee 1964) to capture the value of future operating flexibility associated with many projects. Proponents (Hodder and Riggs 1985; Hodder 1986) have argued that the problem arises from misuse of DCF techniques as they are commonly applied in practice. Myers (1987), while confirming that part of the problem results from various misapplications of the underlying theory, acknowledges that traditional DCF methods have inherent limitations when it comes to valuing investments with significant operating or strategic options (e.g., in capturing the sequential interdependence among investments over time), suggesting that option pricing holds the best promise of valuing such investments. Trigeorgis and Mason (1987) clarify that option valuation can be seen operationally as a special, economically corrected version of decision-tree analysis that is better suited in valuing a variety of corporate operating and strategic options. Baldwin and Clark (1992) discuss the importance of organizational capabilities in strategic capital investment, while Baldwin and Trigeorgis (1993) propose remedying the underinvestment problem and restoring competitiveness by developing specific adaptive capabilities viewed as an infrastructure for acquiring and managing corporate real options. (Capital budgeting is reviewed in chapter 2 of the present volume.[7])

A New Direction: Conceptual Real-Options Approaches

Building on Myers's (1977) idea of thinking of discretionary investment opportunities as "growth options," Kester (1984) conceptually discusses strategic and competitive aspects of growth opportunities. Other general conceptual real-options frameworks are presented by Mason and Merton (1985), Trigeorgis and Mason (1987), Trigeorgis (1988), Brealey and Myers (1991), and Kulatilaka and Marcus (1988, 1992). Mason and Merton (1985) provide a good discussion of many operating and financing options, and integrate them in a discussion of the financing of a hypothetical large-scale energy project.

Foundations and Building Blocks

The quantitative origins of real options derive from the seminal work of Black and Scholes (1973) and Merton (1973) in pricing financial options. Cox, Ross, and Rubinstein's (1979) binomial approach enabled a more simplified valuation of options in discrete time. Margrabe (1978) values an option to exchange one risky asset for another, while Stulz (1982) analyzes options on the maximum (or minimum) of two risky assets and Johnson (1987) extends it to several risky assets. These papers opened up the potential to help analyze the generic option to switch among alternative uses and related options (e.g., abandon for salvage value or switch among alternative inputs or outputs). Geske (1979) values a compound option (i.e., an option to acquire another option), which in principle may be applied in valuing growth opportunities that become available only if earlier investments are undertaken. Carr (1988) combines the above two building blocks to value sequential (compound) exchange options, involving an option to acquire a subsequent option to exchange the underlying asset for another risky alternative. The above line of work has the potential, in principle, to value investments with a series of investment outlays that can be switched to alternative states of operation, and particularly to eventually help value strategic interproject dependencies.

Risk-Neutral Valuation and Risk Adjustment

The actual valuation of options in practice has been greatly facilitated by Cox and Ross's (1976) recognition that an option can be replicated (or a "synthetic option" created) from an equivalent portfolio of traded securities. Being independent of risk attitudes and of considerations of capital-market equilibrium, such risk-neutral valuation enables present-value discounting, at the risk-free interest rate, of expected future payoffs (with actual probabilities replaced by risk-neutral ones), a fundamental characteristic of "arbitrage-free" price systems involving traded securities. Rubinstein (1976) further showed that standard option-pricing formulas can be alternatively derived under risk aversion, and that continuous trading opportunities enabling a riskless hedge or risk neutrality are not really necessary. Mason and Merton (1985) and Kasanen and Trigeorgis (1994) maintain that real options may, in principle, be valued similar to financial options, even though they may not be traded, since in capital budgeting we are interested in determining what the project cash flows would be worth if they were traded in the market (that is, their contribution to the *market* value of a publicly traded firm). The existence of a traded "twin security" (or a dynamic portfolio of traded securities) that has the same risk characteristics (i.e., is perfectly correlated) with the non-traded real asset in complete markets is sufficient for real-option valuation. More generally, Constantinides (1978), Cox, Ingersoll, and Ross (1985, lemma 4), Garman (1976), and Harrison and Kreps (1979), among others, have suggested that any contingent claim on an asset, traded or not, can be priced in a world with systematic risk by replacing its expectation of the cash flow (or actual growth rate) with a certainty-equivalent growth rate (by subtracting a risk premium that would be appropriate in market equilibrium) and then behaving as if the world were risk neutral. This is analogous to discounting certainty-equivalent cash flows at the risk-free rate, rather than actually expected cash flows at a risk-adjusted rate. For traded assets in equilibrium or for real assets with no systematic risk (e.g., R&D and exploration or drilling for certain precious metals or natural resources), the certainty-equivalent or risk-neutral growth rate just equals the risk-free interest rate (minus any "dividends"). However, if the underlying asset is not traded, as may often be the case for capital-budgeting-associated options, its growth rate may actually fall below the equilibrium total expected return required of an equivalent-risk traded financial security, with the difference or "rate-of-return shortfall" necessitating a dividend-like adjustment in option valuation (McDonald and Siegel 1984, 1985). If the underlying asset is traded on futures markets, though, this dividend-like (or convenience-yield-like) return shortfall or rate of forgone earnings can be easily derived from the futures prices of contracts with different maturities (Brennan and Schwartz 1985). In other cases, however, estimating this return shortfall may require use of a market-equilibrium model (McDonald and Siegel 1985).

Valuing Each Different Real Option Separately

A series of papers gave a boost to the real-options literature by focusing on valuing quantitatively—in many cases deriving analytic, closed-form solutions—one type after another of a variety of real options, although each option was typically analyzed in isolation. As summarized in table 1.1, the option to defer or initiate investment has been examined by McDonald and Siegel (1986), by Paddock, Siegel, and Smith (1988) in

valuing offshore petroleum leases, and by Tourinho (1979) in valuing reserves of natural resources. Ingersoll and Ross (1992) reconsider the decision to wait in light of the beneficial impact of a potential future interest
rate decline on project value. Majd and Pindyck (1987) value the option
to delay sequential construction for projects that take time to build, or
there is a maximum rate at which investment can proceed. Carr (1988)
and Trigeorgis (1993a) also deal with valuing sequential or staged (compound) investments. Trigeorgis and Mason (1987) and Pindyck (1988)
examine options to alter (e.g., expand or contract) operating scale or capacity choice. The option to temporarily shut down and restart operations
is analyzed by McDonald and Siegel (1985) and by Brennan and Schwartz
(1985). Myers and Majd (1990) analyze the option to permanently
abandon a project for its salvage value seen as an American put option.
Options to switch use (e.g., outputs or inputs) are examined by Margrabe
(1978), Kensinger (1987), Kulatilaka (1988), and Kulatilaka and Trigeorgis
(1994). Baldwin and Ruback (1986) show that future price uncertainty
creates a valuable switching option that benefits short-lived projects.
Future investment opportunities seen as corporate growth options are
discussed by Myers (1977), Brealey and Myers (1991), Kester (1984,
1993), Trigeorgis and Mason (1987), Trigeorgis (1988), Pindyck (1988),
and Chung and Charoenwong (1991).

Multiple Options and Interdependencies

Despite its enormous theoretical contribution, the earlier literature is of
limited practical value because it focuses on valuing individual real options (i.e., one type of option at a time). Real-life projects are often more
complex in that they involve a collection of multiple real options, whose
values may interact. An early exception is the work of Brennan and
Schwartz (1985), who determine the combined value of the options to
shut down (and restart) a mine and to abandon it for salvage. They recognize that partial irreversibility resulting from the costs of switching the
mine's operating state may create a hysteresis or inertia effect, making it
optimal in the long term to remain in the same operating state even if
short-term cash-flow considerations seem to favor early switching. Although hysteresis is a form of interaction between early and later decisions, Brennan and Schwartz do not explicitly address the interactions
among individual option values. Trigeorgis (1993a) focuses explicitly on
the nature of real option interactions, pointing out that the presence of
subsequent options can increase the value of the effective underlying asset

for earlier options, while the exercise of prior real options may alter (e.g., expand or contract) the underlying asset itself, and hence the value of subsequent options on it. Thus, the combined value of a collection of real options may differ from the sum of separate option values. Trigeorgis identifies conditions for when option interactions are small or large, negative or positive. Kulatilaka (1995b) examines the impact of interactions among such options on their optimal exercise schedules. The recent recognition of the interdependencies of real options should make possible a smoother transition from a theoretical stage to an application phase.

The General Environment: Competition and Strategy

Real options have the potential to make a significant difference in the area of competition and strategy. Sustainable competitive advantages resulting from patents, proprietary technologies, ownership of valuable natural resources, managerial capital, reputation or brand name, scale, and market power empower companies with valuable options to grow through future profitable investments and to more effectively respond to unexpected adversities or opportunities in a changing technological, competitive, or general business environment. A number of economists addressed several competitive and strategic aspects of capital investment early on. Roberts and Weitzman (1981) find that in sequential decision making it may be worthwhile to undertake investments with negative NPV when early investment can provide information about the project's future benefits, especially when their uncertainty is greater. Baldwin (1982) finds that optimal sequential investment for firms with market power facing irreversible decisions may require a positive premium over NPV to compensate for the loss in value of future opportunities that results from undertaking an investment. Pindyck (1988) analyzes options to choose capacity under product price uncertainty when investment is, again, irreversible. Dixit (1989) considers a firm's entry and exit decisions under uncertainty, showing that in the presence of sunk or costly switching costs it may not be optimal in the long term to reverse a decision even when prices appear attractive in the short term. Bell (1995) combines Dixit's entry and exit decisions with Pindyck's capacity options for a multinational firm under volatile exchange rates. Kogut and Kulatilaka (1994) analyze the international plant-location option in the presence of mean-reverting exchange-rate volatility. Kulatilaka and Marks (1988) examine the strategic bargaining value of flexibility in a firm's negotiations with input suppliers.

From a more explicit real-options perspective, Myers (1987), Kester (1984, 1993), Trigeorgis and Mason (1987), Trigeorgis (1988), Brealey and Myers (1991), and Trigeorgis and Kasanen (1991) have initially dealt with competitive and strategic options rather conceptually. For example, Kester (1984) develops qualitatively various competitive and strategic aspects of interproject growth options, and Kester (1993) proposes a planned sequential (rather than parallel) implementation of a collection of interrelated consumer products when learning results from early product introductions (e.g., about shelf space needed for similar subsequent products) and when competitive advantage is eroding. Trigeorgis and Kasanen (1991) examine sequential project interdependencies and synergies as part of an ongoing process of strategic planning and control. Kasanen (1993) also deals with the strategic problem of the interaction between current investments and future opportunities, using a spawning matrix to determine the optimal mix of strategic and operating projects. Trigeorgis uses quantitative option-pricing techniques to examine early investment that may preempt anticipated competitive entry (1991a) and to value the option to defer investment when impacted by random competitive entry (1990b). Ang and Dukas (1991) incorporate both competitive and asymmetric information, arguing that the time pattern of discounted cash flows also matters because of the possibility of premature project termination as a result of random competitive entry. Further departing from the common assumption of perfect competition, Kulatilaka and Perotti (1992) and Smit and Trigeorgis (1993) examine how the investment decisions of a firm will influence competitive reactions and the equilibrium market price or quantity when early investment generates a strategic (e.g., cost) advantage. Smit and Ankum (1993) offer a simpler game-theoretic treatment of competitive reactions under different market structures in a real-options framework. Supplementing options analysis with game-theoretic tools capable of incorporating strategic competitive counteractions promises to be an important and challenging direction for future research.

Numerical Techniques

In the more complex real-life situations, such as those involving multiple interacting real options, analytic solutions may not exist and one may not even be always able to write down the set of partial differential equations describing the underlying stochastic processes. The ability to value such complex option situations has been enhanced, however, by various numerical analysis techniques, many of which take advantage of risk-neutral valuation. Generally, there are two types of numerical techniques for option valuation: (1) those that approximate the underlying stochastic processes directly, and are generally more intuitive, and (2) those that approximate the resulting partial differential equations. The first category includes Monte Carlo simulation, used by Boyle (1977), and various lattice approaches, such as Cox, Ross, and Rubinstein's (1979) standard binomial lattice method and Trigeorgis's (1991b) log-transformed binomial approach; the latter methods are particularly well suited to valuing complex projects with multiple embedded real options, a series of investment outlays, dividend-like effects, and option interactions. Boyle (1988) shows how lattice frameworks can be extended to handle two state variables. Hull and White (1988a) suggest a control-variate technique to improve computational efficiency when a similar derivative asset with an analytic solution is available. Examples of the second category include numerical integration and the implicit or explicit finite-difference schemes used by Brennan (1979), Brennan and Schwartz (1977, 1978), and Majd and Pindyck (1987). A number of analytic approximations are also available.

For a comprehensive review of numerical techniques, see Geske and Shastri 1985, Trigeorgis 1991b, and Hull 1989. We discuss numerical analysis in chapter 10. Other comprehensive treatments of real options can be found in Mason and Merton 1985, Trigeorgis and Mason 1987, Sick 1989, Pindyck 1991, Dixit and Pindyck 1994, and Trigeorgis 1995a. The spring 1987 issue of the *Midland Corporate Finance Journal* (vol. 5, no. 1), a 1991 special issue of *Managerial Finance* (vol. 17, no. 2/3), and part of the autumn 1993 special issue of *Financial Management* (vol. 22, no. 3) are also devoted to real options and capital budgeting.

Suggested Readings

Baldwin, C., and L. Trigeorgis. 1993. Real Options, Capabilities, TQM, and Competitiveness. Working paper 93-025, Harvard Business School.

Hayes, R., and D. Garvin. 1982. "Managing as if tomorrow mattered." *Harvard Business Review* 60, no. 3: 71–79.

Kester, W. C. 1984. "Today's options for tomorrow's growth." *Harvard Business Review* 62, no. 2: 153–160.

Myers, S. C. 1987. "Finance theory and financial strategy." *Midland Corporate Finance Journal* 5, no. 1: 6–13.

Trigeorgis, L., and S. P. Mason. 1987. "Valuing managerial flexibility." *Midland Corporate Finance Journal* 5, no. 1: 14–21.

2   Traditional Capital Budgeting

This chapter reviews the essential concepts and several traditional approaches to capital budgeting. The concept of net present value (NPV) and its "correctness" are examined on the basis of value maximization as the primary financial objective of the firm, first under certainty and then in various forms under uncertainty. Subsequently, other approaches dealing with uncertainty and complexity are examined, with simulation and decision-tree analysis emphasized. These approaches are practically useful in dealing with uncertainty and with the modeling of interdependent variables and decisions, but they stumble on the problem of the appropriate discount rate. The chapter can be glossed over or skipped by readers well acquainted with these issues.

2.1   The Financial Objective of the Firm

Capital budgeting is concerned with the allocation of resources among investment projects on a long-term basis. It involves sacrificing current consumption (making an immediate investment outlay) in order to achieve consumption in future periods. The tradeoff between consumption today and consumption in the future (or, to put it another way, between consumption and investment) is at the heart of the choices that an individual or a firm must directly or implicitly make every day.

The financial objective of an individual should thus be to choose between alternative patterns of consumption and investment opportunities so as to achieve the greatest satisfaction—i.e., to maximize his or her satisfaction or *utility* of consumption across time. The financial goal of a firm should be to help its owners achieve their objective—i.e., to maximize the utility of each of its owners. The usual focus in finance is on the residual owners of the firm, i.e., its stockholders.[1] It would be impossible, however, for a firm to directly maximize the utilities of a variety of individual stockholders having different levels of wealth, different preferences for current versus future consumption, and different attitudes toward risk (i.e., each having a different utility function). However, a firm can avoid such conflicts of interest and rest assured that it has done its best to enable each of its many owners to maximize his own utility simply by adopting as its goal the maximization of its owners' wealth.[2] In a perfect and complete capital market, the individual owners can then adjust their income flows and investment portfolios by borrowing or lending, selling or buying in the market in the amounts that would maximize each owner's particular satisfaction. If, for instance, a particular shareholder's received cash flows from the firm were insufficient for his particular preferred level of current consumption, he could borrow in the market (using his stock as collateral, if necessary) or sell the stock (or a portion thereof) to achieve his preferred balance; if the stockholder instead preferred delayed consumption, he could reinvest the excess income by lending it or purchasing stocks of low-dividend-paying firms.

How, then, can a firm help its owners maximize their wealth, which in perfect markets would subsequently enable them to maximize their utility? A firm clearly cannot maximize its residual owners' total wealth if part of this wealth is in the form of holdings in other assets or firms which may themselves be managed suboptimally. But it is a necessary condition to the maximization of its owners' wealth that the firm maximizes the part of their wealth represented in the firm itself, i.e., the market value of their shares.[3] The market value of the stockholders' shares derives, of course, from the dividends they expect to receive over time, including the final liquidation dividend (any intermediate appreciation in market value from selling the shares can be thought of as a function of expected remaining future dividends and the ultimate liquidation value), all of which depend on cash flows. It is cash flows, and not accounting profits, that the firm owners can withdraw for consumption or reinvest to generate future cash flows. Thus, the amount, timing, and riskiness of cash flows eventually determine the market value of the residual owners' stock. Any measure of performance of capital investments should therefore be consistent with the criterion of maximizing the market value of the firm's stock—which would enable the firm's owners to maximize their wealth, and subsequently their utility of consumption over time. The goal of maximizing the value of the firm is well accepted in the standard finance literature.

2.2   The Concept of Net Present Value and Its "Correctness"

In the absence of managerial flexibility, net present value (NPV) is the only currently available valuation measure consistent with a firm's objective of maximizing its shareholders' wealth, thus enabling individual shareowners to maximize their particular utilities through an associated financial decision in the capital markets. Other valuation measures used in industry, such as payback period, accounting rate of return, and internal rate of return, are acknowledged by standard finance textbooks to be inferior to NPV.

NPV under Certainty

Let us first consider the concept of NPV in a certain, two-period world (which will later be extended in a multi-period world).[4] As has been noted, the tradeoff between current consumption and future consumption lies at the heart of an individual's (or a firm's) decision problem. The combinations of income for current consumption and future consumption that would leave an individual equally satisfied can be represented by a time-preference (or utility-indifference) curve, such as U_1 in figure 2.1. Based

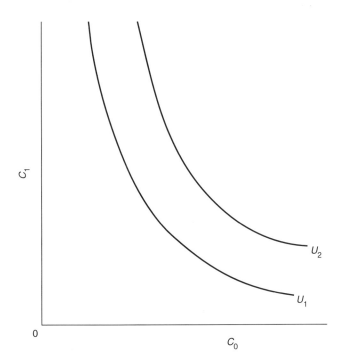

Figure 2.1
An individual's time-preference (utility) curves. Here and in the following figures, C_0 is income for current consumption and C_1 is income for future consumption.

on the assumption that the average individual prefers early consumption rather than late, the utility curves have the indicated convex shape to the origin, showing that the individual is willing to forgo current consumption only in exchange for a greater amount of future consumption. Assuming also that, other things being the same, the individual would prefer more income for consumption in any period to less, his objective should be to achieve the highest utility possible (i.e., to move away from the origin as much as possible, indicating preference for U_2 over U_1).

The individual's opportunity to consume today or in the future so as to achieve higher and higher utility is limited only by two constraints: his productive investment opportunities (to forgo current consumption and make productive investments in real assets that will be transformed into increased future wealth) and his market opportunities (to exchange between current and future income, such as when borrowing or lending in the financial markets).

The combinations of income available for current consumption and income for consumption in the next period that an individual can achieve by investing his current wealth (starting at P) in productive opportunities are represented in figure 2.2 by the productive-opportunity curve PP'. Its slope is the marginal rate of return on the productive investment (which also happens to be identical to the internal rate of return (IRR) in this certain, two-period world). Since the best or highest-return investments would be taken first (imagining that projects are lined up starting from the best at point P and turning increasingly less attractive as we move counterclockwise), the curve's steeper-at-first concave shape indicates diminishing returns on investment.

In the absence of market opportunities, the optimal investment for each individual would have been to invest to the point where his productive-opportunity curve is just tangent to the highest attainable time-preference (utility) curve, equating his marginal return on investment to his marginal utility. Thus, stockholders in the same firm facing identical productive-investment opportunities but having different utilities would actually follow different criteria for *optimal* investment. Such would be the case of individuals E (the Ephemeral) and S (the Saver) in figure 2.3: E demands that the firm invest an amount PI_1, while S wants it to invest a greater amount, PI_2.

Individuals, however, have access to market or exchange opportunities as well. Assuming that individuals can borrow or lend without limit at the same constant interest rate, r, in perfectly competitive capital markets, we can represent their market opportunities by a straight line such as mm' in

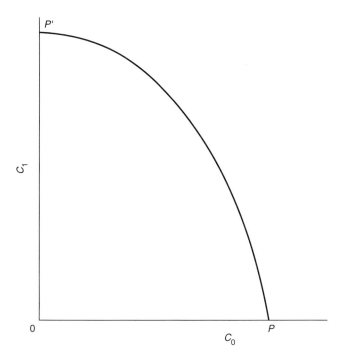

Figure 2.2
The productive-opportunity curve PP'.

figure 2.4, with slope equal to $1 + r$. Thus, an individual may lend one dollar out of his current income, C_0, in exchange for $(1 + r)$ dollars of C_1 next period (or he may use C_0 to purchase a capital asset entitling him to future income C_1); alternatively, he may borrow an amount $C_1/(1 + r)$ today against C_1. In this certain, two-period world, the total present value of the individual's income (C_0 in the current period, and C_1 in the next period discounted at the market interest rate, r) is $PV = C_0 + C_1/(1 + r)$. Thus, the market-opportunity line is an iso-wealth line representing constant present value of wealth for the individual.

With market opportunities to borrow or lend also available, each individual can now achieve a higher level of satisfaction (utility) by following a two-step process (figure 2.5). The first step, the productive-investment decision, can be achieved by any individual, regardless of his particular utility, by investing in productive capital projects (up to an amount PI) until his market-opportunity line shifts out as much as possible to become just tangent to his production-opportunity curve at A. A unique investment solution is thus obtained. The importance of this solution cannot be

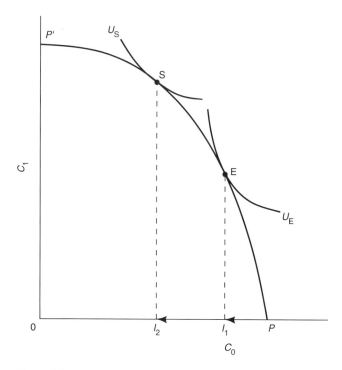

Figure 2.3
Conflicting "optimal" investment rules when market opportunities are not available.

overemphasized: It allows separation of ownership and management in a firm; Ephemeral and Saver shareholders can put aside their conflicting interests resulting from differing utilities and can now safely delegate authority to management to invest the unambiguous amount *PI*. (See also Brealey and Myers 1991.)

The last step, the market or *financing* decision, is then left up to the individual shareholder to achieve in a way consistent with his or her own time preferences for consumption. Starting from the common productive-investment decision at *A*, each shareholder can now move along the market line *MM'* to a point maximizing his particular utility. The Ephemeral can borrow (move down the market line) until he reaches point *E'* at his higher utility U'_E. The Saver can lend (move up the line) until she best satisfies her own time preferences at *S'*. Any point along the market line *MM'* can now be reached by exploiting both market and productive-investment opportunities. Notice that both shareholders are now better off than if each undertook productive investments to the point of directly

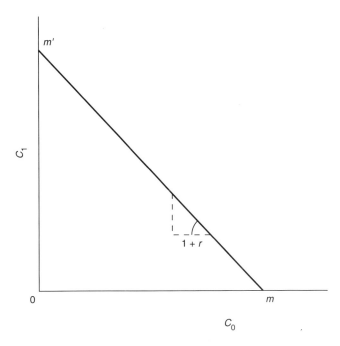

Figure 2.4
The market-opportunity (iso-wealth) line mm'.

satisfying his or her own utilities by disregarding market opportunities ($U'_E > U_E$ and $U'_S > U_S$), or if they invested only in capital-market opportunities ($U'_E > U''_E$ and $U'_S > U''_S$).

The NPV of the investment is the difference between the present value of future income discounted at the market interest rate or the opportunity cost of capital, $AI/(1 + r)$ or IM, and the investment cost IP; that is, it is equal to the amount PM. In fact, the same amount, PM, represents the increase in the present value of shareholders' wealth (as shown by the market-opportunity or iso-wealth line shifting to the right from mm' to MM' by this amount) as a result of undertaking the productive investment. Actually, shifting the market-opportunity line until it is just tangent to the productive-opportunity curve guarantees the maximum possible increase in the NPV of the investment and in the shareholders' wealth (by the same amount); investing in real, productive assets at a greater or lesser amount can easily be seen to produce a suboptimal result. Shareholders' wealth is therefore maximized by maximizing the NPV of total investment, i.e., by first taking those projects with highest NPV until all projects with positive NPV are accepted; since NPVs are additive, any positive-

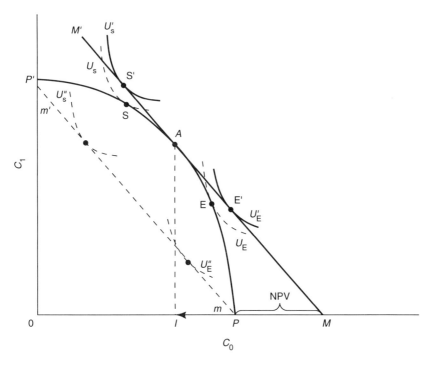

Figure 2.5
A common optimal investment decision when market opportunities are exploited.

NPV project undertaken would increase total investment NPV and share-holders' wealth by that positive amount.

The optimal production solution of tangency between the productive-opportunity curve and the market line at A (at which the slopes of the two curves become equal) can alternatively be attained by moving along the productive-opportunity curve PP' (starting at P) as long as the slope of the curve PP' (the marginal return on investment, or the IRR in the certain two-period case) is greater than the slope of the market line MM' (the market interest rate, r). In other words, shareholders' wealth can also be maximized in this certain two-period world by following the IRR rule: invest as long as the IRR of the next unit of productive investment exceeds the rate of return on comparable investments in the capital market (or the opportunity cost of capital). NPV and IRR do give identical results in the certain two-period case. In the more general case of a multi-period or uncertain world, however, IRR may no longer be identical to the marginal return on productive investments and the IRR rule may fail.

The NPV criterion, however, maintains its validity in multi-period situations. NPV can be extended from its two-period certainty form

$$NPV = \frac{C_1}{1+r} - I \quad (C_0 \equiv -I)$$

to a certain T-period form in a similar manner:

$$NPV = \sum_{t=1}^{T} \frac{C_t}{(1+r)^t} - I, \tag{2.1}$$

where r is the (risk-free) opportunity cost of capital, C_t is the (certain) net cash inflow in year t, I is the (single initial) investment outlay, and T is the number of years of the project's life.

If a series of investment outlays (as opposed to a single investment) is required, we instead subtract the present value of cash outflows from the present value of cash inflows above to arrive at the NPV; that is,

$$I \equiv \sum_{t=0}^{T} \frac{O_t}{(1+r)^t},$$

where O_t is the cash outflow in year t and C_t now represents the (net) cash inflow in year t.

Example 1   A pharmaceutical company is presented with the opportunity to purchase an exclusive patent on a proven technology for producing a new drug developed by a small biotech firm at a cost of $I_0 = \$0.1$ million. The patent will allow the firm to build a plant in 3 years at an additional cost of $I_3 = \$0.9$ million for commercializing the product. The government, wishing to support the new drug, guarantees to purchase the entire output, paying an annual cash flow of $0.15 million for 11 years starting in year 5; the firm will also get $0.3 million at the end (in year 15) for salvage value. The rate of return on similar traded assets without risk (e.g., government bonds) is 5% ($r = 0.05$). The firm must decide immediately whether to accept, or else the biotech firm will approach someone else. What is the value of this investment opportunity?
From equation 2.1,

$$NPV = \left[\sum_{t=5}^{15} \frac{C_t}{(1+r)^t} + \frac{S_{15}}{(1+r)^{15}} \right] - \left[I_0 + \frac{I_3}{(1+r)^3} \right]$$

$$= \left[\sum_{t=5}^{15} \frac{0.15}{(1+0.05)^t} + \frac{0.3}{(1+0.05)^{15}} \right] - \left[0.1 + \frac{0.9}{(1+0.05)^3} \right]$$

$$= [0.15(15.380 - 3.546) + 0.3 \times 0.864] - 0.877$$

$$= 1.157.$$

Since the opportunity has a positive NPV ($1.157 million), the firm would be justified to go ahead with the purchase.

In a more general case where the discount rate may vary from period to period,

$$\text{NPV} = \sum_{t=1}^{T} \frac{C_t}{(1 + r_1) \cdots (1 + r_t)} - I, \qquad (2.1')$$

where r_t is the riskless interest rate in year t.

Even in the multi-period case, the concept of NPV makes it possible to separate the productive and the financing decisions of an individual shareholder. A variety of shareholders with conflicting time preferences for current versus future consumption can agree on the same criterion for the productive-investment (or capital-budgeting) decision and delegate authority to the firm's management—allowing separation of ownership and management—with a clear mandate: maximize the shareholders' wealth by accepting all productive investments with positive NPV, using as a discount rate the rate of return offered by comparable investment opportunities in the capital market (the opportunity cost of capital). In so doing, management can be content that it enables each individual shareholder to attain his highest personal satisfaction without having to worry about matching the cash flows from the investment with each shareholder's preferred pattern of consumption; in perfectly competitive capital markets, each individual shareholder can make the associated *financing* decision on his own by borrowing or lending or by buying or selling capital assets in the market.

NPV under Uncertainty: Allowing for Risk

So far we have basically assumed away or suppressed the existence of risk. We have seen that under certainty, in the absence of managerial flexibility, a firm should select the subset of proposed investments with positive NPV; this criterion was found to be consistent with the maximization of the market value of the firm's stock, leading to the maximization of its shareholders' wealth, which would subsequently allow maximization of their utility of consumption in a perfect and complete capital market. However, the real world within which business decisions must be made is unavoidably characterized by risk and uncertainty. Uncertainty is typically resolved gradually, and the forecasting of cash flows (unless they are contractually guaranteed) is imperfect and subject to error. Thus, risk and investors' attitudes toward it must be accounted for in the process of capital budgeting, and particularly in the NPV criterion.

Under uncertainty, a future variable is characterized not by a single value but by a probability distribution of its possible outcomes. The amount of dispersion or variability of possible outcomes is a measure of how risky that uncertain variable is. Where does risk in an investment project arise? Under uncertainty, the future cash flows used to calculate NPV are estimated, almost invariably, from forecasts of other *primary* variables, such as the costs of labor and materials, the prices and quantities of products sold, assumptions about competition, the firm's market share, the size and growth of the market, effective tax rates, expected inflation rates, and the project's lifetime. These primary variables are uncertain and subject to variability, usually more so the more remote in the future they are; thus they cause variability in the estimates of the cash flows and consequently in the NPV estimate. Why should we be concerned about the dispersion surrounding the cash flows or the NPV? The basic reason is that the average investor prefers less risk to more risk, other things being the same. That people are willing to pay a premium to buy insurance, that they tend to avoid large *fair* gambles, that they diversify their portfolios to avoid "putting all their eggs in one basket," and that they demand higher returns from more uncertain investments all testify to the assertion that investors are generally risk averse. Under uncertainty, the example given above is modified as follows.

Example 2   Instead of the external offer to purchase the technology for a new drug that management feels is necessary to maintain the firm's strategic position, the pharmaceutical firm of example 1 is now faced with an internal opportunity to accept or reject a 3-year R&D proposal requiring an immediate $100,000 investment ($I_0 = 0.1$ million) but providing only a small (30%) chance at discovering (or reengineering) the drug. If at the end of the 3 years the R&D project proves successful, management may then build a plant expected to cost $3 million and to generate expected annual cash flows of $500,000 a year (starting in year 5) for the next 11 years (until year 15), after which time it would be sold for an expected salvage value of $1 million. The opportunity cost of capital or expected return offered by other traded assets of similar risk in the market is 10% ($k = 0.10$). What is the value of the R&D opportunity?

Certainty-Equivalent Approach to Risk Adjustment
The NPV criterion under certainty of preferring those projects with the highest NPVs as given by equation 2.1 can be extended in a straightforward manner under uncertainty. The now-uncertain cash flow in each year, c_t, is replaced by its _certainty-equivalent_ amount, $\hat{c}_t$—i.e., the certain cash flow in year t that has the same present value as the uncertain cash flow in that year. Thus, NPV under uncertainty may be written as

$$NPV = \sum_{t=1}^{T} \frac{\hat{c}_t}{(1+r)^t} - I, \qquad (2.2)$$

where r is the riskless interest rate. Thus,

$$PV = \frac{\hat{c}_t}{(1+r)^t} = \frac{E(c_t)}{(1+k)^t},$$

where $E(c_t)$ is the expected cash flow in year t and k is the opportunity cost of capital or the risk-adjusted discount rate. For example, if $r = 0.05$ and $k = 0.10$ in each year, the certainty-equivalent cash flow in year 5 in example 2 can be determined as follows:

$$\hat{c}_5 = E(c_5)\left(\frac{1+r}{1+k}\right)^5 = 0.3 \times 0.5 \left(\frac{1.05}{1.10}\right)^5 = 0.15 \times 0.7925 = \$0.119 \text{ million.}$$

Notice that the certainty-equivalent approach disaggregates the effects of time (time value of money under certainty) and uncertainty (risk aversion) on the NPV of an investment by discounting for the time value of money at the risk-free interest rate in the denominator, and by accounting for risk aversion by the certainty equivalents, $\hat{c}_t$, in the numerator.

Defining _risk premium_ as the uncertain outcome's expected value minus its certainty-equivalent amount, $p_t \equiv E(c_t) - \hat{c}_t$, we can rewrite each certainty-equivalent cash flow in any year t in terms of the expected cash flow in that year and a risk premium, i.e., $\hat{c}_t = E(c_t) - p_t$. For example, the risk premium or deduction for risk in year 5 is

$$p_5 = E(c_5) - \hat{c}_5 = 0.15 - 0.119 = 0.031.$$

The relevant risk premium is, of course, that of the average investor in the market, or the _market's risk premium_. Later, the equivalence of this approach to the capital asset pricing model's approach to risk adjustment for determining the NPV will be shown by noting that the relevant market premium is the _market price of risk_, λ, times the covariance of the period's uncertain cash flow, c_t, with the expected market rate of return, r_m:

$p_t = \lambda_t \, \text{cov}(c_t, r_{mt})$.

Note that, in general, the cash flows in each period may be associated with different levels of risk compared to other periods, so there may be a different risk premium in each period, p_t. As will be discussed shortly, using a single constant risk-adjusted opportunity cost of capital to adjust for risk implicitly assumes constant resolution of uncertainty over time, so that the riskiness of cash flows and the risk premium, p_t, increase at a constant rate over time.

If we let $p_t \equiv (1 - \alpha_t)E(c_t)$, then the certainty-equivalent cash flow is expressed as a proportion of the expected cash flow, $\hat{c}_t = \alpha_t E(c_t)$, leading to the conventional form of the certainty-equivalent NPV first proposed by Robichek and Myers (1966):

$$\text{NPV} = \sum_{t=1}^{T} \frac{\alpha_t E(c_t)}{(1+r)^t} - I, \tag{2.2'}$$

where r is the risk-free interest rate (assumed to remain constant over the investment's life T), and α_t is the *certainty-equivalent coefficient* (CEC), defined as the ratio $\hat{c}_t/E(c_t)$, or as $1 - p_t/E(c_t)$.

The CEC compensates for the business and financial risks related to the investment, allowing discounting at the risk-free rate as opposed to a risk-adjusted opportunity cost of capital. It typically ranges in value from 0 to 1, with higher values showing a lower risk penalty associated with the uncertain cash flows. If a future cash flow has no (systematic) risk associated with it, the CEC becomes 1 and the certainty equivalent becomes the cash-flow estimate.

If the risk-free interest rate changes from year to year (being r_t in year t), the certainty-equivalent form of NPV can be extended to

$$\text{NPV} = \sum_{t=1}^{T} \frac{\alpha_t E(c_t)}{(1+r_1)\cdots(1+r_t)} - I. \tag{2.2''}$$

Let us now explore the relationship between the certainty-equivalent approach and the more widely used risk-adjusted-discount-rate approach to capital budgeting, especially its more popular form of using a single constant discount rate or opportunity cost of capital. Let us assume that the risk borne per period is constant (i.e., that the total riskiness of future cash flows and hence the risk premium p_t increase at a constant rate, s, over time)—an assumption that is shown to be implicitly made when a single opportunity cost of capital is used under uncertainty. This assump-

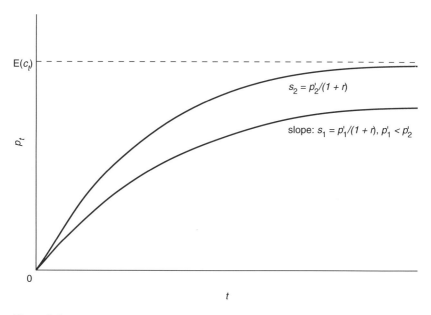

Figure 2.6
Risk premium increasing at a constant rate as implied by a constant discount rate (opportunity cost of capital). Here p_t, the risk premium, is plotted versus time (t).

tion is reasonable for most projects for which uncertainty-resolving events occur randomly and the times between such random events are exponential so that the riskiness of cash flows builds up in a constant or memoryless fashion. Let the risk premium increase at the constant rate s as a proportion of each period's expected cash flows, as shown in figure 2.6 and as described by the equation

$$p_t = E(c_t)(1 - e^{-st}),$$

where s, the slope of the risk premium curve in figure 2.6, is a measure of how fast riskiness builds up; the higher s, the higher the risk premium necessary to compensate for the increased risk. Thus, assuming a constant risk-free interest rate, r, we can define $s \equiv p'/(1 + r)$, where p' is a measure of the required incremental risk premium per period. The discrete form of the above equation for the risk premium at time t then becomes

$$p_t = E(c_t)[1 - (1 + s)^{-t}] = E(c_t)\left[1 - \left(1 + \frac{p'}{1+r}\right)^{-t}\right].$$

Rearranging terms, we obtain

$$1 - \frac{p_t}{E(c_t)} = \left(1 + \frac{p'}{1+r}\right)^{-t},$$

which gives

$$\frac{E(c_t)}{E(c_t) - p_t} = \left(\frac{1 + r + p'}{1 + r}\right)^t.$$

Recognizing that $E(c_t) - p_t = \hat{c}_t$, we obtain

$$\frac{\hat{c}_t}{(1+r)^t} = \frac{E(c_t)}{(1 + r + p')^t}.$$

Finally, by taking sums of each side over the investment's life and subtracting the initial cost from each side, we establish the equivalence between the certainty-equivalent approach and the single risk-adjusted-discount-rate form of NPV under the assumption that risk increases at a constant rate over time:

$$\sum_{t=1}^{T} \frac{\hat{c}_t}{(1+r)^t} - I = \sum_{t=1}^{T} \frac{E(c_t)}{(1+k)^t} - I,$$

where $k \equiv r + p'$. It can be easily seen that this equivalence alternatively implies that

$$\alpha_t = \left(\frac{1+r}{1+k}\right)^t = \frac{E(c_t)/(1+k)^t}{E(c_t)/(1+r)^t}.$$

In example 2, if $r = 0.05$ and $k = 0.10$ in each year,

$$\alpha_t = \left(\frac{1.05}{1.10}\right)^t = 0.95455^t,$$

where $t = 5, \ldots, 15$ (e.g., $\alpha_5 = 0.793, \alpha_6 = 0.756, \alpha_7 = 0.722$, etc.). Thus, a constant (risk-adjusted) opportunity cost of capital (e.g., $k = 0.10$) suggests that α_t—which can be interpreted here as the percentage reduction in present value as a result of risk, being the proportion of present value of expected cash flows discounted for both the time value of money and risk (i.e., at the risk-adjusted rate) to the present value of expected cash flows discounted for time alone (at the riskless rate)—decreases at a constant rate over time. Alternatively, it is assumed that the market risk borne *per period* is constant or that the total risk increases at a constant rate.

In practice it is rather difficult to determine a certainty equivalent (or a market risk premium) by traditional methods, especially when risk per period does not remain constant (as in multi-stage projects or projects involving expansion, abandonment and other real options). However, the modern options approach presented in this book effectively solves the problem of determining certainty equivalents using market prices to derive "certainty-equivalent" (or risk-neutral) expectations under risk-neutral valuation.

Risk-Adjusted-Discount-Rate Approach
It was shown above that under certainty the goal of maximizing the market value of a firm was achieved by selecting investment projects in accordance with the NPV criterion of discounting the future cash flows at the (risk-free) opportunity cost of capital or the required rate of return that the firm and investors in the market demand of comparable investments, r. The same idea can be used under uncertainty, provided that "comparable investments" is interpreted to mean investments also having similar risk characteristics (belonging to the same *risk category*). This opportunity cost of capital of a particular project under uncertainty can be determined as the cost of funds or the required rate of return demanded by investors of an all-equity firm engaged exclusively in the same type of business as the project under consideration. Notice that—unlike the certainty-equivalent approach, which separates the effects of time and risk—the risk-adjusted-discount-rate (RADR) approach accounts, through the discount rate in the denominator, both for the time value of money and for risk aversion. Thus, the risk-adjusted discount rate, k, is the sum of the risk-free interest rate r (typically approximated by the yield of three-month Treasury bills, considered to be default-free) used to discount for the time value of money (pure discount) and a discount risk premium, p', used to compensate for the risk associated with the project—i.e., $k = r + p'$. (In the above example, $p' = k - r = 0.10 - 0.05 = 0.05$.)

If a constant discount rate (opportunity cost of capital) k is used, the static RADR form of NPV (assuming passive management) is, of course,

$$\text{NPV} = \sum_{t=1}^{T} \frac{\text{E}(c_t)}{(1+k)^t} - I. \tag{2.3}$$

Example 3   In the previous R&D example, the traditional (static or passive) expected NPV is

$$\text{NPV} = \left(\sum_{t=5}^{15} \frac{E(c_t)}{(1+k)^t} + \frac{E(S_{15})}{(1+k)^{15}} \right) - \left(I_0 + \frac{E(I_3)}{(1+k)^3} \right)$$

$$= \left(\sum_{t=5}^{15} \frac{0.3 \times 0.5}{(1.10)^t} + \frac{0.3 \times 1}{(1.10)^{15}} \right) - \left(0.1 + \frac{0.3 \times 3}{(1.10)^3} \right)$$

$$= 0.037.$$

Based on this negative NPV, management would be inclined to reject this opportunity.

As a practical guideline, normal projects in the same line of business as the firm and having the same risk characteristics (belonging to the same *risk class*) do not affect the firm's total riskiness and therefore should be discounted at the firm's average opportunity cost of capital (representing the expected return commensurate with the firm's riskiness required by the providers of funds). Projects with other than average riskiness tend to change the firm's total risk posture (or risk class) and should be discounted at a rate other than the firm's average cost of capital—the correct discount being the marginal opportunity cost of capital for the particular project under consideration (or for investments with similar risk characteristics). Thus, projects with above-average risk (such as the introduction of a new product in an uncertain market) require a discount rate in excess of the firm's average cost of capital—the higher (than average) the risk, the higher the required discount rate. Similarly, projects exhibiting less risk than the firm's normal operations (e.g., contractual projects) should be discounted at a lower rate.

Many firms, rather than determine a unique risk-adjusted discount rate for each project, attempt to simplify the capital-budgeting process by classifying projects according to risk characteristics and then assign a discount rate for each risk category—for example, a discount rate of 10% for cost-reduction projects, 15% for ongoing or plant-expansion investments, and 20% for R&D projects or new-product introductions. These risk classifications, of course, entail the danger of failing to account for important differences in risk between investments belonging to the same general risk class. Not only may the riskiness associated with a particular project be ignored; in addition, when the same constant discount rate k (or constant discount risk premium p') is used over the project's entire lifetime, changes in the project's own riskiness over time may not be properly accounted for. That is so because the use of such a constant discount rate is predicated on the implicit assumption that the riskiness of the project's cash flows is increasing at a constant rate over time. This problem could be surmounted, of course, by looking at the riskiness associated with the yearly cash flows of each individual project and determining different risk-adjusted discount rates to reflect each period's riskiness in the extended NPV form

$$\text{NPV} = \sum_{t=1}^{T} \frac{\text{E}(c_t)}{(1 + k_1) \cdots (1 + k_t)} - I, \tag{2.3'}$$

where k_t is the risk-adjusted discount rate in year t.

The Capital Asset Pricing Model
We have seen that the objective of a firm's management under uncertainty should be to employ market-oriented risk attitudes to maximize the shareholders' wealth. We have also seen that the average shareholder, as the average investor in the market, would avoid "putting all his eggs in one basket" and would attempt to reduce risk through diversification by holding a portfolio of different securities.

— The basic underlying idea of risk reduction via diversification is that, when prices of different stocks do not move exactly together (or returns are not perfectly correlated), opposite moves among different stocks in a portfolio tend to offset one another, so that the variability of the portfolio can be substantially less than the average variability of the individual stock returns. In the simplest mathematical form, the variance (a measure of dispersion or total risk) of the returns of two assets r_1 and r_2 combined (in equal proportions) can be less than the sum of the individual variances if their returns are negatively correlated, since

$$\text{Var}(r_1 + r_2) = \text{Var}(r_1) + \text{Var}(r_2) + 2\,\text{cov}(r_1, r_2)$$

$$< \text{Var}(r_1) + \text{Var}(r_2) \qquad \qquad \text{if cov}(r_1, r_2) < 0.$$

More generally, if the proportional weights invested in each asset are x_1 and x_2, respectively, the variance of a portfolio is given by

$$\text{Var}(x_1 r_1 + x_2 r_2) = x_1^2\,\text{Var}(r_1) + x_2^2\,\text{Var}(r_2) + 2x_1 x_2\,\text{cov}(r_1, r_2),$$

so that less-than-perfect (even positive) correlation is sufficient to bring about risk reduction via diversification. The above idea can be easily extended to a combination of many assets, confirming that the total risk (variance) of a portfolio of assets may be less than the average variability of the individual securities, depending on the extent of correlation between asset returns. Therefore, the relevant risk of an asset's returns when diversification opportunities are available is that asset's contribution to the portfolio's total risk. Thus, from the point of view of the firm's shareholder or the average investor in the market who can select any of the securities traded in the market in constructing his portfolio, the relevant risk of a new security or investment project for which the investor requires a premium is that asset's marginal contribution to the riskiness of the market portfolio, which depends on the covariance between the asset returns and the returns of the market portfolio; no premium would be required for the part of an asset's risk (i.e., the unique or firm-specific risk) that can be diversified away.

There is a difference between diversification by investors and diversification by a firm, however. Since a firm can be thought of as a portfolio of assets or projects, one might think that the relevant risk, and hence the value of a proposed new investment, should depend on its effect on the total riskiness of the firm, and in particular on the covariance of that investment's returns with the returns of other existing or proposed projects. This would be a disheartening situation, because in this case NPVs would no longer be additive. However, except for situations where the firm is in such a risky business and the new investment is large enough that it might significantly affect the probability of bankruptcy, or the firm is closely held (with its owner-managers "putting all their eggs" in the firm), or when there exist physical interdependencies (economic synergies) between the investment under consideration and other existing or proposed investments, corporate diversification is not a legitimate objective from the shareholders' viewpoint; since the firm's shareholders can diversify more efficiently in the capital market on their own simply by buying the individual firms' stock, they should pay no extra premium for firms to diversify for them. Thus, the value of a given project is, in general, independent of the risks of (or correlations with) other existing or proposed investments, and hence of the firm undertaking it, so that NPVs do generally add up. However, the covariance of the project's returns with the market (driven by the same macroeconomic forces affecting all securities or firms in the economy) remains relevant in determining the risk premium demanded by investors in the market.

The capital asset pricing model (CAPM) provides a method to simultaneously relate the required return of a project or security to its relevant nondiversifiable risk, seen as a function of the covariance of the asset's return with the return of the securities market as a whole. To see the insight behind the CAPM in a simplified way, consider the (single-factor) market model postulating a linear relationship between the asset's returns and the

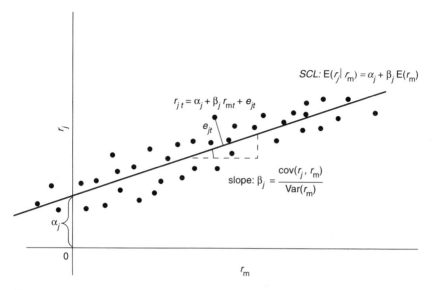

Figure 2.7
The security characteristic line (SCL), postulating a linear relationship between the returns
from an individual asset (r_j) and the returns from the market (r_m).

returns of the entire market (e.g., as proxied by the Standard & Poor's 500
index of common stocks):

$$r_j = \alpha_j + \beta_j r_m + \varepsilon_j, \tag{2.4}$$

where r_j is the return on asset (project or security) j during a particular
period, r_m is the return on the market (e.g., the S&P 500 stock index) during the same period, and α_j and β_j are parameters characteristic of asset j.

In a regression of r_{jt} as the dependent variable against the market re-
turn, r_{mt}, as the explanatory variable, $r_{jt} = \alpha_j + \beta_j r_{mt} + \varepsilon_{jt}$, the coefficients
α_j and β_j represent the intercept and the slope of the security characteristic
line (SCL) shown in figure 2.7, best describing the relationship between r_j
and r_m:

$$E(r_j|r_m) = \alpha_j + \beta_j E(r_m).$$

The slope, β_j, determined from ordinary least-squares (OLS) regression
analysis, is equal to $\text{cov}(r_j, r_m)/\text{Var}(r_m)$ and indicates the sensitivity (percent change) of the asset's returns to a given (1%) variation in the market
return. ε_j is the residual (firm-specific) or random error, representing the
deviation of the actual returns of asset j from its expected returns as pre-

dicted by the regression, incorporating the effects of other factors unique to asset j, its firm, or its industry.

The total risk of asset j, as can be measured by the variance of its returns, can then be expressed as

$$\mathrm{Var}(r_j) = \mathrm{Var}(\alpha_j + \beta_j r_m + \varepsilon_j)$$

$$= \mathrm{Var}(\alpha_j) + \mathrm{Var}(\beta_j r_m) + \mathrm{Var}(\varepsilon_j)$$

$$= \beta_j^2\, \mathrm{Var}(r_m) + \mathrm{Var}(\varepsilon_j) \quad (\text{since } \mathrm{Var}(\alpha_j) = 0);$$

that is,

Total risk = Market risk + Firm-specific risk.

The total risk of asset j can thus be seen to consist of two distinct parts:

A part that can be attributed to aggregate market movements (explained by the regression), given by $\beta_j^2\, \mathrm{Var}(r_m)$. This part of risk is known as *market, systematic,* or *nondiversifiable* risk, since it arises from the correlation between the asset returns and the market return driven by economy-wide forces affecting all securities in the market (e.g., the budget deficit or inflation), which therefore cannot be diversified away.

Unique or firm-specific risk driven by factors other than the market (which cannot be explained by the regression), given by $\mathrm{Var}(\varepsilon_j)$. This risk results from variability in factors unique to the particular firm or its industry (e.g., the risk that the firm's chief executive officer may quit or die). It is known as *unsystematic* or *diversifiable* risk since the effect of these firm-specific or unsystematic factors beyond the market can be diversified away (e.g., with the risk that one firm's CEO may resign offset by a positive R&D discovery by another firm) by holding a portfolio of (roughly 15 or more) securities.

Since a well-diversified investor can eliminate the unsystematic component of risk, the only relevant risk for which he or she would demand a premium in terms of a higher required return is the systematic risk, $\beta_j^2\, \mathrm{Var}(r_m)$. With $\mathrm{Var}(r_m)$ constant for all assets, the extent to which the individual asset's returns move with the market, β_j, can be used as a distinguishing measure of that asset's systematic risk; since $\beta_j = \mathrm{cov}(r_j, r_m)/\mathrm{Var}(r_m)$ with the denominator again constant for all assets, $\mathrm{cov}(r_j, r_m)$ can also be used as a proxy for asset j's systematic risk.

Having shown that a well-diversified investor would require a premium in terms of a higher expected return to be compensated only for an asset's systematic risk as measured by its beta coefficient, β_j, it is useful to describe the standard assumptions underlying the one-period CAPM:

(1) Investors are rational, having as their objective the maximization of the single-period expected utility of their terminal wealth.

(2) Investors are risk averse and diversify their portfolios efficiently on the basis of the mean and variance of portfolio returns.[5]

(3) Investors have homogeneous expectations, i.e., identical estimates of the expected values, variances, and covariances of returns for risky assets.

(4) There exists a risk-free interest rate, r, at which investors can borrow or lend any amounts.

(5) There are no taxes or transactions costs, and the cost of bankruptcy is negligible; furthermore, information is freely available to investors.

(6) All assets are perfectly divisible and liquid.

(7) The market is competitive so that investors do not believe they can influence through their actions the prices of any assets (i.e., investors are price takers), and the amount of each asset is given.

The first three of these assumptions concern the behavior of investors; the last four concern the functioning of perfect and competitive capital markets.

Based on these assumptions, we can determine the expected return required by investors to be compensated for bearing any level of systematic risk for any asset (or portfolio) in equilibrium in a competitively perfect capital market. If the market portfolio is efficient (offering the highest expected return for a given risk level), there must be a linear relationship between each asset's expected return and its marginal contribution to (market) portfolio risk (β_j). This is represented by the security market line (SML) shown in figure 2.8, suggesting that the expected risk premium on asset j over the risk-free return, $E(r_j) - r$, is directly proportional to its beta, β_j, and the expected market risk premium, $E(r_m) - r$, i.e.,

$$E(r_j) = r + \beta_j[E(r_m) - r]. \tag{2.5}$$

Alternatively, the same expected return-beta relationship can result without some of the above restrictive CAPM assumptions (e.g., that investors are mean-variance optimizers). With no arbitrage opportunities and a single-factor market, the same expected return can be achieved by combining two basic benchmark portfolios in specific proportions: a risk-free asset (e.g., a money-market fund or Treasury bills) and a market index (e.g., a

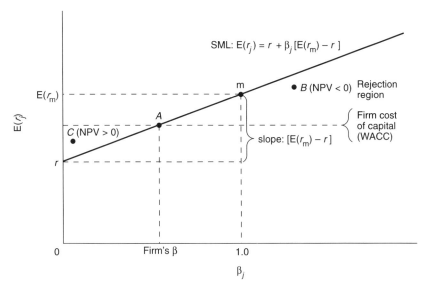

Figure 2.8
The security market line (SML), illustrating the relationship between the expected return on an individual asset j, $E(r_j)$, and that asset's systematic risk, β_j.

stock mutual fund). For assets with no systematic risk ($\beta_j = 0$), investors demand an expected return equal to the risk-free rate, r, thus determining point $[0, r]$ on the SML. For assets with an average systematic risk ($\beta_j = 1$), investors require a return equal to the return on the market portfolio, determining point $[1, E(r_m)]$ on the SML. Since investors can invest a specific proportion ($\beta_j\%$) of their *own money* in the risky market portfolio, offering $E(r_m)$, and can borrow or lend the remainder ($1 - \beta_j\%$) at the risk-free interest rate, r, they can achieve any combination along the SML and obtain an expected portfolio return with the same β_j given by

$$E(r_j) = \beta_j E(r_m) + (1 - \beta_j)r = r + \beta_j[E(r_m) - r].$$

Thus, an investor will be willing to hold an asset with a particular β only if he can receive a compensating return as given by the SML, so that all assets in equilibrium should be represented as combinations (points) along the line. The SML, having intercept r and slope $E(r_m) - r$, is a graphical representation of the known CAPM equation

$$E(r_j) = r + \beta_j[E(r_m) - r], \tag{2.5'}$$

where $E(r_j)$ is the expected (required) return from asset j, $E(r_m)$ is the expected return from the market portfolio, r is the risk-free interest rate, and

$\beta_j \equiv \text{cov}(r_j, r_m)/\text{Var}(r_m)$ is the asset's volatility relative to the market (i.e., the percent change in the asset's return associated with a 1% increase in the market).

Example 4   In example 2, suppose that the β of the project's cash flows is 0.625, that the expected return on the market portfolio, $E(r_m)$, is 13%, and that the risk-free interest rate offered by 3-month Treasury bills is 5%. What is the opportunity cost of capital for discounting the project's expected cash flows?

Straightforward application of CAPM equation 2.5' gives

$$k = E(r) = 5 + 0.625(13 - 5) = 10\%,$$

as used above.

— The CAPM equation gives the return that any asset (or portfolio) in equilibrium must earn to compensate for its systematic risk, thus offering a cutoff criterion or hurdle rate for the project's acceptance (or, alternatively, specifying the project's risk-adjusted discount rate or opportunity cost of capital). Any project plotting on the SML, such as A in figure 2.8, is a marginal project in that its expected return is precisely what is required by investors to be just compensated for the project's particular systematic risk. Any project below the SML, such as B, should be rejected, since its expected return is less than the return that is normally required (or that can be earned) by investors from investments with its given level of systematic risk, i.e.,

$$E(r_j) < r + \beta_j[E(r_m) - r].$$

On the other hand, any project above the SML, such as C, would improve the value of the firm and should be accepted since it offers an expected return that more than compensates for the project's particular systematic risk, i.e.,

$$E(r_j) > r + \beta_j[E(r_m) - r].$$

A firm can, of course, expect to find positive-NPV investment opportunities plotting above the SML in the short run if it enjoys some competitive advantage (such as patents, an advantageous location, better relations with its customers, suppliers or employees, or an entrenched position with high barriers to entry for competitors); in the long term, as the particular competitive advantage erodes, market forces will tend to reduce the excess return over that given by the SML toward zero. Unless the project is of the same riskiness as the firm, the firm's weighted average cost of capital (WACC) is, in general, inappropriate as a cutoff criterion or discount rate for appraisal of projects; represented as a horizontal line in figure 2.8, it may lead to incorrect decisions, such as accepting project B (lying above the horizontal WACC line) when it should be rejected (as lying below the SML line) or rejecting project C when it should be accepted according to the CAPM.

As noted, the basic message of the CAPM is that the relevant risk premium that investors would pay for a risky capital asset in equilibrium is directly related to that asset's systematic risk as given by its beta or the covariance of its returns with the market. Alternatively, note that the risk premium per period,

$$p' \equiv E(r_j) - r = [E(r_m) - r]\beta_j$$

$$= [E(r_m) - r] \frac{\mathrm{cov}(r_j, r_m)}{\mathrm{Var}(r_m)}$$

$$= \frac{E(r_m) - r}{\mathrm{Var}(r_m)} \, \mathrm{cov}(r_j, r_m)$$

$$= \lambda \, \mathrm{cov}(r_j, r_m),$$

where $\lambda \equiv [E(r_m) - r]/\mathrm{Var}(r_m)$ is the *market price of risk* (or reward-to-variability ratio) for the period, representing the premium (excess return) per unit of risk in the market (portfolio).

Since the expected rate of return of a project given by the CAPM is the minimum return required by investors from securities having the same systematic risk, the CAPM return specifies the hurdle rate or the risk-adjusted discount rate for determining the NPV of the project. The CAPM form of the NPV criterion is of course equivalent to (and can be derived from) its certainty-equivalent form. Since CAPM is a one-period model (involving rates of return over a single period), let us first show this equivalence for a one-period project requiring an outlay, I, at the beginning of the period and offering a single cash inflow, c_1, at the end of the period. The certainty-equivalent form of the NPV criterion in such a case reduces to

$$\mathrm{NPV} = \frac{\hat{c}_1}{1+r} - I,$$

where the certainty equivalent is $\hat{c}_1 \equiv E(c_1) - p_1$ and the relevant market risk premium of the cash flow is $p_1 = \lambda \, \mathrm{cov}(c_1, r_m)$. Thus, the present value of the cash flow, V_0, is

$$V_0 = \frac{E(c_1) - \lambda \operatorname{cov}(c_1, r_m)}{1 + r}.$$

Noting that

$$\operatorname{cov}(r_j, r_m) = \operatorname{cov}(c_1/V_0 - 1, \ r_m) = \operatorname{cov}(c_1, r_m)/V_0,$$

and rearranging, we get

$$V_0(1 + r) = E(c_1) - \lambda V_0 \operatorname{cov}(r_j, r_m),$$

and by collecting the V_0 terms we obtain

$$V_0 = \frac{E(c_1)}{1 + r + \lambda \operatorname{cov}(r_j, r_m)}.$$

This results in the RADR form of NPV:

$$\text{NPV} = \frac{E(c_1)}{1 + k} - I,$$

where the discount rate is given by the CAPM:

$$k = r + \lambda \operatorname{cov}(r_j, r_m) = r + \beta_j [E(r_m) - r].$$

Most capital-budgeting investments, of course, involve discounting of cash flows over multiple future periods, so that using the single-period CAPM for discounting one period at a time would necessitate certain additional assumptions concerning the evolution of its variables over time. Fama (1977) shows that the present value of a future net cash flow is its current expected value discounted at risk-adjusted discount rates given by the CAPM. The discount rates must be known and nonstochastic (i.e., they must evolve in a deterministic fashion through time), and in general they will differ from period to period (and across cash flows for a given period). Thus, market parameters (such as the risk-free interest rate r_t and the market price of risk λ_t or the project's β_{jt}) are assumed to evolve deterministically through time, so that any intermediate uncertainty about the value of a cash flow arises from uncertainties concerning reassessments of the cash flow's expected value through time (and the covariance between these reassessments and those for the market). The NPV of an investment project is then simply the sum of the present values of all its future net cash flows.

To better appreciate the conditions under which we can use the CAPM for discounting in a multi-period setting, let us examine the relationship between the certainty-equivalent and CAPM risk-adjusted-discount forms of NPV for multi-period investments, while trying to keep the arguments as simplified as possible. First, we can see why the discount rates have to be deterministic if the expected NPV of a multi-period investment under uncertainty is to assume its standard risk-adjusted discount form. The expected NPV, denoted E[NPV] and defined as

$$E\left[\sum_{t=1}^{T} \frac{c_t}{(1 + k_1) \cdots (1 + k_t)} - I\right],$$

will be identical to its conventional form,

$$\sum_{t=1}^{T} \frac{E(c_t)}{(1 + k_1) \cdots (1 + k_t)} - I.$$

(That is, the expectation can "go through" the summation only if the discount rates, k_t, are deterministic.) Also, in perfectly competitive markets, the portfolio opportunities facing investors are independent of any individual firm's decisions so that r_t and λ_t are market-determined parameters that are deterministic from the point of view of an individual firm. Since from the CAPM

$$k_t = r_t + \lambda_t \operatorname{cov}(r_{jt}, r_{mt}),$$

deterministic k_t, r_t, and λ_t imply that the covariance and β_t should also be deterministic. Thus, from the certainty-equivalent form of the market value (at the beginning of a period, $t - 1$) of a single uncertain future cash flow (to accrue at the end of the period, t),

$$V_{t-1} = \frac{E_{t-1}(c_t) - \lambda_t \operatorname{cov}(c_t, r_{mt})}{1 + r_t},$$

we can see that, in a world where the CAPM holds in each period, the basic intermediate uncertainty in the value of a cash flow can only result from investors' reassessments through time of their expectations concerning the cash flow (where $E_{t-1}(c_t)$ represents investors' expectation of the uncertain cash flow at time t, given the information available as of time $t - 1$).

In the case of a multi-period investment generating a sequence of uncertain future cash flows until the end of a specified life, T, the present value of the investment at the beginning of a period will depend on the uncertain cash flow at the end of the period, c_t, and on the uncertain end-of-period value of the investment representing the present value at that time of the subsequent stream of uncertain future cash flows. The certainty-equivalent form of the value of the investment at the beginning of any period $t - 1$ is then given by

$$V_{t-1} = \frac{E_{t-1}(V_t + c_t) - \lambda_t \, \text{cov}(V_t + c_t, r_{mt})}{1 + r_t}.$$

Noting that

$$\text{cov}(r_{jt}, r_{mt}) = \text{cov}\left(\frac{V_t + c_t}{V_{t-1}} - 1, \, r_{mt}\right) = \frac{\text{cov}(V_t + c_t, r_{mt})}{V_{t-1}}$$

and rearranging terms, we get

$$V_{t-1}(1 + r_t) = E_{t-1}(V_t + c_t) - \lambda_t V_{t-1} \, \text{cov}(r_{jt}, r_{mt}),$$

or

$$V_{t-1}[1 + r_t + \lambda_t \, \text{cov}(r_{jt}, r_{mt})] = E_{t-1}(V_t + c_t),$$

which gives

$$V_{t-1} = \frac{E_{t-1}(V_t + c_t)}{1 + k_t},$$

with the deterministic risk-adjusted discount rate, k_t, given by the CAPM-required rate of return for the period, i.e.,

$$k_t = r_t + \lambda_t \, \text{cov}(r_{jt}, r_{mt}).$$

Similarly, for the previous period,

$$V_{t-2} = \frac{E_{t-2}(V_{t-1} + c_{t-1})}{1 + k_{t-1}}$$

$$= \frac{E_{t-2}(c_{t-1})}{1 + k_{t-1}} + \frac{E_{t-2}E_{t-1}(c_t)}{(1 + k_{t-1})(1 + k_t)} + \frac{E_{t-2}E_{t-1}(V_t)}{(1 + k_{t-1})(1 + k_t)}.$$

Thus, starting from the last period, T, and working backward in a dynamic-programming fashion, we can obtain the generalized RADR form of present value:

$$V_0 = \sum_{t=1}^{T} \frac{E_0(c_t)}{(1 + k_1) \cdots (1 + k_t)},$$

where the last cash flow, c_T, incorporates the expected salvage value so that $E_0(V_T) = 0$. We have thus shown the equivalence of the certainty-equivalent form of NPV with its generalized risk-adjusted discount rate form (as in equation 2.3')

$$NPV = V_0 - I = \sum_{t=1}^{T} \frac{E_0(c_t)}{(1 + k_1) \cdots (1 + k_t)} - I,$$

where the discount rates are determined according to the CAPM under the condition that k_t, r_t (the risk-free interest rate), λ_t (the market price of risk), and β_t (the project's systematic risk) evolve deterministically through time.

If the discount rates not only are deterministic but also can be assumed to be constant through time, i.e., $k_t = k$, the simplified textbook NPV formula with a single risk-adjusted rate or opportunity cost of capital (in equation 2.3) can then be obtained:

$$NPV = \sum_{t=1}^{T} \frac{E(c_t)}{(1 + k)^t} - I.$$

According to Fama (1977), this is valid provided the portfolio investment opportunity set facing investors (i.e., the combinations of expected return and variance obtainable from efficient portfolios) remains unchanged so that the risk-free interest rate and the market price of risk are constant (i.e., $r_t = r$, $\lambda_t = \lambda$), and provided the project's systematic risk as given by its beta also remains constant through time (i.e., $\beta_t = \beta$). As we saw earlier, the use of a constant discount rate, k, implicitly assumes that the relevant total risk increases at a constant rate through time or that the same incremental uncertainty is resolved in each period. Since in the multi-period CAPM world, in the absence of real options, the basic intermediate uncertainty results from reassessments through time of investors' expectations of cash flows, it may not be unreasonable for projects or firms of a given *type* or for those expected to maintain the same nature of activities throughout their life to assume that the risks in the reassessments of the expected value of cash flows are the same in each period and use a single CAPM risk-adjusted discount rate or cost of capital. However, the presence of managerial flexibility in the form of embedded real options changes the nature of risk and invalidates the use of a constant discount rate.

Although the beta of many assets can be found to be fairly stable over time, in general beta may be very difficult to determine accurately, even in the absence of real options. Apart from statistical measurement difficulties, Myers and Turnbull (1977) point out that a project's true beta depends on

its life, the growth rate of its expected cash flows, the pattern of the expected cash flows over time, the characteristics of any individual underlying components of these cash flows, the procedure by which investors
revise their expectations of cash flows, and the relationship between forecast errors for the cash flows and those for the market return. If the project's beta to be used in obtaining its cost of capital and the NPV is to be
determined by measuring the beta of a security in the same risk class as
the project, then, to be strict, the project and the security should be
matched on all the above factors. Moreover, if the security represents a
firm with growth opportunities (real options), the observed beta of the
growth firm's stock (which can be looked at as an option on the firm's assets) would actually be an overestimate of the true beta of the firm's assets, leading to undervaluation of the project when its beta is carelessly
derived from observed common-stock betas of growth firms. If a project's
beta cannot be reasonably assumed to be constant in each period of its life
(or if risk does not increase at a steady rate over time), then the generalized RADR form of NPV with different discount rates in various periods
is more appropriate in principle than the more widely used textbook single cost of capital approach. The presence of contingencies introduced by
managerial flexibility poses more serious problems, necessitating the use
of option-based valuation.[6]

2.3   Other Approaches Dealing with Uncertainty and Complexity

Other approaches (such as sensitivity analysis, simulation, and decision-
tree analysis) that attempt to deal with uncertainty and complexity, and
furthermore to account for the possibility of later decisions that could be
taken by the firm's management have been proposed which, although
helpful in improving management's understanding of the structure of the
investment decision, nevertheless stop short of offering a manageable,
consistent solution.

Sensitivity Analysis

We have already seen that the estimates of the cash flows used in capital
budgeting to determine NPV are invariably derived from (oftentimes
most likely) forecasts of other primary variables (the project's life, salvage
value, production costs, the price of the product, the size and growth of
the market, the firm's market share, etc.). Sensitivity analysis is the process
of delving into these forecasts to identify the key primary variables and

determining the impact upon NPV (or sometimes IRR) of a given variation (or misestimation) in each key variable at a time, with other variables
held constant; it is also sometimes called "what if" analysis, since it addresses questions of the form "What is the consequence or effect on the
investment decision (NPV) if there is an error or misestimation of variable
x by a certain amount, assuming other variables are estimated correctly?"

Sensitivity analysis thus starts with a base-case scenario where management determines the base-case (usually most likely) estimates of the
key primary variables from which it can calculate the base-case NPV.
Then, while keeping all other variables equal to their base-case or most
likely values, each variable is changed by a certain percentage below and
above its base-case value (or, alternatively, is set to its *pessimistic* and *opti-
mistic* estimates); the resulting *perturbed* NPV values can then give a pic-
ture of the possible variation in or sensitivity of NPV when a given risky
variable is misestimated.

Sensitivity analysis is useful in identifying the crucial variables that
could contribute the most to the riskiness of the investment. A variable
may itself be very risky (in having a large variance relative to other variables) but may nonetheless make an insignificant contribution to the riskiness of the project's NPV, in which case the investment decision does not
crucially depend on the accuracy of its estimate; on the other hand, a less
risky variable (having a small variance) may be crucial if even marginal
errors in its estimate could have a significant impact on NPV. Whether a
variable is crucial or not would indicate whether it is worth investing additional time and money to gather additional information that could reduce the uncertainty surrounding the variable, or whether we should bother
with estimating (the probability distribution describing) that uncertainty
in the first place. Sensitivity analysis also indicates how bad a misestimation (or how large the forecast error) of a variable can be before the investment becomes unacceptable.

Sensitivity analysis has its limitations as well. First, as we saw, it considers the effect on NPV of only one error in a variable at a time, thus
ignoring combinations of errors in many variables simultaneously—a
definite drawback when, as happens with most real-life projects, management's forecasts of different variables err in concert. Moreover, examining
the effect of each variable in isolation is even less meaningful when there
are interdependencies among the variables, in which case knowing the
value of one variable would influence the estimates of another; if two
variables are positively (negatively) interdependent, whenever one has a
high value exceeding its most likely estimate the other will then quite

probably also have a high (low) value above (below) its own expectation, so that it is inappropriate to consider the effect of each variable in isolation. In addition, estimates of a variable may be serially dependent over time so that a forecast error in one year may propagate higher errors in subsequent years, causing a greater impact on NPV.

If variables are interdependent, it will be an improvement over sensitivity analysis—which considers the impact of varying only one variable at a time—to examine the project under alternative scenarios that examine the impact on NPV of a limited number of different, internally consistent (in terms of accounting for dependencies) combinations of variables. A bigger step forward that considers the impact of all possible combinations of variables is achieved through Monte Carlo simulation, considered next.

Traditional Simulation

Traditional simulation techniques use repeated random sampling from the probability distributions for each of the crucial primary variables underlying the cash flows of a project to arrive at output probability distributions or *risk profiles* of the cash flows or of NPV (sometimes of IRR) for a given management strategy. Simulation attempts to imitate a real-world decision setting by using a mathematical model (consisting of operating equations or identities) to capture the important functional characteristics of the project as it evolves through time and encounters random events, conditional on management's prespecified operating strategy. A Monte Carlo simulation usually follows these steps:

(1) Modeling the project through a set of mathematical equations and identities for all the important primary variables, including a description of interdependencies among different variables and across different time periods.

(2) Specifying probability distributions for each of the crucial variables, either subjectively or from past empirical data. Sensitivity analysis should precede simulation to determine which variables are important (so that special care can be taken to obtain their precise probability distributions) and which are not (in which case a single estimate of the variables may suffice). To deal with dependencies between two variables, in principle a single probability distribution can be determined for the independent variable while several distributions can be specified for the dependent one, each conditional on the independent variable falling within a given

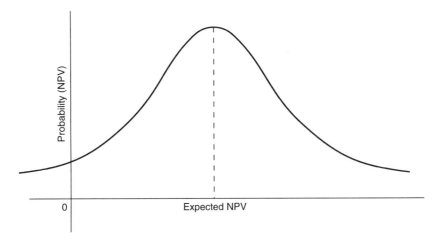

Figure 2.9
A (symmetric) probability distribution of NPV.

range—although in practice this may sometimes place unreasonable demands on management's ability to furnish realistic estimates.

(3) A random sample is then drawn (using a computer random number generator) from the probability distribution of each of the important primary variables enabling (with the help of the modeling equations and identities) the calculation of net cash flows for each period (from which the NPV for the sample can also be determined).

(4) The process is repeated many times (until, say, 500 random samples are obtained), each time storing the resulting cash flow or NPV sample observations so that finally a probability distribution for the project's cash flows or of NPV (such as the one shown in figure 2.9) can be generated (along with its expected value, standard deviation, and other statistics).

Although simulation can handle complex decision problems under uncertainty with a large number of input variables, which may even interact with one another or across time, it is not without its own limitations. First, even if the analysts responsible for estimating the probability distributions are unbiased, it will be very difficult and complex to correctly capture all the inherent interdependencies. The existence of substantial complexity may then induce management to delegate model building to experts, with the resulting danger that management's understanding of and consequently faith in and commitment to the simulation results may be substantially reduced. Second, when the outcome of simulation is a risk profile of NPV rather than of the intermediate cash flows, the meaning of an outcome probability distribution of NPV is questionable, since it is not clear what discount rate should be used. To quote Myers (1976): "If NPV is calculated using an appropriate risk adjusted discount rate, any further adjustment for risk is double-counting. If a risk-free rate of interest is used instead, then one obtains a distribution of what the project's value would be tomorrow if all uncertainty about the project's cash flows were resolved between today and tomorrow. But since uncertainty is not resolved in this way, the meaning of the distribution is unclear." Also, if a project can have many possible "present values"—one for each point on the distribution—then we can no longer interpret present value as the price the project would command in competitive capital markets. Third, even if management wants to base a decision on the probability distribution or risk profile of NPV, it still has no rule for translating that profile into a clear-cut decision for action; it can only stare at the fake *expected* NPV (discounted at the riskless interest rate) and its surrounding variance until it receives inspiration from above on how to trade them off. Fourth, simulation users may be tempted to use as a relevant measure of risk the variability of project outcomes (i.e., the project's own, or *total*, risk) instead of its *systematic* risk, which we saw to be the relevant risk from the point of view of the firm's shareholders who have opportunities to diversify away part of that risk by buying other securities in the market; Lewellen and Long (1972) point exactly to this inability to reveal how the resulting distribution interacts with the distribution of returns faced by the firm in its other projects or by investors in their personal portfolios as the major shortcoming of simulation. Furthermore, using the total variability of the NPV distribution violates value additivity and enables managers to successfully promote unrelated projects as a group, when each project alone might be unacceptable.

Myers (1976) points to other problems of interpretation of simulation output, such as the unreliability of extreme values of simulated probability distributions. Finally, Monte Carlo simulation is a *forward-looking* technique based on a predetermined (built-in) operating strategy offering roughly symmetric probability distributions, and as such it may be an appropriate model for path-dependent or history-dependent problems; however, it cannot handle well the asymmetries in the distributions introduced by management's flexibility to review its own preconceived operating strategy when it turns out that, as uncertainty gets resolved over time, the realization of cash flows differs significantly from initial expectations. Management, in reality, can adapt to surprises (e.g., abandon a project if it turns out to perform surprisingly poorly), but a computer-simulated model cannot; it will faithfully and blindly continue obeying the business-as-usual operating strategy that it was programmed to follow, based on management's expectations and information at the very outset. Thus, as will become clear later, simulation is limited in dealing with the options or *free-boundary* problems that enter the valuation of real investment opportunities (such as determining the optimal timing policies for undertaking or abandoning a project), whose solution requires a backward-induction or dynamic-programming approach.

Despite the above shortcomings, in many real-life problems when making use of dynamic programming is difficult (e.g., when there are many state variables), simulation and numerical-lattice approaches constitute the primary practical approaches to valuation. A more appropriate role for simulation in traditional capital budgeting would be to assess the probability distribution not of NPV but of cash flows, from which the expected value of cash flows and the appropriate risk-adjusted discount rates can be determined and used to derive a single-value expected NPV that can be used for clear-cut decision making. Thus, simulation should be used not instead of but rather as an aid to implementing NPV. When real options are involved, simulation may be a powerful tool for determining the relevant "certainty-equivalent" or risk-neutral probability distributions within a backward risk-neutral valuation process.

Decision-Tree Analysis

Another approach that attempts to account for uncertainty and the possibility of later decisions by management is decision-tree analysis (DTA). DTA helps management structure the decision problem by mapping out all feasible alternative managerial actions contingent on the possible states of nature (chance events) in a hierarchical manner. As such it is particularly useful for analyzing complex sequential investment decisions when uncertainty is resolved at distinct, discrete points in time. Whereas conventional NPV analysis might be misused by managers inclined to focus only on the initial decision to accept or reject the project at the expense of subsequent decisions dependent on it, DTA forces management to bring to the surface its implied operating strategy and to recognize explicitly the interdependencies between the initial decision and subsequent decisions.

The basic structure of the decision setting is as follows: Management is faced with a decision (or a sequence of decisions) of choosing among alternative courses of action; the consequence of each alternative action depends on some uncertain future event or state of nature which management can describe probabilistically on the basis of past information—or additional future information obtainable at some cost. Management is finally assumed to select a strategy consistent with its preferences for uncertain consequences and its probabilistic judgments concerning the chance events. This means that management should choose the alternative that is consistent with maximization of expected utility—or, in a capital-budgeting context, the one that maximizes the risk-adjusted expected NPV.

Example 5   Let us now revisit the earlier R&D example, in which if the initial $0.1 million investment proves successful (with a 30% chance), management can build a base-scale plant expected to generate annual cash flows of $0.5 million. This time we will delve deeper into the conditional nature of the cash-flow forecasts. In particular, the marketing department believes there is a 20% chance that the market will be highly (H) receptive of the new drug in its first year (offering, at the assumed 10% cost of capital, an expected value as of year 5 of subsequent cash flows, including the salvage value, of approximately $8 million), a 60% chance that the product will meet medium (M) market reception (offering a year-5 expected value of about $4 million), and a 20% chance that the product will meet low (L) acceptance (offering a year-5 expected value of −$0.1 million).

Figure 2.10 shows the basic decision tree describing pictorially the decision problem facing the firm. There are two kinds of nodes (decision points) on the tree. Squares represent separate decision points for management (decision nodes); circles represent decision points for nature or points in time when outcomes outside the control of management are revealed by nature (outcome nodes). It is as if management is playing a "game" (say, chess) against nature, taking turns to make their "moves." (Nature, of course, is a nonthinking opponent making its moves randomly so such a game against nature presents management with an optimization problem; this is in contrast to problems of strategy or games against competition in which calculated countermoves can be made.) Management has to move first by making an initial decision at node A as to whether to accept the R&D project or reject it (as shown by the branches emanating from that node). If management decides to accept the project, nature will then make its move, revealing the outcome of the R&D effort (at node a). In the event that R&D is successful—which has a 0.3 probability of occurrence, as shown in parentheses next to the appropriate

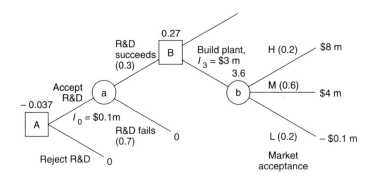

Year 0   3   4   5   . . .

Figure 2.10
A decision-tree representation of the R&D problem. The static base-case NPV (ignoring management flexibility) is negative, implying (inappropriate) rejection of the project.

branch—management must make a subsequent decision at node B if it is to invest an additional $3 million to build a base-scale plant[7] to produce the product. Nature will then reveal at node b whether the product will meet high (H), medium (M), or low (L) market acceptance with associated probabilities of 0.2, 0.6, and 0.2 and associated values of cash-flow consequences of $8 million, $4 million, and—$0.1 million, respectively.

Although management need only make the current decision (of accepting or rejecting the R&D project) for the time being, it should realize that the current choice will in effect determine (and eventually be determined by) the feasibility and attractiveness of future events and possible later decisions by management. Since a decision at any stage can be long-term optimal (in the light of possible later decisions) only if all subsequent decisions are themselves optimal, the optimal initial decision must be determined by starting from the end (the right side) of the tree and working backward to the beginning. This dynamic-programming, average-out-and-fold-back, or roll-back procedure involves determining at each stage, as we move backward, the expected risk-adjusted discount NPV (or expected utility) by multiplying all the NPV (or utility) values calculated at the previous (although chronologically following) stage with their respective probabilities of occurrence and summing up. (Expected NPVs are, of course, obtained after discounting at the appropriate risk-adjusted discount rate or opportunity cost of capital for securities with similar risk characteristics, here assumed to be 10%.)

Starting from the back of the tree in figure 2.10, it can be seen that the expected present value of subsequent cash flows as of year 5 (as given by summing the products of the values of expected NPV at the time, conditional on market acceptance's being high, medium, or low, with their associated probabilities) is

$$E_5(PV) = 0.2 \times 8 + 0.6 \times 4 + 0.2(-0.1) = 3.98.[8]$$

Rolling back at node b and discounting at the cost of capital, $k = 0.10$, we get for the expected NPV as of year 4

$$E_4(NPV) = \frac{E_5(PV)}{1+k} = \frac{3.98}{1+0.10} = 3.6.$$

(The expected NPV of subsequent cash flows as of any year will subsequently be shown above the corresponding node or square in that year—in the present case, 3.6 is shown above node b in figure 2.10.) Folding back one more period at node B, we get

$$E_3(NPV) = \frac{E_4(NPV)}{1+k} - I_3 = \frac{3.6}{1.10} - 3 = 0.27.$$

Finally, we arrive at the node of the initial decision A, obtaining the expected NPV as of year 0 (the present):

$$E_0(NPV) = \frac{E_0 E_3(NPV)}{(1+k)^3} - I_0$$

$$= \frac{0.3 \times 0.27 + 0.7 \times 0}{(1.10)^3} - 0.1$$

$$= -0.037, \text{ or } -\$37,000 \text{ (base-case expected NPV).}$$

This is roughly the same value yielded by the traditional NPV calculation earlier in this chapter. On the basis of this negative static or passive base-case expected NPV, management would be inclined to reject the R&D project.

However, in real life management may not actually have to be committed to a project for its entire pre-estimated expected life. In fact, it may have the flexibility to abandon a once-undertaken simple project when its abandonment value (net salvage value) exceeds the NPV of the project's

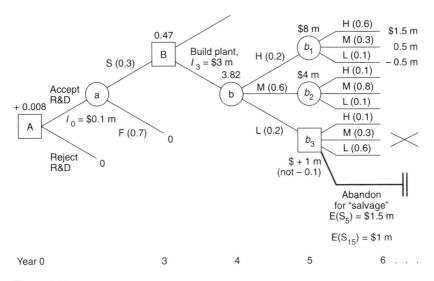

Figure 2.11
"Expanded expected NPV" when management has the option to abandon a once-undertaken simple project (in this case, the plant) for its "salvage" value.

expected subsequent cash flows at any time before the end of its useful life, or to abandon a compound (multi-stage) project with a series of investment "installments" just before the next "installment" is due if the value from continuing (the present value of subsequent expected cash flows plus any subsequent options) is not adequate to cover the upcoming costs.

Let us next consider the first case, i.e., the flexibility to abandon a simple project, once undertaken, before the end of its pre-estimated expected life when its salvage value at any time exceeds the present value of expected subsequent cash flows (including the abandonment value at the end of the estimated useful life). Figure 2.11 delves deeper into the estimates used for the static base case of building the plant in figure 2.10, focusing particularly on the stage (or project) following the introduction of the product in the market (years 5–15). In addition to showing the probabilities of high, medium, and low market acceptance in the year of the product's introduction (which we saw earlier to be 0.2, 0.6, and 0.2 respectively), figure 2.11 shows management's subjective probabilities of H, M, or L market acceptance in the second stage (years 6–15) of the product's expected life. Specifically, management believes that if the market is highly receptive of the product (which has a 0.2 probability of occurring) in its first year, then the probabilities of H, M, and L acceptance in subsequent years are 0.6, 0.3 and 0.1, respectively; conditional on a medium first-year market acceptance (with a 0.6 probability) the probabilities of H, M, and L acceptance in subsequent years are 0.1, 0.8, and 0.1; and the conditional probabilities given low first-year acceptance (having a 0.2 probability) are 0.1 for H, 0.3 for M, and 0.6 for L market acceptance in subsequent years, respectively. In any of the 11 years the product is expected to be sold in the market, management expects to receive net annual cash flows of $1.5 million if market acceptance is H, $0.5 million if it is M, and −$0.5 million if it is L in that year. In any case, management can abandon the project at the end of its expected useful life in year 15 for an expected net salvage value of $1 million ($E(S_{15}) = 1$); if, however, it were to abandon the project after year 5 (after observing the market's reception of the product in its year of introduction), management would expect to receive a net salvage value of $1.5 million (i.e., $E(S_5) = 1.5$).

The expected cash flows in any subsequent year t ($t = 6 - 15$) conditional on H, M, or L first-year acceptance are

$$E(c_t|H) = 0.6 \times 1.5 + 0.3 \times 0.5 + 0.1 \times (-0.5) = 1,$$

$$E(c_t|M) = 0.1 \times 1.5 + 0.8 \times 0.5 + 0.1 \times (-0.5) = 0.5,$$

and

$$E(c_t|L) = 0.1 \times 1.5 + 0.3 \times 0.5 + 0.6 \times (-0.5) = 0,$$

giving an unconditional expected (average) cash flow in each year (for $t = 6 - 15$) of

$$E(c_t) = \Pr(H)E(c_t|H) + \Pr(M)E(c_t|M) + \Pr(L)E(c_t|L)$$

$$= 0.2 \times 1 + 0.6 \times 0.5 + 0.2 \times 0$$

$$= 0.5 \text{ per year,}$$

and (for $t = 5$)

$$E(c_5) = 0.2 \times 1.5 + 0.6 \times 0.5 + 0.2 \times (-0.5) = 0.5,$$

verifying that the expected cash flow in each year of the product's life (years 5–15) is $500,000, as stated earlier. Also, the expected value as of year 5 of all subsequent cash flows (including salvage value at the end) after high market acceptance in the first year is

$$E_5(V_5|H) = \sum_{t=1}^{10} \frac{1}{(1.10)^t} + \frac{1}{(1.10)^{10}} = 6.1 + 0.4 = 6.5.$$

Similarly, $E_5(V_5|M) = 3.1 + 0.4 = 3.5$ and $E_5(V_5|L) = 0 + 0.4 = 0.4$. (If we include the cash flow expected to occur in the same year, the expected values as of year 5 of all cash flows from that year onward, conditional on H, M or L first-year market acceptance, are

$E_5(c_5 + V_5|H) = 1.5 + 6.5 = 8$,

$E_5(c_5 + V_5|M) = 0.5 + 3.5 = 4$,

and

$E_5(c_5 + V_5|L) = -0.5 + 0.4 = -0.1$,

which are roughly in agreement with the values given in figure 2.10.)

Looking at the unconditional expected value as of year 5 of the subsequent cash flows based on information available at time 0 (which is $E_5(V_5) = 0.2 \times 6.5 + 0.6 \times 3.5 + 0.2 \times 0.4 = 3.5$), management may be tempted to decide at time 0 that it should continue with the project after year 5 (since the expected value of subsequent cash flows from continuing, based on information at time 0, is $3.5 million, which exceeds the expected salvage value of $1.5 million from abandoning the project right after year 5). This reasoning is wrong, however, since in reality management has the flexibility to wait until right after year 5 (and benefit from any intermediate resolution of uncertainty, in particular from the information provided by the market concerning the product's first-year acceptance) before it has to actually make the subsequent decision of continuing or abandoning the project after year 5. The only decision management has to commit to at time 0 is the initial decision whether to accept or reject the initial R&D project; any time-0 operating policy (based on information available at the time of the first decision) concerning subsequent decisions may be revised later as uncertainty is resolved and more information is gathered along the way. Thus, if market acceptance of the product turns out to be low, management may find it desirable to abandon the project since the expected value of continuing after year 5 (including the salvage value at the end), $E_5(V_5|L) = 0.4$, is less than the $1.5 million salvage value management could obtain from abandoning the project immediately after year 5; the project should otherwise continue since the expected values of subsequent cash flows following M first-year acceptance ($3.5 million) or following H first-year acceptance ($6.5 million) both exceed the $1.5 million salvage value from immediate abandonment. The asymmetry introduced by the flexibility to abandon early for the salvage value provides management with a downside protection consisting of the option to choose the maximum of the expected value from continuing or the salvage value from abandoning the project, i.e., max(0.4, 1.5). Including the cash flow in year 5, the expected value of the project at the end of year 5, including abandonment when the first-year acceptance turns out to be low, now becomes

$$E_5(c_5 + S_5|L) = -0.5 + 1.5 = +1$$

(instead of -0.1 without abandonment). Essentially, with the flexibility to abandon now present, the static base-case tree in figure 2.10 should be modified by changing the value of the low branch from -0.1 to $+1$ (or, alternatively, by adding a decision node after period 5 at the end of the low market acceptance branch, followed by two branches with values -0.1 and $+1$, only the better of which will actually be pursued). The (unconditional) expected present value as of year 5 then becomes

$$E_5(NPV) = Pr(H)E_5(c_5 + V_5|H) + Pr(M)E_5(c_5 + V_5|M)$$
$$+ Pr(L)E_5(c_5 + S_5|L)$$
$$= 0.2 \times 8 + 0.6 \times 4 + 0.2 \times 1$$
$$= 4.2$$

(instead of 3.98 without abandonment). The value of the flexibility to abandon in present-value (time 0) terms (which we refer to as *abandonment value*) is

$$\frac{0.3(4.2 - 3.98)}{(1.10)^5} = 0.041.$$

The expanded expected NPV, when the flexibility to abandon is present, is thus more valuable than the base-case static (or passive) expected NPV without abandonment by the amount of the premium for the flexibility to abandon (or abandonment value), i.e.,

Expanded $E_0(NPV)$, with abandonment for salvage

$$= Static\ E_0(NPV) + Abandonment\ value$$
$$= -0.037 + 0.041$$
$$= +0.004,\ or\ \$4000.$$

On the basis of this positive expanded NPV, which incorporates the flexibility to abandon the plant for its salvage value before the end of its anticipated useful life, the initially undesirable R&D project now becomes acceptable.

So far we have considered abandoning a once-undertaken project for its salvage value in one particular year (in our specific case, the end of year 5) if that year's salvage value exceeds the expected NPV of subsequent cash flows (including later abandonment). The total abandonment value may, of course, be higher if the flexibility to abandon exists in more (or all) years. If the project's expected salvage value were to exceed the expected NPV of subsequent cash flows (including later abandonment) for more than one year, then it would not necessarily be optimal that management should abandon the project in the first such year; instead, management must also determine the year in which abandonment would be optimal jointly with determining abandonment value. In such a case, the optimal year for abandonment is the year in which expanded NPV (i.e., the sum of the static base-case NPV and the abandonment value) is maximized.

In addition to abandoning a simple project for its salvage value, management may have the flexibility to abandon a compound or multi-stage project (consisting of a chain of contingent stages or subprojects) at the end of one stage and before it has to incur a new investment-cost "installment" to proceed to the next stage; management would find such an opportunity to *default* (or abandon by defaulting on an "installment" outlay) desirable when the expected present value of subsequent cash flows is not sufficient to cover the expected costs to be incurred (or, alternatively, when the expected NPV of subsequent cash flows—including any subsequent options—turns out negative in any such year). The R&D project in figure 2.11 is an example of such a multi-stage project (or compound option): accepting the R&D project (by paying the first investment cost installment of $0.1 million) provides an initial option to engage in the research effort; if it proves successful, it may be followed by another option to construct a production plant (by incurring another outlay), with the opportunity that the project will be commercialized and the product sold in the market to generate the expected cash revenues.

The flexibility to abandon the project by defaulting on planned investment installments may exist at several points during the project's life, such as right after year 3 (if the R&D effort fails) or at the end of year 4 (since there is no obligation to proceed with building a plant). The more such flexibility there is, the greater the total abandonment value and the greater the total value of the project as given by the following equation:

Expanded expected NPV

= Static expected NPV + Total abandonment value.

In summary: The problem facing management is a sequence of decisions: the initial decision (which is the only decision management has to commit to now) is whether to accept the R&D project immediately or to reject it (node A). If the R&D project proves a success, management will then be faced with deciding whether to build a plant and later sell its product for all the years of its useful life or to abandon the project early.

Based on information available at the time of the initial decision (year 0), management determines its optimal operating strategy according to the criterion of maximizing the expanded expected NPV (incorporating the flexibility to abandon the project early at specific times) as follows: Management immediately accepts the R&D project. With respect to its later decisions, management now anticipates (although, as time progresses and future uncertainty gets resolved, it may find it desirable to revise its anticipated future decisions) that if its research effort proves successful it will proceed to build the plant and introduce the product in the market; if, however, the results are discouraging, it will abandon the project by defaulting on the planned investment outlays. Finally, if the product's first-year market acceptance is low, management will abandon the plant for its salvage value, otherwise it will continue selling the product for the remaining years.

The above discussion shows that, in principle, decision-tree analysis is well suited for analyzing sequential investment decisions when uncertainty is resolved at discrete points in time, and that it forces management to recognize explicitly the interdependencies between immediate decisions and subsequent ones, bringing to the surface management's implied operating strategy based on its current information. DTA is able to accommodate in principle the flexibility to abandon a project at certain discrete prespecified points in time based on the expectation of cash flows and their probabilistic estimates that can be quantified at the time of the initial decision. But although it goes a long way, it has practical limitations in the real world.

First of all, decision-tree analysis can easily become an unmanageable "decision-bush analysis" when actually applied in most realistic investment settings, as the number of different paths through the tree (or bush) to be evaluated expands geometrically with the number of decisions, outcome variables, or states considered for each variable. In the examples above, we considered only two or three states for each outcome variable.

In reality, market demand does not have just "high" or "low" values; there are quite a few intermediate values. Also, in the real world chance events may not simply occur at a few discrete points; rather, the resolution of uncertainty may be continuous. Similarly, decision choices, such as the option to abandon a project early, may not just present themselves at a few discrete points in time but may require management's continuous attention. In our R&D project, for example, the option to abandon for the project's salvage value may present itself in any year, including the first 3 years of research or any of the last 10 years of selling the product in the market—not just after the product's first year—if unanticipated unfavorable events come up in the future. It should thus be clear that a continuous-time version of decision-tree analysis might be in a better position to describe real-world problems in a more compact manner.

A more serious problem is how to determine the appropriate discount rate (or utility). In our earlier example we avoided this problem by assuming the risk-adjusted discount rate to be 10% in each year. To be strict, of course, using a constant discount rate presumes that the risk borne per period is constant and that uncertainty is resolved continuously at a constant rate over time, not (as the example suggested) at discrete lumps; if discrete chance events were appropriate, then different discount rates should have been used in different periods (or at different stages in the project's life). Even then, the problem of finding the proper discount rate remains.

For example, in the case of investment opportunities involving multiple follow-on stages, even for a decision maker willing to accept a constant discount rate for the cash flows in the last stage (the "underlying asset") it would not be appropriate to use a constant rate for the preceding stage, since it is essentially an option on the value of cash flows from the following stage.[9] In the R&D example above, even if we are willing to assume a constant discount rate of 10% for the expected cash flows from the commercialization stage (the sale of the product in the last 11 years) it may be incorrect to use the same constant discount rate for the first 3 years of the research effort. Even in a simple (single-stage) project (or in the last stage of a multi-stage investment), the presence of a real option would alter the project's riskiness, hence altering the discount rate that would prevail without the option. For example, a put option to abandon would clearly reduce the project's risk and lower the discount rate. In the extreme case where a put option (such as that provided by a government guarantee to purchase the product in case of low demand, as in the example of chapter 1) would completely eliminate risk, the proper discount rate would reduce to the lower risk-free interest rate. (In example 1, with $r =$ 5%, the base-case NPV is \$1.157 million rather than $-\$0.037$ million.) Using the higher 10% (risk-adjusted) cost of capital that may be appropriate for the naked project (without the abandonment option) in the DTA would clearly undervalue the project's true worth when risk is reduced via an abandonment option or a guarantee.

Some authors have attempted to get around the problem by discounting at the risk-free rate and then trying to arrive at a decision by examining the probability distribution of NPV. As was discussed under simulation above, the meaning of such a distribution and its expected value are not clear. In any case, it is inconsistent to build the tree forward in DTA using the actual probabilities and expected rate of return but to then move backward discounting at the risk-free rate (without using certainty-equivalent or risk-neutral probabilities). In principle one may alternatively use expected utility maximization instead, but determining the appropriate utility to use is no easier. Traditional DTA is on the right track, but although mathematically elegant it is economically flawed because of the discount-rate problem. An options approach can remedy these problems.

Suggested Readings

Bierman, H., Jr., and S. Smidt. 1993. *The Capital Budgeting Decision*. Eighth edition. Macmillan.

Brealey, R., and S. C. Myers. 1991. *Principles of Corporate Finance*. Fourth edition. McGraw-Hill.

Fama, E. 1977. "Risk-adjusted discount rates and capital budgeting under uncertainty." *Journal of Financial Economics* 5, no. 1: 3–24.

Fischer, I. 1930. *The Theory of Interest*. Macmillan.

Hertz, D. 1964. "Risk analysis in capital investment." *Harvard Business Review* 42 (January-February): 95–106.

Magee, J. 1964. "How to use decision trees in capital investment." *Harvard Business Review* 42 (September-October): 79–96.

3

Option-Pricing Theory and Financial-Options Applications

This chapter reviews the basic concepts and tools of option-pricing theory and contingent-claims analysis, along with some financial-options applications. Sections 3.1 and 3.2 explain the basic nature of options and the basic replication idea underlying option valuation. Section 3.3 presents the basic rational properties of option pricing based on distribution-free dominance arguments and lists the standard assumptions. Section 3.4 describes the general multiplicative binomial process in discrete time. A review of basic stochastic processes in the context of stock-price behavior is given in section 3.5. Section 3.6 describes the continuous-time Black-Scholes option-pricing model. Adjusting for dividend effects is discussed in section 3.7. Section 3.8 describes a general approach to the valuation of contingent claims, whether the underlying asset is traded or not. Section 3.9 describes various applications to corporate liabilities and other financial securities. The appendix summarizes useful solutions for later reference. Much of this chapter can be skipped by well-informed readers.

3.1 The Basic Nature of Options

An *option* is defined as the right, without an associated symmetric obligation, to buy (if a *call*) or sell (if a *put*) a specified asset (e.g., common stock) by paying a prespecified price (the *exercise* or *strike price*) on or before a specified date (the *expiration* or *maturity* date). If the option can be exercised before maturity, it is called an *American* option; if only at maturity, a *European* option.

The beneficial asymmetry deriving from the right to exercise an option only if it is in the option holder's interest to do so—with no obligation to do so if it is not—lies at the heart of an option's value. Options differ from *futures contracts*, which involve a commitment to fulfill an obligation undertaken to buy or deliver an asset in the future at terms agreed upon

Table 3.1
Extract from listed stock options quotations, April 20, 1995.

Option (N.Y. close)	Strike price	Expiration date	Call	Put
AT&T	45	May	—	$\frac{1}{8}$
$49\frac{1}{8}$	45	July	$4\frac{7}{8}$	$\frac{1}{4}$
$49\frac{1}{8}$	50	April	$\frac{1}{16}$	$\frac{3}{4}$
$49\frac{1}{8}$	50	May	$\frac{13}{16}$	$1\frac{3}{16}$
$49\frac{1}{8}$	50	July	$1\frac{5}{8}$	$1\frac{5}{8}$
$49\frac{1}{8}$	50	October	$2\frac{1}{4}$	$2\frac{1}{8}$
$49\frac{1}{8}$	55	May	$\frac{1}{16}$	—
$49\frac{1}{8}$	55	July	$\frac{1}{4}$	—

Source: *Wall Street Journal*, April 21, 1995.

today whether the holder likes it or not. Thus, unlike the potential payoff to futures contracts, which are symmetric with regard to up or down movements of the underlying asset, the payoff to options is asymmetric or one-directional.

The underlying asset to an option may be one of a large variety of financial or real assets. For example, there are options traded on individual shares of common stock (e.g., IBM); on stock indexes (e.g., the Standard and Poor's 500 index in the United States, the Nikkei 225 index in Japan, the FT 100 index in Europe); on various types of bonds (effectively, on the interest rate); on oil, metals, and various types of commodities (e.g., wheat or potatoes); on foreign currencies; on various corporate liabilities (convertible or callable securities, warrants, etc.); on real assets or capital projects (real options); and so on.

Table 3.1 shows how options on individual shares of common stock would be listed in the financial press (e.g., in the *Wall Street Journal* under the heading "Listed Options Quotations" in the Money and Investing section). The underlying stock's name (e.g., AT&T) and New York closing price are listed in the first column. Options for various exercise or strike prices, typically in increments of $5 around the stock's current price (e.g., $45, $50, or $55), are listed in the second column. The third column lists the available (closest) expiration dates (by convention, the third Friday of the listed expiration month). The last two columns show the prices (or premiums) for calls and for puts for each strike price and expiration. Stock options typically have maturities of 3, 6, and 9 months. By convention,

one option contract is for the purchase or sale of 100 shares of the underlying stock; therefore it costs 100 times the quoted price.

Consider, for example, the call option on the AT&T stock in table 3.1
with a strike or exercise price (E) of $55 and 3 months to maturity
(expiring in July 1995). Since the stock is currently selling for $S = \$49\frac{1}{8}$
(below the exercise price), the option holder would not find it desirable to
exercise immediately (i.e., would not want to pay the exercise price of
$E = \$55$ to acquire an asset worth less). Nevertheless, the call option has a
positive value ($\$\frac{1}{4}$) since there is roughly an even chance that the stock
may move up or down by maturity. Suppose, for simplicity, that on the
last day the stock will be worth either $S^+ = \$60$ (if the market moves up)
or $S^- = \$40$ (if it moves down). If the stock were to move down, the call
option would not be exercised (since no such obligation is involved), and
would therefore expire worthless (i.e., $C^- = 0$). However, if the stock
were to move up to $60, the call option at maturity would be worth the
difference between the price of the stock (that would be acquired) and the
set exercise price (that would be paid), i.e.,

$$C^+ = S^+ - E = 60 - 55 = \$5.$$

This possibility of a positive future payoff is reflected in a positive current
price (premium) for the option. If the stock were more volatile, moving up
to, say, $70 or down to $35 by maturity, the option would be even more
valuable. On the downside, although the stock price may drop lower, the
losses on the option are limited to the same amount (i.e., the option still
expires worthless, with the total loss again limited to the premium paid to
purchase the option up front); the upside profit potential is improved,
however, with the payoff to the option in this case increased to $70 − 55,
or $15. Thus, contrary to conventional wisdom that uncertainty is harm-
ful, the basic asymmetry in the case of options—both calls and puts—
makes uncertainty beneficial.

Unlike call options, which increase in value with favorable movements
in the underlying asset price (i.e., are more valuable on the upside), put
options—just like *insurance*—pay off when the asset drops in value (i.e.,
are more valuable on the downside). In the case of a put option on the
above stock with the same maturity (July) and an exercise price $E = \$45$,
for example, the put would expire worthless if the stock at maturity were
to move up to $60, but would pay off $E - S^- = 45 - 40$ or $5 if the stock
were to move down to $40 (or $10 if it were to drop to $35). The possi-
bility of a positive payoff on the down side is reflected in a positive
premium for the put option. Put options can be used like insurance to

provide protection against a decline in the value of the underlying asset. A government guarantee or a product warranty is, in effect, a put option.

In fact, options are like a double-edged knife: used by themselves, *naked* options can be used to *speculate* or gamble about ones' beliefs on the direction of the underlying asset value, with amplified potential returns (as well as risks); for example, if one believes that oil prices are on the rise one can buy call options on crude oil, or if the U.S. stock market is headed for a decline one can buy put options on the Standard and Poor's 500 stock index. On the other hand, used in conjunction with other assets, options can be used to reduce or *hedge* risk; for example, if a person is heavily invested in the U.S. stock market and is concerned about his exposure to potential adverse movements in the market, he can *insure* his stock wealth against a potential decline below a given floor level by buying an appropriate amount of put options on the S&P 500 index (or by creating a home-made put-option position synthetically using a dynamic trading strategy known as *portfolio insurance*, along the principles shown in the next section). Similarly, options on government bonds can be used to hedge against fluctuations in interest rates, and options on foreign currency can hedge against foreign exchange risk.

The following notation will be employed in the next sections:

$C \equiv C(S, \tau; E)$: value of an American call option

$c \equiv c(S, \tau, E)$: value of a European call option

$P \equiv P(S, \tau; E)$: value of an American put option

$p \equiv p(S, \tau; E)$: value of a European put option

$S \equiv S_t$: underlying stock price at time t

T: maturity (expiration date of the option)

τ: time to expiration of the option $(= T - t)$

E: exercise (strike) price of the option

r : risk-free interest rate (for maturity T)

3.2   The Basic Valuation Idea: Option Replication with Synthetic Options

The basic idea enabling the exact pricing of options is that one can construct a portfolio consisting of buying a particular number, N, of shares of the underlying asset (e.g., common stock) and borrowing against them an appropriate amount, $B, at the riskless rate, that would exactly replicate the future returns of the option in any state of nature. Since the option and this equivalent portfolio (effectively, an appropriately levered position in the stock) would provide the same future returns, to avoid risk-free arbitrage profit opportunities they must sell for the same current price. Thus, we can value the option by determining the cost of constructing its equivalent replicating portfolio, that is the cost of a *synthetic* or homemade option equivalent.

Suppose that the price of the underlying stock (currently at $S = \$100$) will move over the next period either up to $S^+ = 180$ (i.e., with a multiplicative up parameter, $u = 1.8$) or down to $S^- = 60$ (with a multiplicative down parameter, $d = 0.6$), with probabilities q and $(1 - q)$, respectively, i.e.,

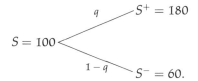

$$S = 100 \quad \overset{q}{\underset{1-q}{\diagup\diagdown}} \quad \begin{matrix} S^+ = 180 \\ \\ S^- = 60. \end{matrix}$$

The value of the option over the period would then be contingent on the price of the underlying stock. Assuming $E = \$112$ (and $r = 0.08$),

$$C \quad \overset{q}{\underset{1-q}{\diagup\diagdown}} \quad \begin{matrix} C^+ = \max(S^+ - E, 0) \\ = 68 \\ \\ C^- = \max(S^- - E, 0) \\ = 0 \end{matrix}$$

where C^+ and C^- are the values of the call option at the end of the period if the stock moves up or down, respectively.

Suppose now we construct a portfolio as described above, consisting of (a) buying N shares of the underlying stock at its current price, S, financed in part by (b) borrowing an amount of B at the riskless interest rate (e.g., selling short Treasury bills), for a net out-of-pocket cost of $NS - B$. That is,

Call option $\approx$ (Buy N shares at S & Borrow B at r),

or

$$C \approx (NS - B). \tag{3.1}$$

After one period, we would need to repay the principal amount borrowed at the beginning (B) with interest, or $(1+r)B$, for certain. The value of this portfolio over the next period will thus be

$$N S - B \begin{cases} \overset{q}{\nearrow} & N S^+ - (1+r)B \\ \underset{1-q}{\searrow} & N S^- - (1+r)B. \end{cases}$$

If the portfolio is to offer the same return in each state at the end of the period as the option, then

$$N S^+ - (1+r)B = C^+$$

and

$$N S^- - (1+r)B = C^-.$$

Solving these two equations (conditions of equal payoff) for the two unknowns, N and B, gives

$$N = \frac{C^+ - C^-}{S^+ - S^-} = \frac{68 - 0}{180 - 60} = 0.56 \text{ shares} \tag{3.2}$$

and

$$B = \frac{S^- C^+ - S^+ C^-}{(S^+ - S^-)(1+r)} = \frac{N S^- - C^-}{1+r} = \frac{0.56 \times 60 - 0}{1.08} = \$31. \tag{3.3}$$

The number of shares of the underlying asset that we need to buy to replicate one option over the next period, N, is known as the option's *delta* or *hedge ratio*, and is simply obtained in the discrete case as the difference (spread) of option prices divided by the spread of stock prices. That is, we can replicate the return to the option by purchasing $N(= 0.56)$ shares of the underlying stock at the current price, S, and borrowing the amount $\$B$ ($= \$31$) at the riskless rate, r.

When substituted back into equation 3.1, $C = N S - B$, equations 3.2 and 3.3 finally result in

$$C = \frac{pC^+ + (1-p)C^-}{1+r} = \frac{0.4 \times 68 + 0.6 \times 0}{1.08} = \$25, \tag{3.4}$$

where

$$p \equiv \frac{(1+r)S - S^-}{S^+ - S^-} = \frac{1.08 \times 100 - 60}{180 - 60} = 0.4 \tag{3.5}$$

is a transformed or *risk-neutral probability*, i.e., the probability that would prevail in a risk-neutral world where investors are indifferent to risk.

Risk-Neutral Valuation

Intuitively, equation 3.1 can be rearranged into $NS - C = B$, i.e., creating a portfolio consisting of (a) buying N shares of the underlying stock and (b) selling (writing) one call option would provide a certain amount of $(1+r)B = \$33$ next period, regardless of whether the stock moves up or down:

$$
\begin{array}{ccc}
& & NS^+ - C^+ = (1+r)B \\
& q \nearrow & 0.56(180) - 68 = 33 \\
NS - C = B & & \\
0.56(100) - 25 = 31 & & \\
& 1-q \searrow & NS^- - C^- = (1+r)B \\
& & 0.56(60) - 0 = 33.
\end{array}
$$

Through the ability to construct such a *riskless hedge*, risk can effectively be "squeezed out" of the problem, so that investors' risk attitudes do not matter. Therefore, we can equivalently—and more conveniently—obtain the correct option value by *pretending* to be in a *risk-neutral world* where risk is irrelevant. In such a world, all assets (including stocks, options, etc.) would earn the risk-free return, and so *expected* cash flows (weighted by the risk-neutral probabilities, p) could be appropriately discounted at the risk-free rate.

Denoting by $R^+ \equiv u - 1 = S^+/S - 1$ $(= 0.80$ or $80\%)$ the return if the stock moves up $(+)$, and by $R^- \equiv S^-/S - 1$ $(= -0.40$ or $-40\%)$ the down $(-)$ return, the risk-neutral probability, p, can be alternatively obtained from the condition that the *expected* return on the stock in a risk-neutral world must equal the riskless rate, i.e.,

$$pR^+ + (1-p)R^- = r.$$

Solving for p yields

$$p = \frac{r - R^-}{R^+ - R^-} = \frac{0.08 - (-0.40)}{0.80 - (-0.40)}$$

or

$$p = \frac{(1+r) - d}{u - d} = \frac{1.08 - 0.6}{1.8 - 0.6} = 0.4. \tag{3.5'}$$

Similarly, the expected return on the option must also equal the risk-free rate in a risk-neutral world, i.e.,

$$\frac{pC^+ + (1-p)C^-}{C} - 1 = r,$$

resulting in equation 3.4.

A number of points are worth reviewing about the above call-option valuation:

It provides an exact formula for the value of the option in terms of S, E, r, and the stock's volatility (spread).

With no dividends, $C > S - E$, so an American call option should not be exercised early; when dividends are introduced, early exercise may be justified, however.

The motivation for the pricing of the option rests with the absence of arbitrage profit opportunities, a strong economic condition.

The actual probability of up and down movements, q, does not appear in the valuation formula. Moreover, the value of the option does not depend on investors' attitudes toward risk or on the characteristics of other assets—it is priced only relative to the underlying asset, S.

The value of the option can be equivalently obtained in a risk-neutral world (since it is independent of risk preferences). Actually, p is the value probability q would have in equilibrium if investors were risk neutral. As the above valuation formula confirms, in such a risk-neutral world—where all assets are expected to earn the riskless rate of return—the current value of the option can be obtained from its expected future values (using the risk-neutral probability, p), discounted at the risk-free interest rate.

A put option can be valued similarly, except that we would need to *sell* (instead of buy) shares of the underlying stock, and *lend* (instead of borrow) at the riskless interest rate (i.e., buy government bonds), i.e.,

Put option $\approx$ (Sell N shares at S & Lend $\$B$ at r).

The hedge ratio or delta for a put option is simply the delta of the corresponding call option minus 1, giving $0.56 - 1 = -0.44$ in the above example (with the minus sign indicating selling, rather than buying, 0.44 shares of the underlying stock). Applying equation 3.3 in the case of a similar put option where $P^- = E - S^- = 112 - 60 = 52$, the amount to lend is given by

$$B = \frac{N S^- - P^-}{1 + r} = \frac{-0.44 \times 60 - 52}{1.08} = -\$72.6.$$

Thus, to replicate a put option we need to sell 0.44 shares of stock at $S = \$100$ and lend (minus sign in B) \$72.6 at the riskless rate (i.e., buy Treasury bills with that face value). Thus, the current value of the put option should be

$$P = NS - B = -0.44 \times 100 - (-72.6) = \$28.6.$$

3.3 Rational Properties and Standard Assumptions of Option Pricing

Basic Rational Properties

Based on a set of weak assumptions concerning rational behavior of investors (that is, free of distributional assumptions about the underlying stock price process), Merton (1973) develops a set of restrictions or consistency criteria for options. The basic assumption used is that of dominance. Security (portfolio) A is dominant over B if over a given period the return of A is at least as large as that of B for all states of the world, and strictly larger in at least one state. Thus, if investors prefer more wealth to less, they would all choose A over B. In equilibrium, no security can be dominant or dominated, leading to the following basic rational properties:

P1 The value of options is non-negative, i.e.,

$C(S, \tau; E) \geq 0,$

$c(S, \tau; E) \geq 0,$

$P(S, \tau; E) \geq 0,$

$p(S, \tau; E) \geq 0.$

Options have limited liability, since exercise is voluntary and will be undertaken only if it is in the best interest of the holder.

P2 At expiration, a call option is worth the maximum of $S - E$ (if $S > E$) or 0 (i.e., it would expire worthless if $S \leq E$):

$$C(S, 0; E) = c(S, 0; E) = \max(S - E, 0).$$

Similarly, a put option at expiration is worth the maximum of $E - S$ (exercised if $S < E$) or 0 (worthless if $S \geq E$):

$$P(S, 0; E) = p(S, 0; E) = \max(E - S, 0).$$

P3 An American option must sell for at least its exercise value (of $S - E$ if a call, or $E - S$ if a put); else there exists an arbitrage opportunity to buy and exercise:

$$C(S, \tau; E) \geq \max(S - E, 0),$$

$$P(S, \tau; E) \geq \max(E - S, 0).$$

P4 An American option with a longer time to expiration is worth at least as much as an otherwise identical option with a shorter time to maturity:

$$C(S, \tau_1; E) \geq C(S, \tau_2; E) \text{ if } \tau_1 > \tau_2.$$

P5 An American option is worth at least as much as an otherwise identical European option (since it gives all the rights of the European option plus the additional right of early exercise):

$$C(S, \tau; E) \geq c(S, \tau; E),$$

$$P(S, \tau; E) \geq p(S, \tau; E).$$

P6 A call option with a lower exercise price is worth at least as much as an otherwise identical option with higher exercise price (by dominance):

$$C(S, \tau; E_1) \geq C(S, \tau; E_2),$$

$$c(S, \tau; E_1) \geq c(S, \tau; E_2) \text{ if } E_1 \leq E_2.$$

P7 A call option cannot be worth more that its underlying stock:

$$C(S, \tau; E) \leq S.$$

From P4 and P6, it follows that $C(S, \tau; E) \leq C(S, \infty; 0) \leq S$.

P8 A call option is worthless if its underlying stock is worthless:

$$C(0, \tau; E) = c(0, \tau; E) = 0.$$

This follows directly from P1 and P7. (A put option, however, will be surely exercised if $S = 0$, and so it would be worth the exercise price E.)

P9 The value of a call option (on a non-dividend paying stock) is worth at least as much as the stock price minus the present value of the exercise price:

$$c(S, \tau; E) \geq \max(S - B(\tau)E, 0),$$

where $B(\tau) \equiv e^{-r\tau}$ is the price of a riskless (default-free) pure-discount bond paying \$1 in τ years. To see this, consider the following two portfolios:

Table 3.2
Illustration for P9.

	Portfolio	
	A	B
If $S < E$	$0 + E$	S
If $S \geq E$	$(S - E) + E = S$	S

(A) Buy one European call for $c(S, \tau; E)$, and E bonds at a price of $B(\tau)$ each, for a total investment of $c(S, \tau; E) + B(\tau)E$.

(B) Buy the stock for S.

At expiration, we have the payoffs illustrated by table 3.2 in each state. Since portfolio A dominates portfolio B ($E > S$ if $S < E$), $c(S, \tau; E) + B(\tau)E \geq S$, which along with P1, proves property P9.

P10 An American call option on a non-dividend paying stock should never be exercised before its expiration, and therefore should have the same value as an identical European option:

$$C(S, \tau; E) = c(S, \tau; E).$$

From P1 and P9, and since $B(\tau) < 1$ for $r, \tau > 0$,

$$C(S, \tau; E) \geq c(S, \tau; E) \geq \max(S - B(\tau)E, 0) > \max(S - E, 0).$$

Thus, the American call option is worth more alive than exercised. That is, it would never be optimal to exercise it early (i.e., the privilege of premature exercise is valueless), and should thus be worth the same as its European counterpart. Unfortunately, this property does not hold for American puts, since there is a positive probability of exercising before maturity. This is most clear if S drops to 0, in which case the put will be exercised for sure. Therefore, an American put, $P(S, \tau; E)$, has a strictly greater value than its European counterpart, $p(S, \tau; E)$.[1]

P11 The payment of dividends (D) may justify early exercise of an American call option. This can be seen by repeating the argument in P10 but buying ($E + D$) instead of E bonds in portfolio A.

P12 A perpetual call option on a non-dividend-paying stock has the same value as the underlying stock:

$$C(S, \infty; E) = S.$$

This follows from P9 with $\tau = \infty$ (i.e., $C(S, \infty; E) \geq \max(S - B(\infty)E, 0) = S$), and from P7.

Table 3.3
Illustration for P13.

	Portfolio	
	A	B
If $S \le E$	$S + (E - S) - E = 0$	0
If $S > E$	$S - E$	$S - E$

P13 The following *put-call parity* relationship holds between the values of European puts and calls with identical exercise prices and time to expiration. The value of the European put is equal to the value of a portfolio consisting of a European call with the same terms, a stock held short, and riskless bonds of face value E:

$$p(S, \tau; E) = c(S, \tau; E) - S + B(\tau)E. \tag{3.6}$$

To demonstrate, consider the following two portfolios:
(A) Buy a stock at S; buy a put at p; and borrow $\$E$ for τ periods. The total investment is $S + p(S, \tau; E) - B(\tau)E$.
(B) Buy a call with the same terms at $c(S, \tau; E)$.
Then, at expiration, the payoffs of each portfolio in each state are as illustrated in table 3.3. Since the two portfolios offer the same payoff in each state, to avoid risk-free arbitrage profit opportunities they must have the same investment costs, i.e.,

$$S + p(S, \tau; E) - B(\tau)E = c(S, \tau; E).$$

This put-call parity relationship is very important since it enables determining (restrictions on) the price of European puts from call-option pricing.

These rational properties require that the value of options as a function of the underlying stock price is within certain bounds and has a shape consistent with what is shown in figures 3.1 (for calls) and 3.2 (for puts). Based on the above rational properties, note the following in figure 3.1 regarding bounds for the call option value:

(1) From P1, $C \ge 0$, the absolute lower bound is 0 (horizontal line OE). Even at A (where $S = E$) the option's value is non-negative ($AE > 0$), since there is a positive chance of a positive gain if by maturity $S > E$.

(2) From P3, $C \ge \max(S - E, 0)$, the option's value is bounded from below by the kinked (45° at E) line OEF. The lower-bound value $(S - E)$ is the value from immediate exercise or at maturity; hence, it is called the intrinsic, exercise, or maturity value.

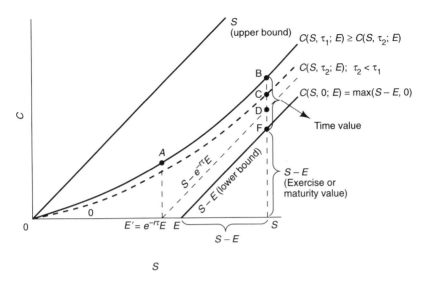

Figure 3.1
Determinants (bounds) for call option values: Variation of call-option value C with underlying asset (stock) price S.

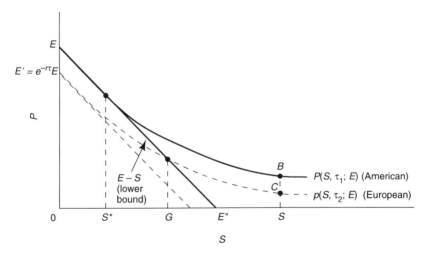

Figure 3.2
Determinants (bounds) for put option values: Variation of put-option value P with underlying asset (stock) price S.

(3) From P4, $C(S, \tau_1; E) \geq C(S, \tau_2; E)$ for $\tau_1 > \tau_2$, curve OB (with more time to maturity) is above curve OC (with lower maturity).

(4) From P7, $C \leq S$, the call has the underlying stock price (i.e., the $45°$ line OS) as an upper bound ($S = C(S, \infty; E)$).

(5) From P8, when $S = 0$ then $C = 0$ (going through the origin, at point 0). That is, when the stock is worthless, so is the call option.

(6) From P9, $C(S, \tau; E) \geq \max(S - e^{-r\tau}E, 0)$ [$> \max(S - E, 0)$ from P3]. Thus, the option value has as a tighter lower bound the line $OE'D$ ($45°$ at $E' = e^{-r\tau}E$), and approaches $S - e^{-r\tau}E$ (point D) in the limit as $S \to \infty$. That is, when the stock price rises substantially, the call option will almost surely be exercised (with E paid in the future), so that the option value would approach the stock price less the present value of the exercise price (S – PV of E). As we saw, buying a call option can be thought of as equivalent to buying the stock with risk-free borrowing, to be paid back at the future exercise time. It is like a delayed purchase of the stock financed with a loan in installments. As such, it is more valuable the higher the risk-free rate (implicit in the installment loan), r, and the longer the time to maturity, τ.

The above bounds suggest that the call-option value increases with the underlying stock price in a manner consistent with the indicated curve OAB. Note that in the case of a call option on a stock without dividends, the value of the option alive (from waiting to exercise) always exceeds its intrinsic or lower-bound value from immediate exercise, and so it is not optimal to exercise a call option without dividends before maturity. Clearly, the option value is higher for a higher asset volatility (σ) since the option holder has the same downside loss but a higher upside gain potential, as well as for a longer time to maturity (τ). In summary, call-option value (C) increases with S, r, τ, and σ and declines with the exercise cost (E), other things being constant.

Figure 3.2 illustrates the appropriate bounds and shape for a put option. At maturity the put is worth $\max(E - S, 0)$, represented by the kinked line $EE''S$ (at $135°$). The put-option value (P) declines with the price of the underlying stock (S) that would be given up in exchange for the specified exercise price (E) and with r, while it increases with τ, σ, and E. However, unlike calls, early exercise of American puts may be optimal even when the underlying stock pays no dividends. As figure 3.2 shows, when the stock price drops below a critical level (when $S < S^*$), the put is worth its immediate exercise value (i.e., $P = E - S$). Thus, for low S the curve representing the American put becomes one with the line representing the intrinsic or immediate exercise value ($E - S$). At an extreme, when S drops to 0 the put will surely be exercised early, since the most it can be worth is E. (Waiting can bring at most E, but at a later time and with a lower present value.) Note also that since the American put is at least as valuable as a similar European put, the latter may be worth less than its intrinsic value $(E - S)$ for low stock prices (for $S < G$); in figure 3.2 the European put curve crosses the intrinsic-value line when $S = G(> S^*)$ and meets the vertical axis (where $S = 0$) at $E' = e^{-r\tau}E(< E)$.

The above properties provide bounds and consistency criteria for option valuation based on dominance arguments, free from distributional assumptions. A set of basic assumptions, including a distributional assumption concerning stock-price movement, however, must be made if exact pricing formulas are to be obtained.

Standard Assumptions

Standard option valuation typically relies on the following assumptions:

A1 Frictionless markets (for stocks, bonds, and options). This means that (a) there are no transactions costs or (differential) taxes; (b) there are no restrictions on short sales (such as margin requirements), and full use of proceeds is allowed; (c) all shares of all securities are infinitely divisible; and (d) borrowing and lending (at the same rate) are unrestricted. These assumptions allow continuous trading.

A2 The risk-free (short-term) interest rate is constant over the life of the option (or known over time).

A3 The underlying asset (stock) pays no dividends over the life of the option. (This assumption is later removed, with appropriate dividend adjustments.)

A4 (distributional assumption concerning the stock-price process) Stock prices follow a stochastic diffusion Wiener process of the form

$$\frac{dS}{S} = \alpha \, dt + \sigma \, dz, \tag{3.7}$$

where α is the instantaneous (total) expected return on the stock, σ is the instantaneous standard deviation of stock returns (assumed constant), and dz is the differential of a standard Wiener process (with mean 0 and variance dt). The diffusion process in equation 3.7 is explained later in section 5. In the discrete-time case, discussed below, this diffusion process is replaced by a multiplicative binomial process or *random walk* which in the limit, as the trading interval gets smaller and smaller, becomes equivalent to the log-normal distribution underlying the process in equation 3.7.

3.4   The Multiplicative Binomial Process: Discrete Time

The general multiplicative binomial option-pricing approach was popu-
larized by Cox, Ross, and Rubinstein (1979). It is based on the replication argument described in section 3.2 above, except that the stock-price
movements follow a more strict multiplicative binomial process. Here A4
is replaced by the following:

A4′ The underlying stock price follows a stationary multiplicative binomial process over successive periods described by

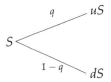

where the stock price at the beginning of a given period, S, may increase
(by a multiplicative factor u) with probability q to uS or decrease with
complementary probability $(1 - q)$ to dS at the end of the period. Thus u
and d represent the (continuously compounded or logarithmic) rate of return if the stock moves up or down, respectively, with $d = 1/u$. (Since
riskless borrowing at the rate r is also available (from A2), to avoid riskless arbitrage profit opportunities, $u > (1 + r) > d$.)

In our earlier notation, $S^+ \equiv uS$ and $S^- \equiv dS$ with $d = 1/u$, so that

$$u \equiv \frac{S^+}{S} = 1 + R^+, \text{ where } R^+ \text{ is the up } (+) \text{ return,}$$

and   (3.8)

$$d \equiv \frac{S^-}{S} = 1 + R^-, \text{ where } R^- \text{ is the down } (-) \text{ return.}$$

Thus, expressions 3.2, 3.3, 3.4, and 3.5 would now become

$$N = \frac{C^+ - C^-}{(u - d)S}, \tag{3.2'}$$

$$B = \frac{dC^+ - uC^-}{(u - d)(1 + r)}, \tag{3.3'}$$

$$C = \frac{pC^+ + (1 - p)C^-}{1 + r}, \tag{3.4'}$$

and

$$p = \frac{(1+r) - d}{u - d} = \frac{1.08 - 0.6}{1.8 - 0.6} = 0.4. \tag{3.5'}$$

The above valuation procedure can be easily extended to multiple periods. If the time to expiration of the option, τ, is subdivided into n equal sub-intervals, each of length $h \equiv \tau/n$, and the same valuation process is repeated starting at the expiration date and working backward recursively, the general multiplicative binomial option-pricing formula for n periods will be

$$C = \frac{\displaystyle\sum_{j=0}^{n} \frac{n!}{j!(n-j)!} p^j (1-p)^{n-j} \max(u^j d^{n-j} S - E, 0)}{(1+r)^n}.$$

The first part, $[n!/j!(n-j)!]p^j(1-p)^{n-j}$, is the binomial distribution formula giving the probability that the stock will take j upward jumps in n steps, each with (risk-neutral) probability p. The last part, $\max(u^j d^{n-j} S - E, 0)$, gives the value of the call option at expiration conditional on the stock following j ups each by $u\%$, and $n - j$ downs each by $d\%$ within n periods. The summation of all the possible ($j = 0, \ldots, n$) option values at expiration, multiplied by the probability that each will occur, gives the expected terminal option value, which is then discounted at the riskless rate over the n periods.

If we let m be the minimum number of upward moves j over n periods necessary for the call option to be exercised or to finish in the money (i.e., $u^m d^{n-m} S > E$, or by logarithmic transformation m is the smallest non-negative integer greater than $\ln(E/Sd^n)/\ln(u/d)$), and break up the resulting term into two parts, then the binomial option-pricing formula can be more conveniently rewritten as

$$C = S\Phi[m; n, p'] - \frac{E}{(1+r)^n} \Phi[m; n, p], \tag{3.9}$$

where Φ is the complementary binomial distribution function (giving the probability of at least m ups out of n steps):

$$\Phi[m; n, p] \equiv \sum_{j=\alpha}^{n} \frac{n!}{j!(n-j)!} p^j (1-p)^{n-j},$$

and

$$p' \equiv \left(\frac{u}{1+r}\right) p,$$

with p and m as defined above.

One may initially object to this discrete period-by-period binomial valuation approach, since in reality stock prices may take on more that just two possible values at the end of a given period, while actual trading in the market takes place almost continuously and not on a period-by-period basis. However, the length of a "period" can be chosen to be arbitrarily small by successive subdivisions.

As the length of a trading period, h, is allowed to become increasingly smaller (approaching 0) for a given maturity, τ, continuous trading is effectively approximated. In the continuous-time limit, as the number of periods n approaches infinity, the multiplicative binomial process approximates the log-normal distribution or *smooth* diffusion Wiener process of equation 3.7, so that distributional assumption A4' is effectively replaced with A4.

By choosing the parameters (u, d, and p) so that the mean and variance of the continuously compounded rate of return of the discrete binomial process are consistent in the limit with their continuous counterparts, the stock price will become log-normally distributed and the (complementary) binomial distribution function, $\Phi[\cdot]$, will converge to the (cumulative) standard normal distribution function, $N(\cdot)$. Specifically, by setting

$$u = e^{\sigma\sqrt{h}},$$

$$d = 1/u, \tag{3.10}$$

$$p = \tfrac{1}{2} + \tfrac{1}{2}(\mu/\sigma)\sqrt{h},$$

where $\mu \equiv \ln r - \tfrac{1}{2}\sigma^2$, τ is the time to expiration, n is the number of subperiods, and $h \equiv \tau/n$ is the interval or length of a trading period (typically expressed as a fraction of a year), Cox, Ross, and Rubinstein (1979) show that, as $n \to \infty$,

$$\Phi[m; n, p'] \to N(x),$$

so that the above binomial formula converges to the continuous-time Black-Scholes formula[3]

$$C = SN(x) - E(1+r)^{-\tau}N(x - \sigma\sqrt{\tau}), \tag{3.11}$$

where

$$x \equiv \frac{\ln(S/E(1+r)^{-\tau})}{\sigma\sqrt{\tau}} + \tfrac{1}{2}\sigma\sqrt{\tau}.$$

For example, if $\tau = 3$ months $= 0.25$ years and $n = 12$, a discrete multiplicative binomial process with $u = 1.1$ and weekly intervals ($h = \tau/n = $

0.02 years) would be consistent in the limit with a log-normal diffusion process with annual standard deviation,

$$\sigma = \ln u / \sqrt{h} = \ln(1.2) / \sqrt{0.02} = 0.66, \text{ or } 66\%.$$

The Black-Scholes solution for a call option can also be derived using the earlier distributional assumption concerning the underlying stock price process of equation 3.7 and making use of Ito's lemma when constructing a riskless hedge. (See section 3.6.)

3.5* Stock-Price Behavior and Stochastic Processes

Stock prices (and gross project values) are assumed to follow a *stochastic process*, i.e., their value changes over time in an uncertain manner. Stochastic processes can be "discrete-time" (changing only at certain discrete intervals) or "continuous-time" (subject to change at any time). A particular type of a stochastic process is the *Markov process*, where only the present state of the process (i.e., the current stock price) is relevant for predicting the future; the past history of the process is irrelevant (i.e., the process is memoryless). This is consistent with the weak form of the efficient-markets hypothesis. Competition among thousands of competent, rational analysts ensures that the latest new information is immediately impounded into the current stock price. If the current stock price already reflects all the information contained in the record of past prices, stock prices will change only in response to new, unpredictable information; price changes (or returns) will thus be independent over time.

A particular type of a Markov process is the *Wiener process* or *Brownian motion*, which has been used to describe collisions of particles in physics. If a variable $z(t)$ follows a Wiener process, then changes in z, Δz, over small time intervals, Δt, must satisfy two important properties:

(1) Δz over small (nonoverlapping) time intervals are independent. That is, the process can be thought of as the continuous limit of a discrete-time random walk.

(2) Δz are *normally distributed*, with mean $E(\Delta z) = 0$ and a variance that increases linearly with the time interval, i.e., $\text{Var}(\Delta z) = \Delta t$. Specifically, $\Delta z = \varepsilon_t \sqrt{\Delta t}$, where ε_t is a normally distributed random variable with zero mean and standard deviation of 1. In continuous time, as $\Delta t \to 0$, the increment of a standard Wiener process becomes $dz = \varepsilon_t \sqrt{dt}$, with $E(dz) = 0$ and $\text{Var}(dz) = dt$.

Although stock prices can be assumed to satisfy the Markov property and have independent increments, price changes are clearly not normally distributed (otherwise, we would observe negative prices). Stock prices are closer to being log-normally distributed, so it is more reasonable to assume that the (natural) logarithm of price follows a Wiener process. Stock prices also have a (nonzero) drift and some volatility (other than 1), so that a more generalized Wiener process would be more appropriate. This can be represented by

$$dS = \alpha(S, t)dt + \sigma(S, t)dz,$$

where dz is the increment of a standard Wiener process (with mean 0 and variance dt) and where $\alpha(S, t)$ and $\sigma(S, t)$ are the drift and variance coefficients expressed as functions of the current state and time. The continuous-time stochastic process S is called an *Ito process*; its mean and variance are $E(dS) = \alpha(S, t)dt$ and $Var(dS) = \sigma^2(S, t)dt$.

An important special case is the *geometric Brownian motion* with drift, or the *standard diffusion Wiener process*, where $\alpha(S, t) = \alpha S$ and $\sigma^2(S, t) = \sigma^2 S^2$ (with α and σ constant), given by

$$dS = \alpha S\, dt + \sigma S\, dz,$$

or by

$$\frac{dS}{S} = \alpha\, dt + \sigma\, dz$$

(i.e., equation 3.7), where α is the (constant) instantaneous expected return on the stock, σ is the (constant) instantaneous standard deviation of stock returns, and dz is the differential of a standard Wiener process (with mean 0 and variance dt).

The above equation is the most widely used model of stock-price behavior. Note that $E(dS) = \alpha S\, dt$, and $Var(dS) = \sigma^2 S^2 dt$. Thus, the expected stock price drift as a *proportion* of the current stock price is assumed to be constant. With a constant instantaneous expected stock return, α, the expected increase in stock price within a small time interval, Δt, is $\alpha S\, \Delta t$.

The discrete-time version of the above model is

$$\frac{\Delta S}{S} = \alpha\, \Delta t + \sigma \varepsilon \sqrt{\Delta t}, \tag{3.7'}$$

where ΔS is the change in the stock price in a small time interval, Δt, ε is a random sample from a standardized normal distribution, α is the expected (multiplicative) stock return per unit of time, and σ is the volatility of stock price.

Before we can proceed to use the above stochastic process for stock-price behavior to derive the value of a call option on a stock, we need to make use of Ito's lemma. Consider an option or a contingent claim, $F(S, t)$, as a function of an underlying state variable, S, and time, t, only. To value the contingent claim, we need to determine how it changes in a small interval of time as a function of the underlying state variable. Ito's lemma is easier to understand as a Taylor-series expansion:

$$F(S + \Delta S, t + \Delta t) = F(S, t) + \frac{\partial F}{\partial t} \Delta t + \frac{\partial F}{\partial S} \Delta S + \frac{1}{2} \frac{\partial^2 F}{\partial S^2} (\Delta S)^2 + \cdots,$$

or

$$\Delta F \equiv F(S + \Delta S, t + \Delta t) - F(S, t)$$

$$= \frac{\partial F}{\partial t} \Delta t + \frac{\partial F}{\partial S} \Delta S + \frac{1}{2} \frac{\partial^2 F}{\partial S^2} (\Delta S)^2 + \cdots.$$

In the limit, as higher-order terms disappear,

$$dF = \frac{\partial F}{\partial t} dt + \frac{\partial F}{\partial S} dS + \frac{1}{2} \frac{\partial^2 F}{\partial S^2} (dS)^2.$$

If S follows the standard diffusion (Ito) process in equation 3.7, $(dS)^2$ behaves like $\sigma^2 S^2 dt$, so that Ito's lemma becomes

$$dF = \frac{\partial F}{\partial t} dt + \frac{\partial F}{\partial S} dS + \frac{1}{2} \frac{\partial^2 F}{\partial S^2} (\sigma^2 S^2 dt).$$

3.6 Black-Scholes Option Pricing: Continuous Time

In their seminal paper, Black and Scholes (1973) showed that the continuous application of a dynamic portfolio replication strategy under assumptions A1–A4 (with σ assumed constant) results in a fundamental partial differential equation that must be satisfied by the value of the call option, $F(S, t) \equiv C(S, t; E)$. The above stochastic processes tools can be used to derive the Black-Scholes p.d.e.

Derivation of Black-Scholes Differential Equation*

Consider constructing an equivalent replicating portfolio as was done in the binomial case, $C = NS - B$, where in the limit $N = \partial C / \partial S$. Alternatively, a riskless hedge portfolio can be constructed, $NS - C = B$, by selling short one call option and purchasing $N = \partial C / \partial S$ shares of the underlying stock at the current price, S. Since the Wiener processes (or the dz terms) underlying S and C are the same, the Wiener-process uncertainty can be eliminated in a small time interval dt. From $dC = N\,dS - dB$ (or $N\,dS - dC = dB$) with $N = \partial C/\partial S$ and using the expression for dC from Ito's lemma above,

$$\frac{\partial C}{\partial t}dt + \frac{\partial C}{\partial S}dS + \frac{1}{2}\frac{\partial^2 C}{\partial S^2}\sigma^2 S^2 dt = \frac{\partial C}{\partial S}dS - dB,$$

or

$$dB = -\left(\frac{\partial C}{\partial t} + \frac{1}{2}\frac{\partial^2 C}{\partial S^2}\sigma^2 S^2\right)dt.$$

Since this portfolio is riskless, it should earn the risk-free return, i.e., $dB/B = r\,dt$. Thus,

$$dB = Br\,dt = \left(\frac{\partial C}{\partial S}S - C\right)r\,dt.$$

Equating the above two expressions for dB and using subscripts to denote partial derivatives (with $C_\tau = -C_t \equiv -\partial C/\partial t$), results in the following p.d.e., which must be satisfied by the value of the call option, $C(S, \tau; E)$:

$$\tfrac{1}{2}\sigma^2 S^2 C_{SS} + rSC_S - C_\tau - rC = 0, \tag{3.12}$$

subject to the terminal condition

$$C(S, 0; E) = \max(S - E, 0),$$

and the lower and upper boundary conditions

$$C(0, \tau; E) = 0$$

and

$$C(S, \tau; E)/S \to 1 \text{ as } S \to \infty.$$

Similarly, the value of a European put option satisfies the same p.d.e. (with p simply replacing C),

$$\tfrac{1}{2}\sigma^2 S^2 p_{SS} + rSp_S - p_\tau - rp = 0, \tag{3.13}$$

but subject to a different set of conditions: the terminal condition

$$p(S, 0; E) = \max(E - S, 0)$$

and the lower and upper boundary conditions

$$p(0, \tau; E) = E$$

and

$$\frac{p(S, \tau; E)}{S} \to 0 \text{ as } S \to \infty.$$

The Black-Scholes Option-Pricing Model

Black and Scholes solved the p.d.e. in equation 3.12, obtaining their now-famous formula—also shown earlier as the limit of the multiplicative binomial process, and rewritten here in more conventional notation as

$$C(S, \tau; E) = SN(d_1) - Ee^{-r\tau}N(d_2), \tag{3.14}$$

where

$$d_1 = \frac{\ln(S/E) + (r + \frac{1}{2}\sigma^2)\tau}{\sigma\sqrt{\tau}},$$

$$d_2 = d_1 - \sigma\sqrt{\tau},$$

and $N(\cdot)$ is the cumulative standard normal distribution function. (A more convenient alternative derivation of the Black-Scholes formula can be obtained using the risk-neutral valuation approach, as shown in equations 3.21–3.23 below.)

Although at first glance it may look awesome, the Black-Scholes formula in essence represents nothing more than the continuous application (in the limit) of the replicating portfolio hedge described above. Interpreting the Black-Scholes formula in terms of the riskless portfolio hedge, the call option is equivalent to a levered position in the stock where the number of shares of the stock held in the replicating portfolio (the option hedge or delta), N, is here given by $N(d_1)$, and the amount borrowed is given by the second term, i.e., $B = Ee^{-r\tau}N(d_2)$. Since N and B fluctuate continuously with the underlying stock price (and with time), they would require frequent (theoretically, continual) adjustment in order to maintain the above equivalence.

It can be confirmed from the above formula that, other factors being constant, the value of a call option is higher (1) the higher the value of the underlying asset (e.g., the stock), S; (2) the longer the time to expiration, τ; (3) the lower the exercise price, E; (4) the higher the variance of asset returns, σ^2; and (5) the higher the riskless interest rate, r. Clearly, the call option would be higher the higher the "reward" to be received (S) and the lower the cost to be paid (E). The greater the time to expiration (τ) and the greater the volatility (σ), the greater the chances that the stock price would move around more, which is beneficial because of the favorable asymmetry of having the right to benefit more from higher upside movements, while being subject to the same limited losses on the down side (since no obligation to exercise is involved). Finally, since the exercise price does not need to be paid until a later time when the option would in fact be exercised—which effectively gives a risk-free credit loan to the option holder—the present value of the cost (E) would be lower the higher the interest rate (r).

To obtain Black-Scholes option values in practice, one may use as a short-cut tabulated values as shown in tables A.1 and A.2 in the appendix to this volume. First, calculate $\sigma\sqrt{\tau}$ to specify the appropriate column; then calculate $S/PV(E)$ (either from $S/[Ee^{-r\tau}]$ or from $S/[E/(1+r)^\tau]$) to identify the proper row. The table entry at their intersection would then give the value of the option relative to the underlying asset price, so we need to multiply the tabulated entry by the asset price S to obtain the option value. For a European call option one should use table A.1; for a European put option one should use table A.2 (or use the put-call parity of equation 3.6). The value of the hedge ratio for a call option can be obtained from a similar table. Note also that, for a put,

Put delta = Call delta − 1.

The Black-Scholes solution for the European put option (obtained readily from the put-call parity relationship, P13) is given by

$$p(S, \tau; E) = -SN(-d_1) + Ee^{-r\tau}N(-d_2), \tag{3.15}$$

where d_1, d_2, and $N(\cdot)$ are as given in equation 3.14.

For the American put option we need to check for early exercise (i.e., whether the value of the option alive exceeds its value from early exercise) by imposing the condition that $P(S, \tau; E) \geq \max(E - S, 0)$. This option does not have a closed-form solution for a finite maturity, although various numerical approximations are feasible. However, for the perpetual put option (with $\tau \to \infty$ and $P_\tau \to 0$), Merton (1973) provides the solution (which can serve as an upper-bound approximation):

$$P(S, \infty; E) = E\left(\frac{(1+\gamma)S}{\gamma E}\right)^{-\gamma}, \tag{3.16}$$

where $\gamma \equiv 2r/\sigma^2$ (> 0).

3.7 Adjusting for Dividend Effects

Without dividends, as Merton (1973) has shown, it is never optimal to exercise an American call option prematurely, and so the value of an American call would equal the value of its European counterpart.[4] If the underlying asset pays dividends, however, then its value would be reduced after each dividend payment, and it may become optimal to exercise an American call option early in order to acquire ownership of the asset and capture the dividend. Dividends generally affect the drift of the underlying stochastic process as well as the risk-neutral probability (p).

Discrete Dividends

Adjusting for discrete dividends can generally be problematic since the nodes in the binomial lattice (tree) do not generally recombine and the number of nodes can grow exponentially with the number of dividends. The following approximation, however, is often found useful.

If a finite number of known discrete dividends are anticipated (D_j, $j = 1, 2, \ldots, n$) at given times, then we can adjust the current asset value by subtracting the present value of the known future dividends anticipated during the life of the option, i.e., $S^* = S - \Sigma_j D_j e^{-r \tau_j}$, and the adjusted price (S^*) can then be used in the Black-Scholes formula to give an approximate value for the call option. This assumes that the option is not exercised prematurely and the value of the stock reflects its capital appreciation and the "escrowed" dividends due before maturity. Intuitively, if the option is not exercised early, the claimant will miss the dividends and thus should deduct their present value from the current asset price. Since this would be a precise adjustment if early exercise were not optimal, it actually offers a lower-bound approximation when early exercise is indeed valuable. An American call option, of course, may potentially be optimally exercisable just before an upcoming ex-dividend date so as to capture the dividend. Thus, it may be a reasonably good approximation to consider exercising only at the limited anticipated ex-dividend times (a *pseudo-American option*), and to select the one giving the maximum option value.[5]

When using binomial option valuation (see Hull 1993), we can generate an adjusted or "shadow" binomial tree projected forward (with the same binomial parameters as the actual tree) starting from S^* (instead of S) at $t = 0$, and then add the PV of each discrete dividend D_j at each node along the way at whatever time (j) a dividend is paid, i.e., $S^* + D_j e^{-r \tau_j}$.

We can then value the option on the basis of the values obtained from this adjusted shadow tree.[6]

Constant Dividend Yield

If the call option is written on an asset paying a continuous constant dividend payout D (which is lost for the owner of the option), then the Black-Scholes solution for the value of a call option on a non-dividend-paying asset (as in equation 3.14) can still be used, but with V replaced by $Ve^{-D\tau}$. This again equals the current value of the asset minus the present value of the (stochastic) future dividends over the life of the option, and represents the "capital appreciation" value of the option. This adjustment makes sense because the payment of a continuous dividend yield at rate D reduces the growth rate of the asset V by a constant amount D (such that the nodes in the binomial tree do indeed recombine). Since the resulting p.d.e. does not depend on any variables affected by risk preferences, standard risk-neutral valuation still applies directly. Since the total return in a risk-neutral world must be the riskless rate r (including the dividend yield D), the expected growth rate in V must be $(r - D)$.[7] The option therefore satisfies a p.d.e. similar to that in equation 3.12, with r replaced by $r - D$:

$$\tfrac{1}{2}\sigma^2 S^2 C_{SS} + (r - D)SC_S - C_\tau - rC = 0. \tag{3.17}$$

Using risk-neutral valuation results in the following dividend-adjusted Black-Scholes solution for a European call option with a constant dividend yield D, as derived by Merton (1973):

$$C(S, \tau; r, \sigma^2, E, D) = Se^{-D\tau} N(d_1') - Ee^{-r\tau} N(d_2'), \tag{3.18}$$

where

$$d_1' = \frac{\ln(S/E) + [(r - D) + \tfrac{1}{2}\sigma^2]\tau}{\sigma\sqrt{\tau}}$$

and

$$d_2' = d_1' - \sigma\sqrt{\tau}.$$

For a general American call option, however, the above adjustment provides only a reasonable lower-bound approximation, since early exercise cannot be precluded. Once more, the pseudo-American valuation technique can be used for a limited number of known ex-dividend dates with stochastic dividends.

Stock indices, foreign currencies, commodities, and many futures contracts are examples of traded assets paying a continuous constant dividend yield, D. In the case of a foreign currency, D is the foreign risk-free interest rate. For an investment-type commodity (e.g., gold or silver) with zero convenience yield, D is equal to the negative of the storage costs (negative dividend). In the case of a futures contract that involves no agreement costs (S is a futures price), D equals the risk-free interest rate (r).

3.8* A General Approach to Valuing Any Contingent Claim (on Traded or Nontraded Assets)

The early option-pricing formulas were derived based on the ability to use a traded underlying security with riskless borrowing in a dynamic portfolio that replicates the payoff of the option in any state of the world, thereby allowing risk-neutral valuation. In real-option valuation, however, the underlying asset is often not traded. Still, any contingent claim on an asset, whether traded or not, can be priced in a world with systematic risk by replacing the expectation of cash flow with a certainty-equivalent rate (by subtracting a risk premium that would be appropriate in market equilibrium) and then behaving as if the world were risk neutral. This section derives the fundamental p.d.e. that any derivative security or claim whose value is contingent on the values of other underlying assets (or state variables) must satisfy, whether the underlying assets are traded or not. This discussion, which follows the no-arbitrage arguments of Garman (1976), Cox, Ingersoll, and Ross (1985), and Hull and White (1988b), leads to a general valuation model that encompasses various special cases with known results and to an extension of the basic risk-neutral-valuation argument of Cox and Ross (1976) to cover nontraded assets.

The Fundamental Pricing Equation

Consider a general contingent claim, F, that depends on the values of n underlying assets or state variables, $V_1, V_2, \ldots, V_n$, as well as on time, t. The n state variables are assumed to follow diffusion processes of the form[8]

$$\frac{dV_i}{V_i} = \alpha_i dt + \sigma_i dz_i \quad \text{for } i = 1, 2, \ldots, n, \tag{3.19}$$

where α_i and σ_i are the expected growth rate (drift) and standard deviation of variable V_i (typically assumed constant) and dz_i are the differentials of standard Wiener processes (with mean 0 and variance dt). We assume complete financial markets with at least $n + 1$ traded securities (without or with reinvested dividends) whose prices, $F_j(V_1, \ldots, V_n, t)$, depend on the n underlying variables and time, in addition to the standard Black-Scholes assumptions listed above.[9] From the extended form of Ito's lemma,

$$dF_j(V_1, \ldots, V_n, t) = \frac{1}{2} \sum_i \sum_k \left(\frac{\partial^2 F_j}{\partial V_i \partial V_k} \right) dV_i \, dV_k + \sum_i \frac{\partial F_j}{\partial V_i} dV_i + \frac{\partial F_j}{\partial t} dt$$

(with $dV_i dV_k$ defined by the multiplication rules $dz_i dz_k = \rho_{ik} dt, dz_i dt = 0$, and $(dt)^2 = 0$), if V_i follow the diffusion processes in equation 3.19, whereby $dV_i \, dV_k = \rho_{ik} \sigma_i \sigma_k V_i V_k \, dt$,

$$dF_j = \frac{1}{2} \sum_{i,k} \rho_{ik} \sigma_i \sigma_k V_i V_k F^j_{ik} dt + \sum_i F^j_i (\alpha_i V_i dt + \sigma_i V_i dz_i) - F^j_\tau dt$$

$$= \left(\frac{1}{2} \sum_{i,k} \rho_{ik} \sigma_i \sigma_k V_i V_k F^j_{ik} + \sum_i F^j_i \alpha_i V_i - F^j_\tau \right) dt + \sum_i (F^j_i \sigma_i V_i) dz_i,$$

where

$$\sum_{i,k} \equiv \sum_i \sum_k,$$

$$F^j_i \equiv \frac{\partial F_j}{\partial V_i},$$

$$F^j_\tau \equiv \frac{\partial F_j}{\partial \tau} = -\frac{\partial F_j}{\partial t},$$

and

$$F^j_{ik} \equiv \frac{\partial^2 F_j}{\partial V_i \partial V_k}.$$

It can thus be seen that F_j follows diffusion processes given by

$$\frac{dF_j}{F_j} = \mu_j \, dt + \sum_i s_i \, dz_i \quad \text{for } j = 1, 2, \ldots, n + 1, \tag{3.20}$$

where the expected return offered by F_j, μ_j, and the component of asset F_j's standard deviation attributable to variable (factor) V_i, s_i, are given by

$$\mu_j = \frac{\frac{1}{2} \sum_{i,k} \rho_{ik} \sigma_i \sigma_k V_i V_k F^j_{ik} + \sum_i \alpha_i V_i F^j_i - F^j_\tau}{F_j} \tag{3.21}$$

and

$$s_i = \left(\frac{F_i^j V_i}{F_j}\right)\sigma_i,$$

with $F_i^j \equiv \partial F_j/\partial V_i$, $F_\tau^j \equiv \partial F_j/\partial \tau$, and $F_{ik}^j \equiv \partial^2 F_j/\partial V_i \partial V_k$. With n under-lying variables (following diffusion processes) and $n+1$ traded securities, a riskless hedge portfolio, P, can be set up over any interval dt with pro-portions w_j invested in each security F_j, having a cost $P = \Sigma_j w_j F_j$.

If the proportions w_j are selected such that the stochastic component (from equation 3.20) is eliminated (i.e., $\Sigma_j w_j s_i F_j = 0$), then the portfolio return over the next period dt $(dP = \Sigma_j w_j \mu_j F_j dt)$, in order to avoid ar-bitrage profit opportunities, must equal the risk-free return (r), requiring $\Sigma_j w_j(\mu_j - r)F_j = 0$.[10] Consistency between these two sets of conditions (involving $n+1$ equations in the $n+1$ w_j's) then requires that

$$\mu_j - r = \sum_i \lambda_i s_i. \tag{3.22}$$

The above is basically a multi-factor asset-pricing model. The parameter $\lambda_i \equiv (\mu_i - r)/\sigma_i$ (where μ_i is the total return, including any dividends D_i) is asset i's market price of risk (or reward to variability ratio), defined as the excess total return above the risk-free rate per unit of risk. It captures the degree to which investors require a higher excess return for bearing the risk associated with asset (factor) i. Alternatively, if asset i pays a con-stant dividend yield D_i (so that $\mu_i = \alpha_i + D_i$),

$$RP_i \equiv (\alpha_i + D_i) - r = \lambda_i \sigma_i \tag{3.23}$$

measures the risk premium (or excess total return above r) of asset i ex-pressed as the market price of risk for asset i (λ_i) times its volatility (σ_i). For most traded financial securities, $\lambda_i > 0$, so that $RP_i > 0$ or $\alpha_i + D_i > r$. If an asset (e.g., a capital-investment project) or a variable (e.g., an interest rate or temperature) is not traded, its market price of risk λ_i would equal the market price of risk of an equivalent traded financial security whose price depends on that asset (or variable) and time alone. In some cases, the market price of risk of a nontraded variable (e.g., an interest rate) can be negative, in which case investors require a negative risk premium and the expected return is less than the riskless interest rate. If the market price of risk (e.g., for an R&D project or for temperature) is zero $(\lambda_i = 0)$, investors would be neutral to the asset's risk and $\alpha_i + D_i = r$. Note that the above analysis was based on arbitrage arguments and did not rely on general-equilibrium assumptions. If the CAPM holds, in particular, then $\lambda_i = \lambda_m \rho_{im}$, or $RP_i = \lambda_m \rho_{im} \sigma_i$, where $\lambda_m \equiv (\mu_m - r)/\sigma_m$ is the market price of risk of the market portfolio (m) and ρ_{im} is the correlation of asset (variable) i with the market. In this case, variables that are uncorrelated with market movements (i.e., have no systematic risk), such as an R&D project, will have zero λ_i and RP_i, and can be priced as if investors are risk neutral. The CAPM can thus be seen as a special case of the multi-factor model (equation 3.22) above, where λ_i captures the correlation between changes in variable i and the market return.

Finally, substituting the expressions for μ_j and s_j from equation 3.21 into the multi-factor model in equation 3.22 and rearranging yields

$$\tfrac{1}{2} \sum_{i,k} \rho_{ik}\sigma_i\sigma_k V_i V_k F^j_{ik} + \sum_i (\alpha_i - \lambda_i\sigma_i) V_i F^j_i - F^j_\tau - rF = 0.$$

Focusing on the particular contingent claim F (dropping the subscript j), and assuming that the contingent claim itself pays a constant payout d (that is received while the contingent claim is held but would be forgone when exercised), we obtain the fundamental p.d.e. that any derivative security whose value is contingent on n underlying state variables V_i $(i = 1, 2, \ldots, n)$ and time t must satisfy

$$\tfrac{1}{2} \sum_{i,k} \rho_{ik}\sigma_i\sigma_k V_i V_k F_{ik} + \sum_i (\alpha_i - \lambda_i\sigma_i) V_i F_i - F_\tau - rF + d = 0, \qquad (3.24)$$

with $\alpha_i = \mu_i - D_i$, $F_i \equiv \partial F/\partial V_i$, $F_\tau \equiv \partial F/\partial \tau$, and $F_{ik} \equiv \partial^2 F/\partial V_i \partial V_k$. The value of a particular contingent claim can then be completely specified and derived after imposing appropriate $(2n + 1)$ terminal and boundary conditions.

Some Special Cases

Two State Variables
Consider, for example, the case that there are two (not necessarily traded) underlying state variables, V and S. Then the general p.d.e. in equation 3.24 reduces to

$$(\tfrac{1}{2}\sigma_V^2 V^2 F_{VV} + \rho_{VS}\sigma_V\sigma_S VSF_{VS} + \tfrac{1}{2}\sigma_S^2 S^2 F_{SS})$$

$$+ [(\alpha_V - \lambda_V\sigma_V) VF_V + (\alpha_S - \lambda_S\sigma_S) SF_S] - F_\tau - rF + d = 0, \qquad (3.25)$$

subject to an appropriate number (five) of terminal and boundary conditions.

When the underlying stochastic variables V and S are the prices of *traded* assets with constant dividend payout rates D_V and D_S respectively (potentially $D_V = D_S = 0$), they must satisfy the equilibrium condition (equation 3.23) that $(\alpha_i + D_i) - r = \lambda_i \sigma_i$ $(i = V, S)$, which implies $\alpha_V - \lambda_V \sigma_V = r - D_V$ and $\alpha_S - \lambda_S \sigma_S = r - D_S$. Thus, for traded dividend-paying risky assets, equation 3.25 for the value of a contingent claim becomes

$$(\tfrac{1}{2}\sigma_V^2 V^2 F_{VV} + \rho_{VS}\sigma_V\sigma_S VS F_{VS} + \tfrac{1}{2}\sigma_S^2 S^2 F_{SS})$$

$$+ [(r - D_V)VF_V + (r - D_S)SF_S] - F_\tau - rF + d = 0. \tag{3.25$'$}$$

Risk-neutral valuation can be applied, with closed-form solutions obtaining in certain cases of European-type options, such as when there are no dividend-like payouts. For example, Stulz (1982) derived closed-form solutions for European options on the maximum or minimum of two non-dividend-paying risky assets that satisfy equation 3.25$'$ (with $D_V = D_S = d = 0$). Generally, these types of solutions involve integrals of the bivariate cumulative standard normal distribution. Similarly, Margrabe (1978) obtains a closed-form solution for the option to exchange one non-dividend-paying risky asset, V, for another, S. Myers and Majd (1990) also analyze the similar problem of a put option to abandon where V is a dividend (cash-flow) paying project and S its uncertain salvage value.

A useful solution procedure in these two-variable exchange problems is to transform them by exploiting the fact that these exchange options are homogeneous of degree 1 (i.e., they satisfy $F(cV, cS) = cF(V, S)$), so that $F(V, S, t) = S F(V/S, 1, t)$. This motivates expressing the option (F) and the first asset (V) using the second variable (S) as numeraire (i.e., use $f \equiv F/S$ and operate on the *relative* underlying asset value, $X \equiv V/S$, having variance $s^2 = \sigma_V^2 + \sigma_S^2 - 2\rho_{VS}\sigma_V\sigma_S$). Then the exercise price of the second asset in terms of itself is known and equal to unity $(I = 1)$. The riskless return (on a loan denominated in units of the second asset) will be zero $(r = 0)$ if there are no dividends; it will be the return on this riskless asset, D_S, if the second asset involves a dividend payout or a return shortfall. That is, the yield on the numeraire asset, D_S, will replace r as the riskless interest rate. With the above type of adjustments the p.d.e. in equation 3.25 is transformed into an equivalent single stochastic variable (X) problem of the form

$$\tfrac{1}{2}s^2 X^2 F_{XX} + (D_S - D_V)XF_X - F_\tau D_S F + d = 0,$$

where $s^2 = \sigma_V^2 + \sigma_S^2 - 2\rho_{VS}\sigma_V\sigma_S$. With the terminal condition $\max(X - 1, 0)$, a call option on the relative value X must then satisfy Merton's (1973) dividend-adjusted Black-Scholes solution given in equation 3.18 (with $S = X$, $E = 1$, $\sigma = s$, $D = D_V$ and $r = D_S$), i.e.,

$$C(X, \tau; D_S, s^2, 1, D_V) = Xe^{-D_V \tau} N(d_1') - 1 e^{-D_S \tau} N(d_2').$$

Given that $F(V, S, \tau) = S\,C(X, \tau)$ and $X = V/S$, the solution for the European call option to exchange one risky asset S (paying dividend payout D_S) for another asset V (with payout D_V) is a dividend-adjusted extension (with D_S replacing r) of Merton's (1973) formula for the Black-Scholes dividend-adjusted solution in equation 3.18:

$$F(V, S, \tau) = Ve^{-D_V \tau} N(d_1') - Se^{-D_S \tau} N(d_2'), \qquad (3.18')$$

where

$$d_1' = \frac{\ln(V/S) + [(D_S - D_V) + \frac{1}{2}s^2]\tau}{s\sqrt{\tau}}$$

and

$$d_2' = d_1' - s\sqrt{\tau}.$$

(Note that $Se^{-D_S \tau}$ above can be interpreted as the futures price for uncertain variable S with yield D_S. If S is constant, it reduces to $Se^{-r\tau}$ as in equation 3.18; that is, r replaces D_S.) McDonald and Siegel's (1985) problem of analyzing a firm's operations as a series of European options to exchange the uncertain variable production costs (S) for the uncertain revenues (V) is one application of this model. The put option to abandon a dividend-paying project (V) for its salvage value (S) analyzed by Myers and Majd (1990) is an American exchange option with a constant proportional dividend payout that has no closed-form solution, however, so that numerical analysis becomes necessary.

In the case that $D_V = D_S = d = 0$, equation 3.18′ reduces to Margrabe's (1978) solution for the option to exchange two non-dividend-paying assets. In this special case without dividends, early exercise is not optimal and so the value of an American exchange option equals its European counterpart. Unless their payoffs depend on r, the prices of exchange options (which describe many real-option situations) and other contingent claims that are homogeneous of degree 1 are independent of r and thus are the same whether r is constant or stochastic.[11]

If the second variable is, in particular, the (instantaneous) short-term interest rate r (i.e., $S = r$, with volatility σ_r), which is nontraded, and if the first variable is a traded security, V, then equation 3.25 becomes

$$(\tfrac{1}{2}\sigma_V^2 V^2 F_{VV} + \rho_{Vr}\sigma_V\sigma_r VrF_{Vr} + \tfrac{1}{2}\sigma_r^2 r^2 F_{rr})$$

$$+ (rVF_V + rF_r) - F_\tau - rF + d = 0. \qquad (3.26)$$

Brennan and Schwartz (1982) analyze the term structure of interest rates using a model with two state variables, with V the inverse of the consol rate (a traded asset) and r the short-term interest rate (nontraded). Hull and White (1987) and others also examine two-state-variable problems where the first variable is a traded security (e.g., stock) and the second its volatility (nontraded).

A Single State Variable
In the case of a single underlying variable, V, *whether traded or not*, the fundamental equation 3.24 that must be satisfied by any contingent claim, $F(V, \tau)$, reduces to

$$\tfrac{1}{2}\sigma^2 V^2 F_{VV} + (\alpha - \lambda\sigma)VF_V - F_\tau - rF + d = 0, \tag{3.27}$$

subject to a terminal condition and to a lower and an upper boundary condition.[12]

When the underlying variable, V, is the price of a *traded* security with a constant dividend rate D (potentially D being 0), it must satisfy the equilibrium condition (equation 3.23) that $(\alpha + D) - r = \lambda\sigma$, which implies $\alpha - \lambda\sigma = r - D$. Thus, for a single traded underlying asset, equation 3.25' for the value of a contingent claim becomes

$$\tfrac{1}{2}\sigma^2 V^2 F_{VV} + (r - D)VF_V - F_\tau - rF + d = 0, \tag{3.28}$$

subject to appropriate terminal and boundary conditions. The call and put stock option p.d.e.'s in equations 3.12 and 3.13 are straightforward applications of this with $d = 0$ (since a stock option itself earns no dividends). Using the terminal and boundary conditions described in equations 3.12 and 3.13, this results in the standard Black-Scholes call and put option solutions we saw in equations 3.14 and 3.15.

If the single underlying state variable is the interest rate r (a nontraded variable), then substituting r for V in equation 3.27 gives[13]

$$\tfrac{1}{2}\sigma_r^2 r^2 F_{rr} + (\alpha_r - \lambda_r\sigma_r)rF_r - F_\tau - rF + d = 0. \tag{3.29}$$

Although this is more difficult to solve than equation 3.28, since the value of the claim must first be determined conditional on each interest-rate path (and then averaging over their probability distribution), analytic solutions are feasible (e.g., see Cox, Ingersoll, and Ross 1985).

Nontraded Assets (with Below-Equilibrium Return) and Extended Risk-Neutral Valuation

If the underlying asset or variable is not traded in limited supply for investment purposes by a large number of investors (e.g., if it is a reproducible commodity), then its growth rate, α, may actually fall *below* the equilibrium total expected rate of return required in the market by investors from an equivalent-risk traded financial security, α^* (McDonald and Siegel 1984, 1985).[14] The resulting rate-of-return shortfall between the equilibrium return on a similar financial security and its actual growth rate is analogous to a constant dividend yield, $\delta \equiv \alpha^* - \alpha$.[15] In fact, in complete markets one can hypothesize the existence of a similar traded security, S, that maintains the same price as V while it pays a constant dividend yield δ (i.e., $\alpha^* - \delta = \alpha$). This equivalent traded security must satisfy the equilibrium relationship (equation 3.23) $(\alpha + \delta) - r = \lambda\sigma$, so that $(\alpha - \lambda\sigma) = r - \delta$. Even though this security may not really exist, it could exist without generating arbitrage profit opportunities and so it must satisfy the fundamental p.d.e. (equation 3.28) above (with $r - \delta$ replacing $r - D$). The same, of course, also holds for the nontraded asset V (since it maintains the same price), i.e.,

$$\tfrac{1}{2}\sigma^2 V^2 F_{VV} + (r - \delta)VF_V - F_\tau - rF + d = 0. \tag{3.30}$$

Equation 3.30 is independent of investors' risk attitudes and can therefore be more conveniently solved using risk-neutral valuation, whether the underlying asset is traded or not. Given that $\alpha^* - \delta = \alpha$, it is obvious that $\alpha - \lambda\sigma$ (equation 3.27) is equivalent to $(\alpha^* - \lambda\sigma) - \delta = r - \delta$ (equation 3.30).[16] This is equivalent to risk-neutral valuation (Cox and Ross 1976; Harrison and Kreps 1979) in which the actual growth rate, α, is replaced with a risk-neutral equivalent drift, $\hat{\alpha}$. Such a world, where expected growth rates are adjusted downward from α to $\hat{\alpha} \equiv \alpha - \lambda\sigma = r - \delta$, is referred to as an (extended) "risk-neutral" world. In this world, instead of using the actual probabilities and expectations operator, E, expectations are formulated using equivalent "risk-neutral" probabilities and a risk-neutral expectations operator, $\hat{E}$ (Harrison and Kreps 1979; Cox and Ross 1976; Trigeorgis and Mason 1987). For traded securities earning an equilibrium return ($\delta = 0$) without dividends ($D = 0$), $\hat{\alpha} = r$. For those real assets with no systematic risk ($\lambda = 0$), such as R&D, exploration, or drilling for certain precious metals or natural resources, $\hat{\alpha} = \alpha$ ($= r$ if traded without dividends). For traded securities paying dividends at a rate D, $\hat{\alpha} = r - D$. For nontraded assets earning a below-equilibrium return (with return shortfall δ) while paying a constant dividend yield D, the risk-neutral growth rate is generally given by $\hat{\alpha} = \alpha - \lambda\sigma = r - (D + \delta)$.

The above confirms—as suggested earlier by Constantinides (1978), by Cox, Ingersoll, and Ross (1985a, lemma 4), by Hull and White (1988b), and by others—that any contingent claim on an asset, whether traded or not, can be priced in a world with systematic risk by replacing its actual growth rate, α, with a certainty-equivalent rate, $\hat{\alpha}$, by simply subtracting a risk premium ($RP = \lambda\sigma$) that would be appropriate in market equilibrium (i.e., $\hat{\alpha} \equiv \alpha - RP$) and then behaving as if the world were risk neutral. Intuitively, since in a risk-neutral world all assets would be expected to earn just the risk-free return (i.e., risk premia would not be offered), equilibrium expected growth rates would therefore be less in the risk-neutral world that they actually are in our risk-averse world by the risk premia. The above adjustment is analogous to discounting certainty-equivalent cash flows at the risk-free rate, rather than actually expected cash flows at a risk-adjusted rate. In other words, the current value of a general contingent claim, F, can still be obtained by discounting "certainty-equivalent" or risk-neutral expectations of the future payoff, F_T, using the risk-free interest rate (r):

$$F = e^{-r\tau} \hat{E}(F_T), \tag{3.31}$$

where $\hat{E}$ is the expectations operator in a risk-neutral world (in which the actual growth rate, α, is replaced with a certainty-equivalent or risk-neutral rate, $\hat{\alpha} = \alpha - RP$).[17, 18]

Futures, Convenience Yield, and the Pricing of Contingent Claims on Nontraded Assets

Nonfinancial assets that are not traded in limited supply for investment purposes by many investors, such as many capital-investment projects and most commodities that are reproducible and are held mostly for consumption purposes, are not considered "traded" securities. In cases of such nontraded assets, there may be a rate-of-return shortfall from the equilibrium return (δ); the market price of risk (λ) and the expected growth rate (α) for such nontraded assets generally depend on investors' risk preferences and can therefore enter into the valuation of contingent claims. For traded securities these parameters drop out and standard risk-neutral valuation applies directly.

Luckily, though, in the case of certain nontraded assets (such as many commodities or capital projects involving commodities) that are traded in futures markets (i.e., when futures prices are available) these parameters can be estimated directly from the prices of futures contracts with varying maturities. In other cases, however, estimating the return shortfall may require use of a market-equilibrium model, such as the CAPM (see McDonald and Siegel 1985).

Briefly, a *futures contract* represents an agreement (i.e., a commitment, as opposed to a discretionary right as in options) to buy or sell a specified asset (e.g., a commodity) at a certain future time at a delivery price (the *futures price*) and other terms (e.g., amount, quality, delivery place) specified in advance.[19] No costs are involved up front to either buy (take a *long position*) or to sell (take a *short position*), since delivery and payment take place at the future delivery time. In effect, a futures contract is a delayed purchase or sale. At any point in time, t, the prevailing futures price, f_t, is the delivery price that would make the value of the futures contract at that time, F_t, zero for both parties (i.e., a zero-NPV transaction). At the time the contract is initially agreed upon, the delivery price I is chosen equal to the futures price (i.e., at $t = 0$, $I = f$, and $F = 0$). Although the up-front agreed-upon delivery price (f) remains constant during the life of the contract, both F_t and f_t fluctuate as the underlying asset value (or spot price) V_t changes. At maturity, T, the then-prevailing futures price must converge to the spot price at that time ($f_T = V_T$). When the spot price of the underlying asset will be V_T at maturity, the value of a long position in a futures contract will be ($V_T - I$); for a short position it will be ($I - V_T$).

From the risk-neutral valuation relationship (equation 3.31), assuming the (instantaneous) short-term interest rate (r) and the asset's expected growth rate (α) are constant, the current value of a (long) futures contract (with $F_T = V_T - I$) is then given by

$$F = e^{-r\tau}\hat{E}(V_T - I) = e^{-r\tau}(Ve^{\hat{\alpha}\tau}) - Ie^{-r\tau} = Ve^{-\delta\tau} - Ie^{-r\tau} \qquad (3.32)$$

(since the expected growth rate in the risk-neutral world is given by $\hat{\alpha} = \alpha - \lambda\sigma = r - \delta$), where V is the value (spot price) of the underlying asset that has a continuous "dividend" yield (an explicit payout and/or an implicit return shortfall) δ and where τ is the time to maturity of the futures contract with delivery price I and current value F. The futures price, f, being the value of the delivery price I such that $F = 0$, is therefore

$$f = \hat{E}(V_T) = Ve^{\hat{\alpha}\tau} = Ve^{(\alpha - \lambda\sigma)\tau} = Ve^{(r-\delta)\tau}. \qquad (3.33)$$

The above *spot-futures parity* or *cost-of-carry* relationship must hold because, in essence, buying a futures contract (and an amount of Treasury bills equal to the present value of the futures price, $fe^{-r\tau}$) is an alternative way to acquire the underlying asset rather than buying it directly at the future date, and so the two strategies must have the same current cost. If the relationship were violated (i.e., if f were to sell for a different price than the one given in equation 3.33), then arbitrage profit opportunities would result. Note also that the futures price, f, is the expected future spot price in a *risk-neutral* world (where the actual growth rate is reduced by the risk premium from α to $\alpha - \lambda\sigma$).

In the case of commodities, the "dividend" yield δ represents the convenience yield (i.e., the benefits or services derived from physical ownership of the commodity for consumption purposes, such as avoiding disruptions in operations by holding inventory), y, net of the storage costs, s. That is, δ is the *net* convenience yield ($\delta = y - s$). For those exceptional commodities held mainly for investment (rather than for consumption) purposes (e.g., gold and silver), the convenience yield is zero ($y = 0$), resulting in a negative "dividend" (minus the storage costs, s).

When futures prices are available on contracts of varying maturities on the same commodity, the risk-neutral growth rate, $\hat{\alpha}$, or the return shortfall (net convenience yield), δ, can be easily estimated. Since the futures price, f_i, of each contract with maturity τ_i (e.g., for $i = 1, 2$) on the same asset (with common spot price V) must satisfy the parity equation 3.33, i.e.,

$$f_2 = V e^{\hat{\alpha} \tau_2},$$

$$f_1 = V e^{\hat{\alpha} \tau_1},$$

simple division and rearranging gives the commodity's expected growth rate in a risk-neutral world:

$$\hat{\alpha} = \frac{\ln(f_2/f_1)}{\tau_2 - \tau_1}. \tag{3.34}$$

For example, consider the futures prices on crude oil on April 20, 1995 (from the Money and Investing section of the *Wall Street Journal*, under Futures Prices) for the following maturities (in dollars per barrel):

May 1995	20.52
June 1995	20.19
July 1995	19.86
September 1995	19.22.

For the one-month period ($\tau_2 - \tau_1 = 1/12$ year) May–June 1995, the equilibrium risk-neutral expected growth rate of crude oil was

$$\hat{\alpha} = \ln\left(\frac{20.19}{20.52}\right) \times 12 = -0.195,$$

or -19.5% per year. Since crude oil futures contracts are available for longer periods, we can similarly obtain longer-horizon estimates. For the four-month period May–September 1995 ($\tau_2 - \tau_1 = 4/12 = 1/3$ year),

$$\hat{\alpha} = \ln\left(\frac{19.22}{20.52}\right) \times 3 = -0.196,$$

again about -19.5% per year. From $\hat{\alpha} = r - \delta$, we can also estimate the convenience yield for crude oil (or rate-of-return shortfall for an oil company project), δ, simply by subtracting the risk-neutral growth rate, $\hat{\alpha}$, from the short-term interest rate, r.

If the underlying variable, V, is some commodity (e.g., oil) whose growth rate cannot be assumed to remain constant but is rather a function of the state variable itself, $\alpha(V)$, then the return shortfall may also be state and time dependent: $\delta(V, t)$. Suppose, for example, that the commodity (or some other variable, such as the continuously compounded yield to maturity of a discount bond) can be assumed to follow a mean-reverting (Ornstein-Uhlenbeck) process of the form

$$\frac{dV_t}{V_t} = \alpha(V_t)dt + \sigma\, dz, \qquad (3.35)$$

where

$$\alpha(V_t) = \frac{\varepsilon(V^* - V_t)}{V_t}.$$

Thus, when the commodity price deviates from some long-term mean equilibrium value, V^*, it becomes subject to elastic forces (e.g., purchasing-power parity) that make it revert back to this mean with a speed of adjustment given by the elasticity parameter ε. If $V_t = V^*$, the drift becomes 0, whereas if $V_t > V^*$ the drift is negative as it approaches the mean. There is no reason for the expected growth rate in the price of such a commodity, $\alpha(V_t)$, at a particular point in time to be in line with the equilibrium return offered in the financial markets by a similar financial security of comparable risk, α^* (e.g., as given by the CAPM). In this case the resulting rate-of-return shortfall will depend on state and time; i.e.,

$$\delta(V_t) = \alpha^* - \alpha(V_t).$$

In such cases, the estimates obtained from equation 3.34 from the futures prices of varying maturity contracts may vary significantly from one period to another. Nevertheless, any approximation error from estimating and using δ to price a contingent claim on such a commodity, or a capital project involving such a commodity, will likely be far more accurate than the fruitless attempt to use a constant discount rate derived from some equilibrium model (such as the CAPM) to price such a contingent claim.[20] Such a discount rate would better be applied directly to capture the relatively more stable commodity risk and determine the gross present value of a commodity-based capital project, which could serve as the underlying asset in properly valuating the contingent claim using the δ or $\hat{\alpha}$ estimates.

3.9 Corporate Liabilities and Other Financial-Options Applications[21]

Option valuation or contingent-claims analysis (CCA) can be applied to corporate securities that can be seen as packages of claims or options on the total value of the firm. Thus, the underlying asset in this case is the total value of the firm's assets, V; the various corporate securities, such as equity, debt, warrants, and convertible bonds, can then be valued as claims contingent on V. We would thus replace assumption A4 above with the following distributional assumption:

A4″ The value of the firm's assets follows over time a diffusion process of the form

$$\frac{dV}{V} = (\alpha - D)dt + \sigma\,dz. \tag{3.36}$$

Here α denotes the (instantaneous) *total* expected rate of return on the firm[22]; D is the *total* net payout by the firm (including both dividends paid to equity and coupon payments to debtholders), expressed as a percentage of V; σ is the instantaneous standard deviation of the firm's return; and dz is a standard Wiener process.

As was derived in equation 3.28 above and in Merton 1977b, any claim $F(V, \tau)$ whose value is contingent on a traded asset (portfolio) with value V, a dividend payout D, and time to maturity τ must satisfy the fundamental p.d.e.[23]

$$\tfrac{1}{2}\sigma^2 V^2 F_{VV} + (r - D)VF_V - F_\tau - rF + d = 0, \tag{3.37}$$

where d is the payout from the firm to the claim F. Each individual contingent claim (corporate liability) is uniquely represented by specifying its particular terminal and boundary conditions, along with the payout d it receives.

A Simple Firm with Equity, Zero-Coupon Debt, and Loan Guarantees

To illustrate the correspondence between corporate liabilities and options, consider first the case of a simple firm with only two kinds of liabilities: equity with market value E, and a single issue of zero-coupon debt with market value D, which prohibits the payment of dividends until after the promised face value of the bond, B, is paid off at maturity τ years from now. The economic balance sheet (in market rather than book values) of such a simple firm would list the assets (on the left side) as V, which would be equal to $D + E$ (the sum of the debt and the equity, on the right side). On the debt's maturity, if the value of the firm exceeds the face value of the debt, $V > B$, the bondholders will receive the promised payment, $D = B$, and the equityholders will receive the residual claim, $V - B$. If $V < B$, the stockholders will find it preferable to exercise their limited liability rights, i.e., default on the promised payment and instead surrender the firm's assets to its bondholders, $D = V$, receiving nothing: $E = 0$.

Equity
At the debt's maturity ($\tau = 0$), equity will thus be worth either $V - B$ or 0, whichever is to the equityholders' greater advantage; i.e.,

$$E(V, 0; B) = \max(V - B, 0).$$

The equity of such a levered firm is therefore analogous to a European call option on the value of the firm's assets, V, with exercise price equal to the bond's promised payment, B, and time to expiration equal to the debt's maturity. Substituting V for S and B for E (while interpreting τ as the time to maturity of the debt and σ^2 as the variance of the firm's return) in the Black-Scholes solution for a call option in equation 3.14 gives as the value of equity

$$E(V, \tau; B) = V N(d_1) - Be^{-r\tau} N(d_2). \tag{3.38}$$

This can also be verified to be the solution to the p.d.e. in equation 3.37 applied to the equity claim ($F = E$) when the firm pays no dividends to equity ($d = 0$) or coupon payments to debt ($D = 0$), i.e.,

$$\tfrac{1}{2}\sigma^2 V^2 E_{VV} + rVE_V - E_\tau - rE = 0 \tag{3.39}$$

s.t.

$E(V, 0) = \max(V - B, 0),$

$E(0, \tau) = 0,$

$E(V, \tau)/V \to 1$ as $V \to \infty.$

Zero-Coupon Debt

Similarly, the debtholders at maturity will receive either the promised payment, B, or the value of the firm's assets, V, whichever is less; i.e.,

$D(V, 0; B) = \min(V, B).$

Since the value of the firm's assets must equal the sum of its liabilities, i.e., $V = E + D$, the value of the debt can be determined from $D = V - E$. Thus, both the value of equity and the value of debt claims are contingent on the value of the firm, V. Figures 3.3 and 3.4 show the value of equity and the value of risky debt as they depend on the firm's value at the debt's maturity.

The zero-coupon risky debt must also satisfy the same fundamental p.d.e. described by equation 3.37 with $F = D$, $d = 0$, and $D = 0$:

$$\tfrac{1}{2}\sigma^2 V^2 D_{VV} + r V D_V - D_\tau - r D = 0 \tag{3.40}$$

s.t.

$D(V, 0) = \min(V, B),$

$D(0, \tau) = 0,$

$D(V, \tau) \to Be^{-r\tau}$ (i.e., the value of a riskless bond) as $V \to \infty.$

The solution can be seen from $D = V - E$ (with E as given by the Black-Scholes European call solution in equation 3.38) to be

$$D(V, \tau; B) = Be^{-r\tau} N(h_1) + V N(h_2), \tag{3.41}$$

where

$$h_1 = \frac{\ln(V/B) + (r - \tfrac{1}{2}\sigma^2)\tau}{\sigma\sqrt{\tau}}$$

and

$$h_2 = \frac{-\ln(V/B) - (r - \tfrac{1}{2}\sigma^2)\tau}{\sigma\sqrt{\tau}}.$$

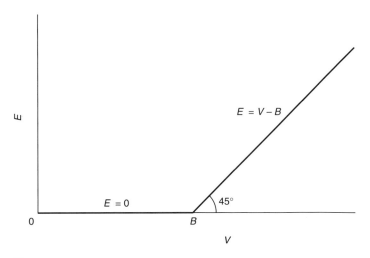

Figure 3.3
Value of equity E $(= \max(V - B, 0))$ at maturity, where $V =$ firm value.

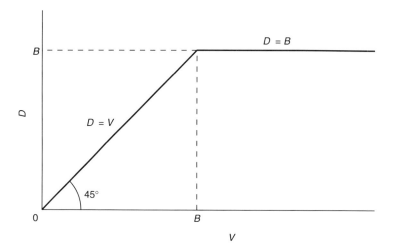

Figure 3.4
Value of risky debt D $(= V - E = \min(V, B))$ at maturity, where $V =$ firm value.

The above valuation has some interesting implications for the firm's claim-holders:

An increase in the value of the firm reduces the probability of default, increasing the value of the risky debt.

The longer the maturity of the debt or the higher the riskless rate, the lower the present value of the promised payment, and hence the less valuable the debt.

Increasing the promised payment increases the value of the debt.

The higher the volatility of the firm, the higher the probability of default (i.e., $V < B$) and the lower the debt value.

Since equity's claims are complementary to those of the debtholders, these factors affect equity in exactly the opposite manner, giving rise to conflicts of interest among the two groups and motivating the use of safety covenants.

By issuing debt, the stockholders have essentially given ownership of the firm's assets to the bondholders (for the proceeds of the issue) while maintaining a call option to buy them back by paying the promised face value of the debt as an exercise price.

Loan Guarantee

Consider now the value of a loan guarantee paying any shortfall in the value of the firm that is necessary to fully repay the promised debt payment (which is similar to having insurance). As depicted in figure 3.5, if at maturity the value of the firm is less than the promised payment, $V < B$, the loan guarantee will have to make up the difference between the promised payment and the value of the firm, $B - V$; however, if the value of the firm exceeds the promised payment, $V > B$, the guarantee will not have to pay anything. That is,

$$G(V, 0; B) = \max(B - V, 0).$$

The loan guarantee is thus equivalent to a European put option on the value of the firm, V, with an exercise price equal to the promised payment, B. The value of the loan guarantee is therefore given by the Black-Scholes European put pricing solution (equation 3.15) with G replacing p, V replacing S, and B replacing E:

$$G(V, \tau; B) = -V N(-d_1) + Be^{-r\tau} N(-d_2). \tag{3.42}$$

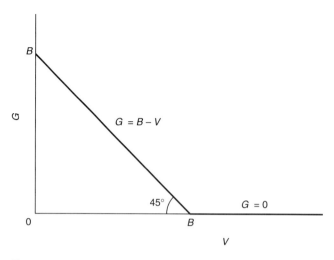

Figure 3.5
Value of loan guarantee $G(= \max(B - V, 0))$ at maturity, where $V = $ firm value.

Restating the put-call parity relationship in equation 3.6,

$$p(S, \tau; E) = Ee^{-r\tau} + c(S, \tau; E) - S,$$

in the current case, where the value of the firm is the underlying asset (i.e., V replaces S), the debt's promised payment is the exercise price (B replaces E), equity is the European call option (E replaces c), and the loan guarantee a corresponding European put with the same terms (G replaces p), and recognizing that $E - V = -D$, gives

$$G(V, \tau; B) = Be^{-r\tau} - D(V, \tau; B). \tag{3.43}$$

This verifies that the value of the loan guarantee (representing the discount due to default risk in corporate bonds) can be determined as the difference between the price of a risk-free bond and the value of risky debt with the same terms. In a different context, Mason and Baldwin (1988) describe loan guarantees by the government to large-scale energy projects. Loan guarantees by parent companies to their subsidiaries, other forms of government subsidies, and insurance contracts (e.g., federal deposit insurance) can be similarly analyzed (see, e.g., Merton 1977a).

Pricing More Complex Corporate Securities

The same valuation approach can be used to analyze more complex corporate securities, such as (multiple issues of) coupon bonds, convertible bonds and warrants. Other refinements such as call provisions, subordination features, sinking fund requirements, and other bond covenants can also be incorporated.

If we allow the bond to receive coupon payments (like "dividends"), equity in the presence of the coupon bond would then be analogous to a European call option on a dividend-paying asset (or, in another sense, like a compound option where each coupon payment made by stockholders represents the exercise price to acquire an option on an option on V).

Callable Coupon Debt

If the coupon bond is callable under a known schedule of call prices, $K(\tau)$, where $K(0) = B$, the equity becomes equivalent to an American call option on a dividend-paying asset (with variable exercise price $K(\tau)$). The value of the call provision (i.e., the value of early exercise) to equity is given by the difference between the values of the American call option and a similar European call option (with exercise price varying according to $K(\tau)$). The value of a call protection feature for the first portion of the debt's maturity would similarly be given by the difference between the values of two American call options (on a dividend-paying asset) with different maturities.

If the firm pays both dividends to equity, δ, and coupon payments to the bondholders, d, for a total payout of $D = (d + \delta)/V$, then the value of the callable coupon bond, $F(V, \tau; B)$ satisfies

$$\tfrac{1}{2}\sigma^2 V^2 F_{VV} + (rV - d - \delta)F_V - F_\tau - rF + d = 0 \qquad (3.44)$$

s.t.

$$F(V, 0) = \min(V, B),$$

$$F(0, \tau) = 0,$$

$$F(V^*(\tau), \tau) = K(\tau),$$

where $V^*(\tau)$ is the schedule of firm values (free boundary) above which it would be optimal for the firm to call the bonds at the call price $K(\tau)$ (i.e., when early exercise of this American call by the equityholders becomes optimal). The solution to both the debt value, F, and the optimal schedule, $V^*(\tau)$, must be determined simultaneously (through numerical analysis).

Convertible (Callable) Debt

If the bondholders are given the right at maturity to either receive the promised payment B or, at their option, convert the bond into new shares

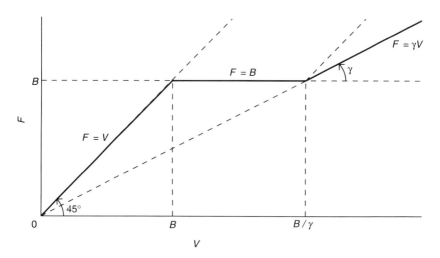

Figure 3.6
Value of convertible debt $F(= \min(V, \max(B, \gamma V)))$ at maturity, where V = firm value.

of equity equivalent to $\gamma\%$ of firm value V, then the value of the convertible bonds at maturity will be

$$F(V, 0) = \min(V, \max(B, \gamma V)). \tag{3.45}$$

As illustrated in figure 3.6,

$$F(V, 0) = V \text{ if } 0 \leq V \leq B \text{ (receive the firm if default)}$$

$$= B \text{ if } B \leq V \leq B/\gamma \text{ (receive payment if not convert)}$$

$$= \gamma V \text{ if } V \geq B/\gamma \text{ (receive } \gamma V \text{ if convert)}.$$

The convertible bond can thus be seen as a combination of (1) a straight bond (without the conversion feature), $D(V, \tau; B)$, as determined in equation 3.41 and (2) a call option on $\gamma\%$ of V with exercise price equal to the face value, B, i.e.,

$$F(V, \tau; B) = D(V, \tau; B) + c(\gamma V, \tau; B). \tag{3.46}$$

If the debt is a callable convertible bond, it satisfies the same fundamental p.d.e. as the callable bond in equation 3.44 except that the terminal condition is replaced by equation 3.45 and the last boundary condition becomes

$$F(V^{**}(\tau), \tau) = \gamma V^{**}(\tau),$$

where $V^{**}(\tau)$ is the value (schedule) above which the firm would find it optimal to call the convertibles and force conversion. Ingersoll (1977) and Brennan and Schwartz (1977b) show that it will be optimal for the firm to call the convertible when the stock first reaches the call price, i.e., when

$$V^{**}(\tau) = \frac{K(\tau)}{\gamma}.$$

This reduces the problem from a free-boundary one (which would have required numerical analysis) to one that allows for a closed-form analytic solution.

Simply stated, the value of a risky callable convertible bond can be seen as equivalent to a portfolio consisting of the following:

Equivalent risk-free bond − Loan guarantee

− Call option + Conversion option + Residual influences.

Further Financial-Options Applications and Some Qualifications

Other financial-options applications of contingent-claims analysis include the pricing of various bond indentures (e.g. safety covenants) and of subordinated debt by Black and Cox (1976); the pricing of sinking fund provisions in multiple callable coupon bonds by Jones, Mason, and Rosenfeld (1983); the pricing of warrants, rights, and underwriting contracts by Smith (1977); the determination of the risk structure of interest rates and the pricing of collateralized loans by Merton (1974); the pricing of dual-purpose funds by Ingersoll (1976); and the valuation of bank-loan commitments (i.e., options on loans) by Bartter and Rendleman (1979). Finally, Galai and Masulis (1976) examine the effects of various corporate policies, such as acquisitions, mergers, increased scale of operations, and spinoffs, on the redistribution of the firm's value between its stockholders and its bondholders.

Despite the close correspondence between corporate liabilities and options, the following differences must be kept in mind (see Cox and Rubinstein 1985):

The underlying asset in the case of corporate liabilities is the total firm value (the sum of all equity and liability claims of the firm), V, which (unlike a stock price) is not observable. This may create a problem in practice: to price any corporate liability we need as input to estimate V by adding up all equity and liability claims of the firm, including the one whose price we wish to determine (a circular process). This problem may be circumvented if a twin traded asset closely correlated with V can be identified or if enough of the firm's liabilities are traded.

The owners of corporate securities (unlike the owners of stock options) receive the payouts made by the firm (like "dividends" to the option).

The owners of corporate securities (unlike the individuals owning stock options) may influence the fundamental determinants of option value through the financing (capital structure), dividend, and investment policies of the firm. For example, the firm's equityholders can affect the exercise price (the face value of the debt) by changing the capital structure (e.g., issuing more bonds while using the proceeds to retire stock), can affect the dividend payments by changing the firm's dividend policy, or can affect the firm's volatility by pursuing a riskier investment policy. The total value of the firm may thus get redistributed from bondholders to stockholders, necessitating the use of protective covenants.

When a convertible security is exercised, new shares of stock are issued (unlike the exercise of stock options). Moreover, any exercise price paid upon conversion is received by (and increases the total value of) the firm. For this reason, it is not necessarily optimal to exercise all identical (American-type) convertible securities simultaneously.

The value of an option (corporate liability) issued by the firm (unlike options sold by individuals) may be affected by other options it may have issued. Also, the value of corporate liabilities (unlike stock options) may depend on factors other than the underlying asset (e.g., reorganization provisions).

Since the identity of the issuer is known, the act of issuing corporate liabilities (unlike stock options) may in itself signal information.

Despite these differences, the pricing of corporate securities seen as collections of options has proven extremely valuable, and is becoming increasingly more so in corporate liability planning and analysis.

3.10 Summary of Useful Solutions

This section summarizes a few solutions that will prove useful for reference in succeeding chapters.

First, an option $F(V, \tau)$ on a non-dividend-paying asset V that follows the diffusion Wiener process

$$\frac{dV}{V} = \alpha \, dt + \sigma \, dz$$

must satisfy the p.d.e.

$$\tfrac{1}{2}\sigma^2 V^2 F_{VV} + rV F_V - F_\tau - rF = 0$$

subject to appropriate terminal and boundary conditions; for example, in the case of a call option ($F = C$) with exercise price I the terminal condition is

$$C(V, 0; I) = \max(V - I, 0).$$

The Black-Scholes solution to such an American call option is

$$C(V, \tau; r, \sigma^2, I) = V N(d_1) - I e^{-rt} N(d_2),$$

where

$$d_1 = \frac{\ln(V/I) + (r + \tfrac{1}{2}\sigma^2)\tau}{\sigma\sqrt{\tau}}$$

and

$$d_2 = d_1 - \sigma\sqrt{\tau}.$$

Similarly, a put option ($F = p$) satisfies the same p.d.e. with a different terminal condition: $p(V, 0; I) = \max(I - V, 0)$. The Black-Scholes solution to the European put is given by

$$p(V, \tau; r, \sigma^2, I) = -V N(-d_1) + I e^{-r\tau} N(-d_2).$$

A claim $F(V, \tau)$ contingent on a single asset V paying a constant "dividend" yield δ (with a payout d accruing to the claim owner) must satisfy the fundamental p.d.e.

$$\tfrac{1}{2}\sigma^2 V^2 F_{VV} + (r - \delta)V F_V - F_\tau - rF + d = 0,$$

subject to one terminal and two boundary conditions.

The adjusted Black-Scholes solution for an American call option with a constant dividend payout δ (which is lost for the owner of the option, i.e., $d = 0$) is given by

$$C(V, \tau; r, \sigma^2, I, \delta) = V e^{-\delta\tau} N(d_1') - I e^{-r\tau} N(d_2'),$$

where

$$d_1' = \frac{\ln(V/I) + [(r - \delta) + \tfrac{1}{2}\sigma^2]\tau}{\sigma\sqrt{\tau}}$$

and

$$d'_2 = d'_1 - \sigma\sqrt{\tau}.$$

The "dividend" yield δ may represent an explicit dividend payout in the case of a traded security, the net convenience yield in the case of commodities, or, in the case of a nontraded state variable, the rate-of-return shortfall between its expected growth rate (α) and the total return expected in equilibrium from an equivalent-risk traded financial security (α^*). If futures prices are available, δ can be estimated from $\delta = r - \hat{\alpha}$, where

$$\hat{\alpha} = \frac{\ln(f_2/f_1)}{\tau_2 - \tau_1}.$$

Alternatively, the risk-neutral drift $\hat{\alpha}$ can be determined from $\hat{\alpha} = \alpha - \lambda\sigma$, given the asset's volatility (σ) and its market price of risk (λ) obtainable from an equivalent-risk traded financial security whose value depends on the asset's price and time only. In some cases, an equilibrium model (such as the CAPM) may be needed to determine the expected equilibrium total return α^* and then estimate δ directly from $\alpha^* - \alpha$. In any event, it is more reliable to use risk-neutral valuation to value the contingent claim than to use the underlying asset's α to discount the claim's cash flows.

With two risky underlying assets, V and S, involving constant dividend payouts δ_V and δ_S, respectively, the fundamental p.d.e. becomes

$$\left(\tfrac{1}{2}\sigma_V^2 V^2 F_{VV} + \rho_{VS}\sigma_V\sigma_S VSF_{VS} + \tfrac{1}{2}\sigma_S^2 S^2 F_{SS}\right)$$
$$+ \left[(r - \delta_V)VF_V + (r - \delta_S)SF_S\right] - F_\tau - rF + d = 0.$$

If the underlying assets are not traded, the dividend payouts may represent below-equilibrium return shortfalls, $\delta_V = \alpha_V^* - \alpha_V$ and $\delta_S = \alpha_S^* - \alpha_S$, where α_V^* and α_S^* are the equilibrium returns (e.g., from the CAPM). The value of a European call option to exchange one risky asset S (paying dividend payout D_S) for another asset V (with payout D_V) is given by

$$F(V, S, \tau) = Ve^{-\delta_V\tau}N(d'_1) - Se^{-\delta_S\tau}N(d'_2),$$

where

$$d'_1 = \frac{\ln(V/S) + [(\delta_S - \delta_V) + \tfrac{1}{2}s^2]\tau}{s\sqrt{\tau}},$$

$$d'_2 = d'_1 - s\sqrt{\tau},$$

and

$$s^2 = \sigma_V{}^2 + \sigma_S{}^2 - 2\rho_{VS}\sigma_V\sigma_S.$$

In general, any claim F contingent on n underlying state variables V_i ($i = 1, 2, \cdots, n$), whether traded or not, must satisfy the general p.d.e.

$$\tfrac{1}{2} \sum_{i,k} \rho_{ik}\sigma_i\sigma_k V_i V_k F_{ik} + \sum_i (\alpha_i - \lambda_i\sigma_i) V_i F_i - F_\tau - rF + d = 0,$$

where $\alpha_i = \mu_i - \delta_i$ (μ_i being the total return and δ_i the dividend yield of asset i), $F_i \equiv \partial F/\partial V_i$, $F_\tau \equiv \partial F/\partial \tau$, and $F_{ik} \equiv \partial^2 F/\partial V_i \partial V_k$, subject to $2n + 1$ terminal and boundary conditions.

Thus, the ability to create a riskless replicating portfolio if the underlying assets are traded, or to obtain "certainty-equivalent" expected growth rates by subtracting appropriate risk premia ($RP_i = \lambda_i\sigma_i$) makes valuation more convenient in a risk-neutral world, in which "certainty-equivalent" or risk-neutral expectations of some future payoff, F_T, can be discounted using the risk-free interest rate r, i.e.,

$$F = e^{-r\tau}\hat{E}(F_T),$$

where $\hat{E}(\cdot)$ is the expectations operator in a risk-neutral world in which the actual growth rate, α, is replaced with a certainty-equivalent or risk-neutral rate, $\hat{\alpha} = \alpha - RP$.

Suggested Readings

Black, F., and M. Scholes. 1973. "The pricing of options and corporate liabilities." *Journal of Political Economy* 81 (May–June): 637–659.

Garman, M. 1976. A General Theory of Asset Valuation Under Diffusion State Processes. Working paper, University of California, Berkeley.

Hull, J., and A. White. 1988. "An overview of contingent claims pricing." *Canadian Journal of Administrative Sciences* (September): 55–61.

Mason, S. P., and R. C. Merton. 1985. "The role of contingent claims analysis in corporate finance." In *Recent Advances in Corporate Finance*, ed. E. Altman and M. Subrahmanyam. Irwin.

Merton, R. C. 1973. "Theory of rational option pricing." *Bell Journal of Economics and Management Science* 4, no. 1: 141–183.

Smith, C. 1976. "Option pricing: A review." *Journal of Financial Economics* 3, no. 1/2: 3–51.

4

A Conceptual Options Framework for Capital Budgeting

This chapter describes qualitatively a general conceptual framework for viewing real investment opportunities as collections of options on real assets (an expanded or strategic NPV framework) that integrates the important operating options (e.g., the options to defer or abandon a project early) with competitive and strategic interactions. Sections 4.1 and 4.2 provide the rationale for an expanded (strategic) NPV and for viewing capital investment opportunities as collections of real options. Sections 4.3 and 4.4 elaborate on the similarities and limitations of the options analogy. Section 4.5 presents an alternative, options-based project classification scheme. Section 4.6 discusses competitive interaction and develops competitive strategies under different kinds of competitive reaction (contrarian or reciprocating). Section 4.7 presents strategic questions for the analysis of capital budgeting. Section 4.8 illustrates the classification scheme in actual cases. Section 4.9 discusses the link between the proposed options classification, management's implicit operating strategy, and various value components.

4.1 Managerial Flexibility, Asymmetry, and Expanded (Strategic) NPV

As was noted in chapter 1, the basic inadequacy of the NPV approach and other DCF approaches to capital budgeting is that they ignore, or cannot properly capture, management's flexibility to adapt and revise later decisions (i.e., review its implicit operating strategy). The traditional NPV approach, in particular, makes implicit assumptions concerning an "expected scenario" of cash flows and presumes management's commitment to a certain "operating strategy." Typically, an expected pattern of cash flows over a prespecified project life is discounted at a risk-adjusted rate (derived from the prices of a twin traded financial security, usually employing the CAPM) to arrive at the project's NPV. Treating projects as independent investment opportunities, an immediate decision is then made to accept any project for which NPV is positive. In effect, it is as if management makes at the outset an irrevocable commitment to an "operating strategy"—e.g., to initiate the project immediately, and operate it continuously until the end of its prespecified expected useful life—from which it cannot depart, whether nature remains faithful to or deviates from the expected scenario of cash flows.

In the real world of uncertainty and competitive interactions, however, the realization of cash flows will probably differ from what management originally expected. As new information arrives and uncertainty about future cash flows is gradually resolved, management may find that various projects allow it varying degrees of flexibility to depart from and revise the operating strategy it originally anticipated. For example, management may be able to defer, expand, contract, abandon, or in various other ways alter a project at various stages during its useful life.

Management's flexibility to adapt its future actions depending on the future environment introduces an asymmetry or skewness in the probability distribution of NPV that expands the investment opportunity's true value by improving its upside potential while limiting downside losses relative to management's initial expectations under passive management (see figure 4.1). In the absence of such managerial flexibility, the probability distribution of NPV would be reasonably symmetric, in which case the static (or passive) expected NPV (or mean of the symmetric distribution) would coincide with its mode or most likely estimate (see upper part of figure 4.1). When managerial flexibility (such as the options to defer or abandon a project early) is significant, however, by basically providing a better adaptation to (or protection against) future events' turning out differently from what management expected at the outset, it introduces a trancation (typically below the mode) with enhanced upside potential so that the resulting actual distribution is skewed to the right (see lower part of figure 4.1). The true expected value of such an asymmetric distribution (which will be referred to as the *expanded* (or *strategic*) expected NPV—"expanded" in that it incorporates managerial operating flexibility and strategic adaptability) exceeds its mode (the same as the mode of the corresponding symmetric distribution, which equals the static or passive expected NPV) by an *option premium*, reflecting the value of managerial flexibility.

This asymmetry introduced by managerial adaptability calls for an expanded (or strategic) NPV criterion (NPV*) that reflects both components

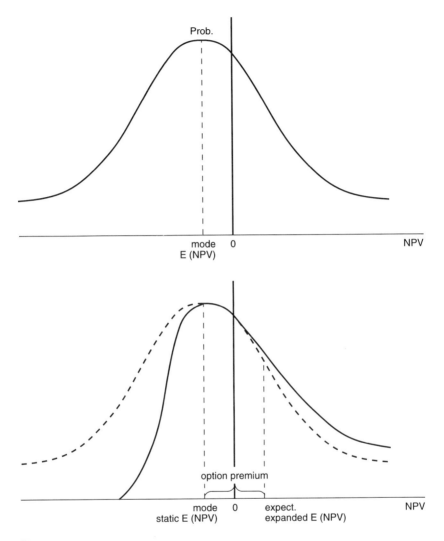

Figure 4.1
Managerial flexibility or options introduce an asymmetry in the probability distribution of NPV. Top: Symmetric distribution of NPV in absence of managerial flexibility. Static expected NPV coincides with the mode (or most likely estimate). Bottom: Asymmetric (skewed to right) distribution of NPV caused by managerial flexibility (e.g., options to defer or abandon). The (expanded) expected net present value exceeds the mode (=static expected NPV): Expanded NPV = Static NPV + "Option premium."

of an investment opportunity's value: the traditional "static" or "passive" NPV of directly measurable expected cash flows and an option premium capturing the value of operating and strategic options under active management and interaction effects of competition, synergy, and interproject dependence. That is,

Expanded (strategic) net present value (NPV*)

   = Standard (static, passive or direct) NPV of expected cash flows

   + Option premium (value of operating and strategic options from
   active management and interaction effects of competition,
   synergy, and interproject dependence).   (4.1)

The motivation for using an options-based approach to capital budgeting arises from its potential to conceptualize and quantify the "option premium" or flexibility (adaptability) component of value. This does not mean that traditional static (passive) NPV should be scrapped; rather, it should be seen as a crucial and necessary input to an options-based "expanded NPV" framework.

4.2   Investment Opportunities as Collections of Real Options

As was noted in chapter 2, the operating flexibility and strategic value aspects of various projects cannot be properly captured by traditional DCF techniques, because of their discretionary asymmetric nature and their dependence on future events that are uncertain at the time of the initial decision. Nevertheless, we can properly analyze these important aspects by thinking of investment opportunities as collections of options on real assets (or real options) through the options-based technique of contingent-claims analysis. Just as the owner of an American call option on a financial asset has the right—but not the obligation—to acquire the asset by paying a predetermined price (the exercise price) on or before a predetermined date (the exercise or maturity date), and will exercise the option if and when it is in his or her best interest to do so, so will the holder of an option on real assets. The owner of a discretionary investment opportunity has the right—but not the obligation—to acquire the (gross) present value of expected cash flows by making an investment outlay on or before the anticipated date when the investment opportunity will cease to exist.[1] Thus, as figure 4.2 illustrates, there exists a close analogy between such real investment opportunities (or real options) and call options on stocks.[2,3]

Call option on stock	Real option on project
Current value of stock	(Gross) PV of expected cash flows
Exercise price	Investment cost
Time to expiration	Time until opportunity disappears
Stock value uncertainty	Project value uncertainty
Riskless interest rate	Riskless interest rate

Figure 4.2
Comparison between a call option on a stock and a real option on a project.

Even if no other associated real options exist, the flexibility to defer investment or to decide when to initiate the project after receiving additional information (as may be provided by a lease to drill for oil, by the property rights to extract mineral reserves, or by a patent to develop a new product) has a positive value even if immediate undertaking of the project would have a negative (static or passive) NPV of cash flows. Such flexibility gives management the right to wait until more information arrives and make the investment (i.e., exercise the option) only if (for instance, the price of oil or the mineral rises, or the demand for the new product develops enough so that) the value of the project turns out to exceed the necessary outlay, without imposing any symmetric obligation to invest and incur losses if the opposite scenario occurs.

More generally, when other real options in addition to the option to defer the investment are present, a discretionary investment opportunity can be seen as a call option on a collection or portfolio consisting of the gross project value, V, and other real call or put options. For example, the option to expand the scale of a project by $e\%$ by making an additional investment outlay I_E can be formally seen as analogous to a call option to acquire $e\%$ of the project's gross value (the underlying "asset") with an exercise price of I_E. If market conditions are uncertain, management may, for example, find it preferable to build excess production capacity that will enable it to produce at a faster rate, on a larger scale, or for a longer period if, as uncertainty resolves itself, it turns out that the product is more enthusiastically received in the market than originally anticipated.

Similarly, the option to contract the scale of a project's operation by $c\%$ to save on certain planned advertising or maintenance expenditures of magnitude I_C can be seen as a put option on $c\%$ of the project's value with exercise price I_C. For instance, management may find it justifiable to build a plant with lower initial construction costs and higher maintenance expenditures in order to acquire the flexibility to contract operations by cutting down on maintenance costs if the product turns out to do worse than initially expected. Management may also have the flexibility to temporarily shut down production (or not to operate) in any given year if cash revenues are not adequate to cover the variable costs of operating in that year. One may thus look at operation in each year as a call option on that year's cash revenue, the exercise price being the variable cost of operating.

Management may also have the flexibility to terminate a project in its current use earlier than initially expected by switching to its future best alternative use (switching between alternative inputs and/or outputs) or by selling its assets on the secondhand market for their salvage value. Consider, for example, the choice between building a rigid plant having lower initial construction costs that can use only electricity to produce a single output (say, vitamins) and building an otherwise identical plant having somewhat higher costs (and higher resale value) but capable of using either electricity or coal to produce a variety of outputs (vitamins or aspirin). Even though the first plant may have a higher (static) NPV, management may find the flexible plant more desirable as market conditions change and the relative prices of inputs, outputs, or the plant resale value fluctuate, as it may switch to a cheaper input or a more profitable output or may sell the plant's assets on the secondhand market. This option to switch use or abandon for salvage value can be seen as a put option on the opportunity's value (in its current use), having as an exercise price its value in the best alternative use (or salvage value). Furthermore, management may also have the option to abandon a project during construction by "defaulting" on subsequent planned investment cost "installments" if a coming installment outlay exceeds the value from continuing the project. This option to abandon can be looked at either as a compound call option on the investment opportunity (with exercise prices the set of individual investment "installments") or as a put option on the opportunity (the cumulative value of subsequent cost savings being the exercise price).

Most of the important payoffs of managerial flexibility can be captured in a simplified way by combining these simple options as building blocks. If many such real options are present simultaneously, then the total investment opportunity can be seen as a collection of such real call and put options and can be, in most cases, analyzed numerically via a more involved contingent-claims analysis.[4] But even in complex cases where analytical solutions or numerical routines are not available, an options-based conceptual framework can offer significant payoffs to qualitative understanding.

4.3   Justification of the Options Analogy

Can the standard techniques of valuing options on the basis of a no-arbitrage equilibrium, using portfolios of traded securities to replicate the payoff to options, be justifiably applied to capital budgeting where projects may not be traded? As Mason and Merton (1985) point out, the answer is affirmative if we adopt the same assumptions used by standard DCF approaches—including NPV—which attempt to determine what an asset or project would be worth if it were to be traded. Recall that in DCF analysis we identify for each project a twin security with the same risk characteristics which is traded in the financial markets, and use its equilibrium required expected rate of return—typically by estimating the project's covariability with the market from the prices of a twin security and applying the CAPM—as the appropriate discount rate. The "correctness" of using NPV (value maximization) rests, of course, on the assumption of market completeness (i.e., the firm's decisions should not expand the investors' opportunity set), so that all that is needed here for the options analogy to hold is the existence of sufficient substitutes.[5] Given the prices of the project's twin security, management can, in principle, replicate the returns to a real option by purchasing a certain number of shares of its twin security while financing the purchase partly by borrowing at the riskless rate. Since the absence of arbitrage profit opportunities is a prerequisite for equilibrium, the equilibrium value of an option on a nontraded project must be the no-arbitrage value of the option on its twin traded security. However, nontraded real assets may earn a return below the equilibrium rate of return expected in the financial markets from comparable traded financial securities of equivalent risk, the rate-of-return shortfall necessitating a dividend-like adjustment. More generally, as was discussed in chapter 3, one can apply risk-neutral valuation, whether the asset is traded or not, by replacing the actual growth rate, α, with a "certainty-equivalent" or risk-neutral growth rate, $\hat{\alpha}$, after subtracting an appropriate risk premium ($\hat{\alpha} = \alpha - \text{RP}$).

4.4   Limitations of the Options Analogy

The analogy between real options and call options on stocks is close but not exact. In addition to the main distinction between traded financial securities and nontraded real assets and the resulting dividend-like adjustment, some of the main differences (see also Kester 1993) are the following.

(Non)Exclusiveness of Ownership and Competitive Interaction

A standard call option on common stock is "proprietary" in that it gives its owner an exclusive right of whether and when to exercise; i.e., the option holder does not have to worry about competition for the underlying investment. Similarly, some real options are proprietary in that they provide their holder with such exclusive rights of exercise, uninhibited by competitive threats. A patent for developing a product having no close substitutes, unique knowhow of a technological process, and market conditions that competitors are unable to duplicate for at least some time— all investment opportunities with high barriers to entry for competitors— are examples of such real proprietary options.

Other types of investment opportunities, however, may be jointly held by more than a single competitor. These real options are "shared" in that, as collective opportunities of the industry, they can be exercised by any one of the participants.[6] Examples of such shared real options include the opportunity to introduce a new product unprotected by possible introduction of close substitutes and the opportunity to penetrate a new geographic market without barriers to competitive entry. The nature of competitive reaction may, of course, be different if the investment opportunity is proprietary or shared, as will be explained shortly.

Nontradability and Preemption

Standard call options on stocks, like stocks themselves, can be traded frequently in efficient financial markets at minimal costs. Real options, however, like most investment projects, are not generally tradable.[7] Some proprietary real options—such as investment opportunities related to patents or licensing agreements—may be traded, although possibly at substantial costs in imperfect markets. Of course, certain proprietary projects may be abandoned before the end of their useful lives and traded for their salvage value.

Other real options may inseparably depend on other real or intangible assets with which they may be sold only as a package. On the other hand, shared real options may not be salable at all, since they are already a collective or "public" good of the whole industry; a firm holding a real option shared by competitors cannot easily avoid even anticipated losses in value resulting from competitive entry by just turning around to sell the option. In many cases, the only available protection against such value losses is an early investment on the firm's part, if it can by so doing preempt competitors from exercising their shared rights. (See Spence 1977 and 1979, Dasgupta and Stiglitz 1980, and Dixit 1979 and 1980 for various treatments of preemptive investments.) For example, a firm anticipating an increase in demand—and hence subsequent competitive entry—may rush to expand its own production capacity early in order to preempt competition, whereas in the absence of such competition it might have preferred to wait for the uncertainty surrounding future demand to resolve itself.

ſ Across-Time (Strategic) Interdependencies and Option Compoundness

Standard call options on common stock are simple in the sense that their value upon exercise derives entirely from the received shares of stock. Similarly, some real options (such as maintenance or standard replacement projects) are "simple" in that their value upon exercise is limited to the value of the underlying project. Other real options, however, lead to further discretionary investment opportunities when exercised. In essence, they are options on options, or *compound options* (i.e., options whose payoff is another option).[8] An investment in R&D, a lease on an undeveloped tract with potential oil reserves, or an acquisition of an unrelated company is undertaken not just for the sake of the underlying asset's cash flows but also (perhaps primarily) for the new opportunities that may be opened up (a new technological breakthrough, large reserves of oil, or access to a new market).

Compound real options may have a more strategic impact on a firm than simple real options, and they are more complicated to analyze. They must be looked at not as independent investments but rather as links in a chain of interrelated projects, the earlier of which may be prerequisites for those to follow. Again, compound real options that may invite competitive reaction may involve a more complicated (game-theoretic) analysis than proprietary real options.

4.5   Developing a New Project Classification

In practice, firms often classify projects according to risk or functional characteristics (e.g., replacement or new product introduction) to simplify the process of capital budgeting. These schemes are incomplete, however, in that they often overlook the option aspects of projects. To motivate a new options-based classification and to be better able to appreciate the various elements that it encompasses, let us start from simple NPV and gradually build up the framework, highlighting one aspect at a time. After considering the flexibility to defer or abandon a project, we will focus on the concept of compoundness, first within and later among projects. Finally, interactions introduced by competition will be discussed.

To see things in a broader perspective, let us first distinguish between two basic types of decision problems that a manager may face (as exemplified by the gap between traditional finance theory and strategic planning):

games against nature, in which the manager's problem is to optimize in the face of random fluctuations in the (gross) value of cash flows from the investment V (mostly applicable to highly competitive markets)

strategic games against competition, in which the manager's investment decisions are made with the explicit recognition that they would invite competitive reaction that would in turn impact the value of the investment opportunity (generally found in oligopolistic markets).

Commitment to Invest: The Static (Passive) NPV Approach

Traditional NPV analysis addresses decision problems of the first type since it ignores strategic competitive interactions. But even in dealing with games against nature, naively applied NPV is further limited in that it implicitly presumes that management is passive—i.e., that all decisions are unequivocally taken up front, as if management does not have the flexibility to review its original plans in response to nature's deviation from the expected scenario of cash flows. In the absence of such managerial flexibility, static or passive NPV would be correct: management would make an immediate investment outlay, I (considering for now the simplest case of a single one-time expenditure), only in return for a higher present value of expected cash inflows, V. The difference, i.e.,

$$\text{NPV} = V - I, \tag{4.2}$$

is of course the current value of the *investment* (i.e., of an installed or completed project), provided the manager had no other choice but to take it (immediately) or leave it.

Note that merely delaying the undertaking of an investment does not necessarily confer flexibility on a project. Suppose that the firm has a commitment (e.g., due to environmental regulations) to make an investment, I, in the future (τ years from now). If the investment is traded and involves no intermediate cash flows, this delayed commitment value, as given by the value of a forward contract on a non-dividend-paying traded asset of value V (assuming the investment cost does not escalate), will be[9]

$$F(V, \tau; I) = V - Ie^{-r\tau}. \tag{4.3}$$

For a nontraded real asset with a cash payout or a below-equilibrium rate-of-return shortfall δ (see equation 3.32),

$$F(V, \tau; I) = Ve^{-\delta\tau} - Ie^{-r\tau}. \tag{4.3'}$$

Opportunity to Invest (Flexibility to Defer)

What is really of interest, however, is not the value of the *immediate* investment per se (or of the delayed commitment), but rather the value of the investment *opportunity*. In a world of uncertainty, where nature can "play games" (where V may fluctuate randomly), the opportunity to invest can be more valuable than immediate investment (or delayed commitment), since it allows management the flexibility to defer undertaking the investment until circumstances turn most favorable, or to back out altogether if they turn unsatisfactory. The opportunity to invest is thus formally equivalent to a call option on the value of a completed project, V, with the one-time investment outlay, I, as exercise price. From the Black-Scholes option-pricing formula adjusted for a cash dividend payout (or return shortfall) δ, this value may be expressed as (see equation 3.18)

$$C(V, \tau; I) = Ve^{-\delta\tau}N(d_1') - Ie^{-r\tau}N(d_2'). \tag{4.4}$$

The value of this opportunity to invest therefore exceeds the static NPV of cash flows from immediate investment $(V - I)$ by the value of the flexibility to defer the investment. It also exceeds the value of a delayed commitment due to the future choice to avoid potentially unfavorable outcomes.

Such an investment opportunity may thus be economically desirable even if the investment itself may have a negative NPV (i.e., $V < I$). It would therefore be very useful to distinguish between investment opportunities that allow management the *flexibility* to defer their undertaking and make the choice after receiving additional information (such as projects with patents or leases) and projects that involve a *commitment* (such as an expiring offer to immediately expand capacity to meet extra demand by an impatient client or a required outlay to meet environmental regulations in the near future).

Even if management lacks the flexibility to defer the undertaking of a project when faced with an immediate accept-or-reject decision, it may still have the flexibility to abandon a once undertaken project for its salvage value before the end of its expected useful life if it turns out to perform worse than expected.[10] The flexibility to abandon a project early should therefore be explicitly accounted for in the investment decision whenever appropriate.

Multi-Stage Projects (Intraproject Compoundness)

Let us, for the moment, suppress the flexibility to defer undertaking the project or abandon it for its salvage value. However, consider the investment outlay, I, no longer as a single one-time expenditure at the outset but rather as a sequence of investment-cost "installments," starting immediately and extending throughout much of the life of the investment (e.g., annual maintenance expenditures during the life of a machine or a plant). In such a case the investment can actually be seen as a *compound option*, where an earlier investment-cost installment represents the exercise price required to acquire a subsequent option to continue operating the project until the next installment comes due, and so on. This is the idea of compoundness within the same multi-stage project—an intraproject interaction. If managerial flexibility is reintroduced, then intraproject compoundness highlights a series of distinct points in time (decision nodes)— just before a subsequent investment installment comes due—when the project might be better discontinued if it turns out not to perform satisfactorily. DCF techniques (particularly NPV analysis) that deal with the sequence of investment installments simply by subtracting their present value from the value of the expected cash inflows or even by including all but the first investment installment costs in the "net cash flows" clearly undervalue such compound investments.

Project Interdependence (Interproject Compoundness)

Let us now return to the simple case of a single one-time investment outlay at the start of each project. Consider, however, the case of *contingent* or *interdependent* projects, where undertaking the first project is a prerequisite for the next or where the first project provides the opportunity to acquire at maturity the benefits of the new investment by making a new outlay. For example, a research project, if successful, provides at completion the opportunity to acquire the revenues of the developed,

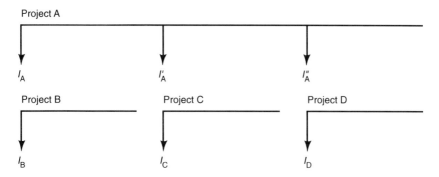

Figure 4.3
Top: Intraproject compoundness (a single project A with many investment-cost installments, I_A, I'_A, I''_A). Bottom: Interproject compoundness (a sequence of many single-outlay interdependent projects B, C, D).

commercialized product upon incurring a production outlay. This idea of *interproject compoundness* is remarkably similar in structure when we look at a sequence of projects to the intraproject compoundness described above (see figure 4.3), with the difference that each investment "installment" now provides the opportunity to begin a new project rather than continue another phase of the same one. Compoundness between projects is an interaction of considerable strategic importance, since it may justify the undertaking of projects with a negative NPV of direct cash flows on the basis of opening up subsequent future investment opportunities (or growth options).

Competitive Interaction

Another dimension to the valuation of investment opportunities is introduced by competitive interaction. Here we may distinguish between two forms of analysis, depending on the type of interaction between competitors. If the impact of competitive entry can be considered *exogenous* and pertains basically to the threat of capturing part of the value of the investment away from the incumbent firm, then its management still faces an optimization problem—although a more complex one—in that it has to incorporate the impact of competition in its own investment decision but can ignore any reciprocal effects of that decision on competitors' actions. If, however, each competitor's investment decisions are contingent upon and sensitive to the other's moves, then a more complex game-theoretic treatment becomes necessary. Investing earlier than one otherwise would to preempt competitive entry is a simple case of such strategic games against competition. Competitive strategy can be analyzed using a combination of option-valuation principles and industrial-organization game-theoretic concepts.

4.6 Endogenous Competitive Reaction and Strategy

For simplicity, suppose that the second stage of the market will result in a duopoly in which either of two competing firms (A and B) may invest in cash-generating followup projects. In this case, instead of the maximum of $(V_t - I, 0)$ or the deferral value in the binomial option-valuation tree, the state value of the investment opportunity would now equal the equilibrium outcome of a simultaneous-investment subgame. We can distinguish four basic cases:

When both firms invest (I) in the second stage, the game ends.

When both firms decide to defer (D), nature moves or market demand (Θ) is revealed, and the game is repeated.

When firm A invests first, nature moves and firm B may then decide whether to invest later (as a follower) or to wait.

When firm B invests first, nature moves and firm A may then decide whether to invest later (as a follower) or not.

The different sets of actions of the two firms would result in project-value payoffs at the end of each branch in the binomial valuation tree, representing the equilibrium outcomes of different competitive market structure games, such as Nash equilibrium (N), a Stackelberg leader/follower game (S), or monopoly (M), as in figure 4.4.

In this competitive context, we can express the expanded NPV criterion in the following form:

Expanded (strategic) net present value (NPV*)

$$= [\text{Direct (passive) NPV} + \text{Strategic value}] + \text{Flexibility value.}$$

$$(4.1')$$

The strategic value may be positive (e.g., if early investment creates a proprietary cost advantage or deters competitive entry) or negative (if early investment "proves" the market or creates shared benefits that a competitor can exploit more). We can refer to the combination of the direct NPV and the net strategic value resulting from an early capital commitment as the *commitment value*. Thus, an early strategic investment in a

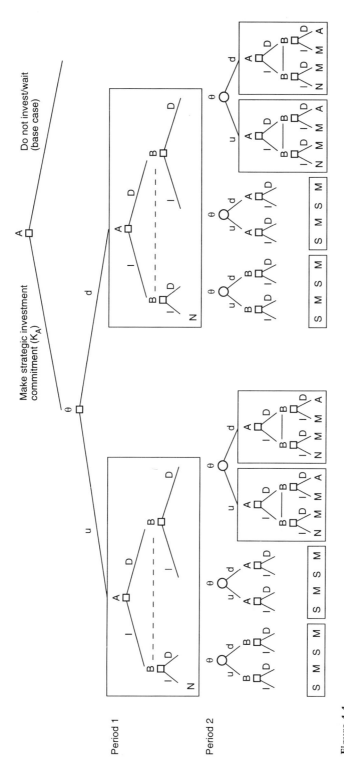

Figure 4.4

The two-stage game in extensive form under different market structures. A or B (square) represents a decision to invest (I) or defer (D) by firm A or B. θ (circle) represents the state of market demand or nature's up (u) or down (d) moves. The combination of competitive decisions (A or B) and market demand moves (θ) may result in one of the following outcomes of the market-structure game: Nash Cournot quantity or price competition equilibrium outcome (N); Stackelberg leader (S_L)/follower (S_F) outcome (S); monopolist outcome (M); abandonment (0 value) (A); deferment flexibility (option value) (D).

pioneering project is seen to have two main effects on value: a *commitment effect* (which influences the firm's competitive position and cash-generating ability in a later stage of the market) and a *flexibility effect* (which captures the firm's ability to alter its future contingent investment decisions under demand uncertainty). Although an early strategic investment necessarily sacrifices flexibility value, it may have either a positive or a negative commitment effect, depending on the sign of the strategic-value effect.

The Strategic Value of Early Commitment

Fudenberg and Tirole (1984) have developed an interesting framework for business strategies to capture strategic interactions. We can integrate these strategic interactions with real-options valuation to develop a two-stage framework for thinking about competitive strategies. Following Fudenberg and Tirole, assume that firm A can make a first-stage strategic capital investment, K_A, in R&D or in a pilot project in a new market. The value of second-stage operating profits for firm i (π_i) in each state of nature (for $i = A$ or B) depends on the strategic investment of the pioneering firm, K_A, as well as on the firm's ability to appropriate the benefits of the strategic investment when investing in follow-on cash generating opportunities, which is a function of competitive reaction. Thus, for firm A

$$\pi_A(K_A, \alpha_A^*(K_A), \alpha_B^*(K_A))$$

and for firm B   (4.5)

$$\pi_B(K_A, \alpha_A^*(K_A), \alpha_B^*(K_A)),$$

where K_A is the first-stage strategic capital investment of pioneering firm A (potentially influencing second-stage operating costs, or market demand Θ), π_i is the value of operating profits of firm i in the second stage of the market, and $\alpha_i^*(K_A)$ is the optimal (*) action of competitor firm i (Q_i in quantity competition, or P_i in price competition), in response to a first-stage strategic investment of K_A by firm A.

In some cases, pioneering firm A may invest in a strategic project in order to deter entry by making firm B's entry unprofitable ($\pi_B < 0$), thereby earning monopoly profits in the later stage of the market. To deter entry, firm A must take a tough stance that would hurt its competitor (i.e., $d\pi_B/dK_A < 0$). If entry deterrence is not feasible or desirable (e.g., if it is too costly), firm A may find it preferable in some cases to follow an accommodating strategy. Firm A's incentive to make the strategic investment then depends on the impact of its incremental investment (dK_A) on its own value from second-stage operating profits, i.e.,

$$\frac{d\pi_A}{dK_A} = \frac{\partial \pi_A}{\partial K_A} + \frac{\partial \pi_A}{\partial \alpha_B} \frac{d\alpha_B^*}{dK_A} \qquad (4.6)$$

(that is, Commitment effect = Direct effect + Strategic effect).

It is a prerequisite for an accommodating strategy that firm A's strategic investment must result in a positive commitment value $(d\pi_A/dK_A > 0)$. Equation 4.6 confirms that the total commitment effect consists of two component effects. The first term captures the direct effect of an incremental strategic investment on firm A's own second-stage profit value, with the competitor's reaction constant. The strategic effect results from the impact of firm A's strategic investment on competitor firm B's optimal second-stage action (e.g., B's output quantity decision), $d\alpha_B^*/dK_A$, and its resulting indirect impact on firm A's profit value. Thus, whether firm A should make the strategic investment or not would depend, in addition to the direct influence on its own profits, on whether the indirect strategic effect via the competitor's reaction is positive or negative.

The sign of this strategic effect depends on whether firm A's strategic investment (K_A) would create incentives for its own followup investment actions, α_A, to hurt $(-)$ or benefit $(+)$ its competitor's second-stage profit value, depending on whether the investment is proprietary or shared[11] and on whether competitor B's reaction to A's action, $R_B(\alpha_A)$, is reciprocating (as often happens in price competition) or contrarian (as is often the case in Cournot-type quantity competition). That is,

Sign of strategic effect $(-$ or $+)$

= Whether investment opportunity is proprietary (hurts competition) or shared (benefits competition)

× Whether competitive actions are reciprocating (complements) or contrarian (substitutes).

Figure 4.5 illustrates the two qualitatively different cases of competitive reaction. The top panel shows competitive reactions that are contrarian (substitutes), involving downward-sloping reaction curves; the right panel illustrates reciprocating (complement) reactions, with upward-sloping reaction functions.[12] When competitive reactions are contrarian, the action of the first-moving firm substitutes for the second-stage action of its competitor, or the competitor's reaction is contrary to the leader's action.

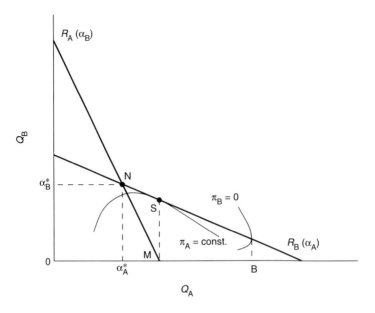

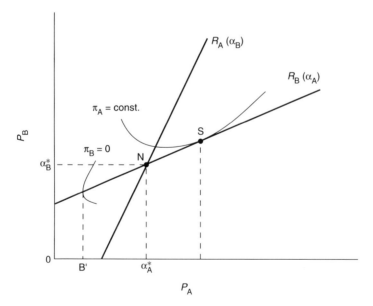

Figure 4.5
Contrarian versus reciprocating competitive reactions. Top: Contrarian competition/substitutes; downward-sloping reaction curves $R_j(\alpha_i)$—e.g., quantity competition ($\alpha_i = Q_i$). Bottom: Reciprocating competition/complements; up-sloping reaction curves, $R_j(\alpha_i)$—e.g., price competition ($\alpha_i = P_i$). α_A: Action of firm A (Q_A or P_A). α_B: Action of firm B (Q_B or P_B).

Often quantity competition, when a larger quantity produced by the leading firm (e.g., capturing a larger market share via economies of scale or a learning cost advantage) results in a lower quantity for its competitor, is regarded as contrarian and involves downward-sloping reaction functions. Competitive reactions are often reciprocating or complementary under price competition. Here, a low price setting by one firm would be matched by a low price by the competing firm (and lower marginal profits for both); both firms may thus be better off if the leading firm sets a higher price instead.

Depending on the nature of competitive reaction (contrarian or reciprocating) and the type of investment (proprietary or shared), different market-structure equilibrium values may result, leading to different optimal competitive strategies.

Market-Structure Outcomes

The market-structure equilibria that can result are, briefly, the following.[13]

Nash (Price or Cournot Quantity) Competition (N)
If both firms decide to invest (I) in the same period, a Nash equilibrium is reached when each firm reacts optimally to the other firm's expected action (as expressed by its reaction function, R), i.e., $\alpha_A^* = R_A(\alpha_B^*)$ and $\alpha_B^* = R_B(\alpha_A^*)$. Thus, the Nash-equilibrium actions (prices or Cournot quantities), α_A^* and α_B^*, are at the intersection of the reaction functions of the two firms, shown as outcomes N in figure 4.5.[14] These Nash-equilibrium actions can be obtained by substituting the expression for $R_j(\alpha_i)$ into $R_i(\alpha_j)$, or by equating the reaction functions $R_A(\alpha_B)$ and $R_B(\alpha_A)$ and solving for the optimal actions α_A^* and α_B^*.

Stackelberg Leadership (S)
If one firm invests earlier in a followup investment and its competitor invests later (e.g., if the follower faces higher operating costs that require waiting until demand has risen more, or if there is a lag while the follower sets up plant capacity), a Stackelberg leader-and-follower game can result. Given that the follower will observe the leader's prior action, the Stackelberg (quantity or price) leader will choose the action on the follower's reaction function, $R_B(\alpha_A)$, that will maximize its own profit, i.e., max $\pi_A(\alpha_A, R_B, (\alpha_A))$.[15] The Stackelberg outcome (shown in figure 4.5 as point S, where firm A's highest isoprofit curve ($\pi_A = $ constant) is

just tangent to firm B's reaction curve) corresponds to a higher profit than the Nash equilibrium.

Monopoly (M)

In some cases (e.g., when the leader has a first-mover cost advantage and/ or realized demand is low), the leader may choose an early action (e.g., a high enough quantity—above the profit-breakeven ($\pi_B = 0$) point B in the top panel of figure 4.5—or a low enough price—below the break- even point B' in the bottom panel) on the follower's reaction curve such that it would become unprofitable for the follower to operate ($\pi_B(\alpha_A, \alpha_B) < 0$, or net of the required outlay, $NPV_B < 0$), preempting the follower's entry and earning monopoly profits (π_m). The monopoly out- come (shown as point M in the top panel of figure 4.5) lies on a higher iso-profit curve than the Stackelberg and Nash outcomes.

Do Not Invest/Defer (D) or Abandon (A)

Of course, management has the option not to invest or to wait if market demand (Θ) is low and undertaking the project would thereby result in a negative value. By deferring investment, management keeps alive the op- portunity that demand may improve and the project may become profit- able. If the firm does not invest until the very last stage, or if it decides to abandon, the value of followup investment will be 0.

The different market-structure games discussed above (N, S, M, D, A) will result in end-state project values (as shown in figure 4.4) that can then be used within a backward binomial risk-neutral option-valuation process to arrive at the *ex ante* optimal competitive strategy.

Competitive Strategies

With an early strategic investment, the firm may enhance its ability to ac- quire a foothold in the market in the form of options to capitalize on fol- lowup investment opportunities. Deterrence strategies are directed at hurting competitors' profit values in the later stage so that they will not enter, creating proprietary profit opportunities for the incumbent. On the contrary, an accommodating strategy depends on the pioneering firm's ability to create valuable followup investment opportunities that can be shared with competitors.[16] Figure 4.6 illustrates various competitive strat- egies, depending on whether the investment opppportunity's benefits are proprietary or shared and hence early strategic investment hurts ($-$) or

		COMPETITION	
		Contrarian (down-sloping reaction/ substitutes) e.g., Quantity competition	*Reciprocating* (up-sloping reaction/ complements) e.g., Price competition
PIONEER	*Proprietary investment* (hurt competition)	C & O Invest (+ strategic effect) (Monopoly profits or Nash Cournot competition)	F & I Don't invest/wait (– strategic effect) (Nash price competition)
	Shared investment (benefit competition)	F & O Don't invest/wait (– strategic effect) (Nash Cournot competition)	C & I Invest (+ strategic effect) (Leader-follower/collusion or Nash price competition)

Figure 4.6
Competitive strategies under contrarian or reciprocating competition for a proprietary or shared investment. C&O: Committing and offensive strategy. F&O: Flexible and offensive strategy. F&I: Flexible and inoffensive strategy. C&I: Committing and inoffensive strategy.

benefits (+) the competitor's second-stage profit value, as well as on whether the competitor reacts in a reciprocating or in a contrarian fashion. Four different competitive strategies can result.

Committing and Offensive Strategy (Proprietary Investment under Contrarian Competition)
An offensive strategic investment commitment may generate a proprietary advantage and make the firm tough, hurting its competitor in the second stage. Under contrarian competition where quantities are substitutes, the competitor will retreat and the pioneering firm can expand its share and gain (Nash Cournot-quantity) leadership as the industry grows. If demand is so low that the competitor's profits would be negative, the pioneer may even enjoy monopoly profits. The strategic effect will be positive.

Flexible and Offensive Strategy (Shared Benefits under Contrarian Competition)
Under contrarian (e.g., quantity) competition, the competitor may take advantage of the pioneering firm's potential accommodating position and capture most of the shared benefits of its strategic investment. The pioneer firm may be better off not investing right away in the strategic

project, in order to prevent the creation of valuable shared opportunities for the competitor. Rather, firm A should maintain an offensive posture via its option (flexibility) to wait to invest in future growth opportunities if uncertainty is resolved favorably over time. If demand grows and both firms choose to invest simultaneously in a later period, a Nash-equilibrium outcome may result. There will be a negative strategic effect and a low commitment value.

Flexible and Inoffensive Strategy (Proprietary Investment under Reciprocating Competition)
Creating proprietary advantage via a strategic investment commitment may hurt competition but can invite a tough reaction by a reciprocating competitor, resulting in intensified rivalry (e.g., price competition in the airline industry). To avoid such intense (and potentially damaging) second-stage competition, firm A will not invest, staying flexible and inoffensive. If demand develops later, both firms can invest; the result will be Nash price equilibrium. The strategic effect is negative.

Committing and Inoffensive Strategy (Shared Investment under Reciprocating Competition)
Here, strategic investment will result in shared banefits with the competitor, who is ready to reciprocate. Thus, the pioneering firm should invest in the strategic project and be accommodating in a later stage of the market, thus avoiding price competition and reaping shared benefits. Through a collusion of high prices and higher profit margins, both firms can enjoy more profitable followup investments. The pioneer firm may act as a Stackelberg leader; the competitor may follow suit. The strategic effect in this case will be positive.

The absence or presence (and the nature) of competitive interaction can therefore serve as another "cut" for classifying and valuing real investment opportunities. We are thus led to propose the set of "strategic questions" for corporate management presented in figure 4.7.

4.7   Strategic Questions for Analysis of Capital Budgeting

The first question that management must address when evaluating an investment refers to the *exclusiveness of option ownership* and to the *effect of competition* on the firm's ability to fully appropriate for itself the option value. If the firm retains an exclusive right as to whether and when to in-

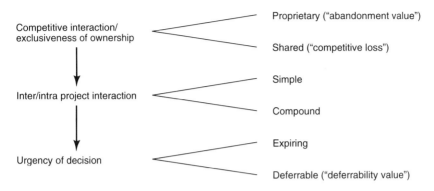

Figure 4.7
Set of strategic questions for analysis of capital budgeting.

vest, unaffected by competitive initiatives, its investment opportunity is classified as a *proprietary option*. Investment opportunities with high barriers to entry for competitors, such as a patent for developing a product having no close substitutes, unique knowhow of a technological process, or market conditions that competitors are unable to duplicate for at least some time, are proprietary real options. In such cases, management may have the flexibility to abandon a project early (i.e., the project has additional *abandonment value*) or even to temporarily interrupt the project's operation in certain "unprofitable" periods.[17] If, however, competitors share the right to exercise and may be able to take part (or all) of the project's value away from the firm, then the option is *shared*.[18] Shared real options can be seen as jointly held opportunities of a number of competing firms or of a whole industry, and can be exercised by any one of their collective owners. Examples of shared real options are the opportunity to introduce a new product unprotected by possible introduction of close substitutes and the opportunity to penetrate a new geographic market without barriers to competitive entry. The loss in value suffered by a firm as a result of competitive interaction when a competitive firm exercises its shared rights will be subsequently called *competitive loss*.[19]

The second strategic question concerns *interproject or intraproject interactions*, specifically compoundness.[20] Is an investment opportunity valuable in and by itself, or is it a prerequisite for subsequent investment opportunities? If the opportunity is a real option leading upon exercise to further discretionary investment opportunities, or an option whose payoff is another option, then it is classified as a *compound* option. Such real options on options may have a more strategic impact on a firm and are more complicated to analyze. They can no longer be looked at as independent investments; they must be seen as links in a chain of interrelated projects, the earlier of which are prerequisites for the ones to follow. A research-and-development investment, a lease for an undeveloped tract with potential oil reserves, and an acquisition of an unrelated company are examples of compound real options that may be undertaken not just for their direct cash flows but also (perhaps primarily) for the new opportunities that they may open up (a new technological breakthrough, large reserves of oil, access to a new market). A project that can be evaluated as a stand-alone investment opportunity is referred to as a *simple option*. Standard equipment-replacement and maintenance projects are examples of independent opportunities whose value upon exercise is limited to the underlying project in and of itself.

The last strategic question refers to the discretionary nature of the decision, focusing specifically on timing or urgency. Management must distinguish between projects that need an immediate accept-or-reject decision (i.e., *expiring* investment opportunities) and projects that can be deferred for future action (i.e., *deferrable* real options).[21] It would also be useful to distinguish deferrable investments that merely represent delayed commitments from future decision (choice) opportunities. We will subsequently refer to the value of the flexibility to defer undertaking a project as the project's *deferrability value*. Discretionary deferrable projects require more extensive analysis of the optimal timing of investment, since management must compare the net value of taking the project today with the net value of taking it at all possible future years. Thus, management must analyze the relative benefits and costs of waiting in association with other strategic considerations; for example, the threat of competitive entry in a shared-deferrable option may justify early capital commitment for preemptive purposes.[22]

This mode of analysis leads us to the real-options-based classification scheme shown in figure 4.8.[23] This eight-fork classification scheme is intended to focus management's attention on the important characteristics of investment opportunities as options on real assets. Although the distinctions between the various categories may at times be relative rather than absolute, most real investment opportunities, including strategic ones, can find a place in one of the eight branches of the options-based classification tree. For example, routine maintenance could be classified and analyzed as a proprietary-simple-expiring (P-S-E) option, plant modernization as proprietary-simple-deferrable, bidding for purchase of assets as shared-simple-expiring, a new-product introduction with close substi-

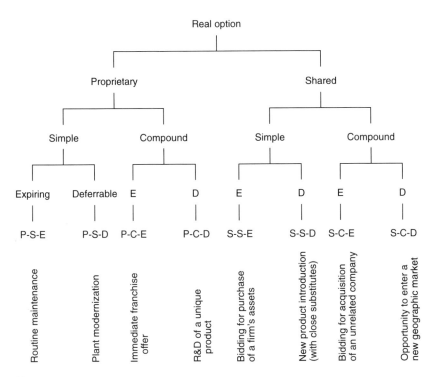

Figure 4.8
Proposed classification of investment opportunities (real options).

tutes as shared-simple-deferrable, an immediate franchise offer as proprietary-compound-expiring, research and development of a unique product as proprietary-compound-deferrable, bidding for the acquisition of an unrelated company as shared-compound-expiring, and the opportunity to enter a new geographic market as shared-compound-deferrable.

Under this classification scheme, conventional (static) NPV investments are properly seen as a special case under the leftmost branch of proprietary-simple-expiring options, since such investments are typically evaluated as if they were exclusively owned (i.e., ignoring competitive interaction, hence proprietary), independent (hence simple), and immediate (hence expiring) opportunities.

4.8 Cases Illustrating the Classification

To illustrate how the proposed classification of options would work in realistic settings, consider the following examples of real situations—

although slightly modified to protect the companies involved—faced by
U.S. companies.

The first example concerns the Upton Company, a producer of a wide
variety of basic materials and one of the country's largest public manufacturing firms.[24] One of the proposals in Upton's 1975 capital budget
was to construct and manage a plant producing a potentially dangerous
substance. The proposal was made by one of Upton's major customers,
which offered to undertake a contractual obligation to purchase all of the
output (and absorb any extra costs that might be imposed on Upton for
environmental cleanup) provided construction were to start immediately;
otherwise the offer would expire and the customer would turn elsewhere
or produce the substance by itself. Upton's opportunity is proprietary
(since it is exclusive and unaffected by competition), simple (since it has
no interdependencies with other investments and can be evaluated as a
stand-alone project—Upton anticipated no other future use for the toxic
substance), and expiring (since an immediate accept-or-reject decision is
required). Even abandonment options are negligible, since Upton is pro-
tected against unfavorable circumstances by its customer's guarantee.
Valuation of such an investment opportunity reduces to the determination
of its conventional NPV of expected cash flows. If the customer were not
to practically eliminate uncertainty in the value of Upton's future cash
flows by its guarantee, if Upton were not to feel committed to serve its
customer until the end of the project's expected useful life, and if the proposed facility were not uniquely suited for the production of the toxic
substance alone but were to have alternative future uses, then abandonment might acquire importance in case of unfavorable developments (e.g.,
environmental problems or reduced demand for the output).

Suppose now that the customer does not really need the product immediately and can wait up to 2 years before construction of a facility to
produce it must be started. However, the customer wants to plan ahead
and is determined to secure a source of the product as soon as possible.
Thus, suppose that if Upton were not to accept the proposal immediately
the offer would remain in effect for 2 years, but that the customer expressed a clear intention to approach Upton's competitors with the same
offer in the meantime. Upton would then classify this opportunity as a
shared-simple-deferrable real option.

Consider next the case of Kelor Chemical Corporation, a U.S. company
with only a moderate share of any of the four markets in which it competed.[25] Back in 1967 Kelor had the opportunity to build and operate a
sulfur recovery plant that promised to greatly expand its output and im-

prove its share of and its competitive position in the sulfur industry. The proposed facility was to exploit a unique new process, developed and tested by Kelor in a pilot plant, for the recovery of sulfur from gypsum. Kelor seemed to enjoy exclusive rights to the process through patent protection, well-guarded technical knowhow, company ownership of 80-year reserves of gypsum, and the availability of other cheap raw materials. Buyers were willing to subsidize the new process by contracting to purchase a certain percentage of the output and guaranteeing a minimum price (i.e., taking the downside risk themselves in exchange for the upside potential of increased total supply and therefore lower future prices). Investors also showed a strong interest in the new process, with Kelor enjoying a high price/earnings ratio thought to be more a reflection of the future earnings potential of the new process than of the proposed specific plant. Clearly, everyone involved looked at the new facility not in isolation but as the first in a series of similar facilities Kelor might build in the future (i.e., as a compound option). But although Kelor maintained exclusivity in producing sulfur by this method (giving it the flexibility to defer the investment), it still faced competition from the existing substitute methods of producing sulfur. Thus, Kelor's opportunity to produce sulfur was actually a shared-compound-deferrable real option. Suppose, however, that not only was the process new but also the product was new and unique, with a variety of potential new applications. Other things the same, the real option would then be proprietary (since Kelor would have exclusive rights to the opportunity to produce a new substance without facing competitive interaction through substitute products), compound, and deferrable.

4.9   Options Classification, Operating Strategy, and Value Components

The above options-based classification scheme helps uncover management's implicit operating strategy as well as the different value components of the "option premium" part of an investment opportunity's expanded or strategic NPV. Figure 4.9 shows different operating strategies and the corresponding real-option value (expanded NPV) for various simple investment categories under the options-classification scheme. Again, the proposed framework should be seen as a practical aid in recognizing and understanding some frequently recurring combinations of options.

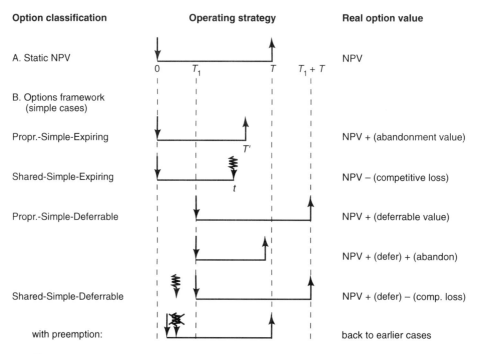

Figure 4.9
Option classification, operating strategies, and components of real option value. T: Expected project life. T_1: Period to defer (e.g., duration of a patent or a lease). ↓: Management's decision to start the project. ↑: Management's decision to end the project. Wiggly arrow: Competitive entry (out of management's control).

Part A of the figure shows the basic operating strategy assumed (appropriately so in the absence of managerial flexibility) by conventional (static or passive) DCF techniques: management starts the project (indicated by ↓) at time 0 and operates it continuously (indicated by a solid line) until the end (indicated by ↑) of its preestimated expected useful life (T). The value of the real opportunity in this case is adequately captured by the static NPV component, since there is no "option premium" in the absence of real options.

In part B of figure 4.9, different operating strategies may be found preferable when circumstances turn out differently from what was originally expected. In a proprietary-simple-expiring opportunity, the possibility of abandonment at an earlier time ($T' < T$) may become valuable. The value of the real opportunity would then be its value if no departure from the expected scenario and operating strategy were to occur (i.e., the static NPV) plus the value of abandonment. In a shared-simple-expiring real option, the project is again taken immediately but competitive entry (de-

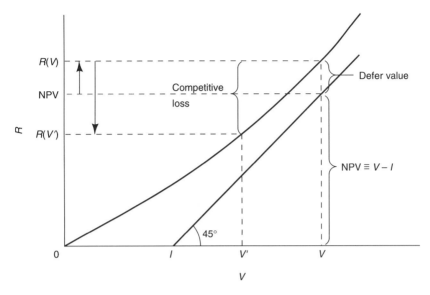

Figure 4.10
Value components for a shared-simple-deferrable investment opportunity. V: Gross project value. R: Investment opportunity (real option) value.

noted by a wiggly arrow) may cause erosion in project value (competitive loss). In a proprietary-simple-deferrable opportunity, the option premium results from management's flexibility to defer the project (until T_1), and possibly from its additional incremental ability to abandon it early. That is,

Option premium = Defererrability value + Abandonment value.

Finally, in a shared-simple-deferrable investment opportunity, the value of the real option is given by

Expanded (strategic) NPV

= Static NPV + (Deferrability value − Competitive loss).

If this expanded (strategic) NPV is positive before the investment opportunity expires, the project should be undertaken. Exactly when, however, depends on the tradeoff between deferrability value and the strategic value of early commitment (see chapter 9), or the competitive loss. The longer management defers the investment, the higher its deferrability value but the greater the risk of competitive loss.

Figure 4.10, based on an analogy with standard call options and intended to give a simplified visual impression of the various components of value for the last case of the shared-simple-deferrable option,[26] shows total real-option value (expanded NPV), R, as a function of (gross) project value, V. This figure is based on the assumption that a competitor's entry causes a drop in project value from V to V', the exact magnitude of the drop (which may, for instance, be due to loss of market share to the competitor) depending on market structure. This drop in the project's value translates into smaller damage to the real-option value attributed to competition from $R(V)$ to $R(V')$ (the competitive loss).

Notice that the real-option value exceeds the static (passive) NPV component of project value (given by the vertical distance to the 45° line, which equals $V - I$), and is non-negative even if the project's NPV is negative. The deferrability value component of the option premium is represented here by the vertical distance equivalent to $R(V) - $ NPV. Observe that either the deferrability value or the competitive-loss part of the option premium may dominate, depending on the severity of the impact of competitive entry on the project's gross value.

Suggested Readings

Kester, W. C. 1984. "Today's options for tomorrow's growth." *Harvard Business Review* 62, no. 2: 153−160.

Kester, W. C. 1993. "Turning growth options into real assets." In *Capital Budgeting under Uncertainty*, ed. R. Aggarwal. Prentice-Hall.

Mason, S. P., and R. C. Merton. 1985. "The role of contingent claims analysis in corporate finance." In *Recent Advances in Corporate Finance*, ed. E. Altman and M. Subrahmanyam. Irwin.

Smit, H. T. J., and L. Trigeorgis. 1993. Flexibility and Commitment in Strategic Investment. Working paper, Tinbergen Institute, Erasmus University, Rotterdam.

Trigeorgis, L. 1988. "A conceptual options framework for capital budgeting." *Advances in Futures and Options Research* 3: 145−167.

5   Quantifying Flexibility in
                       Capital Budgeting:
                       Discrete-Time Analysis

This chapter first utilizes a generic example to confirm that options-based valuation can be seen operationally as a special, though economically corrected, version of decision-tree analysis that recognizes open market opportunities to trade and borrow and explains how option pricing can be practically used in principle to quantify the value of a variety of operating real options. Specifically, it deals with the options to defer an investment, expand or contract the scale of operations, temporarily shut down (i.e., not operate in a given year), switch use (or abandon for salvage value), and abandon project construction by defaulting on planned cost installments. It then extends the analysis to the case of a levered firm and examines the improvement in equityholders' value as a result of additional financial flexibility (project financing), noting interactions with financial flexibility. A general framework, based on the generic option to switch operating "modes" (basically a compound exchange option) that subsumes earlier cases and allows the firm to be viewed as an adaptive system, is presented next. Finally, extensions to capture interproject interactions and the flexibility resulting from interest-rate uncertainty are discussed.

Just as corporate liabilities can be viewed as collections of call or put options on the value of the firm (as described in chapter 3), real investment opportunities can be seen as collections of similar real call and put options on the value of the project. And just as option-based valuation can be useful in quantifying the value of flexibility in financial instruments, it can be useful in quantifying the value of operating flexibility and strategic adaptability implicit in real opportunities. Flexibility is nothing more than the collection of options associated with an investment opportunity, financial or real.

Traditional approaches for the valuation of either financial or real investments were seen to be inadequate in the presence of such flexibility because of the asymmetry caused by the collection of such rights without associated symmetric obligations. In the case of real investments, of course, the basic inadequacy of the NPV and DCF approaches to capital budgeting, in general, is that they ignore or cannot properly capture management's flexibility to adapt and revise later decisions (i.e., review its implicit static operating strategy) when, as uncertainty is resolved, future events turn out differently from what management expected at the outset. This value of managerial adaptability, and the resulting asymmetry, can better be captured by the expanded-NPV rule:

ᐧ Expanded (strategic) NPV = Static (passive) NPV + Option premium.

Traditional NPV, which was initially developed to value bonds or stocks by passive investors, implicitly assumes that corporations hold a collection of real assets passively. In naively applied NPV, managerial choices are thus presumed to be limited to the initial decision (of accepting or rejecting a capital project), as if project value subsequently unfolds through chance events (like outcome nodes in an event tree). The value of active management (i.e., the value of flexibility or the option premium) will be better captured if value is realized within a decision tree, where flexibility is modeled through decision nodes allowing future managerial decisions to be made (and altered) after some uncertainty has been resolved and more information has been obtained, before proceeding to the next stage. Decision-tree analysis (DTA) would thus appear to be better suited, in principle, to value such problems than naively applied NPV. The presence of flexibility embedded in future decision nodes, however, changes the payoff structure and the risk characteristics of an actively managed asset in a way that invalidates the use of a constant discount rate. Unfortunately, classic DTA is in no better position than DCF techniques to provide any recommendations concerning the appropriate discount rate.

ᐧ The motivation for using option pricing or contingent-claims analysis (CCA) in capital budgeting arises from its potential to enable us to quantify properly the option premium or flexibility component of value. This does not mean that static (passive) NPV should be scrapped; rather, it should be seen as a necessary input to an options-based expanded-NPV approach to capital budgeting. An options-based expanded-NPV approach, however, is superior, since it combines the best features of DTA and NPV without their drawbacks. It borrows from DTA the use of decision nodes (rather than passive event nodes) in modeling flexibility while being more careful about using NPV's notion of a comparable security to properly price risk. An option-based expanded NPV can be seen, in fact, as an economically corrected version of a forward-looking dynamic programming process.

Decision scientists have argued that all that is needed to capture the value of managerial flexibility is the use of decision nodes within traditional decision-tree analysis, a technique that has existed for over 30 years. A number of professional managers have been concerned that, although the analogy relating managerial flexibility to options has intuitive appeal, the actual application of option-based techniques to capital budgeting must be too complex for practical application (certainly more complex than DCF techniques).

5.1 Option Pricing vs. Decision-Tree Analysis[1]

A Generic Example with Managerial Flexibility

Suppose we wish to value an opportunity to invest $I_0 = \$104$ million (all equity) in a project (e.g., to build a plant) that a year later will generate an expected value of subsequent cash flows of $180 million if the market moves up ($V^+ = 180$) or $60 million if it moves down ($V^- = 60$). That is, gross project value, V, follows a multiplicative binomial process, each period either increasing by a multiplicative factor $u = 1.8$ or falling to $d = 0.6$ of its earlier value. There is an equal probability ($q = 0.5$) that the project will move up or down in any year. What is the value of this project?

To determine net present value, we need an estimate of the project's opportunity cost of capital. If the project's risk is not the same as that of the company's average project, the company's cost of capital will be inappropriate. Following traditional practice, let S be the price of a "twin security" that is traded in the financial markets and has the same risk characteristics (i.e., is perfectly or highly correlated) with the real project under consideration (e.g., the listed stock price of an identical plant). Recall that the existence of such a "twin security" is implicitly assumed in NPV analysis for purposes of estimating the required rate of return on a project. The twin security's payoffs are proportional to (one-fifth of) the project's, and the twin security is currently priced in the market at $S = \$20$. Consistent with this market pricing, both the project and its twin security have an expected rate of return (or discount rate) of $k = 20\%$. The required return on the twin security can be confirmed from

$$k = \frac{E_0(S_1)}{S_0} - 1 = \frac{0.5 \times 36 + 0.5 \times 12}{20} - 1 = 0.20 = 20\%.$$

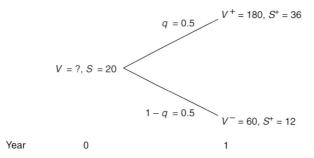

$V^+ = 180,\ S^+ = 36$

$q = 0.5$

$V = ?,\ S = 20$

$1 - q = 0.5$

$V^- = 60,\ S^+ = 12$

Year   0   1

Figure 5.1
Decision tree for the generic project and its "twin security." V: present value of subsequent expected cash flows from project. S: "twin security" price. I: required investment outlay. E: value of investment opportunity to firm's equityholders. k: risk-adjusted discount rate, i.e., expected rate of return. r: risk-free interest rate. Assumptions: $I = 104$, $k = 20\%$, $r = 8\%$.

The risk-free interest rate is assumed to be $r = 8\%$. The above are summarized in figure 5.1.

Traditional Approaches
Traditional DCF techniques, including NPV analysis, would discount the project's expected cash flows using the expected rate of return of the project's twin security as the appropriate discount rate. The discount rate would typically be estimated by determining the project's β coefficient from the prices of its twin security and applying the CAPM. The gross value of the project, V, would then be given by

$$V_0 = \frac{E_0(C_1)}{1+k} = \frac{qV^+ + (1-q)V^-}{1+k} = \frac{0.5 \times 180 + 0.5 \times 60}{1 + 0.20} = 100.$$

Subtracting the present value of investment costs gives the project's NPV:

$$\text{NPV} = V_0 - I_0 = 100 - 104 = -4.$$

Thus, the value of this investment opportunity is $-\$4$ million. In the absence of managerial flexibility, traditional DCF would correctly reject this project. As we will see shortly, however, if managerial flexibility or various kinds of operating options are present, the project may actually become economically desirable, despite its negative static NPV.

Traditional DCF is unable to capture the value of operating options properly, because of their discretionary asymmetric nature and their dependence on future events that are uncertain at the time of the initial decision. As we saw earlier, decision scientists attempt to overcome the shortcomings of conventional DCF analysis by taking into account the possibility of later actions that could be taken by the firm's management as future uncertainty resolves itself. Simulation techniques of the Monte Carlo type, for example, can allow explicit recognition of uncertainty by using repeated random sampling from the probability distributions for the various cash-flow components of a project to generate output probability distributions of NPV (or of IRR) for a given management strategy. Decision-tree analysis helps management structure the decision problem by mapping out all feasible alternative actions contingent on the possible states of nature in a hierarchical, or "tree-like," manner. DTA can actually be seen as an advanced version of DCF or NPV—one that correctly computes unconditional expected cash flows by properly taking account of their conditional probabilities given each state of nature. As such, DTA is correct in principle and is particularly useful for analyzing complex sequential investment decisions. Its main shortcoming is the problem of determining the appropriate discount rate to be used in working back through the decision tree.

As will be shown, the fundamental problem with traditional approaches to capital budgeting lies in the valuation of investment opportunities whose claims are not symmetric or proportional. The asymmetry resulting from operating flexibility options and other strategic aspects of various projects can nevertheless be properly analyzed by thinking of discretionary investment opportunities as options on real assets (or as real options) through the technique of contingent-claims analysis.

Contingent-Claims Analysis

The options-based approach of contingent-claims analysis enables management to quantify properly the additional value of a project's operating flexibility. In the absence of such flexibility, CCA gives results identical to those of traditional DCF. As we saw in chapter 3, the economic foundation of CCA rests with the explicit recognition of market opportunities to trade and create desired payoff patterns through securities transactions.

To confirm what insights CCA can provide, suppose that the gross value of a project (e.g., a fully constructed plant), V, and the price of the project's "twin security," S, move over the next period as follows:

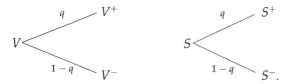

In our example, the gross value of the completed plant should not be confused with the value of the (possibly complex) opportunity to initiate construction of a new plant. The value to equityholders of the opportunity to start construction on a new plant (or the value of the project equity), E, will then move in a manner that is perfectly correlated with the movements in V or S:

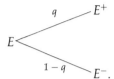

Now consider some of the open-market transactions that would be possible. Specifically, following a standard option-pricing hedging strategy (as described in chapter 3), management could construct an equivalent portfolio consisting of N shares of the "twin security" S partly financed by borrowing of amount B at the riskless rate, r. As we saw, this portfolio can be chosen such that it will exactly replicate the payoffs to equity (i.e., the opportunity to build a new plant) whether the project does well (S^+) or poorly (S^-):

$$
E = NS - B
\begin{cases}
\overset{q}{\nearrow} & E^+ = NS^+ - (1+r)B \\
\underset{1-q}{\searrow} & E^- = NS^- - (1+r)B.
\end{cases}
$$

Thus, if this portfolio can be specified precisely (that is, how many shares, N, financed by how much borrowing, $\$B$), then the investment opportunity, E, must have the same value as the equivalent portfolio, or profitable arbitrage opportunities will exist. Treating the conditions of equal payoffs as two equations, we can solve for the two unknowns N and B (similar to equations 3.2 and 3.3)

$$
N = \frac{E^+ - E^-}{S^+ - S^-}
$$

and

$$
B = \frac{E^+S^- - E^-S^+}{(S^+ - S^-)(1+r)} = \frac{NS^- - E^-}{1+r}.
$$

In other words, management can replicate the payoff to equity (i.e., the new investment opportunity) by purchasing N shares of the "twin security" and by financing this purchase in part by borrowing an amount of $B at the riskless rate.

The current (beginning of the period) value of the opportunity or equity claim (obtained by simply substituting for N and B in $E = NS - B$, and rearranging) is given by

$$E = \frac{pE^+ + (1-p)E^-}{1+r},$$

with

$$p = \frac{(1+r)S - S^-}{S^+ - S^-} = \frac{(1+r) - d}{u - d}.$$

Note again that the value of the investment opportunity does not explicitly involve the actual probabilities, q. Instead, it is expressed in terms of the adjusted or risk-neutral probabilities, p, that allow expected values to be discounted at the risk-free rate. Essentially, instead of using the actual decision tree to discount expected future values (using the actual probabilities of 0.5) at the required risk-adjusted rate of return ($k = 20\%$), CCA uses an equivalent "risk-neutral" decision tree, discounting expected future values (computed using the risk-neutral probability of 0.4) at the riskless rate (here, 8%). To demonstrate, by substituting into the expression for the risk-neutral probability,

$$p = \frac{(1+r)S - S^-}{S^+ - S^-}$$

$$= \frac{1.08 \times 20 - 12}{36 - 12}$$

$$= 0.4 \text{ (as distinct from } q = 0.5),$$

and applying this probability and the risk-free rate, we obtain

$$V = \frac{pV^+ + (1-p)V^-}{1+r} = \frac{0.4 \times 180 + 0.6 \times 60}{1.08} = 100.$$

This is identical with the gross project value obtained earlier using traditional DCF with the actual probability, q, and the discount rate, k,

$$V = \frac{qV^+ + (1-q)V^-}{1+k} = \frac{0.5 \times 180 + 0.5 \times 60}{1.20} = 100.$$

As this example illustrates, in the absence of operating flexibility or asymmetry, CCA gives the same results as traditional DCF. When operating flexibility is present, however, such as when management has the option to defer, abandon, expand, or contract the project, traditional DCF is unable to properly handle the resulting asymmetries and may result in significantly misleading prescriptions for capital budgeting.

Simple Examples of Managerial Flexibility (Operating Options)

Continuing with our basic example, we will assume throughout that the value of the project (i.e., the value in each year of its subsequent expected cash flows appropriately discounted back to that year), V, and its twin security, S, move through time as follows:

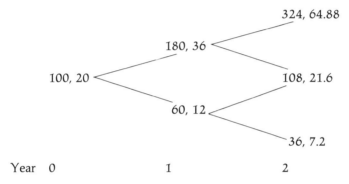

Year   0   1   2

In the examples that follow, we also assume that if any part of the required investment outlay (having present value of $104 million) is to be spent in the future, an allowance for it is made by placing that amount in an escrow account earning the riskless interest rate. (This assumption is intended to make the analysis somewhat more realistic and is not at all crucial to the analysis).

a.   Option to Defer Investment
Suppose the firm has a one-year license granting it the exclusive right to defer undertaking the project for a year (e.g., to construct a new plant of the same kind being considered). What is the value of the investment opportunity provided by the license? Clearly, although undertaking the project *immediately* was shown to have a negative NPV, the license (i.e., the *opportunity* to invest) has to be worth a positive (non-negative) amount to the firm's equityholders. With the flexibility to defer undertaking the project provided by the exclusive license, management— acting on behalf of equityholders—maintains the right to benefit from favorable random movements in project value; at the same time, they

cannot be hurt by unfavorable market circumstances, because they have no symmetric obligation to invest. To determine the exact positive amount of the option to defer (the *deferrability value*) provided by the license, we simply substitute the appropriate values for the payoffs to the investment opportunity (or equity claims), E^+ and E^-, in the risk-neutral valuation relationship above.

Because the option to defer the project for a year gives managers (equityholders) the right, but not the obligation, to make the investment by next year, they will wait and make the investment if the project value next year turns out to exceed the necessary investment at that time. In other words, the option to wait can be seen as a call option on the gross project value V, with an exercise price equal to the required outlay next year, I_1. This translates into the right to choose the maximum of the project value minus the required investment or zero, since management will simply allow the license or option to expire worthless if project value turns out not to cover the necessary costs. That is,

$$E^+ = \max(V^+ - I_1, 0) = \max(180 - 112.32, 0) = 67.68,$$

$$E^- = \max(V^- - I_1, 0) = \max(60 - 112.32, 0) = 0$$

(with $I_0 = 104$ growing in one year at 8% to $I_1 = 112.32$).

Thus, with the option to defer the investment, the payoff structure will be as follows:

$$q \qquad V^+ = 180, \ E^+ = 67.68$$

$$V_0 = 100, \ E_0 = ?$$

$$1 - q \qquad V^- = 60, \ E^- = 0$$

$$I_1 = 112.32$$

Year 0   1

Note how the option to defer (implicit in the license) has asymmetrically altered the structure of the payoffs. Instead of paying $104 million immediately to receive either $180 million or $60 million next period, we are now able to wait and observe if the outcome is favorable, in which case we would go ahead with investing for a net payoff of $67.68 million; or we could decide not to proceed if the outcome is unfavorable, with 0 payoff. Again, with

$$p = \frac{(1+r)S - S^-}{S^+ - S^-} = 0.4,$$

the total value of the investment opportunity (the expanded NPV that incorporates the value of the option to defer) is

$$E_0 = \frac{pE^+ + (1 - p)E^-}{1 + r} = \frac{0.4 \times 67.68 + 0.6 \times 0}{1.08} = 25.07.$$

Although the project per se has a negative (passive) NPV of $4 million if taken immediately, the investment proposal should not be rejected because the *opportunity* to invest in the project within a year (that is, when the value of the license is taken into consideration) is actually worth a positive amount of $25.07 million. The value of the option to defer provided by the license itself is thus given by

Option premium = Expanded NPV − Passive NPV

$$= 25.07 - (-4)$$

$$= 29.07$$

(which, incidentally, is equal to almost one-third of the project's gross value).

It should be clear from the above example that CCA is operationally identical to decision-tree analysis, but with the key difference that the probabilities are transformed so as to allow the use of a risk-free discount rate. Therefore, CCA visits no new implementation problems on DTA.

Of course, one may claim that this value of waiting can be captured equally well by traditional DCF and DTA approaches. Simply recognize that you can wait for a year and then take the project only if its value next year exceeds the necessary investment cost (so that again $E^+ = 67.68$ and $E^- = 0$); then determine its expected value using the actual probabilities and discount back at the expected rate of return ($k = 20\%$) to determine the current value of the investment opportunity (including the value of the option to wait) as follows:

$$E_0 = \frac{qE^+ + (1 - q)E^-}{1 + k} = \frac{0.5 \times 67.68 + 0.5 \times 0}{1.20} = 28.20.$$

Notice that the DCF/DTA value of waiting is different than that given by contingent-claims analysis. The DCF/DTA approach here overestimates the value of the option ($28.20 million vs. $25.07 million) because it uses the constant 20% discount rate required of securities comparable in risk to the *naked* (passive, inflexible) project or its twin security, although the presence of flexibility has dramatically altered the structure of the flexible project's payoffs. (In this case, it would have required a 35% discount rate for the DCF/DTA approach to give the correct answer, although this rate could only be obtained in an ad hoc manner. Discounting back at the lower risk-free rate of 8% while using the actual probabilities also produces an answer, $E = 31.33$, that is different from CCA's.)

To show that the $28.20 million given by the traditional approach is not the correct value for this investment opportunity, simply refer back to the replication, arbitrage-free argument. Would anyone be willing to pay $28.20 million for the license? The answer is "no" because any prospective buyer could instead purchase

$$N = \frac{67.68 - 0}{36 - 12},$$

or 2.82 million, shares of the "twin security" at its current price of $20 per share, for a total cost of $56.40 million, while financing the remaining part of that purchase by borrowing $B = \$31.33$ million at the riskless rate. Next year the investment will be worth $67.68 million or 0:

$$E^+ = N S^+ - (1 + r)B = 2.82 \times 36 - 1.08 \times 31.33 = 67.68,$$

$$E^- = N S^- - (1 + r)B = 2.82 \times 12 - 1.08 \times 31.33 = 0.$$

Thus, an investor would have been able to exactly replicate the payoff of the investment in any state of the world for an out-of-pocket expense of $25.07 million. Clearly, he, or anyone else, would not pay $28.20 million for an opportunity that can be replicated for $25.07 million. Therefore, to eliminate the possibility of riskless arbitrage profit opportunities, the value of this investment opportunity must be $25.07 million, as given by the CCA approach.

The error in the traditional DTA approach arises from the use of a single (or constant) risk-adjusted discount rate. Asymmetric claims on an asset do not have the same riskiness (and hence expected rate of return) as the underlying asset itself. CCA corrects for this error by transforming the probabilities. With the above demonstration CCA can therefore be seen as operationally equivalent to DTA. Following the insights of option pricing, however, it takes account of open market opportunities to buy or sell and borrow or lend. In so doing, it provides an economically corrected version of the conventional DTA. As such, CCA is superior to either traditional NPV or DTA, when applied naively, since it integrates the best features of both, without their drawbacks. It is similar to DTA's use of decision nodes (rather than passive event nodes) in modeling flexibility, while at the same time it is more careful about using NPV's notion of a comparable (perfectly correlated) security to properly price risk.

b.   Option to Expand (Growth Option)

Once a project is undertaken, management may have the flexibility to alter it in various ways at different times during its life. The option to expand is an excellent example of the strategic dimension of a project. Management may find it desirable, for example, to make additional follow-on investment (e.g., by building excess production capacity that would enable it to produce at a faster rate) if it turns out that its product is more enthusiastically received in the market than originally expected. In this sense the original investment opportunity can be thought of as the initial-scale project plus a call option on a future opportunity (i.e., the corporate growth option of Myers (1977)).

Suppose that in our example (assuming that the project was started in year 0) management has the option to invest an additional $80 million outlay (e.g., in excess production capacity and increased advertising expenditures) one year after the initial investment (that is, $I'_1 = \$80$ million) which would double the scale and value of the project (plant). Then in year 1 management has the flexibility either to maintain the same scale of operation (i.e., receive project value, V, at no extra cost) or double the scale and receive twice the project value by paying the additional cost, whichever is higher. That is,

$E = \max(V,\ 2V - I'_1)$

$\quad = V + \max(V - I'_1,\ 0),$

so that

$E^+ = \max(V^+,\ 2V^+ - I'_1)$

$\quad = \max(180,\ 360 - 80)$

$\quad = 280\ \text{(expand)}$

and

$E^- = \max(V^-,\ 2V^- - I'_1)$

$\quad = \max(60,\ 120 - 80)$

$\quad = 60\ \text{(maintain the same scale)}.$

Thus, management will exercise its option to expand if market conditions turn out favorably, but will otherwise let it expire unexercised. The value of the investment opportunity (including the value of the option to expand if market conditions turn better than expected) then becomes

$$E_0 = \frac{pE^+ + (1-p)E^-}{1+r} - I_0 = \frac{0.4 \times 280 + 0.6 \times 60}{1.08} - 104 = 33.04,$$

and thus the value of the option to expand is equal to $33.04 - (-4) =$ $37.04 million, or 37% of the project's gross value.

As noted, the option to expand enables a firm to capitalize on future growth opportunities. When a firm builds excess plant capacity from the outset at some higher-than-otherwise cost, when it buys vacant development land, or when it builds a small negative-NPV plant in a new location (domestic or overseas) to position itself to take advantage of a developing large market, the firm essentially installs an option to expand or grow. This option, which will be exercised only if future market developments are favorable, can make it worthwhile to undertake a base-case investment that would otherwise (on the basis of static NPV) be considered unprofitable.

c. Option to Contract

Analogous to the option to expand a project is the option to contract the scale of a project's operation by forgoing planned future expenditures if the product is not as well received in the market as initially expected. The option to contract can thus be seen as a put option on the part of the project that can be contracted, with an exercise price equal to the part of planned expenditures that can be canceled.

Suppose that in our example a portion of the investment cost necessary to initiate and maintain the given scale of the project's operation (present value: $104 million) is to be spent next year. Specifically, $50 million will have to be paid immediately as a startup cost, and an investment of $58.32 million (the future value of $54 million) is planned in one year.[2]

Suppose also that in one year, as an alternative to making the full $58.32 million investment necessary to maintain the current scale of operations, management has the option to halve the scale and value of the project by making a lower outlay, $I_1'' = \$25$ million (e.g., saving $I_1^* = \$33.32$ million by cutting down on the advertising expense). Clearly, if market conditions next year turn out unfavorably, management may find it valuable to exercise its option to contract the scale of the project's operation. That is,

$$E = \max(V - I_1, 0.5V - I_1'')$$

$$= (V - I_1) + \max(0, I_1^* - 0.5V),$$

so that

$$E^+ = \max(180 - 58.32, \, 90 - 25)$$

$$= (180 - 58.32) + \max(0, \, 33.32 - 90)$$

$$= 121.68$$

and

$$E^- = \max(60 - 58.32, \, 30 - 25)$$

$$= (60 - 58.32) + \max(0, \, 33.32 - 30)$$

$$= 5.$$

The investment opportunity, incorporating the option to contract, is then worth

$$E_0 = \frac{0.4 \times 121.68 + 0.6 \times 5}{1.08} - 50 = -2.16,$$

so that the value of the option to contract is $-2.16 - (-4) = \$1.84$ million, or about 2% of the project's gross value.

The option to contract, like the option to expand, may be particularly valuable in the case of new product introductions in uncertain markets. The flexibility to contract may also be important in cases where management may find it preferable to build a plant with lower initial construction costs and higher maintenance costs in order to acquire the flexibility to contract operations by cutting down on maintenance if the market conditions turn out less favorably than anticipated.

d.   Option to Temporarily Shut Down

Unlike traditional DCF procedures that implicitly assume that sufficient cash flows will occur in every year of a project's life to warrant its operation in each year, management may recognize that it may have the flexibility to temporarily shut down production (or not to operate) in a given year if cash revenues are not adequate to cover the variable costs of operating in that year; thus, operation in each year may be looked at as a call option to acquire that year's cash revenue by paying as exercise price the variable cost of operating.

Suppose that the project in our previous example makes a 30% cash payout, so that the cash revenues in a given year amount to 30% of the project's value ($C = 0.3V$). Next year, for example, the cash revenues will be $C^+ = 0.3 \times 180 = \$54$ million (with the balance representing expected cash revenues in subsequent years) if the market moves up, or $C^- = 0.3 \times 60 = \$18$ million if it moves down. In order to acquire these cash revenues, management will have to pay \$40 million in variable costs (advertising and maintenance expenditures). Management would of course be justified to do so if the market moves up and the cash revenues exceed these variable costs ($54 > 40$), but if the market moves down and the cash revenues next year are not sufficient to cover the variable costs of operating in that year ($18 < 40$) it will be better off to temporarily shut down production. In other words, management has the flexibility to operate in a given year and obtain the project's value (net of fixed costs) minus the variable costs (VC) or to shut down and receive the project's value minus the cash revenue, whichever is higher; i.e.,

$$\max(V - VC, V - C) - FC.$$

Alternatively, the option not to operate enables management to acquire the project's value by paying the minimum of variable costs (if the project does well and management decides to operate) or cash revenues (which would be sacrificed if the project does poorly and management chooses not to operate); i.e.,

$$(V - FC) - \min(VC, C).$$

Thus,

$$E^+ = (180 - 18.32) - \min(40, 54) = 161.68 - 40 = 121.68$$

and

$$E^- = (60 - 18.32) - \min(40, 18) = 41.68 - 18 = 23.68.$$

The value of the investment opportunity (including the option to temporarily shut down next year) is then

$$E_0 = \frac{pE^+ + (1-p)E^-}{1+r} - I_0 = \frac{0.4 \times 121.68 + 0.6 \times 23.68}{1.08} - 50 = 8.22,$$

and the value of the option to shut down next year is $8.22 - (-4) = \$12.22$ million, or 12% of the project's value.

If the variable costs are equally divided between years 1 and 2, then it can be easily shown that, following a down market and a temporary shutdown in year 1, operations will remain temporarily shut in the second year if the market moves down again but will restart if the market moves up. (This is distinct from permanent abandonment of the project.) The option not to operate in a given year, although not often significant in practice, may be important when deciding among mutually exclusive projects or alternative production technologies having different proportions of variable costs. McDonald and Siegel (1985) and Brennan and Schwartz (1985a,b) have valued this type of option.

e. Option to Abandon for Salvage Value or Switch Use

In addition to the option not to operate a once-undertaken project in a given year, management may also have the flexibility to abandon the project in exchange for its salvage value or its value in the best alternative use before the end of its estimated useful life if market conditions turn unfavorable. Consider the case of the chemical plant that can use either electricity or coal as an input and has the flexibility to produce either vitamins or aspirin. It is conceivable that, as market conditions change and as the relative prices of inputs and outputs or the plant's resale value on the secondhand market fluctuate, equityholders may find it preferable to abandon the current project's use by switching to a cheaper input or a more profitable output or to simply sell the plant's assets on the secondhand market. Let the project's value in its best alternative use or the salvage value for which it can be abandoned, A, fluctuate over time as follows[3]:

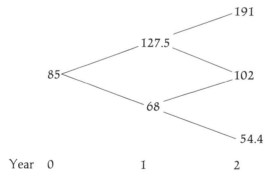

Year   0   1   2

The project's salvage value ($A = 90$) is currently below the project's value in its present use ($V = 100$); otherwise management would have switched use immediately. However, salvage value has a smaller variance; thus, if the market keeps moving up it will not be optimal to abandon the project early for its salvage value, but if it moves down management may find it desirable to do so (e.g., in year 1 to exchange the present-use value, $V_1^- = 60$, for the higher alternative-use value, $A_1^- = 68$). In other words, the option to abandon the project early in exchange for its salvage value translates into the equityholders' flexibility to choose the maximum of the project's value in its present use, V, or its value in its best alternative use, A, i.e., $E = \max(V, A)$:

$$E^+ = \max(V^+, A^+) = \max(180, 127.5) = 180 = V^+ \text{ (continue)};$$

$$E^- = \max(V^-, A^-) = \max(60, 68) = 68 = A^- \text{ (switch use)}.$$

The value of the investment opportunity (including the value of the option to abandon early or switch use in year 1) is then

$$E_0 = \frac{pE^+ + (1-p)E^-}{1+r} - I_0 = \frac{0.4 \times 180 + 0.6 \times 68}{1.08} - 104 = +0.44,$$

so the project with the flexibility to switch use becomes desirable. The value of the option to abandon for salvage or to switch from the project's current use to its best alternative future use in year 1 (S_1) is therefore $0.44 - (-4) = \$4.44$ million (that is, more than 4% of the project's value). The option to switch use can be especially valuable in new-product introductions in highly uncertain markets, particularly in the case of a project that can easily switch between alternative uses or be traded on the secondhand market. Myers and Majd (1990) have analyzed this option as an American put.

f. Option to Default on Planned Cost "Installments" during Construction
In addition to temporarily not operating in a given year or terminating a project in its current use earlier than originally expected in order to either switch to its future best alternative use or sell its assets on the second-hand market, management may find it justifiable to abandon a project during construction to save any subsequent investment costs. This will happen when the current required investment exceeds the value from continuing the project. Thus, when the necessary investment outlay is not simply a single expenditure at the outset but rather a sequence of invest-ment "installments" extending throughout the project's life, the invest-ment opportunity can actually be seen as a compound option where each investment "installment" represents the exercise price that must be paid in order to acquire a subsequent option to continue operating the project for the next stage until the next installment comes due, and so on. (This is the idea of compoundness within the same project—intraproject interaction.)

Suppose again that the investment costs (present value: $104 million) necessary to operate our project will be paid out in a series of "install-ments": $40 million out of the $104 million allocated amount will have to be paid out immediately (in year 0) as a startup cost, with the $64 million balance placed in an escrow account (earning the risk-free rate) planned to be paid in installments in the subsequent years. (For simplicity, assume that all subsequent installments are due as one $69.12 million payment in year 1.) Then next year management will pay the investment-cost "installment" as planned only in return for a higher project value from continuing, else it will default on the "installment" payment and receive nothing. Thus, this option to abandon by defaulting translates into $E = \max(V - I_1, 0)$:

$$E^+ = \max(V^+ - I_1, 0) = \max(180 - 69.12, 0) = 110.88 \text{ (continue)},$$

$$E^- = \max(V^- - I_1, 0) = \max(60 - 69.12, 0) = 0 \text{ (default)}.$$

The value of the investment opportunity (with the option to abandon by defaulting on future investment cost installments) is therefore given by

$$E_0 = \frac{pE^+ + (1-p)E^-}{1+r} - I_0 = \frac{0.4 \times 110.88 + 0.6 \times 0}{1.08} - 40 = 1.07,$$

and the option to abandon by defaulting is $1.07 - (-4) = \$5.07$ million, or 5% of the project's value. This option to abandon can be particularly significant in highly uncertain capital-intensive projects with long development times, such as large energy-generating plants.

5.2 Interaction between Financial and Operating Flexibility

So far we have dealt with operating (or real) options, assuming an all-equity firm. If we allow the introduction of debt financing, then the value of the project to equityholders will be improved by the additional amount of financial flexibility (i.e., the equityholders' option to default on debt payments). Let us examine the value of financial flexibility by reevaluating the original opportunity, in this case with project financing (where the firm consists entirely of this project).

Recall that the investment opportunity requires an immediate outlay, $I_0 = \$104$ million, to acquire the gross value of the project's expected cash flows, V, which moves through time as follows:

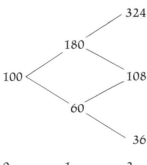

Year   0   1   2

Suppose now that $I_0^D = \$40$ million out of the required $104 million out-lay is borrowed against the project's expected future cash flows to be repaid with interest in 2 years (at an annual interest rate of 10%); the bal-ance of $I_0^E = \$64$ million is to be supplied by the firm's equityholders. Re-call that one may look at equityholders as having an option to acquire the project's value V—which in the meantime is "owned" by the debtholders—by paying back the debt (with interest) as exercise price 2 years later. Thus, in year 2, equityholders will pay back what they owe the debt-holders ($D_2 = 40 \times 1.10^2 = 48.4$) only if the project's value exceeds the promised payment, else they will default (surrender the project's assets to debtholders and receive nothing); i.e.,

$$E_2 = \max(V_2 - D_2, 0).$$

Thus, depending on whether the market moves up in both years (super-script $++$), up in one year and down in the other ($+-$) or down in both years ($--$), the equityholders' claims in year 2 will be

$$E_2^{++} = \max(324 - 48.4, 0) = 275.6,$$

$$E_2^{+-} = E_2^{-+} = \max(108 - 48.4, 0) = 59.6,$$

$$E_2^{--} = \max(36 - 48.4, 0) = 0.$$

According to CCA, the value of equityholders' claims back in year 1, de-pending on whether the market was up or down, would then be

$$E_1^+ = \frac{pE_2^{++} + (1-p)E_2^{+-}}{1+r} = \frac{0.4 \times 275.6 + 0.6 \times 59.6}{1.08} = 135.19$$

or

$$E_1^- = \frac{pE_2^{-+} + (1-p)E_2^{--}}{1+r} = \frac{0.4 \times 59.6 + 0.6 \times 0}{1.08} = 22.07.$$

Finally, moving another step back to year 0, the present value of the in-vestment opportunity (including the financial flexibility provided by the project debt financing) becomes

$$E_0 = \frac{pE_1^+ + (1-p)E_1^-}{1+r} - I_0^E = \frac{0.4 \times 135.19 + 0.6 \times 22.07}{1.08} - 64 = -1.67,$$

so the value of financial flexibility (debt financing) is $-1.67 - (-4) =$ $2.33 million, over 2% of the project's gross value.

Moreover, the combined interactive effects between operating and fin-ancial flexibility can further magnify the amount of undervaluation caused by traditional DCF techniques. Consider, for example, the interaction between the above financial flexibility and the operating default option analyzed earlier.

Suppose that $I_0^D = \$40$ million is borrowed as before to be paid immediately as a project startup cost, but now the $64 million equity money is put in an escrow account (earning the riskless rate) to be paid as an investment "installment" in year 1 (as $I_1^E = 64 \times 1.08 = 69.12$). (This case is identical to the default case in subsection f above, except that the initial outlay is now borrowed money.) Thus, equityholders now have the additional operating flexibility to abandon the project (by not making the equity cost "installment," I_1^E, if it turns out to exceed the project's value) in year 1.

Again, starting from the end and moving backward, the value of equityholders's claims in year 2 (with debt repayment) remains unchanged, but in year 1 the value now becomes the maximum of its value in the previous case (in the absence of any outlay), minus the equity cost "installment" (I_1^E) now due, or zero (if the project performs poorly and equityholders abandon it by defaulting on the debt installment), i.e., $(E_1)' = \max(E_1 - I_1^E, 0)$:

$$(E_1^+)' = \max(135.19 - 69.12, 0) = 66.07,$$

$$(E_1^-)' = \max(22.07 - 69.12, 0) = 0.$$

Finally, the value of the investment opportunity (with both financial and operating abandonment flexibility) becomes

$$E_0' = \frac{p(E_1^+)' + (1-p)(E_1^-)'}{1+r} = \frac{0.4 \times 66.07 + 0.6 \times 0}{1.08} = 24.47,$$

so the value of the combined abandonment with debt financing option is $24.47 - (-4) = \$28.47$ million, amounting to more than 25% of the project's value.

Note that this combined value of the operating option to default on planned cost installments (determined separately to be 5% in subsection f above) and of the financial flexibility (separately estimated at about 2%) far exceeds the sum of separate option values, indicating the presence of substantial positive interaction (i.e., 28% > (5 + 2)%). Such positive interaction effects are typical in compound option situations such as this.[4]

The interactive effects between operating and financial flexibility can be quite significant for large, uncertain long-development investment projects. CCA would therefore be a particularly useful tool to corporate strategists, since it provides a consistent, unified approach toward incorporating the value of both the operating and financial options associated with the combined investment and financing decision of the firm.

5.3   The General Flexibility to Switch Operating "Modes"[5]

Let us now revisit and generalize the option to switch use introduced in subsection e above, allowing for managerial decisions to switch, possibly at specified switching costs, among alternative "modes" of operation (e.g., projects, machines, technologies) at multiple decision points (or in each period). This generalization has natural applications in flexible manufacturing systems, although (with appropriate interpretation of the operating "modes" and switching costs) it may subsume as special cases most of the other real options we discussed so far.

Consider first the case of two alternative projects (e.g., machines whose operation is rigid—that is, restricted just to one technology), A and B, with three decision points ($t = 0, 1, 2$). Let $c_t^s(m)$ be the net cash flow generated in year t if found in state s (where $s = +$ or $-$ in year 1, or $++$, $+-$, $--$ in year 2) when using technology (operating mode) m ($m = A, B$):

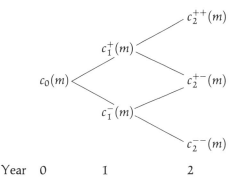

Year   0   1   2

Suppose that the machine with rigid technology A ($m = A$) will generate the following cash flows in each year:

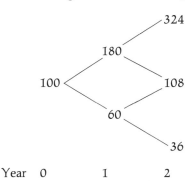

Year   0   1   2

Similarly, the cash flows from the machine using rigid technology B are

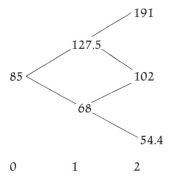

Year   0   1   2

As noted, the present value of cash flows from each project can be equivalently obtained (in the absence of flexibility) either by discounting expected cash flows (using the actual probabilities of 0.5) at the expected
rate of return (e.g., $k = 20\%$ for A) or by discounting risk-neutral expected values (using the risk-neutral probabilities) at the risk-free rate ($r =$
0.08). The risk-neutral probability, obtainable from market information as
shown earlier in this chapter, is $p = 0.4$ for up movements and $1 - p =$
0.6 for down movements in each period. The present value of cash flows
from the machine using rigid technology A can thus be obtained as
follows:

$$PV(A) = 100 + \frac{0.5 \times 180 + 0.5 \times 60}{1.20} + \frac{144}{1.20^2}$$

$$= 100 + \frac{0.4 \times 180 + 0.6 \times 60}{1.08} +$$

$$\frac{0.4^2 \times 324 + 2 \times 0.4 \times 0.6 \times 108 + 0.6^2 \times 36}{1.08^2}$$

$$= 100 + 100 + 100$$

$$= 300.$$

Similarly, for the machine using rigid technology B,

$$PV(B) = 85 + 85 + 85 = 255.$$

No Switching Costs and Option-Value Additivity

Consider now a flexible operating system, F, that can switch between
alternative technologies, A and B. For simplicity, initially assume that

switching involves no costs (i.e., $I = 0$). Obviously, the right (with no ob-ligation) to switch between the two technologies makes the equity value of the flexible system, $E(F)$, greater than the value of either of the rigid machines. That is,

$$E(F) \geq \max(PV(A), PV(B)).$$

Actually, the equity value of the flexible system exceeds that of rigid machine A (which is committed to using only technology A) by the value of the flexibility to switch operation from A to B, denoted by $F(A \rightarrow B)$, whenever the value of cash flows from operating technology B turns out to be higher, i.e.,

$$E(F) = PV(A) + F(A \rightarrow B).$$

In the case with no switching costs, this combined flexibility value is the sum of the three (European) options to switch from A to B, denoted by $S_t(A \rightarrow B)$, in years 0, 1, and 2, respectively. That is,

$$F(A \rightarrow B) = S_0(A \rightarrow B) + S_1(A \rightarrow B) + S_2(A \rightarrow B).$$

(As we will see later, the presence of switching costs creates a *compound-ness* effect that makes this option-value additivity break down.)

To confirm this, let $c_t^s(A \rightarrow B)$ be the *incremental* (additional) cash pay-off from voluntarily switching from technology A to B in year t and state s if it is beneficial to do so. That is,

$$c_t^s(A \rightarrow B) \equiv \max(c_t^s(B) - c_t^s(A), 0).$$

In the above example,

$$S_0(A \rightarrow B) = \max(85 - 100, 0) = 0;$$

i.e., the option to switch from A to B immediately is worthless. Switching from A to B in year 1, however, results in the following incremental cash-flow pattern in each state:

$$c_1^+(A \rightarrow B) = \max(127.5 - 180, 0) = 0$$

$$S_1(A \rightarrow B)$$

$$c_1^-(A \rightarrow B) = \max(68 - 60, 0) = 8.$$

$$t = 0 \qquad\qquad 1$$

Thus, the value of the option to switch from A to B in year 1 is given by

$$S_1(A \to B) = \frac{p\,c_1^+(A \to B) + (1-p)c_1^-(A \to B)}{1+r}$$

$$= \frac{0.4 \times 0 + 0.6 \times 8}{1.08} = 4.4,$$

which confirms the result of subsection e above. Similarly, for switching in year 2,

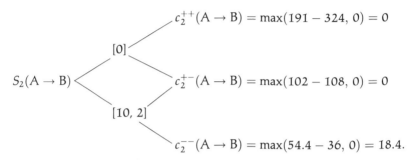

$$c_2^{++}(A \to B) = \max(191 - 324, 0) = 0$$

$$c_2^{+-}(A \to B) = \max(102 - 108, 0) = 0$$

$$c_2^{--}(A \to B) = \max(54.4 - 36, 0) = 18.4.$$

The discounted values of the terminal ($t = 2$) cash flows one year earlier (at $t = 1$), given in brackets, are 0 and 10.2, respectively. For example, for the down state ($-$) in year 1,

$$\frac{0.4 \times 0 + 0.6 \times 18.4}{1.08} = 10.2.$$

Discounting one more time to the beginning, we get

$$S_2(A \to B) = \frac{0.4 \times 0 + 0.6 \times 10.2}{1.08} = 5.7.$$

Thus, the combined value of the flexibility to switch operation from technology A to B at any of the three decision times is

$$F(A \to B) = S_0(A \to B) + S_1(A \to B) + S_2(A \to B)$$

$$= 0 + 4.4 + 5.7$$

$$= 10.1.$$

Thus, flexible system F should be preferred over rigid machine A as long as the incremental cost of acquiring F over A is less than the value of flexibility (of 10.1 above), i.e.,

$$I(F) - I(A) < F(A \to B) \; (= E(F) - PV(A)),$$

or

$$E(F) - I(F) > PV(A) - I(A) \ (\equiv NPV(A))$$

(i.e., as long as the flexible system, F, has a greater "expanded NPV" than the rigid machine). The total value of the flexible system (using either technology A or B) is therefore given by

$$E(F) = PV(A) + F(A \rightarrow B) = 300 + 10.1 = 310.1.$$

Alternatively, the flexible system can be thought of as equivalent (in the absence of switching costs) to operating machine B, with the flexibility to switch (from technology B) to A when profitable, i.e.,

$$E(F) = PV(B) + F(B \rightarrow A).$$

Again,

$$F(B \rightarrow A) = S_0(B \rightarrow A) + S_1(B \rightarrow A) + S_2(B \rightarrow A),$$

where

$$S_0(B \rightarrow A) = c_0(B \rightarrow A) = \max(100 - 85, 0) = 15$$

and

$$c_1^+(B \rightarrow A) = \max(180 - 127.5, 0) = 52.5$$

$$S_1(B \rightarrow A)$$

$$c_1^-(B \rightarrow A) = 0.$$

$$t = 0 \qquad\qquad 1$$

Thus, the value of the option to switch from B to A in year 1 is

$$S_1(B \rightarrow A) = \frac{0.4 \times 52.5 + 0.6 \times 0}{1.08} = 19.4.$$

Similarly, for year 2 switching from B to A:

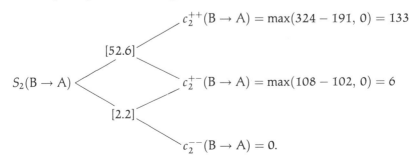

$$c_2^{++}(B \rightarrow A) = \max(324 - 191, 0) = 133$$

$$[52.6]$$

$$S_2(B \rightarrow A)$$

$$c_2^{+-}(B \rightarrow A) = \max(108 - 102, 0) = 6$$

$$[2.2]$$

$$c_2^{--}(B \rightarrow A) = 0.$$

The discounted values of the terminal cash flows at $t = 1$ are again shown in brackets as 52.6 ($= [0.4 \times 133 + 0.6 \times 6]/1.08$) and 2.2, respectively, giving

$$S_2(B \to A) = \frac{0.4 \times 52.6 + 0.6 \times 2.2}{1.08} = 20.7.$$

Thus, the combined value of the flexibility to switch operation from B to A is

$$F(B \to A) = S_0(B \to A) + S_1(B \to A) + S_2(B \to A)$$

$$= 15 + 19.4 + 20.7$$

$$= 55.1.$$

Therefore,

$$E(F) = PV(B) + F(B \to A) = 255 + 55.1 = 310.1,$$

confirming that, in the absence of switching costs,

$$PV(A) + F(A \to B) = E(F) = PV(B) + F(B \to A).$$

Table 5.1 summarizes the breakdown of value into various components (and their additivity) for each rigid machine separately as well as for the flexible system.

Alternatively, the flexible system can be valued directly as a package by noting (as in subsection e above) that its cash flows in each period will be the higher of those from the two technologies, e.g.,

$$c_2^s(F) = \max(c_2^s(A), c_2^s(B)).$$

In this case, this would result in the following decision tree (with the

Table 5.1
Value components for each rigid machine (A and B) and for the flexible system (A/B).

Period	Rigid technology A	Option A → B	Rigid technology B	Option B → A	Flexible system A/B
0	100	0	85	15	100
1	100	4.4	85	19.4	104.4
2	100	5.7	85	20.7	105.7
Total	300	10.1	255	55.1	310.1

brackets in the top lines, added next to the best current cash flow, capturing the value as of that time of subsequent cash flows given optimal future operation):

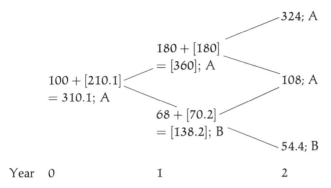

Year   0   1   2

The optimal technology or "mode" to use (A or B) at each decision node is noted (after the semicolon) along with the optimal total value (which is confirmed to be 310.1 at $t = 0$). Basically, without switching costs the general dynamic problem is equivalent to a series of simpler myopic problems, with the combined package value being equal to the sum of the separate component values. This equivalence no longer holds in the presence of asymmetric nonzero switching costs.

With Switching Costs: Compound Interactions

When there are costs associated with switching from one operating mode (e.g., technology) to another, the separate switching options are no longer independent and their separate values no longer add up to the combined flexibility value (that is, option-value additivity breaks down). In contrast with the previous case with no costs, where potential exercise of an earlier switching option affects the current payoff but has no effect on a subsequent option, switching with costs not only affects the current decision and cash payoff but also alters the exercise costs and switching decisions (options) in future periods. Basically, exercise of a prior option (i.e., switching operating modes in an earlier period) creates a series of nested new options (to switch in the future), analogous to a compound option. This invalidates option-value additivity.

Let $I(A \rightarrow B)$ be the cost of switching from operating mode (technology) A to B. In the presence of such switching costs, the incremental cash flow of switching from A to B then becomes

$$c_t^s(A \to B) \equiv \max(c_t^s(B) - c_t^s(A) - I(A \to B), 0).$$

For example, suppose $I(A \to B) = 8$ and $I(B \to A) = 2$. Revisiting our example above with such asymmetric switching costs, each separate switching option is now valued as follows:

$$S_0(A \to B) = \max(85 - 100 - 8, 0) = 0,$$

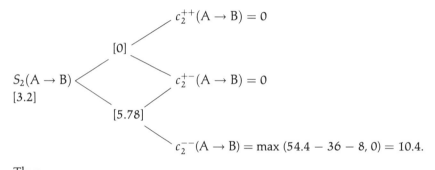

$$c_1^+(A \to B) = \max(127.5 - 180 - 8, 0) = 0$$

$S_1(A \to B)$
$[0]$

$$c_1^-(A \to B) = \max(68 - 60 - 8, 0) = 0$$

so the option to switch from A to B at time 1 by paying an \$8 switching cost also becomes worthless $(S_1(A \to B) = 0)$, and

$$c_2^{++}(A \to B) = 0$$

$[0]$

$S_2(A \to B)$
$[3.2]$

$$c_2^{+-}(A \to B) = 0$$

$[5.78]$

$$c_2^{--}(A \to B) = \max(54.4 - 36 - 8, 0) = 10.4.$$

Thus,

$$S_0(A \to B) + S_1(A \to B) + S_2(A \to B) = 0 + 0 + 3.2 = 3.2.$$

Similarly, the sum of separate option values for switching from B to A is

$$S_0(B \to A) = \max(100 - 85 - 2, 0) = 13,$$

$$c_1^+(B \to A) = \max(180 - 127.5 - 2, 0) = 50.5$$

$S_1(B \to A)$
$[18.7]$

$$c_1^-(B \to A) = 0,$$

and

$$c_2^{++}(B \to A) = \max(324 - 191 - 2, 0) = 131$$

[50.7]

$$S_2(B \to A)$$
[19.6]

$$c_2^{+-}(B \to A) = \max(108 - 102 - 2, 0) = 4$$

[1.5]

$$c_2^{--}(B \to A) = 0.$$

Year   0   1   2

Thus,

$$S_0(B \to A) + S_1(B \to A) + S_2(B \to A) = 13 + 18.7 + 19.6 = 51.3.$$

It therefore can be seen that

$$PV(A) + \sum_{t=0}^{2} S_t(A \to B) = 300 + 3.2 = 303.2,$$

which is no longer equivalent to

$$PV(B) + \sum_{t=0}^{2} S_t(B \to A) = 255 + 51.3 = 306.3.$$

That is, in the presence of asymmetric switching costs, the flexible system can no longer be viewed as being equivalent to one of the rigid machines plus the set (or sum) of simple options to switch to the other technology.

In fact, the value of the flexible system, $E(F)$, differs from either of the above values. Since a current decision (to switch or not) would affect the mode (technology) under which the system would operate as it enters future periods, it would affect the future switching costs (i.e., the exercise price of future options) and the set of future (switching) decisions, necessitating the use of a backward *dynamic programming* process. In such cases the project (i.e., flexible system) *value*, E, must be determined *simultaneously* with the *optimal operating mode* (technology), m. (The optimal operating mode next period depends on the current operating mode, the switching costs, and the probability of switching again in future periods.)

Before proceeding, let us review our notation:

$c_t^s(m)$ represents cash flow at time t (and state s) when operating in mode (technology) m.

$E_t^s(m)$ represents the value of the project (flexible system) as of time t given that state s is entered while operating in mode (technology) m (assuming optimal future switching decisions).

$m_t^s(i)$ represents the optimal operating mode (technology) at time t given that state s is entered while operating in mode i (here $i = $ A or B).

$\hat{E}[\cdot]$ is the risk-neutral expectations operator (using the risk-neutral probability, p).

At any time, the operator of the flexible system has two basic choices: continue operating in the current mode (e.g., technology A) for one more period, and receive the current cash payoff, $c_t^s(A)$ plus any expected future benefits (assuming optimal future operation), or switch immediately (to B) by paying the specified switching cost in exchange for receiving B's current cash flow and its expected future benefits. A mode (technology) switch will be optimal only if the value from switching immediately exceeds the value from delaying potential switching. That is,

$$E_t^s(A) = \max\left(c_t^s(A) + \frac{\hat{E}[E_{t+1}^s(A)]}{1+r}, \; c_t^s(B) + \frac{\hat{E}[E_{t+1}^s(B)]}{1+r} - I(A \to B) \right),$$

where

$$\hat{E}[E_{t+1}^s(i)] \equiv pE_{t+1}^+(i) + (1-p)E_{t+1}^-(i),$$

with $i = $ A or B.

The backward iterative process would start from the terminal time T (here $T = 2$), with the above expression simplified to

$$E_T^s(A) = \max(c_T^s(A), \; c_T^s(B) - I(A \to B))$$

$$= c_T^s(A) + \max([c_T^s(B) - c_T^s(A)] - I(AB), \, 0).$$

(The latter expression resembles a call option to pay the switching costs as exercise price in order to acquire the incremental cash flows of B over A.)

Applying this to our earlier example, we obtain the following terminal values for each state s, $E_2^s(A)$, assuming operation is entered in mode (technology) A:

$E_2^{++}(A) = \max(324, \, 191 - 8) = 324;$ $m_2^{++}(A) = $ A (i.e., stay in A),

$E_2^{+-}(A) = \max(108, \, 102 - 8) = 108;$ $m_2^{+-}(A) = $ A (stay in A),

$E_2^{--}(A) = \max(36, \, 54.4 - 8) = 46.4;$ $m_2^{--}(A) = $ B (switch to B).

Similarly, if operation is entered in mode (technology) B,

$E_2^{++}(B) = \max(191, 324 - 2) = 322$; $m_2^{++}(B) = A$ (switch to A),

$E_2^{+-}(B) = \max(102, 108 - 2) = 106$; $m_2^{+-}(B) = A$ (switch to A),

$E_2^{--}(B) = \max(54.4, 36 - 2) = 54.4$; $m_2^{--}(B) = B$ (stay in B).

The above backward process will then result in the following two decision trees, each with a set of project values, $E_t^s(i)$, and optimal operating modes, $m_t^s(i)$, depending on whether operation is entered in mode (technology) A or B ($i = A, B$). If operation is entered in mode (technology) A,

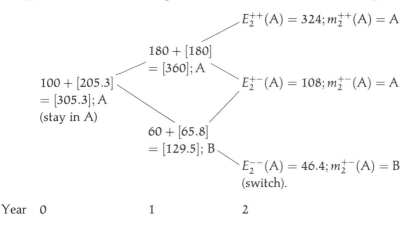

Year   0   1   2

If operation is entered in mode (technology) B,

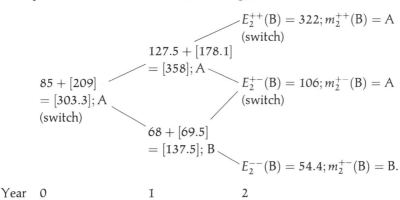

Year   0   1   2

The discounted (risk-neutral) expected value of future payoffs one period earlier is shown in the (top line) brackets at that time. For each operating mode, we would then add to the current cash flow the discounted risk-neutral expectation of the future benefits from operating in that mode (net of any switching costs), and select the mode resulting in the higher project value. That is,

$$E_1^+(A) = \max\left(c_1^+(A) + \frac{pE_2^{++}(A) + (1-p)E_2^{+-}(A)}{1+r}, \right.$$

$$\left. c_1^+(B) + \frac{pE_2^{B++}(B) + (1-p)E_2^{+-}(B)}{1+r} - I(A \to B) \right)$$

$$= \max\left(180 + \frac{0.4 \times 324 + 0.6 \times 108}{1.08}, \right.$$

$$\left. 127.5 + \frac{0.4 \times 322 + 0.6 \times 106}{1.08} - 8 \right)$$

$$= \max(180 + [180], \ 127.5 + [178.1] - 8)$$

$$= \max(360, \ 297.6)$$

$$= 360; \ m_1^+(A)$$

$$= A \text{ (stay in A)}.$$

Similarly,

$$E_1^-(A) = \max\left(c_1^-(A) + \frac{pE_2^{+-}(A) + (1-p)E_2^{--}(A)}{1+r}, \right.$$

$$\left. c_1^-(B) + \frac{pE_2^{-+}(B) + (1-p)E_2^{--}(B)}{1+r} - I(A \to B) \right)$$

$$= \max(60 + [65.8], \ 68 + [69.5] - 8)$$

$$= \max(125.8, \ 129.5)$$

$$= 129.5; m_1^-(A)$$

$$= B \text{ (switch to B)}.$$

If operation is entered in mode (technology) B,

$$E_1^+(B) = \max\left(c_1^+(B) + \frac{pE_2^{++}(B) + (1-p)E_2^{+-}(B)}{1+r}, \right.$$

$$\left. c_1^+(A) + \frac{pE_2^{++}(A) + (1-p)E_2^{+-}(A)}{1+r} - I(B \to A) \right)$$

$$= \max(127.5 + [178.1], \ 180 + [180] - 2)$$

$$= \max(305.6, \ 358)$$

$$= 358; \ m_1^+(B)$$

$$= A \ (\text{switch to A})$$

and

$$E_1^-(B) = \max(68 + [69.5], \ 60 + [65.8] - 2)$$

$$= \max(137.5, \ 123.8)$$

$$= 137.5; m_1^-(B)$$

$$= B \ (\text{stay in B}).$$

Finally, moving similarly one step earlier to the beginning, we find

$$E_0(A) = \max(100 + [205.3], \ 85 + [209] - 8)$$

$$= \max(305.3, \ 286)$$

$$= 305.3; \ m_0(A)$$

$$= A \ (\text{i.e., if enter in A, stay in A})$$

and

$$E_0(B) = \max(85 + [209], \ 100 + [205.3] - 2)$$

$$= \max(294, \ 303.3)$$

$$= 303.3; \ m_0(B)$$

$$= A \ (\text{i.e., if enter in B, switch immediately to A}).$$

(If immediate switching is not possible, then $E_0(B) = 294$.) The current value of the flexible system is, of course, the most beneficial of the above initial operating choices, i.e.,

$$E_0(F) = \max(E_0(A), \ E_0(B)) = \max(305.3, \ 303.3) = 305.3,$$

and the optimal initial operating mode (technology) is A. The optimal operating schedule (or time sequence of optimal $m_i^s(i), i = A$ or B) is

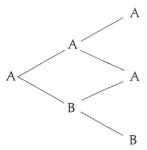

That is, start operating in A; in case of an up state, stay in A; else (if down state), switch to B; if another down state occurs stay in B, else (if up) switch back to A.

We can now confirm that the compoundness effect introduced by switching costs causes the separate switching options to interact, violating their value additivity. For example, the combined switching flexibility afforded by the flexible system beyond rigid machine A (or B) is given by

$$F(A \rightarrow B) = E(F) - PV(A) = 305.3 - 300 = 5.3$$

and

$$F(B \rightarrow A) = E(F) - PV(B) = 305.3 - 255 = 50.3$$

$$(= 294 - 255 = 39, \text{ excluding immediate switching}).$$

That is, to acquire the flexible system with the given switching costs one should be willing to pay \$5.3 beyond the cost of rigid machine A, \$50.3 (or \$39) more than the cost of machine B, and \$4.8 ($= 310.1 - 305.3$) less than the cost of a comparable flexible system with costless switching. The combined flexibility value clearly differs from the sum of separate values determined above:

$$S_0(A \rightarrow B) + S_1(A \rightarrow B) + S_2(A \rightarrow B) = 0 + 0 + 3.2 = 3.2$$

(vs. a combined value of 5.3) and

$$S_0(B \rightarrow A) + S_1(B \rightarrow A) + S_2(B \rightarrow A) = 13 + 18.7 + 19.6 = 51.3$$

(vs. 50.3) (or, $S_1(B \rightarrow A) + S_2(B \rightarrow A) = 18.7 + 19.6 = 38.3$, vs. 39 if immediate switching is excluded). When compound options are involved (as above), there are often positive interactions or complementarities that make the value of the whole greater than the sum of the parts.

A General Framework with Other Real Options as Special Cases

The above approach can be generalized for more than three periods ($t = 0, 1, 2, \ldots, T$) to cover any number of states ($s = 0, 1, 2, \ldots, n$), and for more than just two operating modes ($i = 0, 1, 2, \ldots, M$, rather than just A or B) within a backward iterative process (seen as a discrete, economically adjusted version of the known Bellman equation of dynamic programming). Starting from the end and moving back, the value of a flexible project in state s at any time, $t - 1$, would be obtained from the expected future values in the up ($s + 1$) or down ($s - 1$) states calculated one step earlier (at time t) as follows:

$$E_{t-1}^s(m) = \max_i \left(c_{t-1}^s(i) + \frac{pE_t^{s+1}(i) + (1-p)E_t^{s-1}(i)}{1+r} - I(m \to i) \right),$$

with $I(m \to i) = 0$ for $i = m$ (i.e., there are no costs when staying in the same mode). At $t = T$ when the process starts, the expression becomes

$$E_T^s(m) = \max_i \left(c_T^s(i) - I(m \to i) \right),$$

$c_T^s(i)$ being the terminal cash flow (or salvage value) when entering state s while operating in mode i. The process is applied iteratively, moving back until the beginning ($t = 0$) project value is obtained, along with the optimal operating schedule. Kulatilaka (1988) provides a numerical analysis of this general problem (based on a set of simultaneous stochastic dynamic programs) and considers various known options as special cases.

As we saw, in the absence of switching costs, the solution to the general dynamic problem would be equivalent to a series of simple myopic solutions: in each period, simply choose the operating mode (i) with the highest current cash flow benefit, $c_t^s(i)$; in this case, the value of flexibility can be determined independent of the operating schedule. The presence of asymmetric nonzero switching costs, however, creates a compoundness effect that requires a more complex, forward-looking dynamic analysis, where the value of flexibility must be determined simultaneously with the optimal operating schedule (or switching "exercise" policy). One consequence is that a hysteresis range may arise whereby, even though immediate switching among operating modes may appear attractive based on myopic or short-term considerations (i.e., current cash flows), it may in fact be long-term optimal to wait, owing to dynamic considerations (e.g., a high cost of immediate switching, and/or a high probability and cost of switching back in later stages). By waiting, the firm maintains its option to switch later, if that becomes sufficiently attractive, instead of being "absorbed" into a mode out of which later reswitching, no matter how desirable, would be excessively costly. For example, in the case of irreversible projects, it may be optimal to defer investment (i.e., wait to invest) even though immediately undertaking the project may result in a positive NPV, or it may be optimal to continue operating (i.e., wait to abandon) a currently unprofitable project. Shutting down and reopening operations or switching among alternative inputs or outputs of a production process may be subject to similar "inertia" or "lag" effects.

Let us see now how, with appropriate interpretation of the operating "modes" and switching costs (and other parameters, such as cash flows), most of the real options we have encountered thus far can be valued as special cases of the above generic switching flexibility (being, in essence, a complex compound exchange option). The operating "modes" are now defined more broadly as various decision alternatives, rather than just machines or technologies. For example, one may think of operating a project in the following "modes" (analogous to a car's gears, with switching costs representing the "friction" encountered):

(0) Do not operate (e.g., defer investment or temporarily shut down).

(1) Operate base-scale project (invest or produce).

(2) Expand scale of production.

(3) Contract operations.

(4) Abandon for salvage value, or default during construction.

(5) Switch use (e.g., outputs or inputs).

Given the above definition of operating "modes," let us revisit some of the known real options with appropriate interpretations of switching costs and other parameters.

a. Option to Defer Investment
The firm considers the optimal timing to invest, i.e., when to make the initial investment outlay, I_0. The current operating mode is 0 (i.e., "do not operate" or "wait") and the alternative mode to switch to is 1 ("operate," "invest," or "produce"). The switching cost involved is the initial investment outlay, so $I(0 \rightarrow 1) = I_0$. No reswitching is possible (i.e., investment is irreversible), so $I(1 \rightarrow 0) = \infty$. No cash flows can be generated while in the current waiting mode (0); i.e., $c_t(0) = 0$. After conversion to the production mode (1), a stream of positive cash flows will be generated, $c_t(1) \geq 0$, with a present value of $PV_0(1)$. In the absence of switching

costs, immediate investment will be optimal if $PV_0(1) > I_0$ or $NPV \equiv PV_0(1) - I_0 > 0$. However, the presence of insurmountable reswitching costs ($I(1 \rightarrow 0) = \infty$) may make it long-term optimal for the firm to wait to invest (i.e., remain in an "out-of-the-money" mode), even if immediate investing would generate attractive current benefits in the form of a positive current net present value (i.e., even if $NPV > 0$).

b. Option to Expand

The firm has already made the initial investment enabling it to produce (operate the base-scale project). Given that it is found in the "up" states (e.g., facing a better-than-expected demand for its product in the market), the firm considers whether to make an additional outlay, I_E, that would enable it to increase production (e.g., by adding plant capacity) by $e\%$. That is, the firm is in mode 1 and considers switching to mode 2. The switching cost is the cost of expanding, i.e., $I(1 \rightarrow 2) = I_E$. Switching is irreversible, so $I(2 \rightarrow 1) = \infty$. The cash flows (and the value of the project) in the expanded "mode" would be $e\%$ higher than in the base-scale mode, so $c_t(2) = (1 + e)c_t(1)$.

c. Option to Contract

The firm considers contracting operations by $c\%$ (from the current base-scale production) in order to save on certain variable operating costs (I_C). The switching cost is the operating cost savings, i.e., $I(1 \rightarrow 3) = -I_C$. The cash flows (and value) in the contracted mode (3) are $c\%$ lower than those in the base-scale mode; i.e., $c_t(3) = (1 - c)c_t(1)$.

d. Option to Temporarily Shut Down and Restart Operations

The firm considers switching back and forth between "operating" (mode 1) and "not operating" (mode 0), as in the case of shutting down and re-opening a mine. There are no cash flows generated in the "shut down" mode, so $c_t(0) = 0$. Switching to the "production" mode involves variable operating costs, $I(0 \rightarrow 1) = I_V$, in exchange for positive cash revenues (R), i.e., $c_t(1) = R_t - I_V > 0$. Switching to the "idle" mode may involve specific shutdown costs (I_S), so $I(1 \rightarrow 0) = I_S$. If no switching costs are involved whatsoever (i.e., if $I(0 \rightarrow 1) = I(1 \rightarrow 0) = 0$), the firm will operate whenever profits are positive, and its value will be the sum of simple call options to pay the variable costs and acquire the cash revenues in each year (as in McDonald and Siegel 1985). However, the presence of non-zero switching costs would violate this option-value additivity because of the compoundness effect (discussed earlier in this chapter).

e.   Option to Abandon for Salvage Value
The firm, currently in the production mode but facing bad prospects, considers abandoning in exchange for a specified salvage value, S (i.e., switching to mode 4). Although the firm currently generates positive cash flows $(c_t(1) > 0)$ and would produce no cash flows in case of abandonment (i.e., $c_t(4) = 0$), it is nevertheless facing negative switching "costs" in the amount of the salvage value (i.e., $I(1 \rightarrow 4) = -S$). If abandonment is irreversible, $I(4 \rightarrow 1) = \infty$. This switching-cost asymmetry may induce firms to continue operating currently unprofitable projects.

f.   Option to Default during Construction (Time-to-Build Option)
Once it decides to initiate investment (mode 1), the firm needs to make a series of investment outlays in stages, say I_0 at $t = 0$ and I_1 at $t = 1$, before completing construction at time T (here, $T = 1$). Positive cash revenues will be generated only after project completion (i.e., for $t \geq T + 1$). That is, $c_t(1) = -I_t$ for $t \leq T$ (i.e., $t = 0, 1$); and $c_t(1) \geq 0$ thereafter (i.e., after the project's completion). However, the firm may choose to abandon the project during construction by defaulting on a coming investment outlay, thereby switching to mode 4. In that mode, no cash flows would be produced; i.e., $c_t(4) = 0$ for all t.

In reality, of course, switching among more than just two operating modes may be possible during the life of a project. For example, the opportunity to invest in a mine may collectively involve the following operating modes: wait to invest (mode 0), expand (mode 2) or contract production (mode 3), shut down (mode 0) and reopen (mode 1), or even abandon the mine completely (mode 4). (Brennan and Schwartz (1985a,b) consider the operation of such a mine with the options to open, shut down, and abandon.) As has been noted, the presence of asymmetric switching costs and interactions among various such real options would make their values nonadditive and would render project valuation and optimal operating policy nontrivial.

This generic framework of switching among various operating "modes" finds applications in a variety of situations other than those described in the special cases above. A noted application is the *process flexibility* of switching among alternative technologies for processing inputs as the relative prices of the inputs change over time. Of course, the flexibility to select the cheapest alternative would be acquired or built in at some extra cost, as in the case of a chemical or power plant that can be operated on electricity, coal, gas, or oil as their relative prices fluctuate. Similarly, a firm may maintain relationships with a variety of suppliers, changing the mix as their relative prices change. A multinational firm may locate production facilities in various countries in order to acquire the flexibility to shift production to the lowest-cost producing facilities as the relative labor costs or exchange rates change. Such investments may place the firm at a competitive advantage by becoming a *cost leader* (i.e., the lowest-cost producer in its industry).

By analogy, a multinational firm may develop export markets in various countries for the flexibility to shift its mix of sales among its domestic and the various export markets as their relative profitability (including exchange rate adjustments) changes. More generally, a firm may build in *product flexibility*, enabling it to switch among alternative technologies for producing outputs. The capability to choose the most profitable output would, again, be acquired at some extra cost. This capability would be particularly valuable in an industry, such as automobiles or pharmaceuticals, where product differentiation and diversity are important and/or demand is uncertain. In such cases, it may be worthwhile to install a more costly flexible capacity to acquire the ability to alter the mix of products or the scale of production in response to changing market demands. Additional examples would include chemical plants or oil refineries that can easily vary their output mix (e.g., a refinery may convert crude oil into gasoline, fuel oil, or lubricants) and farms that can easily switch their crops depending on relative prices.

The most natural application of product flexibility is, of course, in the economic justification of flexible manufacturing systems. The basic challenge is how to choose between a more costly but flexible manufacturing system that allows rapid changes in operating mode at very low costs in response to uncertain market developments and a dedicated (specialized) mass-production alternative with economies of scale. Switching costs may arise from retooling and other setup costs, from required changes in inventory, from delays, from training costs, and so on. Intuitively, if the firm operates in a predictable environment, the dedicated system may often prove to be more cost effective. If, however, the firm operates in a highly uncertain environment (e.g., one requiring frequent design changes, varying product styles, or rapid product innovation, as in the automobile industry, or one with uncertain input or output prices due to unpredictable competitive responses), the value of the flexibility to better respond to such market uncertainties may well justify the extra cost.

Of course, the realization of the benefits of a flexible system depends on how well it interacts with and is integrated with the rest of the business (e.g., with the R&D department in capitalizing on new innovations, with the engineering department in utilizing computer-aided design and manufacturing, or with the marketing and distribution department). Thus, the acquisition of a flexible system enhances the firm's overall organizational capabilities (and its strategic ability to respond to changing market and competitive developments). At the same time, the potential value delivered by a flexible system can be strengthened by other existing organizational capabilities, such as the firm's ability to use the system more rapidly, with lower switching costs, or to put it to entirely new uses (i.e., create a wider array of choices) relative to its competitors. For example, an identical flexible manufacturing system (FMS) having the same cost and the same *potential* flexibility value will have a different *realized* value to a certain auto company than to its competitors if that company responds faster to information about customers' needs from the field, comes up with an innovative engineering design, and utilizes computer-aided manufacturing to rapidly produce, and subsequently distribute, an entirely new model with minimal switching costs. The justification of a flexible system must therefore be seen as part of overall corporate strategy.

The Firm as an Adaptive System Converting Inputs into Marketable Outputs

More generally, a firm may be viewed as an adaptive "system" utilizing various organizational capabilities and other resources to *convert* a variety of inputs (e.g., raw material, energy, labor), at some conversion cost, into a profitable mix of output products.

As a simple illustration of the conversion process and the value of active or adaptive management, consider an oil company operating a single plant that converts one factor input (crude oil) into one output product (petroleum).[6] For now, assume no conversion (i.e., switching) costs. Revisiting our earlier example, we may reinterpret the cash flow (per unit of production) in mode A at a given time as the price of the output commodity (petroleum) as of that time (i.e., $c_t(A) = O_t$), and the cash flow in mode B as the price or variable unit cost ($c_t(B) = I_t$) of the input commodity (crude oil). The output and input commodities' price movements are again, respectively, given by

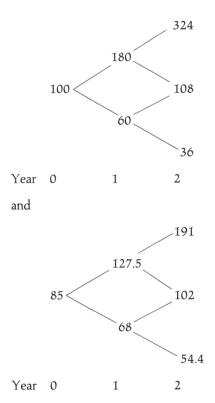

Year   0   1   2

and

Year   0   1   2

Thus, the cash flows from converting the factor input into the output are equivalent to those from switching operation from mode B to mode A in the earlier generic example, with the difference that no reconversion (re-switching) is allowed from mode A (the output) back to B (the input); i.e., $I(A \rightarrow B) = \infty$.

If management were committed to passively and blindly implementing the conversion from inputs into outputs in each period, the *incremental* cash flows from blind conversion (which may also be interpreted as unit profits, equaling revenues minus operating costs), i.e.,

$$c_i^s(B \rightarrow A) = c_i^s(A) - c_i^s(B),$$

would be as follows:

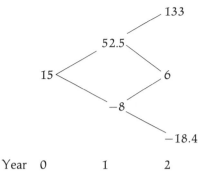

Year   0   1   2

The present value of these incremental cash flows (or profits) resulting from blind conversion is 15 in *each* year (i.e., the difference between the time-0 expected cash revenue, 100, and the expected input cost, 85, in each year), resulting in a total present value for the passive firm of 45:

$$PV(B \rightarrow A) = 15 + \frac{0.4 \times 52.5 + 0.6 \times (-8)}{1.08}$$

$$+ \frac{0.4^2 \times 133 + 2 \times 0.4 \times 0.6 \times 6 + 0.6^2 \times (-18.4)}{1.08^2}$$

$$= 15 + 15 + 15$$

$$= 45.$$

The value from this incremental cash flow approach is, of course, equivalent to the difference in the total present values found earlier, confirming that

$$PV(B \rightarrow A) = PV(A) - PV(B) = 300 - 255 = 45.$$

In reality, however, an active or adaptive management would not implement a conversion that would be unprofitable at any time; instead it would not operate, or it would shut down temporarily. As if it had insurance protection, an active management would truncate the negative incremental cash flows ($c_1^-(B \rightarrow A) = -8$ and $c_2^{--}(B \rightarrow A) = -18.4$) to 0; that is,

$c_t^s(B \rightarrow A) = \max(c_t^s(A) - c_t^s(B), 0):$

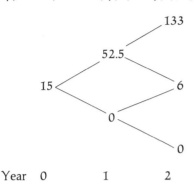

Year   0   1   2

The adjusted present value of the adaptive firm with managerial flexibility to voluntarily convert inputs (B) into outputs (A) when it is profitable to do so is again given by the sum of the three switching (conversion) options in each year:

$$F(B \rightarrow A) = S_0(B \rightarrow A) + S_1(B \rightarrow A) + S_2(B \rightarrow A)$$

$$= 15 + \frac{0.4 \times 52.5 + 0.6 \times 0}{1.08}$$

$$+ \frac{0.4^2 \times 133 + 2 \times 0.4 \times 0.6 \times 6 + 0.6^2 \times 0}{1.08^2}$$

$$= 15 + 19.4 + 20.7$$

$$= 55.1.$$

Thus, the value of the adaptive firm (allowing discretionary conversion of inputs into outputs) exceeds that of a comparable passive firm (whose management is committed to automatic conversion) by the *value of active management*, here given by

$$F(B \rightarrow A) - PV(B \rightarrow A) = 55.1 - 45 = 10.1.$$

If a nonzero conversion cost is involved when transforming inputs into outputs ($I(B \rightarrow A) > 0$) while conversion is still irreversible ($I(A \rightarrow B) = \infty$), then the conversion cost is simply subtracted from each incremental cash flow:

$$c_t^s(B \rightarrow A) = \max(c_t^s(A) - c_t^s(B) - I(B \rightarrow A), 0).$$

For example, if $I(B \rightarrow A) = 2$, the incremental cash flows again become

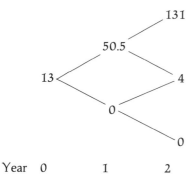

The value of the adaptive firm (or of the revised conversion options) with conversion costs then becomes

$$F(B \rightarrow A) = 13 + 18.7 + 19.6 = 51.3,$$

which is less than the value of costless adaptive (voluntary) conversion (55.1) but is 6.3 higher than the value of costless passive (automatic) conversion (45).

The value of a conversion option (or of the capability to adapt) would generally be higher the higher the individual volatility of the input or the output prices and the lower the correlation between the input and output prices. These factors would increase the spread of the output price relative to the price (or cost) of the input, which would result in higher realized cash revenues under active management. Since management has the flexibility to convert inputs into outputs and will do so only when profitable, it will capitalize on large positive cash revenues when the spread is wide (and positive); it will not convert and cut its losses when the spread turns negative.

Since operation can be entered only in mode B (i.e., from inputs to outputs), and since reswitching (conversion back into inputs) is infeasible, there is no interdependence between current and future conversion decisions. That is, exercising one conversion option in one year does not affect (and is not affected by) options to convert in other years. Therefore, option-value additivity is preserved in this case.

Our firm may, of course, be able to convert crude oil not only into petroleum but also into gasoline, lubricants, and other products. It may have other plants, or it may be able to set up the current plant, at some switching cost, to use gasoline (previously an output) as an input and to produce, say, polyester. In general, a firm may produce a variety of output products, using alternate input combinations for each. In this case, the lowest-cost input combination would be selected (net of necessary conversion costs) for each output, and their (net) incremental cash flow would be determined as above. Then, conditional on using the lowest-cost input combination for each output, the best output (production) mode would be selected. Basically, we would select the (joint input and) output mode set that maximizes not only the current spread between output revenues and input (plus conversion) costs, given the lowest-cost input alternative for that output, but also the value from optimal future switching. That is, the firm will select to produce those outputs, i, that maximize the firm's equity value:

$$E_{t-1}^s(m) = \max_i \left(c_{t-1}^s(i) + \frac{pE_t^{s+1}(i) + (1-p)E_t^{s-1}(i)}{1+r} - I(m \to i) \right),$$

where now

$$c_t^s(i) = \max_i \left(O_t^s(i) - \min_j (I_t^s(j) + C(j \to i)), 0 \right),$$

with $O_t^s(i)$ now denoting the price (or cash revenue) of output product i, $I_t^s(j)$ indicating the price (operating cost) for input j, and $C(j \to i)$ being the cost of converting input j into output i. Again, $I(m \to i)$ is the cost of switching from producing product m to product i, with $I(m \to i) = 0$ for $i = m$ (i.e., there are no switching costs when staying with the same output product). The valuation process would again start from the end ($t = T$). Given the uncertainties in input and output values and the asymmetric costs of switching between production (and input) modes, value additivity would generally be violated.

In reality, of course, effective conversion of low-cost inputs into marketable outputs is not achieved simply through machines. The firm may be endowed with or acquire (at some cost) and nurture a set of *organizational capabilities* (ranging from equipment, technologies, processes, information systems, human skills, strategies, etc.) that would enable it to be more responsive to changing customer needs, market demands, and competitive conditions. This "organizational glue" or infrastructure that enables the firm to be more flexible and more responsive in the market is partly what makes its "package" more valuable than its parts. The more "flexible" it becomes (i.e., the greater its adaptive potential and its ability to turn that potential, through its organizational capabilities, into realized value) in an uncertain business environment, the more successful the firm will be in the long term relative to its competitors. The value of flexibility will be greater the wider the array of low-cost input choices and profitable output choices it can develop, the more rapidly and cost effectively the firm can convert inputs into outputs that meet the needs of the market, the greater the volatility in input and output prices (as well as the lower the correlation between output and their factor input prices), and, generally, the more uncertain and turbulent the business environment.

Any flexible "system" (whether a flexible manufacturing system or an entire adaptive firm) may generally provide many "intangible" (hard-to-quantify) or "strategic" benefits, such as faster response, better adaptation to varying customer needs (resulting in better customer service), higher quality, greater product diversity or differentiation, a stronger cost position with respect to alternative suppliers or factor inputs, and an enhanced ability to respond to technological innovation in either product or factor-input markets, to competitive moves, or to other market developments (e.g., to survive a low market or to capitalize on future growth opportunities). All these capabilities help position the firm at a competitive advantage, which down the road should translate into cash flows and positive-NPV investments.

An options-based expanded or strategic NPV analysis is therefore better suited to capture these aspects of operating flexibility and strategy than a traditional static-NPV analysis. Of course, acquiring and managing organizational capabilities with embedded flexibility would require information, evaluation, control, and reward systems capable of recognizing and rewarding the resulting "intangible" benefits of operating flexibility and strategy.

5.4   Project Interdependence (or Interproject Interactions)

At the strategic level, many projects are not independent, as assumed by traditional DCF procedures; they are better seen as links in a chain of interrelated projects, the earlier of which are prerequisites for the ones to follow. Making an investment outlay to acquire the first project in such a sequence of contingent investments is a prerequisite for opening up the opportunity to acquire the benefits of the next investment in line by paying the next cost installment or "exercise price." In essence, such investment opportunities are *compound* options (i.e., options whose payoff are other options). When one is looking at a sequence of projects, this notion of project interdependence (or *interproject compoundness*) is remarkably similar in structure to the *intraproject* relationships (or compoundness) present in the options to expand or default (described in subsections b and f above) or in the option to switch modes with switching costs; thus, it can be analyzed in essentially the same manner. The principal difference is that each investment-cost "installment" now provides the opportunity to begin a new project rather than to continue with a new stage of the same project.

Project interdependence (or interproject compoundness) may have considerable strategic import, since it may justify acceptance of projects with negative static NPV on the basis of their potential to open up new investment opportunities for the firm in the future. A research-and-development project, a lease for an undeveloped tract with potential oil reserves, and an acquisition of an unrelated company are only a few examples of such compound real options that may be undertaken not only for their directly measurable cash flows (there may be none, as in the case of some speculative research projects) but also (perhaps primarily) for the new opportunities they may open up (a technological breakthrough, large oil reserves, access to a new market). In general, such interproject options are associated with investments intended to place the firm on a growth path or to improve its strategic position in the industry (say, by entering a new geographic market or employing a new technology).

5.5   Flexibility due to Interest-Rate Uncertainty

So far we have focused on managerial flexibility deriving from the uncertainty in project cash flows. Even in the absence of cash-flow-based real options, however, management may still have flexibility to time the initiation (or the abandonment) of a project as a result of uncertainty in the interest rate (or the cost of capital) (Ingersoll and Ross 1992). To illustrate the flexibility due to interest-rate uncertainty, let us, for the moment, assume away any cash-flow uncertainty (and any of the above real options) altogether. Suppose, for example, that at time t ($t = 0$ or 1) we consider investing $I_t = \$104$ in a project that will generate a *certain* cash flow worth $c_{t+1} = \$115$ a year later. Since the future cash flow is riskless, it will be discounted at the risk-free interest rate, r. In the first year the riskless rate is assumed to be 8%, as before (i.e., $r_1 = 0.08$).

If the second-year interest rate will be the same with certainty (i.e., $r_2 = r_1 = 0.08$), then, in the absence of cash-flow uncertainty and real options, it will be optimal to initiate investment immediately, provided the investment has a positive NPV. In the above example, the NPV of initiating investment at time 0 is

$$\text{NPV}^0 = \frac{c_1}{1 + r_1} - I_0 = \frac{115}{1.08} - 104 = 2.5.$$

The NPV as of time 0 of initiating investment in year 1 is

$$\text{NPV}^1 \text{ (flat term structure)} = \frac{c_2/(1 + r_2) - I_1}{1 + r_1} = \frac{115/1.08 - 104}{1.08} = 2.3.$$

Thus, under a flat deterministic interest-rate structure, it is better to invest immediately than to initiate the project next year.

Suppose, however, that the second-year interest rate were to decline with certainty to $r_2 = 0.03$. Then,

$$\text{NPV}^1 \text{ (declining structure)} = \frac{c_2/(1 + r_2) - I_1}{1 + r_1} = \frac{115/1.03 - 104}{1.08} = 7.1.$$

Thus, declining interest rates (opportunity cost of capital) would favor delay in project initiation. By contrast, rising interest rates would favor investing earlier. For example, if management were to be committed to investing in year 1 and the second-year interest rate were to rise for certain to 13%, we would have

$$\text{NPV}^1 \text{ (rising term structure)} = \frac{115/1.13 - 104}{1.08} = -2.1.$$

So far we have examined a non-flat but deterministic interest-rate structure. What happens, though, if there is uncertainty in future interest rates? For example, suppose that the second-year interest rate is again expected to be 8% (i.e., $E(r_2) = r_1 = 0.08$) but in fact has a 50–50 chance of either declining to 3% or rising to 13%. Since management is really not committed to investing in year 1 no matter what, it would actually be beneficial to wait for a year, observe the realization of the future (year 2) interest rate, and then invest only if the interest rate has declined sufficiently. In this way, management would actually avoid the above unfavorable (rising term structure) scenario (receiving a conditional NPV of 0 rather than -2.1 in that case). Therefore,

$$\text{NPV}^1 \text{ (uncertain term structure)} = 0.5 \times 7.1 + 0.5 \times 0 = 3.55.$$

Again, this exceeds the value from immediate investing ($\text{NPV}^0 = 2.5$); thus, the uncertainty in interest rates (like a declining deterministic term structure) will favor delaying the project in hope of a decline in interest rates, even though the project currently has a positive NPV. Thus, with interest-rate uncertainty it may not be optimal to initiate a project until its rate of return substantially exceeds its break-even or zero-NPV rate, r^b

(i.e., until its NPV is sufficiently positive or the investment is "in the money"). We can actually determine an optimal "exercise" policy of the form "invest now if $r \leq r^* < r^b$; wait if $r > r^*$" (where r^* is the optimal acceptance (exercise) rate, selected to maximize project value, which must be determined simultaneously with project valuation).

The value of the flexibility to wait and capitalize on the uncertainty (potential decline) in interest rates in the above example is given by the difference in the two values:

Value of flexibility due to interest-rate uncertainty

$= \text{NPV}^1$ (uncertain term structure) $- \text{NPV}^0$

$= 3.55 - 2.5$

$= 1.05.$

The value of this flexibility to wait, like any option, is higher the greater the uncertainty in future interest rates (implying a lower optimal acceptance rate, r^*) and the longer the project maturity. The value of waiting can alternatively be proxied by the difference between the break-even rate and the optimal acceptance rate, $r^b - r^*$. The latter increases with project duration when interest-rate uncertainty is high. Thus, consistent with option pricing and the payback rule, among projects with the same value of cash flows, one should invest sooner in those projects with shorter duration in an uncertain interest-rate environment.

In reality, of course, situations do not present themselves in such simple scenarios. For example, a parallel upward shift in the level of interest rates (favoring early investment) in the presence of rising interest-rate uncertainty (favoring project delay) would result in an unclear mixed effect. Moreover, if the cash flows of a project are growing and/or the project's life expires at a specified time (e.g., upon expiration of a patent or upon competitive entry), then delaying the project would involve an opportunity cost analogous to a "dividend" effect, reducing the value of the option to wait and favoring earlier initiation. Furthermore, if the cash flows are uncertain and correlated with the interest rate (and the market return), the cost of capital will differ from the risk-free interest rate. A risk-neutral valuation approach will then be necessary, especially if other real options are also present. The risk-neutral probabilities will again be derived from market price and interest-rate information, but now they may vary over time and across states (since they will depend on changing interest rates).

5.6 Concluding Remarks

We have seen that active management of investments in response to changing market conditions confers operating flexibility and strategic value beyond what is traditionally captured by discounted cash flows, and we have seen how to start quantifying this value. Naively applied conventional NPV was seen to be based on a myopic, passive approach to management, as if market developments were unfolding in an event tree without any contingent response on the part of management. Clearly, using single *expected* cash-flow estimates does not capture the dependence of future cash flows on future management decisions, since the cash-payoff structure of a flexible project changes asymmetrically in the presence of real options. Nor can the use of a single risk-adjusted discount rate capture the complex changes in risk that result from management's flexibility to capitalize on success or to cut losses in case of failure. A decision-tree-type analysis capturing the choices conferred by managerial flexibility through decision nodes is therefore an improvement. It is not sufficient, however, simply to condition future cash flows on future optimal decisions and to continue using a constant risk-adjusted discount rate. No ad hoc, exogenously provided, single risk-adjusted discount rate can properly capture the interdependencies between current and future decisions in the presence of managerial flexibility, since risk changes endogenously in time, with the underlying uncertain variable, and with managerial response. Since the value of a flexible project and the optimal operating (exercise) schedule must generally be determined concurrently, the discount rate must, in effect, be imputed *endogenously* within a forward-looking dynamic programming process.

An options-based (expanded-NPV) analysis bypasses the discount-rate problem by relying on the notion of a comparable security to properly price risk while still being able to capture the dynamic interdependencies between cash flows and future optimal decisions. As such, it combines the best features of NPV and of decision-tree analysis and dynamic programming. Its ability to quantify the value of operating flexibility options and strategic benefits has been demonstrated in the cases of the options to defer investment, to expand or contract operating scale, to default during construction, to shut down operations temporarily or abandon for salvage permanently, and to switch between general operating "modes" (e.g., between inputs or outputs), with a variety of potential applications. In fact, a firm may be viewed as a flexible "system" utilizing various organizational capabilities to convert an array of inputs into profitable outputs that meet the needs of the market. Interactions within and among projects, as well as with financial flexibility, have also been pointed out. Finally, even in the absence of any of the above option-like features attached to a project itself, an investment may have timing flexibility (e.g., to wait or to abandon) if interest rates are uncertain, even if there is no uncertainty associated with the project's cash flows.

Suggested Readings

Ingersoll, J., and S. Ross. 1992. "Waiting to invest: investment and uncertainty." *Journal of Business* 65, no. 1: 1–29.

Kensinger, J. 1987. "Adding the value of active management into the capital budgeting equation." *Midland Corporate Finance Journal* 5, no. 1: 31–42.

Kulatilaka, N. 1988. "Valuing the flexibility of flexible manufacturing systems." *IEEE Transactions in Engineering Management* 35, no. 4: 250–257.

Kulatilaka, N., and L. Trigeorgis. 1994. "The general flexibility to switch: Real options revisited." *International Journal of Finance* 6, no. 2: 778–798.

Ritchken, P., and G. Rabinowitz. 1988. "Capital budgeting using contingent claims analysis." *Advances in Futures and Options Research* 3: 119–143.

Trigeorgis, L. 1993. "The nature of option interactions and the valuation of investments with multiple real options." *Journal of Financial and Quantitative Analysis* 28, no. 1: 1–20.

Trigeorgis, L. 1993. "Real options and interactions with financial flexibility." *Financial Management* 22, no. 3: 202–224.

Trigeorgis, L., and S. P. Mason. 1987. "Valuing managerial flexibility." *Midland Corporate Finance Journal* 5, no. 1: 14–21.

6   Quantifying Flexibility: Some Continuous-Time Analytic Models

In recent years a number of authors have used quantitative option-pricing techniques in an attempt to value different types of real options, deriving analytic models whenever possible. McDonald and Siegel (1986) and Paddock, Siegel, and Smith (1988) examined the option to defer (or initiate) investment. Majd and Pindyck (1987) valued the option to delay sequential construction (or the time-to-build option) when there is a maximum rate at which staged contruction can proceed. McDonald and Siegel (1985) examined the option to temporarily shut down operations in a given year. Myers and Majd (1990) viewed the option to permanently abandon a project for its salvage value as analogous to an American put option on a dividend-paying asset. Margrabe (1978) analyzed the simple option to exchange one risky asset for another. Stulz (1982) valued options on the minimum (or maximum) of two risky assets, and Johnson (1987) later extended this analysis to several risky assets. These papers offer the potential of analyzing the option to switch use (e.g., change between alternative inputs or outputs).

Compound options were first analyzed by Geske (1979), who valued a call option on stock (itself seen as an option on the firm's assets). This framework provides insights for the analysis of real compound or growth options. Carr (1988) combined the two elements of compoundness and the option to exchange in his analysis of sequential (compound) exchange options, which involve options to acquire subsequent options to exchange the underlying asset for another risky asset. Kulatilaka (1988) and Kulatilaka and Trigeorgis (1994) analyzed the generic option to switch between broadly defined operating "modes." The latter papers have the potential, in principle, to value investments with a series of investment outlays that can be switched to alternative states of operation, and to eventually help value strategic interdependencies. We will look at this literature in some detail, considering the major existing quantitative results that may be relevant to the valuation of real investment opportunities. The last section of this chapter, devoted to the development of various core relationships and techniques that may be useful in quantifying the values of many complex options and option interactions, includes neat derivations of the results of Black and Scholes (1973), Geske (1979), Margrabe (1978), and Carr (1988).

6.1 The Option to Defer

McDonald and Siegel (1986) study the optimal timing of investing in an irreversible project (i.e., without abandonment flexibility) where the gross project value (and possibly the investment cost) follows a stochastic process of the form

$$\frac{dV}{V} = \alpha \, dt + \sigma \, dz, \tag{6.1}$$

where V is the gross present value of (appropriately discounted) expected cash flows, α is the instantaneous expected return on the project, σ is the instantaneous standard deviation of project value, and dz is an increment of a standard Wiener process. As was discussed in chapter 3 above, in a risk-neutral world α is replaced with $\hat{\alpha} = r - \delta$, where δ is the below-equilibrium return shortfall (i.e., the difference between the equilibrium expected return on a similar traded financial security, α^*, and the actual project drift, α, on the nontraded project).

With a fixed investment cost I necessary to take the project, McDonald and Siegel find a schedule of critical project values, V_t^*, above which (i.e., for $V_t \geq V_t^*$) it would be optimal to make the investment, and otherwise defer. They calculate the investment opportunity value, R, as the expected present value of the project's payoff at the first passage time (t'):

$$R = E(e^{-rt'}(V_{t'} - I)).$$

They then show that, in the special case of a *perpetual* investment opportunity, this gives an explicit analytic solution:

$$R = (V^* - I)(V/V^*)^b, \tag{6.2}$$

where

$$V^* = I\left(\frac{b}{b-1}\right),$$

$$b \equiv (\tfrac{1}{2} - \hat{\alpha}/\sigma^2) + \sqrt{(\hat{\alpha}/\sigma^2 - \tfrac{1}{2})^2 + 2r/\sigma^2},$$

and

$$\hat{\alpha} = r - \delta.$$

In the case where the investment cost is also stochastic, following a process similar to that in equation 6.1,

$$\frac{dI}{I} = \alpha' dt + \sigma' dz', \tag{6.1'}$$

it will then be optimal to invest when the ratio V/I reaches a given boundary, Δ, and the value of the opportunity becomes

$$R = (\Delta - 1)I(V/I\Delta)^{b'}, \tag{6.2'}$$

where

$$\Delta = \frac{b'}{b' - 1},$$

$$b' \equiv [\tfrac{1}{2} - (\hat{\alpha} - \hat{\alpha}')/s^2] + \sqrt{[(\hat{\alpha} - \hat{\alpha}')/s^2 - \tfrac{1}{2}]^2 + 2(r - \hat{\alpha}')/s^2},$$

and

$$\hat{\alpha}' = r - \delta'$$

(with $s^2 = \sigma^2 + \sigma'^2 - 2\rho\sigma\sigma'$, where ρ is the correlation coefficient between V and I).

Based on this type of analysis and simulations of specific examples, McDonald and Siegel conclude that the value of the option to wait can be significant, and that it may be optimal to defer until the gross value of the project is roughly twice the investment costs.

It must be pointed out that explicit closed-form solutions, such as equations 6.2 and 6.2', do not exist in more realistic situations where the project value has an opportunity cost or "dividend payout" (resulting from intermediate project cash flows and a below-equilibrium return shortfall, or competitive erosion) and when the opportunity is finite rather than perpetual.

Paddock, Siegel, and Smith, in their 1988 paper on the valuation of offshore petroleum leases, look at an undeveloped reserve as an option (with current per-unit value $R(V, \tau; I)$) to acquire developed reserves (i.e., reserves with productive capacity) having present value V per unit by paying the random unit development cost, I, as the exercise price. The value of a producing developed reserve (the underlying asset), V, is assumed to follow the diffusion process

$$\frac{dV}{V} = (\alpha - D)\, dt + \sigma\, dz, \tag{6.3}$$

where D is a payout rate (opportunity cost, convenience yield, or "dividend yield"), which Paddock et al. determine from the market equilibrium in petroleum reserves, with other variables as defined above.

The value of the undeveloped reserve seen as a call option on V, $R(V, \tau; I)$, must then satisfy the partial differential equation

$$\tfrac{1}{2}\sigma^2 V^2 R_{VV} + (r - D)VR_V + R_t - rR = 0 \tag{6.4}$$

s.t.

$$R(0, \tau; I) = 0,$$

$$R(V, 0; I) = \max(V - I, 0) \text{ if } V/I < \Delta,$$

and

$$R(V, \tau; I) = V - I \text{ if } V/I \text{ first exceeds the critical boundary } \Delta.$$

Note that for a traded asset like oil (with convenience yield D) the actual drift rate is again replaced in the p.d.e. above with $r - D$ under risk-neutral valuation. After the solution to the option value (the unit undeveloped reserve) is determined via numerical analysis (since no closed-form solution exists for a project of finite life), the expected value of total undeveloped reserves, TR, is then determined as follows:

$$\text{TR} = \int \tilde{Q} R(V, \tau; \tilde{I})\, dF(\tilde{Q}, \tilde{I}), \tag{6.5}$$

where $\tilde{Q}$ represents the (random) quantity of reserves and $F(\tilde{Q}, \tilde{I})$ is the joint probability distribution over $\tilde{Q}$ and $\tilde{I}$, conditional on exploration's taking place.

Finally, the value of the lease giving the opportunity to explore (with probability p) after paying an expected exploration cost E and to subsequently acquire the undeveloped tract, seen as an option on the developed petroleum reserves, is found from

$$L = \max[p(\text{TR} - E), 0].$$

Paddock, Siegel, and Smith note that their option-valuation estimates are much closer to actual industry bids than the government's traditional DCF valuation estimates based on the same data. Their option values are still lower than the actual bids, however, perhaps partly because they have not fully accounted for the compound-option characteristics of the lease.

Majd and Pindyck (1987) examine the option to delay irreversible construction in a project where a series of outlays must be made sequentially but construction cannot proceed faster than a rate k (i.e., it takes time to build) and the project produces no intermediate cash flows until it is complete. They also assume that the market value of a completed project (e.g., a factory or an apartment building), V, evolves according to equation 6.3, i.e.,

$$\frac{dV}{V} = (\alpha - D)\, dt + \sigma\, dz,$$

where D is an opportunity cost (e.g., forgone cash flows from delaying completion of the project).

The investment opportunity ("program") is thus seen as a compound option on V. Interestingly, instead of time, Majd and Pindyck use as the second state variable the total amount of investment costs left for completion, K. With no adjustment costs, they show that the optimal rate of investment is either the maximum rate k or 0 (a "bang-bang" solution), depending on whether V is above or below a cutoff schedule, V^*. Denoting the value of the investment opportunity that is contingent on V as $F(V, K)$ if $V > V^*$ and $f(V, K)$ if $V < V^*$, they show that this value must satisfy the following set of partial differential equations (one for each region):

$$\tfrac{1}{2}\sigma^2 V^2 F_{VV} + (r - D)VF_V - rF - kF_k - k = 0,$$

$$\tfrac{1}{2}\sigma^2 V^2 f_{VV} + (r - D)Vf_V - rf = 0 \tag{6.6}$$

subject to the following boundary conditions[1]:

$$F(V, 0) = V,$$

$$F_V(\infty, K) = e^{-DK/k},$$

$$f(0, K) = 0,$$

$$f(V^*, K) = F(V^*, K),$$

$$f_V(V^*, K) = F_V(V^*, K).$$

Majd and Pindyck finally solve this system using numerical analysis (explicit finite differences) to simultaneously determine both the value of the investment opportunity (program) and the optimal investment rule, $V^*(K)$. They conclude that traditional NPV analysis, which treats the pattern of investment as fixed, may grossly understate the value of such a project.

6.2   Options to Shut Down or Abandon

McDonald and Siegel (1985) also value projects with the option to cost-lessly shut down production temporarily whenever the unit output price, P, would not be sufficient to cover the variable unit production costs, C. Assuming that the output price follows a diffusion process of the form

$$\frac{dP}{P} = \alpha \, dt + \sigma \, dz, \tag{6.7}$$

and viewing operation in each period as an option to acquire P_t by paying C_t as exercise price, they value a current claim, $V_0(t)$, on time-t profits, $\pi_t = \max(P_t - C_t, 0)$, under risk neutrality as

$$V(P, C, t) = e^{-rt} E_0(\pi_t)$$

$$= e^{-rt} E_0(\max(P - C, 0)),$$

where $E_0(\ )$ denotes expectation conditional on time-0 information. They then show that this current claim on time-t profits is equal to

$$V(P_0, C_t, t) = P_0 e^{-Dt} N(d_1) - C_t e^{-rt} N(d_2), \tag{6.8}$$

where

$$d_1 = \frac{\ln(P_0/C_t) + [(r - D) + \frac{1}{2}\sigma^2]t}{\sigma\sqrt{t}},$$

$$d_2 = d_1 - \sigma\sqrt{t},$$

and

$$D = r - \alpha.$$

Thus, the present value of operating a project, R, generating a stream of future profits can be found (in the absence of "switching costs") by summing up the separate values of all such time-t claims over the project's life, T:

$$R = \sum_{t=0}^{T} V(t).$$

McDonald and Siegel subsequently show that the value of the project under risk-aversion would remain essentially the same (as given in equation 6.8), except that D would be replaced, using the CAPM, by $D' = k - \alpha$, where $k = r + \beta[E(r_m) - r]$.

Myers and Majd (1990) calculate the value of the option to permanently abandon a project for its salvage value. They also assume that the gross value of the project, V, follows the diffusion process

$$\frac{dV}{V} = (\alpha - D)\,dt + \sigma\,dz,$$

where D represents the instantaneous cash payout (i.e., $D = CF/V$) from the project (like a "dividend yield"). They then view the option to abandon for the project's salvage value or value in its best alternative use, S, as an American put option on a dividend-paying asset, V ("dividends" being the cash flows), having as an exercise price the salvage value, S. The value of the option to abandon, $A(V, \tau)$, must then satisfy the p.d.e.

$$\tfrac{1}{2}\sigma^2 V^2 A_{VV} + (r - D)VA_V - A_\tau - rA = 0 \qquad (6.9)$$

s.t.

$$A(V, 0) = \max(S - V, 0),$$

$$A(0, \tau) = S,$$

and

$$A(\infty, \tau) = 0.$$

Finally, the possibility of optimal early exercise is examined at each period, giving a schedule of project values, V^*, below which the project should be abandoned, determined simultaneously with the abandonment value.

Because of the free boundary V^* and the payout of cash flows ("dividends") no closed-form solution exists for the American put, so Myers and Majd resort to numerical analysis (an explicit finite-difference approximation to the equation 6.9). Their analysis shows that, other things constant, the value of the abandonment option increases with salvage value (the exercise price), project volatility, and project life (maturity), while it decreases with project value, as predicted by put-option pricing theory.

Myers and Majd subsequently allow for uncertainty in the salvage value, which is assumed to be a market price following a diffusion process similar to that of the project, i.e.,

$$\frac{dS}{S} = (\alpha' - D')\,dt + \sigma'dz', \tag{6.10}$$

where the project and its salvage value are correlated with a correlation coefficient ρ. Through a suitable transformation, using salvage value as a numeraire, they show that the problem with uncertain salvage can be reduced to the one with deterministic salvage above. This transformation involves redefining the state variable as $X = V/S$ (i.e., expressing V in units of S), whose variance now becomes

$$s^2 = \sigma^2 + \sigma'^2 - 2\rho\sigma\sigma';$$

setting the exercise price equal to 1; and substituting the opportunity cost, D', for the risk-free interest rate, r. Myers and Majd finally show that conventional procedures that assign an expected salvage value at the end of a project's life assumed to be fixed do not properly capture this option to abandon early, thus undervaluing such projects.

6.3   The (Simple) Option to Exchange

Margrabe (1978) examines the value of an option to exchange one non-dividend-paying risky asset for another. With no dividends, the prices of assets V and S—which we could interpret as the project value and salvage value in the abandonment problem above had they paid no intermediate cash flows or other "dividend payout"—are assumed to follow diffusion processes of the forms

$$\frac{dV}{V} = \alpha\,dt + \sigma\,dz$$

(equation 6.1) and

$$\frac{dS}{S} = \alpha'dt + \sigma'dz' \tag{6.10'}$$

with correlation coefficient ρ.

Margrabe shows that a position in the option to exchange asset V for S, $F(V, S, \tau)$, can be hedged by a portfolio strategy consisting of selling short F_V units of asset V and buying F_S units of asset S, resulting in a p.d.e. whose solution (a special case of equation 3.18') is

$$F(V, S, \tau) = V N(d_1) - S N(d_2),\tag{6.11}$$

where

$$d_1 = \frac{\ln(V/S) + \frac{1}{2}s^2\tau}{s\sqrt{\tau}},$$

$$d_2 = d_1 - s\sqrt{\tau},$$

and

$$s^2 = \sigma^2 + \sigma'^2 - 2\rho\sigma\sigma'.$$

By thinking of S as a numeraire, this solution can be reduced to the Black-Scholes one. With V expressed in units of S, it can be seen that the value of V becomes $X \equiv V/S$, with variance s^2; that the value of S in terms of itself becomes 1 (the exercise price); and that the interest rate on a riskless loan denominated in units of S becomes 0 (i.e., $r = 0$ with zero dividends, $D' = 0$), since asset S itself will be returned (with its capital appreciation in market equilibrium as full compensation). This transformation readily gives the Black-Scholes value of a call option on $X = V/S$:

$$C(X, \tau) \equiv \frac{F(V, S, \tau)}{S} = X N(d_1) - 1 e^{-0\tau}N(d_2).$$

Margrabe also shows that, in the absence of any dividends, the American option to exchange two risky assets is worth more alive than exercised; thus, since it would not be optimal to exercise early, the American exchange option without dividends should have the same value as its European counterpart. Moreover, since the option to exchange can be seen either as a call or as a put, this results in a put-call parity relationship for such American options.

Margrabe finally describes a few potential applications, including an offer to exchange shares of one unlevered firm for shares in another. (This may increase the price of shares in the offeree firm, since its shareholders are suddenly given a valuable free option to exchange.) Again, a primary problem preventing the direct application of Margrabe's formula to real-option situations is the assumption that the underlying assets pay no cash flows or other dividend-like payouts. With "dividends," no such analytic formulas exist for the American exchange option.

Stulz (1982) examines similar European options on the minimum or maximum of two risky assets, which may have potential implications for some real investment (growth) opportunities involving mutually exclusive uses or risky streams of cash flows. Like Margrabe, Stulz assumes that the underlying assets, V and S, pay no dividends and follow the same diffusion processes as in equations 6.1 and 6.10'. Stulz then shows that a self-financing portfolio replicating the value of a European call option on $\min(V, S)$, with exercise price I, denoted by $M(V, S, \tau; I)$, must satisfy the p.d.e. (equation 3.25, with $d = 0$)

$$(\tfrac{1}{2}\sigma^2 V^2 M_{VV} + \rho\sigma\sigma' VS M_{VS} + \tfrac{1}{2}\sigma'^2 S^2 M_{SS})$$

$$+ (rVM_V + rSM_S) - M_\tau - rM = 0 \tag{6.12}$$

s.t.

$$M(V, S, 0) = \max(\min(V, S) - I, 0),$$

$$M(0, S, \tau) = 0,$$

and

$$M(V, 0, \tau) = 0.$$

The solution to this p.d.e. is of the form

$$M(V, S, \tau; I) = V\, B(a_1, b_1, \rho') + S\, B(a_2, b_2, \rho'') - Ie^{-rt}B(\gamma_1, \gamma_2, \rho), \tag{6.13}$$

where $B(a, b, c)$ is the bivariate cumulative standard normal distribution with upper limits of integration a and b and correlation coefficient c, with

$$\gamma_1 = \frac{\ln(V/I) + (r - \tfrac{1}{2}\sigma^2)\tau}{\sigma\sqrt{\tau}},$$

$$\gamma_2 = \frac{\ln(S/I) + (r - \tfrac{1}{2}\sigma'^2)\tau}{\sigma'\sqrt{\tau}},$$

$$s^2 = \sigma^2 + \sigma'^2 - 2\rho\sigma\sigma',$$

$$a_1 = d_1 + \sigma\sqrt{\tau},$$

$$a_2 = d_2 + \sigma'\sqrt{\tau},$$

$$b_1 = \frac{\ln(S/V) - \tfrac{1}{2}s^2\sqrt{\tau}}{s\sqrt{\tau}},$$

$$b_2 = \frac{\ln(V/S) - \tfrac{1}{2}s^2\sqrt{\tau}}{s\sqrt{\tau}},$$

$$\rho' = \frac{\rho\sigma' - \sigma}{s},$$

and

$$\rho'' = \frac{\rho\sigma - \sigma'}{s}.$$

If the exercise price of the option on the minimum of two risky assets is zero ($I = 0$), the value of this option becomes V minus the option to exchange given in equation 6.11, i.e.,

$$M(V, S, \tau; 0) = V - F(V, S, \tau)$$

$$= V[1 - N(d_1)] + S\,N(d_2). \tag{6.14}$$

Stulz then shows that the price of a European option on the *maximum* of two risky assets (without dividends), whose value at maturity is given by $\max(\max(V, S) - I, 0)$, can be obtained from

$$MX(V, S, \tau; I) = C(V, \tau; I) + C(S, \tau; I) - M(V, S, \tau; I) \tag{6.15}$$

where $M(V, S, \tau; I)$ is given by equation 6.14, and $C(A, \tau; I)$ represents the value of a European call option on asset A with exercise price I.

Equation 6.15 for the European call option on the maximum of two risky assets, or Johnson's (1987) extension to several risky assets, may be useful for valuing real investment opportunities where payment of a future outlay offers the right to choose between two (or more) mutually exclusive risky assets or uses, such as a piece of property that can be used either as a residential building or as an office building, or a factory that can take diverse inputs or can produce a variety of outputs (provided there are no "dividends"). As expected, such an option will be more valuable the lower the correlation between the values of the alternative uses or assets. Moreover, the land or factory will be more valuable with more possible uses rather than fewer. Once more, a main obstacle to application is the existence of cash flows (or other dividend-like payments) and the American option feature in most real opportunities of interest.

6.4   (Simple) Compound Options

Geske (1979) derives a formula for valuing a call option on stock, seen itself as a European call option on the value of the firm's assets. The valuation of such options on options has potential implications for the valuation of compound real (growth) opportunities where earlier investment opportunities are prerequisites for others to follow.

Let C be a European call option providing the right at its maturity T' to acquire, with exercise price E, another (European call) option, S, on an asset V with maturity T and exercise price I. Thus, C is a claim whose value is directly contingent on S and indirectly contingent on V and t, i.e.,

$$C = f(S, \tau) = f(g(V, \tau), \tau).$$

Assuming that the value of the underlying asset (a stock, or potentially a real project), with no cash dividends, follows the diffusion process (equation 6.1)

$$\frac{dV}{V} = \alpha \, dt + \sigma \, dz,$$

Geske shows that a riskless hedge portfolio can be created duplicating the value of the compound option, which must satisfy the p.d.e.

$$\tfrac{1}{2}\sigma^2 V^2 C_{VV} + rVC_V - C_\tau - rC = 0 \tag{6.16}$$

s.t.

$$C_{T'} = \max(S_{T'} - E, 0).$$

This is similar to the Black-Scholes p.d.e., except that the variable entering the boundary condition now is S (instead of V), itself an option on V whose value is given by the Black-Scholes solution. Geske then provides the following closed-form solution for the value of the European compound option in the absence of dividend payouts:

$$C = V \, B(h + \sigma\sqrt{\tau'}, \, k + \sigma\sqrt{\tau}, \rho) - Ie^{-r\tau}B(h, k, \rho) - Ee^{-r\tau'}N(h), \tag{6.17}$$

where

$$h = \frac{\ln(V/V^*) + (r - \tfrac{1}{2}\sigma^2)\tau'}{\sigma\sqrt{\tau'}},$$

$$k = \frac{\ln(V/I) + (r - \tfrac{1}{2}\sigma^2)\tau}{\sigma\sqrt{\tau}},$$

$$\tau = T - t,$$

$$\tau' = T' - t,$$

$N(\ )$ is a (univariate) cumulative standard normal distribution function, $B(a, b, \rho)$ is a bivariate cumulative normal distribution function with upper integral limits a and b and correlation coefficient ρ (where $\rho = \sqrt{\tau'/\tau}$, and V^* is the schedule of asset value V above which the compound option should be exercised (obtained by solving $S(V^*) - E = 0$).

The Black-Scholes formula is actually a special case of equation 6.17, as can be seen by setting $I = 0$ or $T = \infty$. Furthermore, one of the implications of (compound) option valuation is that even if the expected rate of return (discount rate) or the variance of returns of the underlying asset (the value of the firm's assets or the project's gross value, V) are constant, those for the option will generally be nonstationary and will depend in a complex manner on a variety of factors. In such compound option situations, discounting expected future values at a constant discount rate may be grossly inappropriate.

6.5   Compound Exchange (or Switch) Options and Interdependencies

Carr (1988, 1995) combines both elements of compoundness and the option to exchange to analyze European compound (or sequential) exchange options. A compound exchange call option is a call option, $C(S(V, I, \tau)$, $E, \tau')$, giving the right upon paying an exercise price E within time to maturity τ', to acquire a subsequent simple (call) option, $S(V, I, \tau)$, to exchange (give up) an underlying ("delivery") risky asset, I, to receive another ("optioned") risky asset, V, within time τ. Carr assumes that both the compound and the simple options have a common delivery asset, I (by assuming that, although stochastic, E is a fixed proportion ($q\%$) of the delivery asset, i.e., $E = qI$), that the underlying risky assets V and I have no dividend-like payouts, and that they follow standard diffusion processes as in equations 6.1 and 6.1', i.e.,

$$\frac{dV}{V} = \alpha\, dt + \sigma\, dz$$

and

$$\frac{dI}{I} = \alpha' dt + \sigma' dz'.$$

Using Euler's formula (linear homogeneity), implying $C(S, qI, \tau') = VC_V + IC_I$, a costless, riskless portfolio, H, can be created consisting of long one compound exchange option, C, short C_V units of the optioned asset V and short C_I units of the delivery asset I:

$$H = C - C_V V - C_I I.$$

In a risk-neutral (no-arbitrage) equilibrium, C must then satisfy the fundamental p.d.e.

$$(\tfrac{1}{2}\sigma^2 V^2 C_{VV} + \rho\sigma\sigma' VI C_{VI} + \tfrac{1}{2}\sigma'^2 I^2 C_{II}) - C_{\tau'} = 0, \tag{6.18}$$

s.t.

$$C(S, qI, 0) = \max(S - qI,\ 0).$$

But the value of the simple exchange option, S, must also satisfy the same fundamental p.d.e.,

$$(\tfrac{1}{2}\sigma^2 V^2 S_{VV} + \rho\sigma\sigma' VI S_{VI} + \tfrac{1}{2}\sigma'^2 I^2 S_{II}) - S_{\tau} = 0, \tag{6.18'}$$

s.t.

$$S(V, I, 0) = \max(V - I,\ 0).$$

The solution to the latter p.d.e. was already derived by Margrabe (1978):

$$S(V, I, \tau) = V\,N(d_1) - I\,N(d_2), \tag{6.11'}$$

where

$$d_1 = \frac{\ln(X) + \tfrac{1}{2}s^2\tau}{s\sqrt{\tau}},$$

$$d_2 = d_1 - s\sqrt{\tau},$$

$$X \equiv V/I,$$

and

$$s^2 = \sigma^2 + \sigma'^2 - 2\rho\sigma\sigma'.$$

Again using the delivery asset I as a numeraire (along with $E = qI$), we can reduce the dimensionality of the problem to involve a single stochastic variable, $X \equiv V/I$, that enables us to solve equations 6.18 and 6.18' to obtain the value of the compound exchange option:

$$C(S(V, I, \tau), qI, \tau') = [V\,B(d_1^*, d_1, \rho) - I\,B(d_2^*, d_2, \rho)] - (qI)N(d_2^*), \tag{6.19}$$

where

$$d_1 = \frac{\ln(X) + \tfrac{1}{2}s^2\tau}{s\sqrt{\tau}},$$

$$d_2 = d_1 - s\sqrt{\tau},$$

$$d_1^* = \frac{\ln(X/X^*) + \tfrac{1}{2}s^2\tau'}{s\sqrt{\tau'},}$$

$$d_2^* = d_1^* - s\sqrt{\tau'},$$

$$X \equiv V/I,$$

and

$$s^2 = \sigma^2 + \sigma'^2 - 2\rho\sigma\sigma',$$

$N(\ )$ is the (univariate) cumulative standard normal distribution function, $B(a, b, \rho)$ is the bivariate cumulative normal distribution function with upper integral limits a and b and correlation coefficient ρ (where $\rho = \sqrt{\tau'/\tau}$), and X^* is the critical value of $X \equiv V/I$, above which the compound exchange option should be exercised. (X^* can be obtained by solving the indifference condition $S(X^*) = qI$, or, after dividing equation 6.11' by I, from $X^*N(d_1(X^*)) - N(d_2(X^*)) = q$.)

If the compound exchange option can be exercised freely (i.e., $q = 0$ or $E = qI = 0$), the above solution reduces to Margrabe's earlier solution for the exchange option; if the delivery assets (I, E) are deterministic ($\sigma' = 0$), Geske's (simple) compound-option solution results. If both of the above hold, then the standard Black-Scholes formula obtains.

A major impediment to the application of any of the above closed-form solutions to real investment opportunities, however, is that they are generally American options involving dividend-like payments (e.g., in the form of cash flows, a below-equilibrium return shortfall, or competitive erosion), violating one of the basic assumptions made by these models.

The work of Kulatilaka (1988) and Kulatilaka and Trigeorgis (1994) on the generic option to switch among various operating modes was discussed in chapter 5. It should again be noted that compoundness in the above options introduces a form of interaction. Trigeorgis (1991b, 1993a) uses binomial numerical analysis to analyze various forms of interaction among multiple real options. Brennan and Schwartz (1985a,b) also deal with interacting options in their analysis of the options to close and re-open a mine. Brennan and Schwartz look at ownership of the mine as an option to acquire its output by paying the variable cost of production as an exercise price, and they note that the value of the option to shut down and subsequently reopen the mine may constitute a substantial proportion of its total value. Such complex, potentially interacting option situations require a more involved analysis (with multivariate cumulative distribution functions if the underlying variables follow standard diffusion processes).

6.6* Developing Building Blocks for Valuing Various Complex Options Using Risk-Neutral Valuation

This section uses risk-neutral valuation (the so-called *martingale* approach) to develop various basic relationships that can serve as useful building blocks in quantifying the value of complex option situations. It provides neat derivations of earlier results in the literature, including the analytic solutions of Black and Scholes (1973), Geske (1979), Margrabe (1978), and Carr (1988). The relationships developed may also be useful in deriving analytic expressions for option interactions.

Suppose that asset value at time t, V_t, follows a standard diffusion process generated by the stochastic differential equation

$$\frac{dV_t}{V_t} = \alpha\, dt + \sigma\, dz, \tag{6.20}$$

where α is the instantaneous (proportionate) expected return on the asset (e.g., a project), σ is the instantaneous standard deviation of asset returns (project value), and dz is the differential of a standard Wiener process (with mean 0 and variance dt). As was noted in chapter 3, in a risk-neutral world the asset would follow an "equivalent" risk-neutral stochastic process,

$$\frac{dV_t}{V_t} = \hat{\alpha}\, dt + \sigma\, dz, \tag{6.20'}$$

where $\hat{\alpha} = \alpha - \lambda\sigma$ (or $r - D$), where λ is the asset's market price of risk, σ is its volatility, and D is a dividend-like payout (such as a rate of return shortfall, a proportional cash flow yield on an operating project, or the net convenience yield in the case of commodities). In such a world, "equivalent" risk-neutral expectations ($\hat{E}$) of future payoffs can be discounted at the risk-free interest rate, r. As illustrated below, this approach can prove to be a very powerful tool for deriving analytic solutions to various complex option problems.

If the asset has an "equivalent" risk-neutral probability density function $f(V_t|V_0)$, then the risk-neutral probability of a call option with exercise price K expiring in the money is

$$P_L \equiv \text{Prob}(V_t \geq K) = \int_K^\infty f(V_t|V_0)dV_t = N(d_2), \tag{6.21}$$

where $N(\ )$ is the (univariate) cumulative standard normal distribution function, with

$$d_1 = \frac{\ln(V/K) + (r + \frac{1}{2}\sigma^2)\tau}{\sigma\sqrt{\tau}},$$

$$d_2 = d_1 - \sigma\sqrt{\tau}.$$

Similarly, the (risk-neutral) probability of a put option with exercise price K expiring in the money is given by

$$P_F \equiv \text{Prob}(V_t \leq K) = \int_0^K f(V_t|V_0)dV_t = N(d_2) = N(-d_2). \qquad (6.21')$$

The (risk-neutral) expectation of asset value, given that the asset ends in the money (see Jarrow and Rudd 1983, pp. 93–94) is then given by

$$\hat{E}_0[V_t|V_t \geq K]\text{Prob}(V_t \geq K) \equiv \int_K^\infty V_t f(V_t|V_0)\,dV_t = V_0 e^{rt}N(d_1). \qquad (6.22)$$

Similarly, using equations 6.22 and 6.21', the expected asset value given that $V_t \leq K$ is

$$\hat{E}_0[V_t|V_t \leq K]\text{Prob}(V_t \leq K) \equiv \int_0^K V_t f(V_t|V_0)\,dV_t$$

$$= \hat{E}_0[V_t] - \int_K^\infty V_t f(V_t|V_0)\,dV_t$$

$$= V_0 e^{rt} - V_0 e^{rt}N(d_1)$$

$$= V_0 e^{rt}N(-d_1). \qquad (6.22')$$

From equations 6.22 and 6.21, the Black-Scholes value of a simple European call option is

$$C_0(V_0, K; t) = e^{-rt}\int_K^\infty (V_t - K)f(V_t|V_0)\,dV_t$$

$$= V_0 N(d_1) - Ke^{-rt}N(d_2). \qquad (6.23)$$

From equations 6.21' and 6.22 (or from put-call parity), the Black-Scholes value of a European put is

$$P_0(V_0, K; t) = e^{-rt}\int_0^K (K - V_t)f(V_t|V_0)\,dV_t$$

$$= Ke^{-rt}N(-d_2) - V_0 N(-d_1). \qquad (6.23')$$

The following relationships are also useful in quantifying the interdependence between a pair of options (e.g., a first put and a later call):

$$\int_E^\infty N(d_2) f(V_1|V_0) \, dV_1 = \int_E^\infty \int_K^\infty f(V_2|V_1) f(V_1) \, dV_2 dV_1$$

$$= B(d_2^*, d_2; \rho), \qquad (6.24)$$

where $B(d_1^*, d_1; \rho)$ is the bivariate cumulative standard normal distribution function evaluated at d_1^* and d_1 (as upper integral limits) with correlation coefficient $\rho = \sqrt{\tau_1/\tau_2}$, where

$$d_1 = \frac{\ln(V/K) + (r + \frac{1}{2}\sigma^2)\tau_2}{\sigma\sqrt{\tau_2}},$$

$$d_2 = d_1 - \sigma\sqrt{\tau_2},$$

$$d_1^* = \frac{\ln(V/V^*) + (r + \frac{1}{2}\sigma^2)\tau_1}{\sigma\sqrt{\tau_1}},$$

and

$$d_2^* = d_1^* - \sigma\sqrt{\tau_1},$$

and where V^* is the critical value of V (exercise boundary) at which one is indifferent between exercising and not exercising the first option.

The joint cumulative probability of exercising two sequential options (e.g., a first put and a later call), where both the put and the call will expire in the money, is thus given by

$$\int_0^E N(d_2) f(V_1|V_0) \, dV_1 = \int_0^E \int_K^\infty f(V_2|V_1) f(V_1) \, dV_2 dV_1 \equiv P_{F,L}. \quad (6.24')$$

Note that

$$N(d_2) - B(d_2^*, d_2; \rho) = B(-d_2^*, d_2; -\rho)$$

and, in general,

$$N(d) - B(d^*, d; \rho) = B(-d^*, d; -\rho). \qquad (6.24'')$$

The following relationships are also useful in deriving the value of a compound call option, or a put on a subsequent call, and for quantifying potential interactions among pairs of options:

$$\int_E^\infty V_t N(d_1) f(V_t|V_0) \, dV_t = V_0 e^{rt} B(d_1^*, d_1; \rho), \qquad (6.25)$$

$$\hat{E}_0[V_t|V_1 \leq E]P_{F,L} \equiv \int_0^E V_t N(d_1) f(V_t|V_0)\, dV_t$$

$$= V_0 e^{rt} B(-d_1^*, d_1; -\rho). \tag{6.25'}$$

Using equations 6.22, 6.25, and 6.24, we get

$$e^{-rt_1}\hat{E}_0[C_1(V_1, K; t_2 - t_1)|V_1 \geq E]P_{F,L}$$

$$\equiv e^{-rt_1} \int_E^\infty C_1(V_1, K; t_2 - t_1) f(V_1|V_0)\, dV_1$$

$$= e^{-rt_1} \int_E^\infty [V_1 N(d_1) - Ke^{-r(t_2 - t_1)} N(d_2)] f(V_1|V_0)\, dV_1$$

$$= V_0 B(d_1^*, d_1; \rho) - Ke^{-rt_2} B(d_2^*, d_2; \rho), \tag{6.26}$$

where $P_{\bar{F},L}$ is the probability that the latter (call) option is exercised while the first (put) is not. Similarly, using equations 6.23, 6.26, and 6.24'', we get

$$e^{-rt_1}\hat{E}_0[C_1(V_1, K; t_2 - t_1)|V_1 \leq E]P_{F,L}$$

$$\equiv e^{-rt_1} \int_0^E C_1(V_1, K; t_2 - t_1) f(V_1|V_0)\, dV_1$$

$$= C_0(V_0, K; t_2) - e^{-rt_1} \int_E^\infty C_1(V_1, K; t_2 - t_1) f(V_1|V_0)\, dV_1$$

$$= V_0 B(-d_1^*, d_1; \rho) - Ke^{-rt_2} B(-d_2^*, d_2; -\rho). \tag{6.26'}$$

From equations 6.26 and 6.21, the value of a compound call option (see Geske 1979) is

$$CC \equiv C_0(C_1(V, K; t_2 - t_1), E; t_1)$$

$$\equiv e^{-rt_1} \int_E^\infty [C_1(V_1, K; t_2 - t_1) - E] f(V_1|V_0)\, dV_1$$

$$= [V_0 B(d_1^*, d_1; \rho) - Ke^{-rt_2} B(d_2^*, d_1; \rho)] - Ee^{-rt_1} N(d_2^*). \tag{6.27}$$

Similarly, the value of a (compound) put on a call, using equations 6.21' and 6.26', is

$$PC \equiv P_0(C_1(V, K; t_2 - t_1), E; t_1)$$

$$\equiv e^{-rt_1} \int_0^E [E - C_1(V_1, K; t_2 - t_1)] f(V_1|V_0)\, dV_1$$

$$= Ee^{-rt_1} N(-d_2^*) - [V_0 B(-d_1^*, d_1; -\rho) - Ke^{-rt_2} B(-d_2^*, d_2; -\rho)]. \tag{6.27'}$$

This can be alternatively obtained from the put-call parity on the call, $C(V, K; t_2 - t_1)$, by substituting the solutions from equations 6.23, 6.27, and 6.24'':

$$P_0(C_1(V, K; t_2 - t_1), E; t_1)$$

$$= -C_0(V, K; t_2) + C_0(C_1(V, K; t_2 - t_1), E; t_1) + Ee^{-rt_1}. \qquad (6.27'')$$

In the case of options to exchange between two risky assets (V and S) that both follow standard diffusion processes like equation 6.20, we can express the first asset using the second risky asset (or uncertain exercise price), S, as numeraire:

$$R \equiv V/S, \text{ with } \sigma^2 = \sigma_V^2 + \sigma_S^2 - 2\sigma_V \sigma_S \rho_{VS};$$

then the exercise price of the second asset in terms of itself is unity (i.e., $EX = 1$), and the interest rate on a riskless loan denominated in units of the second asset is zero (see Margrabe 1978). With these kinds of adjustments, the above relationships still hold in their basic form.

Let $X_t(V, S; \tau)$ denote the time-t value of a European option to deliver asset S in exchange for receiving asset V, with time to maturity τ (and no dividends). From the homogeneity assumption,

$$\frac{X_0(V_0, S_0; t)}{S_0} = X_0(V_0/S_0, 1; t)$$

is a call option on $R \equiv V/S$ with $EX = 1$ and $r = 0$. Using equation 6.23 with appropriate adjustments, the value of a call option on V with uncertain exercise price, S, is Margrabe's (1978) solution, given by

$$C_0(V_0, S_0; t) = S_0 C_0(V_0/S_0, 1; t)$$

$$= S_0[(V_0/S_0)N(d_1) - 1\,N(d_2)]$$

$$= V_0 N(d_1) - S_0 N(d_2), \qquad (6.28)$$

with

$$d_1 \equiv d_1(1, 0; \tau_2) = \frac{\ln(V/S) + \frac{1}{2}\sigma^2\tau_2}{\sigma\sqrt{\tau_2}},$$

and

$$d_2 = d_1 - \sigma\sqrt{\tau_2},$$

where (more generally)

$$d_1(\mathrm{EX}, r; \tau) \equiv \frac{\ln(V/\mathrm{EX}) + (r + \frac{1}{2}\sigma^2)\tau}{\sigma\sqrt{\tau}}$$

and

$$d_2(\mathrm{EX}, r; \tau) = d_1(\mathrm{EX}, r; \tau) - \sigma\sqrt{\tau}.$$

From put-call parity,

$$P_0(V_0, S_0; t) = (S_0 - V_0) + C_0(V_0, S_0; t),$$

the value of a put option on V with uncertain exercise price (e.g., salvage value) S is given by

$$P_0(V_0, S_0; t) \equiv X_0(S_0, V_0; t) = S_0 N(-d_2) - V_0 N(-d_1). \tag{6.28'}$$

To derive the value of a compound (sequential) exchange call option (i.e., a compound call on another call with uncertain exercise price), or of a call on a put with uncertain exercise price, we will need the following relationships (based on a transformation using S as numeraire, and utilizing equations 6.28, 6.25, and 6.24):

$$e^{-rt_1}\hat{E}[C_1(V, S; t_2 - t_1)|V_1 \geq E]P_{F,L}$$

$$\equiv e^{-rt_1} \int_E^\infty C_1(V, S; t_2 - t_1) f(V_1|V_0) \, dV_1$$

$$= e^{-rt_1} \int_E^\infty [V_1 N(d_1) - S_1 N(d_2)] f(V_1|V_0) \, dV_1$$

$$= V_0 B(d_1^*, d_1; \rho) - S_0 B(d_2^*, d_2; \rho). \tag{6.29}$$

Based on put-call parity, and a transformation with S as numeraire using equations 6.21, 6.22, 6.29, and 6.24'',

$$e^{-rt_1}\hat{E}_0[P_1(V, S; t_2 - t_1)|V_1 \geq E]P_{F,L}$$

$$\equiv e^{-rt_1} \int_E^\infty P_1(V, S; t_2 - t_1) f(V_1|V_0) \, dV_1$$

$$= e^{-rt_1} \int_E^\infty [(S_1 - V_1) + C_1(V_1, S_1; t_2 - t_1)] f(V_1|V_0) \, dV_1$$

$$= S_0[N(d_2) - (V_0/S_0)N(d_1)] + [V_0 B(d_1^*, d_1; \rho) - S_0 B(d_2^*, d_2; \rho)]$$

$$= S_0 B(-d_2^*, d_2; -\rho) - V_0 B(-d_1^*, d_1; -\rho). \tag{6.29'}$$

Then, from the solutions to equations 6.28' and 6.29',

$$e^{-rt_1} \int_0^E P_1(V_1, S_1; t_2 - t_1) f(V_1|V_0) \, dV_1$$

$$= P_0(V_0, S_0; t_2 - t_1) - e^{-rt_1} \int_E^\infty P_1(V_1, S_1; t_2 - t_1) f(V_1|V_0) \, dV_1.$$

$$(6.29'')$$

The value of a compound (sequential) exchange call option then becomes, using equations 6.29 and 6.21,

$$CC \equiv C_0(C_1(V, S; t_2 - t_1), E; t_1)$$

$$\equiv e^{-rt_1} \int_E^\infty [C_1(V_1, S_1; t_2 - t_1) - E] f(V_1|V_0) \, dV_1$$

$$= [V_0 B(d_1^*, d_1; \rho) - S_0 B(d_2^*, d_2; \rho)] - E e^{-rt_1} N(d_2^*), \qquad (6.30)$$

where

$$d_1 \equiv d_1(1, 0; \tau_2) = \frac{\ln R + \frac{1}{2}\sigma^2 \tau_2}{\sigma\sqrt{\tau_2}},$$

$$d_2 = d_1 - \sigma\sqrt{\tau_2},$$

$$d_1^* \equiv d_1(R^*, 0; \tau_1) = \frac{\ln(R/R^*) + \frac{1}{2}\sigma^2 \tau_1}{\sigma\sqrt{\tau_1}},$$

and

$$d_2^* = d_1^* - \sigma\sqrt{\tau_1},$$

and where R^*, the critical value of $R \equiv V/S$ at which one is indifferent as to whether the first (call) option is exercised or not, is obtained from the solution to $C_1(R^*, 1; t_2 - t_1) = E/S$, with the call as in equation 6.28.

Similarly, using equations 6.29' and 6.21, a (compound) call on a put (exchange) option is given by

$$CP \equiv C_0(P_1(V, S; t_2 - t_1), E; t_1)$$

$$\equiv e^{-rt_1} \int_E^\infty [P_1(V_1, S_1; t_2 - t_1) - E] f(V_1|V_0) \, dV_1$$

$$= [S_0 B(-d_2^*, d_2; -\rho) - V_0 B(-d_1^*, d_1; -\rho)] - E e^{-rt_1} N(d_2^*). \qquad (6.30')$$

From the put-call parity on the call $C(V, S; t_2 - t_1)$, a (compound) put on the call (exchange) option is given, using equations 6.28, 6.30, and

6.24″, by

$$PC \equiv P_0(C_1(V, S; t_2 - t_1), E; t_1)$$

$$= -C_0(C_1(V, S; t_2)) + C_0(C_1(V, S; t_2 - t_1), E; t_1) + Ee^{-rt_1}$$

$$= Ee^{-rt_1}N(-d_2^*) - [V_0B(-d_1^*, d_1; -\rho) - S_0B(-d_2^*, d_2; -\rho)]. \qquad (6.30'')$$

If in equation 6.30 the exercise price of the first option, E, is itself uncertain but a proportion of S, i.e., $E = qS$, then Carr's (1988) solution for a sequential exchange call option is obtained:

$$CC \equiv C_0(C_1(V, S; t_2 - t_1), qS; t_1)$$

$$\equiv e^{-rt_1} \int_E^\infty [C_1(V_1, S_1; t_2 - t_1) - qS_1]f(V_1|V_0)\,dV_1$$

$$= [V_0B(d_1^*, d_1; \rho) - S_0B(d_2^*, d_2; \rho)] - qS_0N(d_2^*). \qquad (6.31)$$

The other types of compound options in equations 6.30′ and 6.30″ can be extended similarly. Various other interacting option situations can be modeled using this type of analysis.

6.7 Conclusions

The works reviewed in this chapter and the analytical techniques developed here for valuing complex options offer useful insight into the value of flexibility in investment opportunities and show how specific real options can be modeled analytically under special circumstances (such as when a project has no intermediate cash flows or any other form of "dividend" payouts, or when it has infinite life). These analytic models, however, may be limited in their practical use to more complex real-life problems in which many such real operating options are present simultaneously and interact, or when competitive entry, compoundness within or between projects, and other strategic interactions may be important. We will turn to these issues in subsequent chapters.

Suggested Readings

Carr, P. 1988. "The valuation of sequential exchange opportunities." *Journal of Finance* 43, no. 5: 1235–1256.

Geske, R. 1979. "The valuation of compound options." *Journal of Financial Economics* 7, no. 1: 63–81.

Jarrow, R., and A. Rudd. 1983. *Option Pricing*. Irwin.

Majd, S., and R. Pindyck. 1987. "Time to build, option value, and investment decisions." *Journal of Financial Economics* 18, no. 1: 7–27.

Margrabe, W. 1978. "The value of an option to exchange one asset for another." *Journal of Finance* 33, no. 1: 177–186.

McDonald, R., and D. Siegel. 1985. "Investment and the valuation of firms when there is an option to shut down." *International Economic Review* 26, no. 2: 331–349.

McDonald, R., and D. Siegel. 1986. "The value of waiting to invest." *Quarterly Journal of Economics* 101, no. 4: 707–727.

Myers, S. C., and S. Majd. 1990. "Abandonment value and project life." *Advances in Futures and Options Research* 4: 1–21.

Paddock, J., D. Siegel, and J. Smith. 1988. "Option valuation of claims on physical assets: The case of offshore petroleum leases." *Quarterly Journal of Economics* 103, no. 3: 479–508.

Stulz, R. 1982. "Options on the minimum or the maximum of two risky assets: Analysis and applications." *Journal of Financial Economics* 10, no. 2: 161–185.

7

**Interactions among
Multiple Real Options**

This chapter deals with the nature of option interactions and the valuation of projects involving multiple real options.[1] So far, most work in real options has focused on valuing individual options (i.e., one type of operating option at a time).[2] However, managerial flexibility embedded in investment projects typically takes the form of a *collection* of real options. Interactions among real options present in combination generally make their individual values nonadditive. Although many readers may intuit that certain options do in fact interact, the nature of such interactions and the conditions under which they may be small or large, as well as negative or positive, may not be trivial.

Interactions generally depend on the type, the separation, the degree of being "in the money," and the order of the options involved. The importance of properly accounting for interactions among multiple real options will be illustrated by means of a generic example. Specifically, we will examine the size and type of interactions among the options to defer, abandon, contract or expand investment, and switch use. We will see that the incremental value of an additional option, in the presence of other options, is generally less than its value in isolation, and that it declines as more options are present. Therefore, valuation errors due to the omission of a particular option may be small. Configurations of real options exhibiting precisely the opposite behavior, however, will also be identified.

7.1 An Investment Opportunity with Multiple Real Options

Consider a generic investment opportunity with multiple real options. Construction of the project requires a series of investment outlays at specific times during a "building stage"—for example, an initial outlay of I_1 and subsequent outlays of I_2 and I_3. The project generates its first cash

flows during the "operating stage" that follows the last investment outlay, I_3.

The investment opportunity allows management the flexibility to

defer undertaking the project,

permanently abandon construction, with no recovery, by forgoing subsequent planned investment outlays,

contract the scale of the project by reducing planned investment outlays,

expand the project's scale by making an additional investment outlay,[3]

or

switch the investment from the current to its best alternative use (here
modeled as a specified salvage value).

The above generic investment, with its collection of real options, is
summarized in figure 7.1. This project could characterize many practical
situations. For example, it could describe the case of the large company
engaged in the exploitation of natural resources that is offered the opportunity to purchase a lease on undeveloped land with potential mineral resources. The lease, expiring in T_1 years, would give management the right

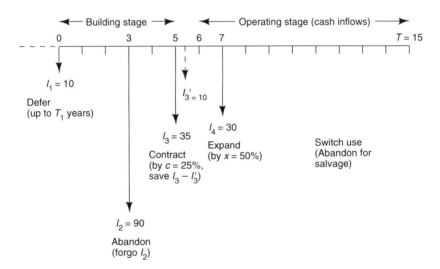

Figure 7.1
A generic project requiring a series of outlays (vertical arrows, I's), allowing management the
flexibility (collection of real options) to defer, to abandon, to contract or expand investment,
and to switch use.

to start the project within that period by making an investment outlay I_1 for construction of roads and other infrastructure. This would be followed by outlays of I_2 for excavation and I_3 for the construction of a processing plant. Reducing this last outlay to I'_3 would result in a contraction of $c\%$ in the operating scale of this plant. If the mineral were later found to enjoy a stronger demand than initially expected, the rate of production could be enhanced by $x\%$ by expanding the processing plant at a cost of I_4. All along, management retains the option to salvage a percentage of its investment.

As another example, the above project could describe the case of the firm that is considering introducing one of its existing patented products into a new geographic market. Management can delay introduction up to the time the patent expires, in T_1 years. Initiating the project requires an outlay of I_1 to purchase land, to be followed by an outlay of I_2 to build a plant in the new area. Upon the plant's completion, management plans a large one-time advertising expenditure of I_3, which, if the product's prospects at that time seem limited, can be reduced to I'_3 with a $c\%$ loss of market share. If a year after introduction the product is more enthusiastically received in the new market than originally expected, management can expand the project by $x\%$ by adding to plant capacity at a cost of I_4. If at any time market conditions deteriorate, management can salvage a portion of the investment by selling the plant and the equipment.

Traditional NPV and Managerial Flexibility

Assume that the generic project is expected to generate annual cash flows during the operating stage, starting in year 6. Under traditional NPV analysis, these expected cash flows and the terminal project value would be discounted at an appropriate risk-adjusted rate. Assume that this calculation results in a "gross" project value of $V = 100$. This is simply the present value of expected cash flows from immediately undertaking the project, not including any required investment outlays or embedded real options. This V (or its modified scale) serves as the underlying asset value for the project's various real options.

Assuming the particular values shown in figure 7.1 and subtracting the present value of the planned investment outlays, $I = 114.7$,[4] the passive NPV of immediately undertaking the above project, in the absence of managerial flexibility, is

NPV $= V - I = 100 - 114.7 = -14.7$.

The project would be rejected because its NPV is negative. The presence of managerial flexibility, however, can make the investment opportunity economically attractive.[5] As we saw, traditional valuation approaches that either ignore real options altogether (e.g., a passive NPV analysis) or attempt to value such investment opportunities using a constant discount rate can lead to significant errors in valuation, since asymmetric claims on an asset do not generally have the same discount rate as the asset itself. This asymmetry can be properly analyzed by viewing flexibility in an options framework.

An options-based approach to this problem, however, must recognize that flexibility seldom takes the form of a single option but instead typically is present as a combination of options. Therefore, proper analysis must account for the possible interactions among multiple options and the extent to which option values are not strictly additive.

Model Specification and Assumptions

The valuation of operating options in this section is based on the log-transformed version of binomial numerical analysis.[6] The gross project value (V_t) is assumed to follow the standard diffusion Wiener process given by[7]

$$\frac{dV}{V} = (\alpha - \delta)\, dt + \sigma\, dz, \tag{7.1}$$

where α is the instantaneous actual expected return on the project, σ is the instantaneous standard deviation of project value, dz is a standard Wiener process, and δ is the rate of return shortfall between the equilibrium total expected return required of an equivalent-risk traded financial asset, α^*, and the actually expected growth rate in the value of a nontraded real asset, α (chapter 3 above; McDonald and Siegel 1984, 1985). In general, the shortfall δ may also capture any proportional cash-flow (dividend-like) payout on the operating project, or even the net convenience yield in the case of commodities.[8]

In discrete time, $\ln V$ follows an arithmetic Brownian motion which can be approximated, over successively smaller intervals, by an equivalent binomial Markov random walk progressing in a triangular lattice as in figures 7.2 and 7.3. Adjustments for cash flows (dividends) and for the asymmetries introduced by real options (the discrete-time equivalent of specifying boundary conditions in continuous-time models with partial differential

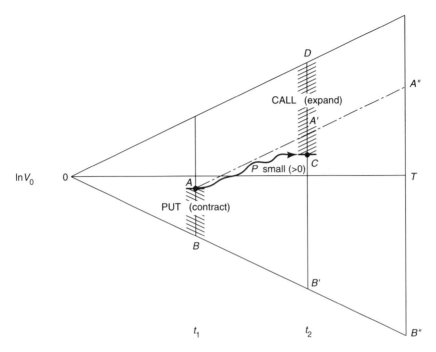

Figure 7.2
Options of different type, approximately additive. Both European out-of-the-money options
(a put and a call) with non-overlapping exercise boundaries and low probability of joint
exercise $(P > 0)$; interactions (proxied by double-shaded area $A'C$) are small, and separate
option values can be approximately added.

equations) are made at appropriate times in a backward risk-neutral iterative process.[9]

The option analysis below is based on the following base-case input
assumptions (see figure 7.1):

The initial gross value of the project, V, is 100.[10]

The annual risk-free interest rate, r, is 5%.

The variance of the project's value, σ^2, is 0.25.

The expected life of the project, T, is 15 years.

The opportunity is deferrable for $T_1 = 2$ years, and the project begins
with an investment outlay of $I_1 = 10$.

Construction can be abandoned, with no recovery, by forgoing the second investment outlay, I_2, of 90 in year 3.

The scale of the project can be contracted by $c = 25\%$ in year 5 by reducing the third investment outlay, I_3, to $I'_3 = 10$.

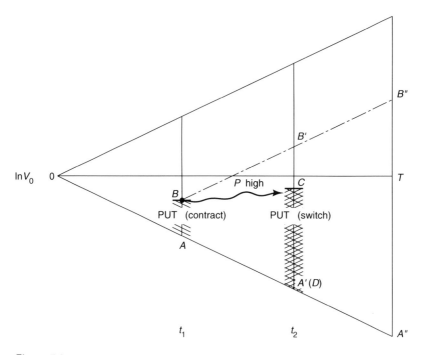

Figure 7.3
Options of similar type, nonadditive. Both out-of-the-money puts with high overlap (area $A'C$) and high probability of joint exercise; interactions are high (and negative if a prior put, as here; positive in case of calls).

The scale of the project can be expanded by $x = 50\%$ by making an additional investment outlay, I_4, of 30 in year 7.

The project's salvage value is $S = 50\%$ of cumulative investment costs (i.e., it "jumps" upward by 50% of each new cost outlay incurred), whereas it declines exponentially at a rate of 10% per year between cost outlays.

7.2   Interactions among Options and Nonadditivity of Option Values

Additivity of individual option values is trivial when options are written on distinct assets (for example, calls or puts on shares of IBM stock). However, option additivity is not trivial when the options are written on the same unique underlying asset. Examples of interacting financial options include putable convertible bonds, callable extendable bonds, and securities callable by the issuer at two distinct times. Real options, of course, more often come as an inseparable package with a single underlying asset (the gross project value, V). In situations where multiple options are embedded in the same asset, options can interact.

The mere presence of subsequent options increases the value of the effective underlying asset for earlier options. In essence, prior real options have as their underlying asset the whole portfolio of gross project value plus the value of any future options at that time. At an extreme, the inseparability of real options from their underlying asset allows also the possibility that exercise of a prior put option on the asset, such as the option to abandon early, may eliminate or "kill" that asset. Owing to the uniqueness of the real asset, this may preclude exercising future options on it (e.g., later contracting the project or switching uses).

More generally, however, exercise of a prior real option may alter the underlying asset itself and hence the value of subsequent options on it, causing a second-order interaction. For example, the option to contract will decrease, while the option to expand will increase the project's scale, affecting the value of other options on it. Further, the (conditional) probability of exercising a later option, in the presence of an earlier option, will be higher or lower than the (marginal) probability of its exercise as a separate option, depending on whether the prior option is of the same or the opposite type, respectively. Real options may thus interact for various reasons and to varying degrees, depending on the probability of their joint exercise during the investment's life.

To illustrate the nature of these interactions, consider a package of two options on the same asset. The degree of interaction and (non)additivity of option values—and the extent to which the underlying asset for a prior or subsequent option is altered—will depend on whether the options are of the same type (e.g., two puts or two calls) or are opposites (i.e., a put and a call), on the degree of separation of their exercise times (which affects their correlation and which is influenced by whether they are European or American options), on their relative degree of being "in or out of the money," and on their sequential order. All these factors affect the degree of overlap between their exercise regions and the probability of joint exercise.

The underlying principle in this analysis is that the value of an option in the presence of other options may differ from its value in isolation. Alternatively, the combined value of two options in the presence of each other may differ from the alternative of evaluating each option separately and adding the results. Two effects may be at work here, each affecting the direction or sign of the interaction as well as its magnitude.

First, recall that the value of a prior option would be altered if followed by a subsequent option because it would effectively be written on a higher underlying asset, V' (equal to the gross project value, V, plus the then-expected value of the subsequent option). Specifically, in terms of sign, if the first option is a put its value will be lower (giving a negative interaction), and if it is a call its value will be higher (exhibiting a positive interaction), *relative to its value as a separate option*. The magnitude of alteration in the *prior* option's value or the degree of its interaction would be larger the greater the joint probability of exercising both options, P, which depends on the similarity of the options.

Second, the effective underlying asset for the *later* option may be lower, conditional on prior exercise of an earlier put option (e.g., to contract the project's scale), V'', than if the prior option were not exercised (i.e., with the project's value, V, maintained). This may lead to a double negative effect if the prior option is a put.[11] If, instead, the prior option is a call (e.g., to expand the project's scale), the interaction can be positive, with the incremental value of both the earlier and the later option greater than their separate values.[12] In either situation, the degree of interaction between the two options will again be directly proportional to the probability of joint exercise.

If the two options are of opposite type (e.g., a put and a call), so that they are optimally exercisable under opposite (negatively correlated) circumstances, then the conditional probability of exercising the later option given prior exercise of the former will be smaller than the marginal probability of exercising the later option alone. The degree of interaction will then also be small, and the options will be approximately additive. If the two options are of the same type (either a pair of puts or a pair of calls), then the conditional probability of exercise and the magnitude of interaction (deviation from option-value additivity) will be higher. Again, the sign of the interaction will depend on whether the prior option is a put (negative) or a call (positive).

We can examine further the possible variations in the magnitude and sign of interaction between two options, starting from situations where option-value additivity holds and progressing to cases with higher degrees of interaction. First, as has already been noted, interactions are small and the separate option values are approximately additive when one option is a put (e.g., the option to contract) and the other is a call (e.g., the option to expand) and are both out of the money.[13] Two such European options would in fact be purely additive (i.e., their interaction would be precisely 0) only if both matured at the same time (i.e., $t_1 = t_2$). In this extreme case, although the marginal probabilities that either option may be exercised independently at (their common) maturity are positive, the joint (or conditional) probability of exercising both options is precisely zero ($P = 0$); with no interaction, each option retains its full, undistorted value as if evaluated independently, and thus their separate values are exactly additive.

The situation depicted in figure 7.2 is similar to the above additive case, except that there is a separation in the exercise times of the two opposite-type, out-of-the-money (European) options, with the put maturing at an earlier time. Although there is again a high positive marginal probability that the put option will be exercised at time t_1 or that the call option may be exercised independently at time t_2, the conditional probability of exercising the later call option, given a prior exercise of the first put ($P_{L|F}$), is nevertheless small—smaller than the marginal probability of exercising the later option alone (P_L). For the put option to be optimally exercised at t_1, the state variable (the logarithm of the asset's value) must drop below the "exercise boundary" into the "exercise region" (shaded in the figure) AB. After exercise of the first option, its subsequent movement will be constrained within the trapezoidal area $ABB'A'$ by t_2 (or $ABB''A''$ by maturity, T), which only partially overlaps with the exercise region (CD) of the subsequent option (the double-shaded area $A'C$)—with only a small chance of reaching the second exercise boundary necessary for triggering exercise of the later call option. The smaller [greater] this overlap ($A'C$), the smaller [greater] the conditional probability of joint exercise and the smaller [greater] the degree of interaction between the two option values. If it is small enough, as in this case of opposite types of options, the separate option values will still be approximately additive. If the order were reversed so that the call option preceded the put, the options would still be of opposite type with nonoverlapping exercise regions and low conditional probability of joint exercise,[14] so their interaction would again be small—though it may be of opposite (i.e., positive) sign—and the separate options could still be approximately added.[15]

If the prior option were also a put instead of a call, as shown in figure 7.3, the separate option values would be far from additive. As the options would then be of similar type (in this case both puts), their exercise regions would overlap significantly and the conditional probability of exercising one put, given earlier exercise of the other (as indicated by the increased double-shaded area $A'C$), would be high (and less than 1). Because exercise of the prior put (e.g., to contract) would reduce the project's scale and value and hence the other put option's (e.g., to switch between uses) with high probability, P, the expected incremental value of the later option would be smaller. The prior put's value may also be somewhat smaller—a double negative effect—than if evaluated separately, because it is written on the project's portfolio with the future put, even though the latter may be reduced by the first-order interaction. Similarly, interactions would again be high—but positive—if the similar-type options were both calls (e.g., to expand the project at two distinct times) instead of puts. Of course, interactions can get more complicated if more than two options are considered. For example, if the pair of European calls (a compound European call)—or, by extension, an American call—were preceded by another put option, potentially dominating negative interactions could arise between the positively interacting pair and the prior put.

Finally, exercising a prior real put option (e.g., to abandon the project by simply forgoing an upcoming investment outlay) may kill other future options. In the extreme case that the exercise regions of two put options overlap fully and the first option can kill the later one with certainty (with $P_{L|F} = 1$), the expected incremental value of the later option will be negligible. The combined value will then simply be the full separate value of the first option (essentially written only on the base-scale project, because the later option is valueless). More generally, however, if the later option (for example, being instead a call with nonoverlapping exercise boundaries, similar to the situation in figure 7.3) were not completely within the "shooting range" of the prior killing put, so that the conditional probability was less than 1, it would not be completely "dead"; it would retain some value as long as there was some chance that it could be exercised without prior exercise of the first killing put (i.e., $P_{L|\bar{F}} > 0$).

Alternatively, if the condition for optimally exercising the one put (e.g., to abandon) also simultaneously satisfies or is a subset of the condition for optimally exercising the other (e.g., switching between uses), the combined value of the two options will simply be the highest of the two separate values—an extreme case of full negative interaction. Such may also be the case when the separation between the exercise times of two similar-type options is negligible.

More generally, the nature of interaction, and hence the extent to which the values of two separate options may or may not approximately add up, can be summarized as follows: There is no [small] interaction, and hence the separate option values will be [approximately additive] additive (i.e., option-value additivity holds), if the conditional probability of exercising both options before maturity is zero [small].[16] Conversely, the interaction will be highest [high], making it most inappropriate to add up the separate option values, if it is certain [likely] that both options will be exercised jointly (or if the conditional probability of a joint exercise, $P_{L|F}$, is 1 [high]). The interaction will typically be positive if the prior option is a call and negative if a put. In the latter case (as when the separation between two similar-type options is negligible), the combined option value may be only [somewhat higher than] the higher of the separate individual values—that is, the incremental value of the lesser option may be negligible [small].

If the underlying asset follows a continuous-time diffusion process, as in equation 7.1, the joint cumulative probability that a pair of real options will be exercised (i.e., that both options will end up in their respective exercise regions, with the first option exercised at t_1 and the second at t_2), P, is more formally given by the bivariate cumulative standard normal distribution function. For European-style options and a log-normal underlying process, the values at the two exercise dates are jointly bivariate log-normal, with variances proportional to the length of each time interval (time to maturity) and correlation proportional to the length of the first time interval divided by the second. This can allow integrating the bivariate normal density to obtain closed-form solutions for certain option values in the presence of other options, and expressing the degree of option interaction as a function of the bivariate cumulative probability of joint option exercise with correlation proportional to the ratio of the two times to maturity. This bivariate cumulative standard normal distribution is of the form $B(a, b; \rho)$, evaluated at a and b (as upper and lower integral limits) with correlation coefficient $\rho = \sqrt{\tau_1/\tau_2}$ (where τ_1 and τ_2 are the times to maturity of the two options). Specifically, for a pair of opposite-type options, such as a first put option to contract and a later call option to expand, P takes the form $B(-d^*, d; -\rho)$ with $\rho = \sqrt{\tau_1/\tau_2}$.[17]

Certain properties of the bivariate distribution (see, e.g., Abramowitz and Stegum 1972, pp. 936—937) are particularly relevant to the nature of these option interactions. When the separation between the exercise times of the pair of options is extremely large (as $\tau_2/\tau_1 \to \infty$), $\rho \to 0$ with $B(-d^*, d, 0) = N(-d^*)N(d)$—where $N(d)$ is the (univariate) cumulative standard normal distribution function, with d as upper integral limit—establishing the stochastic independence condition ($P_{F,L} = P_F P_L$).[18] With finite separation between opposite-type options having low (negative or zero) correlation, $B(-d^*, d; -\rho) \leq N(-d^*)N(d)$; this confirms that $P_{F,L} \leq P_F P_L$, or $P_{L|F} \leq P_L$ (and the interaction effect is relatively small). In the special case that there is no separation between two opposite-type options $(\tau_1 = \tau_2)$, $\rho \equiv -\sqrt{\tau_1/\tau_2} = -1$ with $B(-d^*, d, -1) = 0$; since $P_{F,L} = P_{L|F} = 0$ (as option exercise is mutually exclusive in this case), all interaction effects disappear leading to pure option-value additivity.

If, instead, the two options were of similar type (such as the pair of put options to contract and later to switch use or a pair of call options to expand at two distinct times), $P_{L|F}$ would be relatively high and the interaction effects would become significant. In this case the joint probability instead takes the form $B(d^*, d; \rho)$, with $\rho = \sqrt{\tau_1/\tau_2}$ (see, e.g., the compound call option situations in chapter 6, or in Geske 1979 and Carr 1988). This involves d^* and d as upper integral limits, and it has a positive correlation coefficient, as should be expected when both options are exercisable under positively correlated (e.g., favorable for calls) circumstances. Again, infinite separation ($\rho \to 0$) leads to the stochastic independence condition, $N(d^*)N(d)$. With finite separation, $\rho \geq 0$ and $B(d^*, d; \rho) \geq N(d^*)N(d)$, verifying that $P_{F,L} \geq P_F P_L$. A large (positive) correlation thus leads to a large value for the bivariate probability, and to a correspondingly large value for the degree of interaction. When there is no separation between two similar-type options, we obtain the largest possible correlation with $\rho = 1$ and $B(d^*, d; 1) = N(d)$ [if $d^* > 0$, or $N(d^*)$ if $d^* < 0$]; with $P_{F,L} = P_F$, or $P_{L|F} = 1$, the interaction is therefore highest. As noted, in such cases (e.g., with a pair of puts) the combined option value may just equal one of the separate values.

Values of the bivariate cumulative normal distribution (indicative of the degree of option interaction) for different values of correlation ρ ($= \sqrt{\tau_1/\tau_2}$) using $d = 0$, $B(d^*, 0; \rho)$, are tabulated for the reader's convenience in tables A.4 and A.5 of the appendix for $-1 \leq d^* \leq 1$ (in steps of 0.05)—table A.4 for negatively correlated (primarily opposite-type) options and table A.5 for positively correlated (or similar-type) options. The last column in table A.5 lists the values of the univariate cumulative normal $N(d^*)$ for comparison. More generally, values of $B(d^*, d; \rho)$ with a nonzero d can be expressed in terms of the values $B(d^*, 0; \rho)$ of tables A.4 and A.5 using certain useful relationships.[19]

The earlier observations can thus be confirmed using the values given in tables A.4 and A.5 with $d = 0$ (so that $N(d) = 0.5$). Consider, for example, the case when $d^* = -1$ for opposite-type options (first row in table A.4) and $d^* = 1$ for similar-type options (last row in table A.5). As noted, for opposite-type (negatively correlated) options interaction is 0 when the option maturities coincide ($\tau_1/\tau_2 = 1$ or $\rho = -1$) and remains at

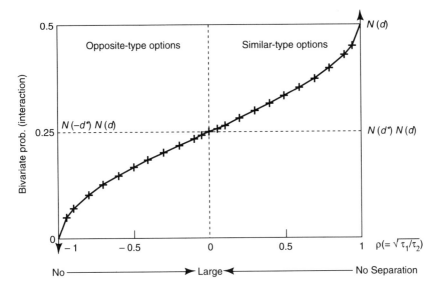

Figure 7.4
Bivariate probability (interaction) versus correlation (separation or exercise times). Bivariate
(joint cumulative probability) distribution ($P \equiv B(d^*, d; \rho)$), assuming $d^* = d = 0$, proxying
for degree of interaction, versus correlation coefficient ($\rho = \sqrt{\tau_1/\tau_2}$), proxying for separation
of exercise times (τ_2/τ_1) between two opposite-type or similar-type options.

low levels (e.g., it equals 0.0313 when the later option's maturity is four
times the earlier option's, or $\rho = -0.5$), not exceeding $N(-1)N(0) =
0.1587 \times 0.5 = 0.0793$ (being highest when their separation is extremely
large or $\rho = 0$). For similar-type (or positively correlated) options, however, as the last row in table A.5 confirms, interaction can be quite high.
In this case it ranges from 0.4207 when separation is high and $\rho = 0$, to
0.4687 when $\tau_2 = 4\tau_1$ and $\rho = +0.5$, to a maximum of $N(0) = 0.5$ when
the two options are exercisable at the same time and $\rho = 1$.

Figure 7.4 illustrates how the degree of interaction, as proxied by
$P_{F,L} = B(d^*, d; \rho)$, depends on the separation of exercise times (τ_2/τ_1) between a pair of options (proxied by the correlation coefficient, $\rho =
\sqrt{\tau_1/\tau_2}$) in the case when $d^* = d = 0$, both for opposite-type and for sim-
ilar-type options. It can be seen that the magnitude of interaction increases with the correlation (and, in the case of opposite-type options
such as those treated here, with separation) at a rate increasing with $|\rho|$ or
declining with separation. (This makes sense, since the bivariate distribution is a function of $\sqrt{1 - \rho^2}$.) Finally, if the two options are of different
orders (and types), one or both interaction effects may change sign.

Table 7.1
Interactions among multiple real options (base case: $V = 100$; $r = 5\%$; $\sigma^2 = 0.25$; life $T = 15$; defer up to $T_1 = 2$ years). NPV of project without real options: -14.7.

Value with one real option				
Defer (D)	Abandon (A)	Contract (C)	Expand (E)	Switch use (S)
26.3^a $(41)^b$	22.1 (36.8)	-7.8 (6.9)	20.3 (35)	24.6 (39.3)
Value with two real options				
D & A	D & C	D & E	D & S	A & C
36.4 (51.1)	27.7 (42.4)	54.7 (69.4)	38.2 (52.9)	22.6 (37.3)
A & E	A & S	C & E	C & S	E & S
50.6 (65.3)	24.6 (39.3)	27.1 (41.8)	25.5 (40.2)	54.7 (69.4)
Value with three real options				
D & A & C	D & A & E	D & A & S	D & C & E	D & C & S
36.8 (51.5)	68.2 (82.9)	38.2 (52.9)	57.1 (71.8)	38.7 (53.4)
D & E & S	A & C & E	A & C & S	A & E & S	C & E & S
71 (85.7)	51.9 (66.6)	25.5 (40.2)	54.7 (69.4)	55.9 (70.6)
Value with four real options				
D & A & C & E	D & A & C & S	D & A & E & S	D & C & E & S	A & C & E & S
69.3 (84)	38.7 (53.4)	71 (85.7)	71.9 (86.6)	55.9 (70.6)
Value with five real options				
D & A & C & E & S (all)				
71.9 (86.6)				

a. Project value including option(s), i.e., expanded NPV.
b. Value of option(s) only.

7.3   Valuation Results for Multiple Options

This section presents the numerical valuation results for the multiple real options of the generic project introduced in section 7.1, first in isolation (i.e., one option at a time) and later in combination.

Valuation of Separate Options

Option to Defer
The option to defer (alone) is basically valued as an American call option on the project, with an exercise price equal to the necessary investment outlays. As shown in table 7.1, this option increases the project's expanded NPV to 26.3, in contrast to the no-flexibility base-case NPV of -14.7. Alternatively, the value of this option is

Option Value $=$ Expanded NPV $-$ Passive NPV $= 26.3 - (-14.7) = 41$,

or 41% of the gross project value V (shown in parentheses in table 7.1).

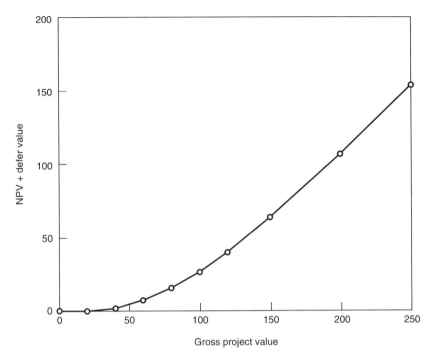

Figure 7.5
Sensitivity analysis of impact of gross project value V on (NPV + defer value).

The sensitivity of the option to defer to various factors is consistent with what one would expect from option pricing theory. Figure 7.5 shows a sensitivity analysis of the impact of gross project value, V, on the total value or expanded NPV, with other things constant. As expected, the total value of the real opportunity with the option to defer increases with V (analogous to a call option). Figure 7.6 illustrates how sensitive the total value of the investment opportunity (with the option to defer included) is to having more or fewer years to defer (i.e., the maturity of the option to defer). As the initially steep and later gradually declining slope of the curve indicates, the option to defer is extremely valuable in the first years and less so later. (There are "diminishing returns to waiting" one more year, so doubling the duration of a lease or a patent would less than double its value.) Figure 7.6 also shows that the value of this project turns from negative (-14.7 if taken immediately) to a moderate positive value if it can be deferred for just a year, and to a substantial positive value if it can be deferred for several years (about 60 for 9 years).

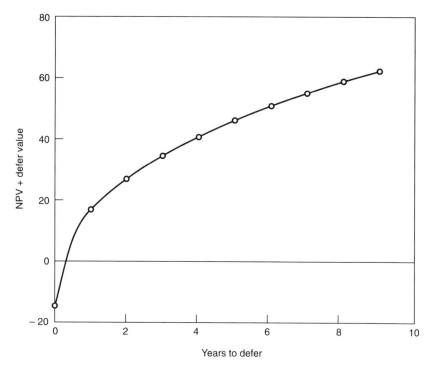

Figure 7.6
Sensitivity analysis of impact of years to defer on (NPV + defer value).

Option to Permanently Abandon during Construction
This option can be valued either as a put or as a compound call option on the project. If management has only this option, then the project has an expanded NPV of 22.1. Thus, the value of the option to abandon during construction amounts to 37% of V. Figure 7.7 shows sensitivity analysis of the impact of V on the option to abandon. As illustrated, the value of this option declines when V increases (similar to a put option).

Option to Contract
The option to contract (i.e., scale down operations) is valued as a European put on part of the project, with exercise price equal to the potential cost savings. Including just this option increases the opportunity's value by 7% of V (from −14.7 to −7.8). Figure 7.8 verifies that the value of this option decreases with V in a manner analogous to a put option.

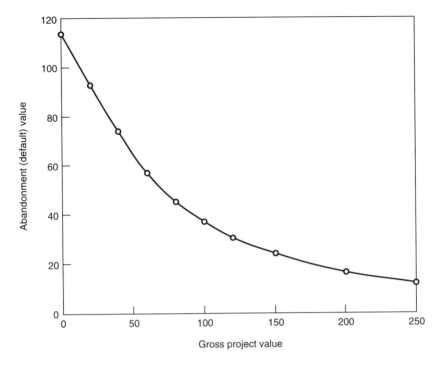

Figure 7.7
Sensitivity analysis of impact of gross project value V on abandonment (default) value.

Option to Expand
The option to expand (i.e., scale up) the base-case project is worth 35% of the project's gross project. This option is valued analogous to a European call option to acquire part of the project by paying the extra outlay as an exercise price, as figure 7.9 illustrates.

Option to Switch Use
This option is valued as an American put on the project, with an exercise price equal to the value in its best alternative use (here assumed to be its salvage value). As shown in table 7.1, its value in isolation is 40% of V. Figure 7.10 shows a sensitivity analysis of this option to changes in various factors. The curve with open circles corresponds to the base-case example, with a salvage value equal to 50% of V, a variance of 0.25, and a project life of 15 years. As predicted from put-option theory, the value of this option to switch use (or abandon for "salvage") increases as the salvage value (or exercise price) increases (curve with open squares), increases

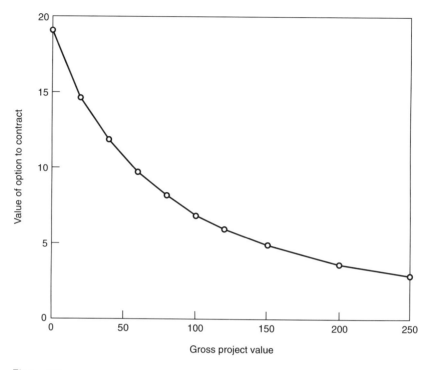

Figure 7.8
Sensitivity analysis of impact of gross project value V on value of option to contract.

as the variance of the project's value rises (solid circles), and decreases as the project's life (maturity) is reduced (solid squares), with other things constant.[20] In the case of uncertain or stochastic salvage value, the option to switch use can become significantly more valuable the lower the correlation coefficient between project value (in its current use) and salvage value. Figure 7.11 shows a sensitivity analysis of the impact of correlation (varying from -1 to $+1$) on the above option value.[21]

Value of Option Combinations with Interactions

The value of an option in the presence of other options may differ from its value in isolation. The presence of subsequent options increases the effective underlying asset for prior options. Moreover, exercise of a prior real option (e.g., expanding or contracting a project) may alter the underlying asset and the values of subsequent options on it. The valuation results for the generic project, when particular real options are valued in the

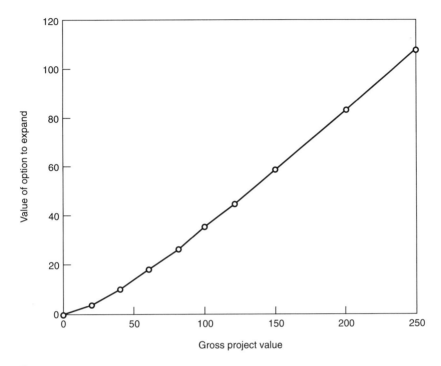

Figure 7.9
Sensitivity analysis of impact of gross project value V on value of option to expand.

presence of others, illustrate option configurations where interactions can be small or large, as well as negative or positive.

Table 7.1 shows the value of the project with different combinations of operating options. For example, the value of the project increases from -14.7 (without any options) to 26.3 with the option to defer only, to 36.4 with the options to defer and abandon (D & A), to 36.8 with the options to defer, abandon, and contract (D & A & C), to 69.3 with the options to defer, abandon, contract, and expand (D & A & C & E), and to 71.9 with all five options. Thus, the combined option value (shown in parentheses in table 7.1) increases from 41 (with only the option to defer) to 51 (D & A), to 52 (D & A & C), to 84 (D & A & C & E), and finally to 86.6 (all five options). These results confirm that the values of real options in the presence of one another are not generally additive. For example, although the value of the option to defer alone is 41 and the value of the option to abandon in isolation is 37, the value of both options present simultaneously is only 51, which shows substantial negative interaction.

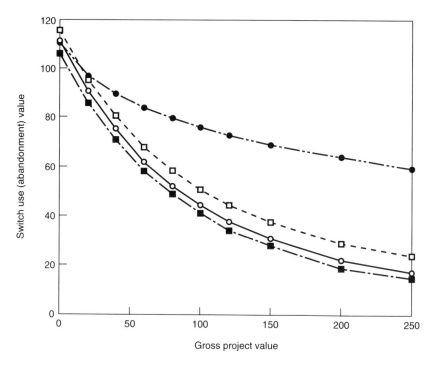

Figure 7.10
Sensitivity analysis of the option to switch use (abandon for "salvage") to changes in various
factors. Open circles: Base case (salvage = 50 percent of V; variance = 0.25; project life
$T = 15$ years). Open squares: Salvage changed to 80% of V. Solid circles: Variance changed
to 1. Solid squares: Project life changed to 10 years.

As has been noted, the degree of interaction is related to the type of
embedded options and the degree of overlap of their exercise regions.
Specifically, recall that options tend to be more additive when the options
involved are of opposite type (i.e., a call option optimally exercised when
circumstances become favorable and a put option optimally exercised
when circumstances become unfavorable), when the times of possible exercise of the two options are close together (e.g., two European options
maturing at the same time, as opposed to having distinctly different maturities or being American options), and when the options are more out of
the money (i.e., when they have relatively high exercise prices for calls
and low exercise prices for puts, which leads to less overlap of their exercise regions). For example, because the options to contract in year 5 and
to expand in year 7 are of different type (i.e., a prior put and a later call)

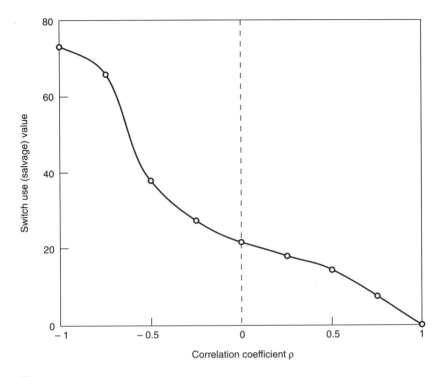

Figure 7.11
Sensitivity analysis of impact of correlation on stochastic "salvage" (switch use) value.

and have no overlap between their exercise regions, their separate values (C = 6.9, E = 35) are basically additive; that is, C & E = 41.8.[22]

Table 7.2 shows the magnitude of interaction as the separation of exercise times varies between the options to abandon construction (in year 3) and to expand (by $x = 50\%$ if $I_E \equiv I_4 = 30$). The maturity of the option to expand, t, is allowed to vary from year 3 to year 13 (so that separation varies from 0 to 10 years). The size of interaction for a given separation is the difference between the combined option value (A3 & Et) and the sum of separate values (A3 + Et). Figure 7.12 shows that for these opposite-type options, negative interaction increases with separation at a decreasing rate.

Table 7.3 illustrates how the size of interaction between the option to abandon construction (in year 3) and the option to expand (by $x = 50\%$ if the firm makes an additional investment of I_E) in year 7 varies as the exercise price (I_E) declines (or, alternatively, the scale of expansion, x, increases) and the option to expand gets relatively deeper in the money

Table 7.2
Interaction between options to abandon and to expand vs. separation of exercise times (as maturity of option to expand increases). The option to abandon in year 3 (A3) is 36.8.

	E3	E4	E5	E7	E9	E11	E13
Option to expand in year t (Et)	28.1	30.2	32.0	35.0	37.4	39.4	41.0
Combined option value (A3 & Et)	64.9	63.0	63.8	65.3	66.5	67.5	68.4
Sum of separate values (A3 + Et)	64.9	67.0	68.8	71.8	74.2	76.1	77.7
Interaction [(A3 & Et) − (A3 + Et)]	0	−4.0	−5.0	−6.5	−7.7	−8.6	−9.3
Separation in years ($= t − 3$)	0	1	2	4	6	8	10

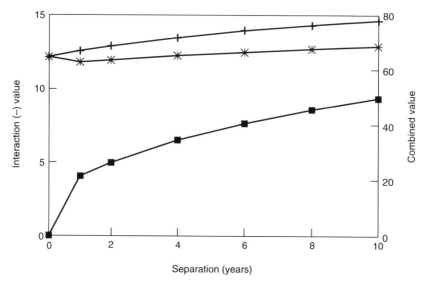

Separation (years)

Figure 7.12
Interaction versus separation. The degree of (negative) interaction between the opposite-type options to abandon (A) and to later expand (E)—i.e., the difference between the combined option value (A & E) and the sum of separate option values (A + E)—increases with the separation of exercise times. Solid squares: Interaction value. +: Sum of separate option values (A + E). ×: Combined option value (A & E).

Table 7.3
Interaction between the options to abandon and to expand vs. depth in the money (as exercise price of option to expand declines). The option to abandon in year 3 (A3) is 36.8.

Exercise price (I_E)[a]	∞	150	75	50	30	20	15
Percentage of scale expansion (x)[b]	0	0.1	0.2	0.3	0.5	0.75	1.0
Depth in the money (xV/I_E)	0	0.333	0.667	1.0	1.667	2.5	3.333
		(out of money)	(at money)		(in money)		
Option to expand in year 7 (E7)	0	3.2	9.7	17.6	35.0	58.3	82.2
Combined option value (A3 & E7)	36.8	39.5	45.1	51.3	65.3	84.3	104.4
Sum of separate values (A3 + E7)	36.8	39.9	46.5	54.3	71.8	95.1	119.0
Interaction [(A3 & E7) − (A3 + E7)]	0	−0.4	−1.4	−3.0	−6.5	−10.8	−14.6

a. Assuming $x = 50\%$ scale expansion in year 7.
b. Assuming $I_E = 30$.

(proxied by xV/I_E). Figure 7.13 confirms that the magnitude of negative interaction between these opposite-type options increases with the relative degree of being in the money.

Furthermore, when operating put options with extensively overlapping exercise regions are considered, there is high negative interaction and the combined value is slightly higher than the separate values. Two examples are the options to contract ($C = 6.9$) and switch use ($S = 39.3$), where C & $S = 40.2$, and the options to abandon ($A = 37$) and switch use ($S = 39.3$), where A & $S = 39.3$.[23] Similarly, there is heavy negative interaction among the values of the options to abandon, contract, and switch use (A & C & $S = 40.2$ vs. $A + C + S = 83$).

In addition to option type, degree of overlap of exercise regions, and depth in the money (or exercise price), the order or sequence of the options affects option-value additivity significantly. As mentioned, if a put precedes a later option, the combined option value will typically exhibit negative interaction. However, if a put follows a prior call, there can be a positive interaction. Finally, the interaction will be positive if a call follows a prior call.

To illustrate the possibility of positive interactions, consider a second (European call) option to expand the project (by 35% with another optional investment of 15) added to the basic example. Table 7.4 shows the total value of the project (including options) and the option values in a number of interesting cases. Note first that if the second option to expand has the same exercise date (i.e., year 5) as the opposite-type option to contract, the purely additive case with precisely zero interaction is obtained: i.e., E5 & C5 = 32.1 = E5 + C5.[24] However, with two options to

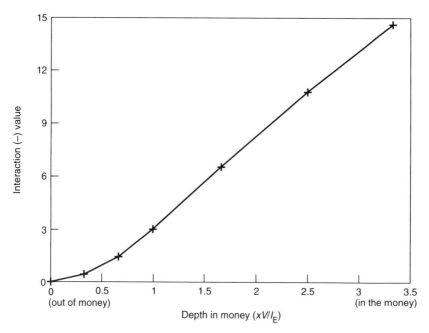

Figure 7.13
Interaction versus depth in money. The degree of negative interaction between the option to abandon and to expand increases with the depth in the money (or as the exercise price of the option to expand, I_E, declines).

Table 7.4
Adding a second option to expand: a case of positive interactions. (NPV of project without real options: -14.7.)

Value with one real option			
Expand year 5 (E5)	Expand year 4 (E4)	Expand year 7 (E7)	Contract year 5 (C5)
10.5[a] (25.2)[b]	9.6 (24.2)	20.3 (35)	-7.8 (6.9)
Value with two real options			
E5 & C5	E4 & C5	C5 & E7	E4 & E7
17.4 (32.1)	16.5 (31.2)	27.1 (41.8)	50.6 (65.3)
Value with three real options			
E4 & C5 & E7			
62 (76.7)			
Value with six real options			
All & E4			
107 (121.7)			

a. Project value including option(s), i.e., expanded NPV.
b. Value of option(s) only.

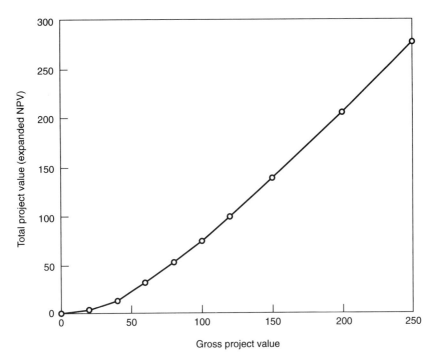

Figure 7.14
Sensitivity analysis of impact of gross project value on total project value (expanded NPV).

expand (a compound call situation), positive interactions are large. As expected, the presence of each call option enhances the other's value, leading to substantial positive interaction.[25] Specifically, the combined value of the options to expand in year 4 and in year 7 exceeds the sum of their individual values: E4 & E7 = 65.3 > E4 + E7 = 59.2. This substantial positive interaction effect is maintained in the presence of the option to contract (E4 & C5 & E7 = 76.7 > E4 + C5 + E7 = 66.1) and when all other options are also jointly considered (All & E4 = 121.7 vs. All + E4 = 111).

Having considered the case of significant positive interactions,[26] let us return to the basic generic project, with just one expansion option in year 7, and examine the marginal effect on project value of having increasingly more options. As a result of predominantly negative option interactions, the combined value of all five options (87) in the basic generic example is slightly more than half the sum of the values of the separate options (159).[27] The value of the combined flexibility is, however, of the same order of magnitude as the value of the project's expected cash inflows (87

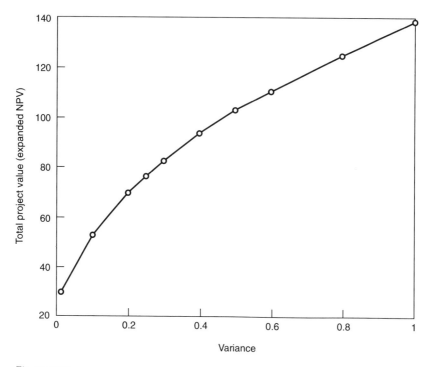

Figure 7.15
Sensitivity analysis of impact of project variance on total project value.

vs. 100). Thus, ignoring the value of all real options would significantly understate the true economic value of such projects (here, by about half). But measuring the value of this flexibility by simply adding the values of the individual options would seriously overstate (almost double) their worth.

However, ignoring certain options (typically, puts) would not necessarily lead to significant valuation errors, because the incremental value of an additional option tends to get lower as the overlap of its exercise region with those of other included options gets greater.[28] As can be seen from table 7.1, having only one option may be nearly half as valuable (e.g., to switch use = 39) as having all five (87), having two may be three-quarters as valuable (e.g., to abandon and expand = 65, or to defer and expand = 69), and having three options may be nearly as valuable (e.g., D & E & S = 86 or D & A & E = 83) as having four (e.g., D & C & E & S = 87 or D & A & E & S = 86) or all five (All = 87). Because of this diminishing marginal option-value effect, although a few particular options may have been neglected in our treatment of the generic project, the valuation

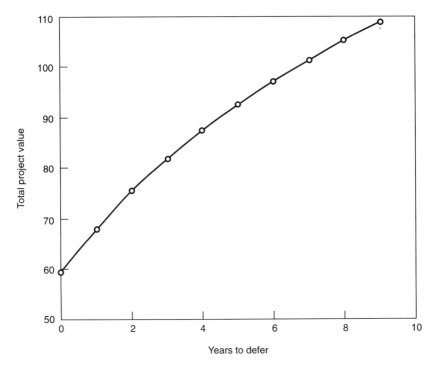

Figure 7.16
Sensitivity analysis of impact of years to defer on total project value.

results may still represent a close approximation to the true value, especially if the options that were included were selected so as to minimize their overlap.[29]

Finally, note that interacting real options maintain a number of the usual option properties. Figures 7.14–7.18 illustrate the sensitivity of the total value of the generic project, including all interacting real options (determined to be 72 in the base-case example above), to changes in various factors that affect option values. With other factors held constant, the total project value increases significantly (almost linearly) with V, increases substantially (at a declining exponential rate) as project variance rises, increases somewhat (in a slightly exponentially declining, almost linear fashion) with more years to defer, increases (in an exponentially increasing manner) as the percentage of costs that can be salvaged rises, and declines (exponentially) as the risk-adjusted discount rate rises (and consequently V declines).[30] In the aggregate, the opportunity to invest with this particular configuration manifests call-option-like properties. It is thus comforting to

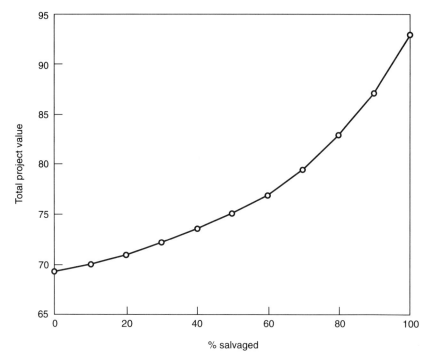

Figure 7.17
Sensitivity analysis of impact of percentage of gross project value that can be salvaged on total project value.

see that this project, valued as a call on a collection of real options, despite various option interactions, preserves many familiar option properties.

7.4   Conclusion

In this chapter we focused on valuing investment opportunities with a collection of embedded real options and quantifying their interactions. We saw that, although the values of real options may not be additive, the combined flexibility that they afford management may be as economically significant as the value of the project's expected cash flows. We considered the nature of option interactions, and examined situations in which option interactions are small and simple option additivity can therefore be a good approximation. Other situations in which large interactions may seriously invalidate option-value additivity were also identified. Interactions were seen to depend on the type, separation, degree of being in or

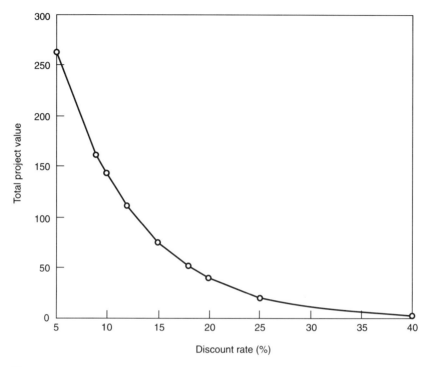

Figure 7.18
Sensitivity analysis of impact of risk-adjusted discount rate on total project value.

out of the money, and the order of the options involved—factors that affect the joint probability of exercise.

The above type of analysis can be useful in deriving rigorous and practical implications for valuing the interdependencies among real options. For example, if the two options are of opposite types and have a given finite separation, the joint probability will be small, and so will be the degree of interaction. As the separation between the exercise times of two opposite-type options becomes large, the degree of their interaction increases. In terms of sign, if the prior option is a put the combined value of both options in the presence of each other is smaller than the sum of their separate values (i.e., the interaction is negative), whereas if the prior option is a call the interaction can be positive. If the two options are of the same type (for a given finite separation), the joint probability will be larger, and so will the degree of deviation from option-value additivity. In the special case where the separation between the exercise times becomes negligible, for opposite-type options the interaction effects disappear (as option exercise becomes mutually exclusive), resulting in straight additivity of option values; for similar-type options, however, the interaction is largest—in cases of full negative interaction the combined value of the options may simply reduce to that of one of the separate option values; that is, the incremental value of the second option may be negligible.

In principle, interactions between two options may be positive as well as negative. In practice, however, where negative interactions are more prevalent within a given project, they may so reduce the incremental value of certain options that simply ignoring them may not create any significant valuation errors. Sensitivity analysis confirms that projects with a variety of such interacting real options do preserve many familiar option properties.

Suggested Readings

Brennan, M., and E. Schwartz. 1985. "Evaluating natural resource investments." *Journal of Business* 58, no.2: 135–157.

Kulatilaka, N. 1995. "Operating flexibilities in capital budgeting: Substitutability and complementarity in real options." In *Real Options in Capital Investment: Models, Strategies, and Applications*, ed. L. Trigeorgis. Praeger.

Trigeorgis, L. 1993. "The nature of option interactions and the valuation of investments with multiple real options." *Journal of Financial and Quantitative Analysis* 28, no. 1: 1–20.

8   Strategic Planning and Control

This chapter introduces an options-based strategic investment planning and control framework, discusses how to integrate various "strategic" sources of value (such as synergy among groups of parallel projects and interdependencies among projects over time) and provides a rationale for the use of control targets. Section 8.1 discusses the valuation of projects in a strategic-planning framework that combines the real-options approach and the strategic-investment-mix approach to capital budgeting. Section 8.2 illustrates how this framework can be used to value project synergies and interdependencies across time. Section 8.3 describes how to design control targets compatible with value maximization. The active management of projects over time is discussed in section 8.4, and implications and concluding remarks are presented in section 8.5.[1]

8.1   A Framework for Strategic Planning

Standard financial theory prescribes selecting individual projects with positive NPV as if management has to make independent decisions to accept or reject investment projects. Under capital-rationing constraints, accepted theory encourages management to examine collections of projects to find the higher total (combined) NPV. In practice, contrary to the simplistic view that each project can generally be valued independent of others, skillful managers value the presence of interactions among various projects. For example, managers see synergies among parallel projects undertaken simultaneously or interdependencies among projects over time (growth options). Even without capital rationing, they understand that entire collections of interacting projects must be valued collectively.

Furthermore, though practicing managers may agree that value maximization (based on NPV, for example) is the proper goal for evaluation purposes, they have to live with the fact that managerial incentive and control schemes are tied to observable, accounting-based measures. Such incentives and control targets are needed to induce and monitor adherence to the desired strategy. But if controls are not set properly, satisfying the cutoff levels (e.g., return on assets $\geq x\%$, growth rate $\geq y\%$) or achieving the best results possible along certain dimensions may not necessarily promote the desired objectives. It is a real challenge to set control targets in a way that is consistent with and enforces the value-maximizing strategy.

Broadly defined, the value-maximizing paradigm can provide a sound basis for rational business decisions.[1] A proper framework for capital budgeting and strategic planning should be able to capture important sources of strategic value missed by standard techniques—for example, collections of operating real options, various competitive interactions, synergies among projects taken simultaneously, and growth opportunities and interdependencies among projects over time.

Integrating the real-options approach with a strategic-investment-mix model may make it possible to quantify the various strategic sources of value embedded in collections of projects. Let us now focus on the strategic-investment-mix approacah and how such an integration can be achieved.

The strategic-investment-mix approach is a model of strategic planning and control based on the following principles[2]:

• Corporate strategic planning, capital budgeting, incentive schemes, and control mechanisms should form an integrated organizational system promoting the primary goal of firm value maximization (figure 8.1). Value, of course, should be broadly interpreted (using the options perspective) as

Strategic (expanded) NPV*

= Traditional (passive) NPV of expected cash flows

+ Value of operating options from active management

+ Interaction effects.

(The interaction effects may be due to competition, synergy, and/or inter-project dependence.)

• The design and use of proper control targets is an essential element in the practical implementation and monitoring of the chosen value-maximizing (NPV*) strategy.

• A crucial task of strategic investment is to create and manage a collection of profitable future investment opportunities (growth options).

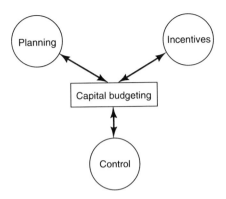

✴ Figure 8.1
An integrated planning/incentives/control approach to capital budgeting.

Figure 8.2 illustrates the three main phases and key elements of strategic capital budgeting. Phase I concentrates on evaluation and planning, phase II on setting optimal control targets, and phase III on active project management. Key elements in phase I include explicit modeling of management's understanding of market conditions and of potential interactions among various individual projects and subsequent modeling of entire categories of projects (for example: cost reduction, maintenance, market development, capacity expansion, research and development, new-product introduction). This approach provides for the building of an integrated corporate model for strategic discussion and analysis. The precise structure of the model should be appropriate for the particular firm or business unit and for its market situation. Any known or anticipated project interactions—parallel (i.e., among projects) or across time—should be taken into account. The outcome of the strategic-investment-mix analysis will be the value-maximizing strategy (NPV*) and the optimal growth path (how much should be invested in each broad project category over time) (figure 8.3).

During phase II, a set of practical control targets (e.g., return on assets and growth rate) can be designed so as to induce and help monitor adherence to the chosen value-maximizing strategy and growth path. Such controls can help in the selection and the active management of individual projects during phase III, and should be adjusted contingent on actual market developments and the exercise of major future options. The results of such active project management will affect the next planning cycle, and so on (figure 8.2).

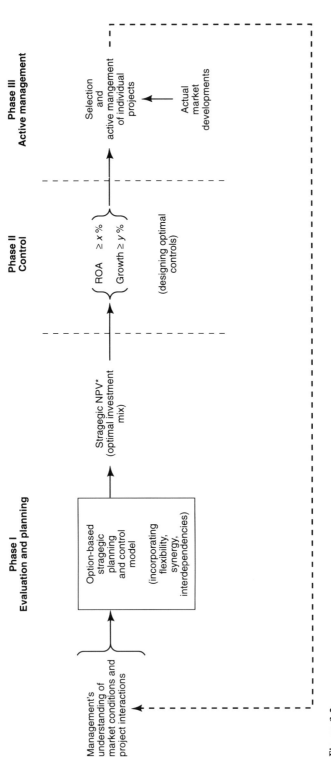

Figure 8.2
The three phases of strategic capital budgeting: evaluation and planning, control, and active management of investment projects.

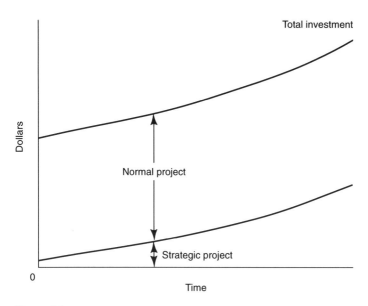

Figure 8.3
The optimal investment mix (normal versus strategic projects) along the growth path.

Such a strategic planning process should, of course, make full use of the concepts and tools of real-option valuation, since they may be able to help better capture operating flexibility, synergy, and certain strategic aspects of project value. In this broader, integrated context, strategic planning can be better viewed as the explicit recognition, creation, and management (optimal exercise) of the firm's portfolio of real options. An options approach to capital budgeting should thus be interwoven with and supportive of the firm's strategic planning process.

8.2   Examples of Strategic Interactions among Sets of Projects

This section discusses interaction effects of synergy among groups of simultaneously undertaken projects and of interproject dependence across time (spawning or growth options). These interactions are considered by many practicing managers to be true ingredients of strategic value. Because of such interactions, however, the combined value of the various operating and strategic real options in practice can often be captured properly only through options-based numerical valuation techniques (such as those presented in chapter 10 below) in a framework of integrated strategic investment planning.

Table 8.1
Present values in base-case operation (maintenance).

Sales (S)	100
Operating costs (C)	(80)
Net cash flows[a] (V)	20

a. For simplicity, depreciation, taxes, and changes in working capital are ignored here.

Table 8.2
Present values for market-expansion and cost-reduction projects taken separately.

	Market expansion	Cost reduction
Sales (S)	150	100
Operating costs (C)	(120)	(72)
Investment (I_E, I_C)	(11)	(10)
Net cash flows (V)	19	18

Synergy among Parallel Projects

Suppose that a mature business unit is expected to produce the financial results shown in table 8.1 if the base-scale operation is maintained. Now consider two new investment opportunities that appear: an advertising expenditure of $I_E = \$11$ million in new-market development (market expansion) that would expand sales by $e = 50\%$ and a cost-reduction investment of $I_C = \$10$ million that would cut unit costs by $c = 10\%$ regardless of the scale of production. Under traditional valuation, taking each project separately would give the results shown in table 8.2. The incremental cash flows from undertaking either project are negative. Standard DCF analysis would therefore suggest that either project would decrease the value of the business unit and should be rejected.

These investment opportunities would look different, however, if seen as real options. The market-expansion project is, of course, better viewed as a call option on V with exercise price the additional outlay I_E, so that the value of the business unit becomes

$$V' = V + \max(eV - I_E, 0) = 20 + \max(0.50 \times 20 - 11, 0)$$

$$= 20 + \max(-1, 0).$$

If exercised, the expansion in scale would be worth -1, and so this project would not be implemented by itself under the present conditions.

Table 8.3
Present values for market-expansion and cost-reduction projects in combination.

Sales (S)	150
Operating costs (C)	(108)
Investment ($I_E + I_C$)	(21)
Net cash flows (V)	21

Similarly, the cost-reduction opportunity is a call option on the cost savings ($c\%$ of C) with exercise price I_C, so

$$V' = V + \max(cC - I_C, 0)$$

$$= 20 + \max(0.10 \times 80 - 10, 0)$$

$$= 20 + \max(-2, 0).$$

Again it is not worth exercising the cost-reduction option by itself, as it would reduce the business unit's value by 2. Consider, however, taking the two projects in combination. Assuming that the unit cost reduction does not depend on whether you expand or not, the combined results (table 8.3) are now encouraging.[3] Viewed as options, the combined market-expansion and cost-reduction investments taken together result in

$$V' = V + \max(eV - I_E + c(1+e)C - I_C, 0)$$

$$= 20 + \max(0.50 \times 20 - 11 + 0.10(1 + 0.50) \times 80 - 10, 0)$$

$$= 20 + \max(+1, 0).$$

The strategic source of value ($+1$) in this example comes from the synergy among the projects when they are taken together.

The value of synergy, which went unnoticed in the standard analysis, can be modeled in a strategic-planning framework as follows[4]:

$$\max_{d_E, d_C \in \{0, 1\}} V' = S' - C' - (d_E I_E + d_C I_C),$$

where

$$S' = \begin{cases} S \text{ if } d_E = 0 \text{ (no expansion)} \\ (1+e)S \text{ if } d_E = 1 \text{ (expansion)} \end{cases}$$

and

$$C' = \begin{cases} \alpha S' \text{ if } d_C = 0 \text{ (no cost expansion)} \\ \alpha(1-c)S' \text{ if } d_C = 1 \text{ (cost reduction)} \end{cases}$$

Table 8.4
Normal project.

Time	0	1	2	3
Book value of assets	21.0	14.0	7.0	0.0
Sales		30.0	40.0	50.0
−Costs		21.0	29.0	34.9
−Depreciation[a]		7.0	7.0	7.0
Before-tax profit		2.0	4.0	8.1
−Tax (50%)		1.0	2.0	4.0
After-tax profit		1.0	2.0	4.0
Investment	(21.0)			
Net cash flow[b]	(21.0)	8.0	9.0	11.0

a. Assuming a straight-line depreciation on initial investment (asset book value) of 21.
b. The NPV (at 10%) of these net cash flows is +2.0.

with $S = 100$, $\alpha = 0.8$,[5] $e = 0.5$, $c = 0.1$, $I_E = 11$, and $I_C = 10$. The problem can be written in compact form as

$$\max_{d_E, d_C \in \{0, 1\}} \quad V' = (1 + e\, d_E)S[1 - \alpha(1 - c\, d_C)] - (d_E I_E + d_C I_C).$$

The decision variables 0 and 1 are needed to capture the asymmetry introduced by active management under uncertainty. The expected value-maximizing strategy can be searched for even if there are hundreds of such market and cost equations in the model. The key point is to capture the important network of interdependencies caused by market feedback from the external environment and cash-flow generation from within the company. The decision variables are the investments in various project categories, and the outcome is the optimal investment mix.

Sequential Project Interdependencies across Time (Growth Options)

Next let us consider the standard practice of classifying investment opportunities as normal or strategic. "Normal" investment typically refers to the production and selling of existing products, whereas "strategic" investment refers mainly to new-market and product-development commitments (R&D, for example). Assume that the standard cash-flow profile of the normal project category for the business unit is as shown in table 8.4. If the risk-adjusted cost of capital for the normal project, k, is 10%, the NPV of expected cash flows from the normal project will be +2.0. The normal project is therefore worth undertaking, since its NPV is positive.

Table 8.5
Strategic project.

Time	0	1	2	3
Book value of assets	3.0	2.0	1.0	0.0
Sales		2.0	3.0	4.0
−Costs		2.0	2.0	1.5
−Depreciation[a]		1.0	1.0	1.0
Before-tax profit		(1.0)	0.0	1.5
−Tax (50%)		(0.5)	0.0	0.75
After-tax profit		(0.5)	0.0	0.75
Investment	(3.0)			
Net cash flow[b]	(3.0)	0.5	1.0	1.75

a. Assuming a straight-line depreciation on initial investment (asset book value) of 3.
b. The NPV (at 10%) of these net cash flows is −0.5.

Similarly, the cash-flow profile of the strategic project category is as shown in table 8.5. If the risk-adjusted cost of capital for the strategic project is 12%, the NPV of the strategic project will be −0.5. Thus, standard NPV analysis will lead to rejection of this strategic investment. However, if the strategic investment would generate future growth opportunities, this standard analysis is myopic.

Suppose, for example, that investing in the strategic project now would generate the opportunity to invest in a normal project, such as the one above, during the next period. Then, in a deterministic world, the value of the strategic project is given by $NPV_S + NPV_N/(1+k)$, or $-0.5 + 2.0/1.1 = 1.3$. Even in the absence of uncertainty, the interaction effect across time (i.e., opening up the opportunity to invest in the future) creates a strategic source of value.[6]

If the project's future value is uncertain, the strategic investment is even more valuable, since it creates an option for management to invest in the normal project next year if the project does well but not to invest if it does poorly. For example, suppose that the normal project's present value of expected cash inflows, currently $V = 23$, is expected to move up or down by 20% next year (to $V^+ = 27.6$ or to $V^- = 18.4$) with equal probability ($q = 0.5$). The required investment of $I_N = 21$ should be incurred next year if the project does well (V^+), but will not be incurred otherwise (V^-). Thus, if the risk-free interest rate, r, is 6% and the risk-neutral probability is

$$p = \frac{(1+r)V - V^-}{V^+ - V^-} = \frac{1.06 \times 23 - 18.4}{27.6 - 18.4} = 0.65,$$

the total value resulting from this strategic investment is

$$NPV^* = NPV_S + \frac{p\max(V^+ - I, 0) + (1-p)\max(V^- - I, 0)}{1+r}$$

$$= -0.5 + \frac{0.65 \times \max(27.6 - 21, 0) + 0.35 \times \max(18.4 - 21, 0)}{1 + 0.06}$$

$$= -0.5 + \frac{0.65 \times 6.6 + 0}{1.06}$$

$$= +3.55.$$

This result contrasts with the earlier result, +1.3, obtained by calculating strict expected values under passive management. Project-value uncertainty and the discretionary-option aspect account for the higher value.

The source of strategic value here is found in the interdependencies among the projects across time. A dynamic model of investment-opportunity generation can thus help analyze the ramifications of these interdependencies. Under uncertainty, the strategic value of such project interdependencies is higher because of the discretionary option. As has already been noted, an earlier investment in a chain of such interdependent projects can be seen as a call option on the next investment, and so on. The strategic-option value of the followup investment may far exceed its own NPV (which may even be negative). Even if the NPV of both projects is negative, however, high future uncertainty may make the strategic option in the followup investment if conditions should turn favorable even more valuable and the negative-NPV strategic investment worth taking.

8.3 Value-Maximizing Control Targets

Once the value-maximizing strategy—defined broadly to incorporate the value of flexibility, synergy, and project interdependencies (NPV*)—has been identified, a compatible system of control targets to help implement that strategy must be set up. It is again crucial that the capital-budgeting system, the incentive schemes, and the control mechanisms form an integrated system that is harmonious with the chosen value-maximizing strategy and that guides management toward that strategy. Even with the best intentions, the business unit may deviate from the optimal strategy. It is thus of paramount importance to be able to discern this early through proper controls. Arbitrarily set (e.g., as a result of an internal political process), control targets may be dysfunctional. However, if properly derived from and consistent with the value-maximizing strategy, control targets can help guide the organization toward the desired strategy.

Consider the situation—found in many companies—where the business strategy calls for growth and product leadership, R&D is expensed in internal calculations, and managers are rewarded on the basis of return on investment (ROI). This seems to constitute a contradiction of objectives, measurement, and incentives.

The design of control targets should be based on the value-maximizing strategy, not on the maximum levels achievable. It may be possible, for example, to increase return on assets if investment is cut, or to increase market share if the profit margin is reduced. But these actions do not necessarily promote value maximization. Because the optimal target levels are typically below the highest feasible levels, the concept of *managerial slack* becomes relevant. The managerial slack of a control target is the set of decisions that can meet or exceed the target.

Consider a typical control target, such as ROA $\geq x\%$, taken alone. There are many sets of investment decisions, in addition to the value-maximizing investment strategy, that can meet this target. Some of these decisions may even be contrary to the desired strategic direction. Consider, however, adding a second target: growth rate $\geq y\%$; now there are fewer investment alternatives that satisfy both constraints simultaneously.

Because the managerial slack of each control target determined according to the value-maximizing strategy contains the value-maximizing investment mix (NPV*), the intersection of the targets narrows down the desired strategy. A typical set of control targets with opposing or contradictory managerial slacks pushing toward the desired strategy could include ROA, growth rate, and even a budget constraint, as illustrated in figure 8.4.

Basically, the initial value-maximization problem can be transformed for purposes of implementation and control into an equivalent set of satisficing constraints (control targets) whose intersection contains the optimum strategy (NPV*). Maximizing value and satisficing a set of control constraints can be made economically equivalent, provided the control cutoff levels are properly chosen.

How tight the controls should be may, of course, depend on the amount of external uncertainty and the quality of management. Creative, competent, and loyal managers may be trusted with greater managerial discretion. Moreover, if the value of the strategy is contingent on the exercise of major future options, then a set of conditional control targets should

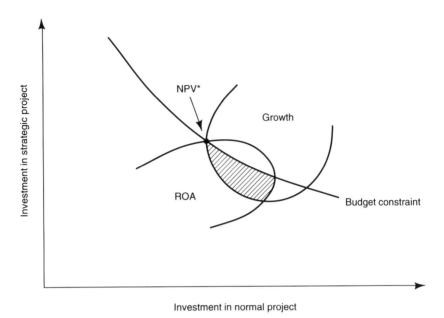

Figure 8.4
The value-maximizing strategy (NPV*) determined by the intersection of the managerial slacks of a combination of control targets (ROA, growth, and a budget constraint).

also be given to lower-level managers. For example, conditional on exercising a major expansion or growth option, the growth target may be increased while the ROA cutoff levels are decreased appropriately. Revisiting the above example of project interdependencies across time from a control point of view, we can verify that setting ROA at 13.5% and the growth rate at 7.7% is consistent with the value-maximizing strategy.

We can also examine whether investment in each project category would make managerial incentive schemes look good or bad in the future, relative to no investing. In this case, it can be shown that the ROA target by itself leads to a negative impact on incentives for the early years, whereas the growth-rate target leads to positive incentives for most years. Set at the optimal levels and used in combination, however, this set of controls can support the desired strategy. Since NPV is appropriate for ex ante project evaluation rather than as an operating control measure, it is useful to derive a proper set of observable control targets and incentives to guide managers on a day-to-day basis toward the value-maximizing strategy.

8.4   Active Management of Investment Projects over Time

The value of active management and project interactions is not captured in the standard framework of an accept-or-reject decision and post-audit analysis. In a turbulent business environment, new opportunities arise and old plans must be revised or abandoned. Option pricing combined with dynamic strategic planning and control models is better able to capture these sources of value.

Active management of investment opportunities means that managers constantly search for opportunities to exercise the built-in options in investment projects, or to create new ones. If major developments occur, or if important options are exercised or created that will change the remaining alternatives, the initial strategy has to be modified. A set of conditional control targets should also be made available to lower-level managers dependent on the exercise of such major future options.

Long-term strategic plans and the search for the value-maximizing strategy should thus be seen as an ongoing process in which the investment mix and the control targets are periodically revised as managers actively try to benefit from new business opportunities or modify old ones. The purpose of planning strategically and using proper control targets is to pursue this value-maximizing strategic path as it evolves through time.

Not only does the corporate strategy have to be flexible and evolve over time; in addition, the control targets compatible with the strategy must be reevaluated whenever the strategy is changed. For example, the current target levels for growth and ROA must reflect the most recent understanding of the value-maximizing strategy.

Market developments should therefore be reflected in the active management of investments and in a regular fine tuning of organizational control targets. The allowed managerial slack should also be a function of the uncertainty in the business environment. In a stable environment, the set of control targets that managers have to meet can be tight and detailed. In a volatile environment, on the other hand, creative and loyal managers may need fewer targets and greater slack or flexibility, so that they can react more swiftly to changing market conditions.

8.5   Implications and Conclusion

A mechanistic determination of the standard NPV of expected cash flows of a single project seen in isolation may overlook several sources of strategic value intuitively grasped by skillful practicing managers. For example, synergies among parallel projects and interdependencies among projects across time create important interaction effects. Operating options and growth opportunities are also major sources of strategic value in an uncertain business environment. These sources of strategic value can be properly quantified by means of an integrated strategic-planning-and-control approach based on the valuation of options.

Furthermore, even if value maximization is properly expanded to capture the above strategic sources of value, it may not be sufficient for the day-to-day management of investment projects at different levels in the organization. Measures for planning, incentives, and control must also be used to guide and support the chosen strategy. It is not necessarily incompatible to search for the NPV*-maximizing strategy while using intermediate indicators and performance measures.

For practical implementation purposes, it may be useful to use several control measures in capital budgeting, as is widely practiced. However, these measures must be derived from and attuned to the value-maximizing strategy. Naturally, the more uncertainty there is in the external environment, the more valuable the option features become and the more managerial discretion in control is needed for active, creative, and properly motivated managers.

Capital budgeting should thus not be treated as a static, mechanistic accept-or-reject lower-level staff function; instead, it should be integrated with strategic planning and control. Business strategy should involve selection of the proper investment mix (e.g., among normal and strategic projects) that leads to the value-maximizing growth path. Top management should actively and continually be involved in shaping the desired investment strategy and setting proper control targets to guide the organization toward the chosen strategy.

In an uncertain business environment, the value-maximizing strategy is not simply a fixed set of decisions taken up front; it is a direction that must be modified when conditions change. Management should periodically examine whether its current organizational control targets and performance measurement schemes are compatible with the new strategic thrust. It should also actively and continually search for opportunities to optimally exercise existing investment options or to create future ones. The full value of these options can be captured only if they are exercised in an optimal way. Option-based valuation can provide optimal exercise policies or guidelines (e.g., expand production in year x when output price exceeds \$$y$, or abandon when value drops below \$$z$). Practical implementation of these policies requires proper managerial incentives and adaptable monitoring controls. A set of conditional control targets, contingent on the exercise of major future options, may support managerial efforts, especially at lower levels in the organization. The succesful integration of incentives, controls, and option-based exercise strategies is a crucial managerial task.

Suggested Readings

Kasanen, E. 1993. "Creating value by spawning investment opportunities." *Financial Management* 22, no. 3: 251–258.

Merchant, K. A. 1982. "The control function of management." *Sloan Management Review* 23, no. 4: 43–55.

Myers, S. C. 1987. "Finance theory and financial strategy." *Midland Corporate Finance Journal* 5, no. 1: 6–13.

Ruefli, T., and J. Sarrazin. 1981. "Strategic control of corporate development under ambiguous circumstances." *Management Science* 27, no. 10: 1158–1170.

Trigeorgis, L., and E. Kasanen. 1991. "An integrated options-based strategic planning and control model." *Managerial Finance* 17, no. 2/3: 16–28.

9   Competition and Strategy

This chapter deals with the valuation of the impact of competitive interactions under exogenous and endogenous competition. The first two sections deal with the valuation of exogenous competitive entry. Section 9.1
deals with the optimal timing of project initiation in a preemptive competitive environment and illustrates how option-based valuation can be
used to determine whether management should exercise a deferrable investment opportunity early in order to preempt anticipated entry by
competitors or whether it should wait despite anticipated competitive
damage. Section 9.2 extends the analysis to value the impact of random
competitive arrivals (modeled as Poisson jumps) on investment opportunity value. In both cases of exogenous competitive entry, the impact of
competitive arrivals on the value of an investment opportunity can be
viewed as analogous to the effect of dividends on American call options.
Section 9.3 uses simple game-theoretic principles from industrial organization to show how endogenous competitive reaction to strategic investment can be analyzed in an options-valuation framework. Section 9.4 is
devoted to implications and conclusions.

9.1   Anticipated Exogenous Competitive Entry and Early
Preemptive Investment

The flexibility to optimally time project initiation is, among other real options, often ignored by naive NPV analysis, which typically assumes that
an immediate accept-or-reject decision must be made. Yet the ability to
"wait and see" is clearly valuable to managers when the value of a project
moves stochastically. The need for an expanded (or strategic) NPV framework incorporating both sources of a project's value—that is, both the
standard or passive NPV of expected cash flows and an option premium
reflecting the value of its operating flexibility and strategic interactions

under active management in an uncertain competitive environment—has already been discussed.

The basic idea of optimal investment timing is not new in the literature of economics (see, e.g., Baldwin 1982; Roberts and Weitzman 1981; Venezia and Brenner 1979).[1] The literature of real options has also dealt with the optimal timing of investment (see, e.g., Tourinho 1979; Siegel, Smith and Paddock 1987; Majd and Pindyck 1987; McDonald and Siegel 1986). Option-based valuation can also be used to determine the optimal time to invest in cases where the timing and the value of the investment opportunity may be affected by competition.

As an example, consider an incumbent firm that has an opportunity to introduce a new patented product in a competitive market. The firm may defer this introduction up to T years, after which time the patent expires and the opportunity disappears. In the meantime, the firm anticipates the introduction by competitors of close substitute products ("competitive arrivals") that may reduce the value of its opportunity (e.g., by reducing prices through excess capacity or by taking market share away from the firm in question). When is it optimal for such a firm to make an investment commitment in this competitive environment? How should it trade off the benefits of waiting afforded by the patent against the danger of competitive damage, especially if the latter can be eliminated if the firm makes an early preemptive investment?

Notation and Assumptions

V is the gross project value or the present value of expected cash inflows from implementing the project, here assumed (between competitive arrivals) to follow the stochastic diffusion Wiener process

$$\frac{dV}{V} = (\alpha - D)\, dt + \sigma\, dz, \tag{9.1}$$

where α is the total instantaneous expected rate of return on the project, σ is the instantaneous deviation of project value (V), dz is an increment of a Wiener process, and D represents continuous intermediate cash flows generated as a proportion of gross project value (like a constant dividend payout).

I is the present value of investment cost outlays required to acquire project V. For simplicity, I is assumed constant here.[2] (Note that immediate implementation of the project gives the standard passive NPV $\equiv V - I$.)

R is the total value of the deferrable real investment opportunity. This is the expanded (strategic) NPV consisting of the passive NPV of the not-yet-implemented project's cash flows plus the value of the option to defer net of the impact of competitive entry.

k_j is the proportion of gross project value just after, versus before, competitive arrival j at time t_j, where $j = 1, 2, \ldots, N$. That is, the project's value is assumed to drop deterministically from V to $k_j V$ after the jth arrival.[3] Alternatively, $1 - k_j$ represents the proportion of the project's current value lost to the jth competitor (like a dividend yield). In general, k is a parameter whose value depends on market-structure characteristics.

T is the life of the project ($\tau \equiv T - t$ is the time to maturity).

r is the real risk-free interest rate.

For the random (uncertain) exogenous arrivals in section 9.2, the following additional notation will be used:

λ is the random competitive arrival rate or instantaneous probability of a competitive entry causing a downward jump. It is an indicator of the intensity of the competitive process. Here we assume for simplicity that λ is constant, although in general it can be $\lambda(V, t)$.

N is the number of competitors sharing the real opportunity with the incumbent.

Early Investment with Preemption of Competitive Erosion (Dividend Analogy)

We have seen that the opportunity to initiate a discretionary deferrable investment by time T (e.g., to introduce a new product or expand capacity) is basically analogous to an American call option on the project's gross value, V. In the absence of any dividend-like effects or costs due to waiting, a firm should wait until close to expiration (T) before deciding whether to exercise.[4] This is because the firm would have no downside risk before implementing the project, whereas it could benefit from a wait-and-see approach in case of favorable future market developments.

In reality, however, a firm may often find it desirable to exercise its real option to invest at an early stage, sacrificing the option value of waiting. This may be justified, for example, in the following cases:

when the value of earlier (or perhaps longer) intermediate cash flows, acting as dividends, exceeds the value of waiting (particularly if there is a set expiration of the investment opportunity) when an early investment can generate information or learning that can improve decisions concerning similar future investments—a justification for sequential or repeatable investments

when the firm can prevent a greater loss, such as when preempting a competitor's entry (and the resulting damage to its own opportunity) by making an early commitment of capital

when an early strategic investment can create a proprietary competitive advantage (or an offsetting gain), such as a lower cost structure ("learning-curve effect") in a later stage of the market under contrarian (e.g., quantity) competition, or sometimes when it can generate shared benefits under reciprocating (price) competition.

This section focuses primarily on the preemptive competitive effect, analyzing investment opportunities whose value can be eroded by anticipated competitive arrivals. Because most real investment opportunities are not tradable, even anticipated competitive losses may not be avoided, since the real option cannot simply be sold in the market. Thus, in many situations the only effective way to avoid such anticipated competitive erosion may be to make an early investment commitment in order to preempt a competitor's entry.

Other economists working in the areas of industrial organization, research and development, and energy have dealt with investments timed to preempt competition.[5] Although the options approach is in agreement with the results of this literature, it offers additional insights into the effects of such variables as uncertainty, interest rates, and investment horizon and into their tradeoffs with potential competitive damage. Accordingly, we will examine when it may be appropriate to make an early preemptive investment and when it may be appropriate to wait despite the damage that competition is anticipated to cause. In nature and in timing, this decision is analogous to the early-exercise decision on a dividend-paying stock call option.

Suppose that the incumbent firm can fully anticipate both the timing and the impact (i.e., percentage damage to its project value, $1 - k$) of competitors' arrivals. For simplicity, consider the anticipated arrivals of two competitors at times t_1 and t_2 before the expiration time (T) of the opportunity to initiate the project ($0 < t_1 < t_2 < T$). This deferrable investment opportunity with anticipated arrivals of competitors resembles an American call option with known dividends[6]: the timing of the anticipated arrivals corresponds to the known ex-dividend times, and the competitive erosion (i.e., the drop in project value due to competition), $d_j =$

$(1 - k_j)V$, with $j = 1, 2$, is similar in magnitude to the known "dividend" payments. In preemptive situations where an early investment by the incumbent firm would successfully prevent competitive arrivals that would otherwise materialize, the analogy to a dividend-paying stock call option holds well. If the incumbent firm owning the real option decides to wait until expiration (i.e., to maintain it as an option rather than exercising it early to preempt competition), it loses the "dividends" (the part of project's value appropriated by competitors), $(1 - k_j)V$, just as the owner of a call option on a dividend-paying stock forgoes any cash dividend payments—which accrue to the owner of the stock—if he or she does not exercise early. If, however, the incumbent firm decides to exercise early and thereby succeeds in preempting competitive entry, it will then "recover" the dividends that would otherwise be lost to competitors. This is analogous to the owner of a stock call option receiving the dividends (since he would then acquire ownership of the stock itself) if he decides to exercise early, which may be optimal "just before" a coming dividend.

Scenarios of Analysis under Anticipated Competition

To help analyze when it would be optimal to exercise such a deferrable investment opportunity with anticipated competitive arrivals, consider the following five "scenarios." Each scenario of analysis and the corresponding total investment opportunity value (including any option value and competitive impact) or expanded NPV, R, is depicted in figure 9.1 as a function of gross project value, V, and other parameters.

Scenario A: Exercise immediately; preempt competition
Under this scenario, the firm would exercise its real option immediately (i.e., initiate the project at $t = 0$) and, through this early commitment of capital, I, would successfully preempt any competitive arrivals. This situation is effectively the same as undertaking a project of value V immediately in the absence of competition; thus, the total opportunity value R (measured by the vertical distance from point A to the horizontal axis and shown along the vertical axis in figure 9.1) is here precisely the project's passive NPV ($\equiv V - I$). This scenario can serve as a benchmark for a comparative analysis of the more complex situations that follow.

Scenario B: Exercise immediately; competition enters
This is the situation whereby competitors would arrive at times t_1 and t_2 despite the firm's immediate exercise of its real option to invest (i.e.,

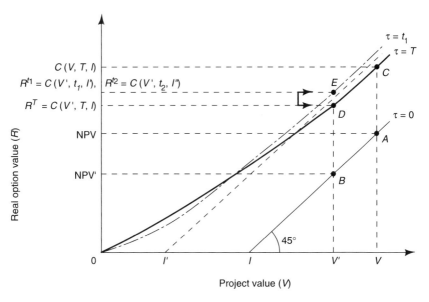

Figure 9.1
Value of a real option (expanded NPV) with anticipated competitive arrivals in five scenarios.
Scenario A: Exercise now, preempt competition. Scenario B: Exercise now; competition enters. Scenario C: Proprietary option (no competition). Scenario D: Maintain option (T); competition enters. Scenario E: Exercise at t_1^- (t_2^-), preempt competition. Here

$$V' = [1 - (1 - k_1)e^{-r\tau_1} - k_1(1 - k_2)e^{-r\tau_2}]V,$$

$$I' = I - [(1 - k_1) + k_1(1 - k_2)e^{-r(t_2 - t_1)}]V,$$

and

$$I'' = I - (1 - k_2)k_1 V,$$

where V = gross project value, I = investment cost outlay, NPV = $V - I$, k_j = new project value (as a proportion of old value) after competitive arrival j at time t_j, T = project life, $\tau \equiv T - t$ = time to maturity, R = total real opportunity value (incorporating option value of waiting and competitive loss), and $C(V,T,I)$ is the Black-Scholes solution for a European call option (adjusted for a constant dividend payout) with asset value V, maturity T, and exercise price I.

preemption would prove unsuccessful). The two competitive arrivals reduce the project's value, V, by the present value of dividends, i.e.,

$$V' = V - (d_1 e^{-r\tau_1} + d_2 e^{-r\tau_2})$$

(with $d_1 = (1 - k_1)V$ and $d_2 = (1 - k_2)k_1 V$) to

$$V' = [1 - (1 - k_1)e^{-r\tau_1} - k_1(1 - k_2 e^{-r\tau_2})]V \qquad (9.2)$$

(with k_j the proportion of project value just after, versus before, competitive arrival j, and with $\tau_j \equiv t_j - t$, where $j = 1, 2$). Thus, the real investment opportunity under scenario B has NPV$' \equiv V' - I$ (which is less than the NPV of scenario A).

Scenario C: Proprietary option (no competition)
The vertical distance to point C in figure 9.1 gives the value of a proprietary real investment opportunity. In the absence of competition, a firm generating no or a low cash-flow payout would tend to delay the introduction of a new product, maintaining its investment opportunity as an option until T rather than exercising it early. If the implemented project would generate a constant cash-flow payout D, the value of this proprietary real option would be given by the Black-Scholes solution for an American call option, $C(\ )$, adjusted for a constant dividend payout D (as in equation 3.18):

$$C(V, t; r, \sigma^2, T, I, D) = V e^{-D\tau} N(d_1') - I e^{-r\tau} N(d_2'), \qquad (9.3)$$

where

$$d_1' = \frac{\ln(V/I) + [(r - D) + \frac{1}{2}\sigma^2]\tau}{\sigma\sqrt{\tau}},$$

$$d_2' = d_1' - \sigma\sqrt{\tau},$$

$\tau = T - t$ (time to maturity),

and $N(\ )$ is the cumulative standard Normal distribution function.

With the arguments t, r, σ^2, and D suppressed for expositional simplicity, the above expression can be rewritten in the more compact form $C(V, T, I)$. Certainly, $C(V, T, I) \geq$ NPV $>$ NPV$'$, or C $\}$ A $\}$ B (i.e., scenario C dominates A, which in turn dominates scenario B).

Scenario D: Wait (maintain the option); competition enters
Here the firm decides to maintain the option (i.e., wait until T rather than exercise early) despite the anticipated competitive arrivals at t_1 and t_2. The total opportunity value is then[7]

$$R^T = C(V', T, I),\tag{9.4}$$

where V' is given by equation 9.2. In other words, R^T is the Black-Scholes solution (adjusted for dividend payout D) with project value V replaced by V', where $V' = V-$ Present value of anticipated future competitive "dividends." This is so because if the real option is not exercised early to preempt competitors then the firm will lose the dividends to competition at times t_1 and t_2. The larger the anticipated loss in project value due to competitive entry (i.e., the larger the competitive dividends, d_j, or the lower k_j, the lower V' and) the lower the value of the opportunity, R^T, when the firm decides to wait despite anticipated competitive entry. Competition, of course, may speed up an incumbent firm's planned investment.

Scenario E: Exercise just before t_j; preempt subsequent competitors
This is the situation where the firm considers exercising "just before" it anticipates a competitive arrival in order to preempt subsequent competitors.[8] If the firm considers exercising only just before t_1 (which would preempt competitive entry both at t_1 and t_2, thus recovering both "dividends," the total value of its investment opportunity is given by

$$R^{t_1} = C(V', t_1, I'),\tag{9.5}$$

where V' is again as given by equation 9.2[9] and where

$$I' = I - [(1 - k_1) + k_1(1 - k_2)e^{-r(t_2-t_1)}]V.$$

Essentially, this is the value of a European call option maturing at t_1, where V is reduced by the present value of all competitive dividends anticipated over the entire life of the option and where the investment cost outlay, I, is reduced by the value of anticipated dividends discounted as of t_1. That is, the incumbent firm makes a preemptive investment I at t_1 and recovers at that time the competitive dividends, d_1 and $d_2e^{-r(t_2-t_1)}$, that would otherwise have been lost to the two competitors had they entered at t_1 and t_2, respectively.

If the firm were to exercise just before t_2 to preempt only the second competitor, then it would lose the first dividend to the first competitor but it would recover the second dividend upon preemption of the second competitor. Again, it can be seen that the value of this real opportunity is given by the Black-Scholes solution for a European call option (adjusted for constant payout, D) with maturity t_2, with the project's value V reduced by the present value of the anticipated dividends over the opportunity's entire life, and with the investment-cost outlay reduced by the second dividend recovered upon exercise at t_2 (i.e., with I replaced by $I'' = I - d_2$):

$$R^{t_2} = C(V', t_2, I''),   (9.6)$$

where V' is again given by equation 9.2 and where

$$I'' = I - (1 - k_2)k_1 V.$$

The firm may, of course, have the flexibility to consider exercising just before any one competitive arrival (in this case either t_1 or t_2), or just before T, whichever is more beneficial. The value of this flexibility (a pseudo-American call option) is given by[10]

$$R = \max(R^{t_1}, R^{t_2}, R^T),   (9.7)$$

where R^{t_1}, R^{t_2}, and R^T are as given in equations 9.5, 9.6, and 9.4, respectively.

Dominating Strategies under Anticipated Entry

The relative rankings or dominance relationships among the various scenarios represented in figure 9.1 serve to illustrate the optimal exercise of the deferrable project with early preemptive investment and the dominating investment strategies.

$C \} D$ (i.e., scenario C dominates scenario D)
The opportunity value at point C in the figure is $R_C = C(V, T, I)$, whereas the opportunity value at D is $R_D \equiv R^T = C(V', T, I)$. Clearly $C(V, T, I) \geq C(V', T, I)$ for $V \geq V'$, since a call option is more valuable for a higher value of the underlying asset, other things being equal. Intuitively, holding a shared opportunity until maturity despite competitive entry (scenario D) is less valuable than a similar opportunity in the absence of competition (i.e., a proprietary real option, as in scenario C).

$D \} B$
First observe that

$$R_C - R_D \leq R_A - R_B,$$

or, equivalently,

$$C - R^T \leq NPV - NPV'$$

(i.e., the option loss due to competitive erosion is less than or equal to the change in NPV).[11] With terms rearranged, this results in

$$R^T - \text{NPV}' \geq C - \text{NPV} \geq 0$$

(because a call option C is always at least as valuable as its immediate exercise value $V - I \equiv \text{NPV}$). Thus, $R^T \geq \text{NPV}'$ or $R_D \geq R_B$. Intuitively, if competitors will come in whether the firm invests early or not, it is preferable to wait rather than invest (i.e., exercise) immediately.

$E \} A$

Given that

$$R_E \geq \max(R^{t_1}, R^{t_2}) = \max(C(V', t_1, I), C(V', t_2, I''))$$

and

$$R_A = \text{NPV},$$

it is rather obvious that $R_E \geq R_A$. Intuitively, if early exercise at any time before a competitive arrival would have the desired preemptive effect, then it is preferable to exercise as late as possible to benefit from the intermediate resolution of uncertainty (as well as earn interest on the exercise cost), i.e., exercise just before a competitive arrival, t_1 or t_2, rather than kill the option immediately.

$A \} B$

NPV > NPV', since $V > V'$. Alternatively, since (as was shown above) $R_A - R_B \geq R_C - R_D$ and $R_C \geq R_D$, it must hold that

$$R_A - R_B \geq R_C - R_D \geq 0, \text{ i.e., } R_A \geq R_B.$$

It is intuitive that exercising this real option by committing capital immediately will be preferable if the investment succeeds in preempting competition.

The analysis so far results in two sets of dominance relationships: C } D } B, and E } A } B. (Here underscores indicate the dominating feasible scenarios.) Since our analysis focuses on a competitive environment, scenario C is infeasible. Thus, either scenario D (maintaining the option to wait until maturity despite competitive arrivals) or scenario E (exercising just before an anticipated competitive entry in order to preempt subsequent competitors) dominates the other scenarios. Whether D or E is the preferable scenario depends on the parameters of the particular situation facing the incumbent firm, and specifically on the relative magnitude of the anticipated competitive loss.

If $D \} E$ (that is, $R^T > \max(R^{t_1}, R^{t_2})$ or $C(V', T, I) > \max(C(V', t_1, I')$, $C(V', t_2, I''))$), the incumbent firm will be justified in waiting (i.e., maintaining the real option) in spite of the arrival of competitors.

If instead $E \} D$ or $R_C - R_E \geq R_C - R_D$ (that is, $\max(R^{t_1}, R^{t_2}) > R^T$), the firm is better off investing early, just before competitors arrive, in order to preempt their entry.

Note that the larger the anticipated loss in project value due to competition that can be preempted (i.e., the larger d_j or the lower k_j) and the more frequent the anticipated arrivals, it becomes relatively less valuable to wait (i.e., the lower is R^T relative to R^{t_1} and R^{t_2} or, alternatively, point D in figure 9.1 shifts down relatively more than point E as V' drops), other factors being constant. Consequently, it becomes more attractive to exercise the opportunity relatively early for preemptive reasons rather than allow it to erode in value at the hands of competitors.

In the case of such a deferrable opportunity with potential competitive damage, expressing the opportunity's total value or expanded NPV as

Expanded NPV

$\quad$ = Passive NPV + [Value of option to wait $\ -\ $ Competitive loss]

makes it clear that, in general, a firm is justified in commiting capital early to preempt exogenous competitive arrivals if the competitive loss preempted, here quantified as

$$R_C - R_D = C(V, T, I) - C(V', T, I),$$

exceeds the value of waiting sacrificed by early exercise or by the cost of killing the option early, $R_C - R_E$. This makes the option premium component of total value lower relative to the passive NPV component, a generalized condition for earlier exercise.

What is relevant in the timing of preemptive investments is the effect of competitive entry on the investment opportunity's total value (i.e., its expanded NPV), and not simply its effect on the passive NPV of its cash flows.[12] Consequently, in order for early exercise to be justified, the savings in a project's net present value resulting from an *immediate* ($t = 0$) preemptive investment, NPV $-$ NPV$'$ (or $R_A - R_B$), must actually exceed the cost of immediately killing the option to wait, $C(V, T, I) -$ NPV (or $R_C - R_A$).[13]

Note again how the options approach looks at uncertainty differently. Whereas conventional approaches typically view uncertainty as damaging the value of an investment's cash flows (NPV), the options approach views uncertainty as beneficial to option value. Thus, other factors being the same, lower project uncertainty implies lower option value of waiting relative to the competitive loss, and hence lower option premium relative to passive NPV.[14] This makes early exercise of less uncertain projects preferable. Similarly, delay is more beneficial, ceteris paribus, for more uncertain investment opportunities (even if their passive NPV is positive), unless the competitive loss is large and can be preempted.

In summary: Option-based analysis suggests that management may be justified in investing relatively early to preempt exogenous anticipated competitive arrivals when the anticipated competitive loss is large and can be preempted, when anticipated competitive entry is more frequent, when project uncertainty is lower, when the anticipated competitive loss preempted exceeds the option value of waiting sacrificed by early investment, or, more generally, when the option premium component of value is low relative to the passive NPV of the project's expected cash flows. Of course, the value of the option can be fully captured only if it is exercised in an optimal way, which is partly contingent on correct anticipation of competitive entry (and the use of proper managerial incentives and controls).

9.2 Uncertain (Random) Exogenous Competitive Arrivals (Poisson Jumps)

Although the analysis so far has been based on the assumption of deterministic timing of competitive entry, the options approach can be extended to handle uncertain exogenous competitive entry as well. In this section we relax the assumption of known (anticipated) timing to briefly illustrate the case where competitors arrive randomly according to an exogenous Poisson distribution. To keep the analysis simple, suppose initially that gross project value, V, follows the pure jump process

$$\frac{dV}{V} = (\alpha - D)\,dt + (k - 1)\,dN, \tag{9.8}$$

where α is the instantaneous actual expected return on the project, D is a proportional cash-flow (dividend-like) payout on an operating project (or a rate-of-return shortfall between the equilibrium total expected rate of return of a similar-risk traded financial asset, α^*, and the actual growth rate of a nontraded real asset). The uncertainty surrounding the random competitive arrivals, N, with instantaneous probability (intensity) λ, is described by the Poisson-jump process

$$dN = \begin{cases} 1 \text{ w.p. } \lambda\, dt \\ 0 \text{ w.p. } 1 - \lambda\, dt. \end{cases}$$

The total real opportunity value, assumed to be a function of V and t alone, would then follow the similar jump process

$$dR(V,t) = \begin{cases} R(kV,t) - R(V,t) \text{ w.p. } \lambda\, dt \text{ (if jump)} \\ R_V\, dV + R_t\, dt \text{ w.p. } 1 - \lambda\, dt \text{ (if no jump)}, \end{cases} \qquad (9.9)$$

where subscripts indicate partial derivatives.

Then, in a risk-neutral world equilibrium, it can be shown (see Trigeorgis 1990b) by extending an argument of Cox and Ross (1975), that the deferrable real opportunity value, $R(V,t)$, must satisfy the following partial differential equation subject to the stated condition:

$$(\alpha^* - D)VR_V + R_t - rR + \lambda[R(kV) - R] = 0 \qquad (9.10)$$

$$\text{s.t. } R(V,T) = \max(V_T - I, 0),$$

where the actual instantaneous growth rate, α, must equal (and be replaced by) the equivalent risk-neutral drift (or required equilibrium return in the competitive-jump world):

$$\alpha^* \equiv r + \lambda(1 - k),$$

where α^* is the equilibrium total expected rate of return required to induce investors to hold an equivalent-risk traded financial security in a risk-neutral world with random competitive jumps.

Thus, a real investment is considered to be in "competitive-jump equilibrium" in a risk-neutral world if it is expected to earn a return exceeding the riskless interest rate, r, by a premium equal to the expected proportional loss (or expected "dividend yield") caused by competitive arrivals, $\lambda(1 - k)$, where λ is the instantaneous probability of an arrival and where $(1 - k)$ is the proportional loss in project value (analogous to a "dividend yield").

The solution to equation 9.10 may be conveniently obtained by employing risk-neutral valuation from the equivalent system:

$$\frac{dV}{V} = [r + \lambda(1 - k) - D]\,dt + (k - 1)\,dN,$$

(9.11)

$$R(V, t) = e^{-r\tau}E[R(V, T)],$$

where $\tau \equiv T - t$ is the time to maturity. The solution to this system is given (see Trigeorgis 1990b) by

$$R(V, t) = Ve^{-D\tau}\Gamma(k\tau, n) - Ie^{-r\tau}\Gamma(\tau, n),$$

(9.12)

where

$$\Gamma(w, n) \equiv \int_w^\infty \gamma(s; \alpha = n + 1, \beta = 1)\,ds$$

is the Gamma complementary distribution function with parameters $\alpha = n + 1$ and $\beta = 1$, with

$$n = \left\| \frac{\ln(V/I) + [r + \lambda(1 - k)D]T}{\ln(1/k)} \right\|$$

and with $\|y\|$ the maximum integer less than y.

Note that both the market-structure parameter, k, and the competitive intensity, λ, affect the value of the real option R (via n and Γ), in addition to the common parameters (V, r, τ, and I) that enter into the Black-Scholes valuation. The comparative statics of the common parameters are similar to those in Black-Scholes valuation. However, in the case of random arrivals without preemption, the greater the drop in V due to a competitive arrival (the lower the k), or the higher the intensity, λ, the more valuable the insurance protection of the real option would be, if other factors were kept constant.

Trigeorgis (1990b) extends this to an equilibrium analysis with a mix of jump and diffusion processes in which equation 9.8 for the underlying process is replaced with the more general mixed diffusion-jump process

$$\frac{dV}{V} = (\alpha - D)\,dt + \sigma\,dz + (k - 1)\,dN,$$

(9.13)

where again α is the instantaneous actual expected return on the project, D is a proportional cash-flow (dividend-like) payout on an operating project, σ is the instantaneous standard deviation of project value, dz is a standard Wiener process, and dN follows the earlier Poisson-jump process.

Assuming that competitive arrivals (e.g., substitute product introductions) essentially affect the specific returns of the firm or its industry but not the entire market, so that the associated competitive jump risk may be diversified away by holding portfolios of firm securities across industries (or portfolios including competitor stocks), Trigeorgis (1990b) shows that the value of the deferrable shared real opportunity with exogenous random competitive arrivals is given by

$$R(V,t) = \sum_{N=0}^{\infty} \frac{e^{-\lambda\tau}(\lambda\tau)^N}{N!} C(V,t;r,\sigma^2,T,I,D+\delta), \tag{9.14}$$

where the last expression, $C(\ )$, is the Black-Scholes value for a (proprietary real) call option adjusted for a constant "dividend" payout $(D+\delta)$:

$$C(V,t;r,\sigma^2,T,I,D+\delta) = Ve^{(-D+\delta)\tau}N(d_1') - Ie^{-r\tau}N(d_2'),$$

where

$$d_1' = \frac{\ln(V/I) + [(r-D-\delta) + \frac{1}{2}\sigma^2]\tau}{\sigma\sqrt{\tau}},$$

$$d_2' = d_1' - \sigma\sqrt{\tau},$$

$\tau = T - t$ (time to maturity),

$\delta = \lambda(k-1) - (N/\tau)\ln k$ (competitive "dividend" payout),

D is the intermediate cash flow payout (as a proportion of V), and $N(\ )$ is the cumulative standard normal distribution function. In other words, the value of a deferrable shared real option with random competitive arrivals is a weighted sum, or an expected value over a Poisson distribution with intensity parameter $(\lambda\tau)$, of Black-Scholes values with a continuous "dividend payout" $(D+\delta)$. Thus, random competitive arrivals can be viewed as causing a continuous "dividend payout" δ (in addition to the project cash-flow payout, D) whose magnitude depends on competitive intensity, λ, and on the market-structure parameter, k. This competitive "dividend" is lost for the owner of the real option, much as a cash dividend is lost for the owner of a call option on a dividend-paying stock.[15]

Note that when there are no competitive jumps (i.e., when $k = 1$) the competitive "dividend payout" disappears ($\delta = 0$) and the value of the shared real option, $R(V,t)$, given in equation 9.14, reduces to the (cash-flow dividend-adjusted) Black-Scholes value for a proprietary option, $C(V,t;r,\sigma^2,T,I,D)$, given in equation 9.3.

The comparative statics of the deferrable shared real opportunity value with uncertain competitive arrivals, R, with respect to the common parameters V, I, r, τ, and σ are again the same as in the Black-Scholes model.

Furthermore, the effects of k and λ are the same as in the earlier pure-jump formulation: the insurance protection and the shared real-option value are higher, other factors being constant, the larger the drop in V (or the lower the k) due to a competitive arrival, and the higher the competitive intensity, λ, for a project earning the "jump equilibrium" return, α^*. This is another example where the options approach gives a different angle on uncertainty and related factors than more conventional approaches. If a nontraded real asset has a below-equilibrium return shortfall, however, other factors (particularly dividend-like effects) may not in fact remain constant (see Trigeorgis 1990b).

9.3 Endogenous Competitive Reaction in Strategic Investment[16]

In this section we relax the exogeneity assumption to deal with strategic games with competition and show how real-option valuation can be supplemented with game-theoretic tools from the field of industrial organization to model strategic investment involving endogenous competitive reaction. Assuming contrarian quantity competition that involves downward-sloping reaction functions, we will see how to develop the equilibrium actions (quantities), profits, and state project values under the various market structures to be used in the binomial option-valuation tree. The case of reciprocating price competition where reaction curves are upward sloping can be analyzed similarly (see Smit and Trigeorgis 1993). Numerical examples are then used to illustrate the implementation of different investment strategies.

Consider first the two-stage game in extensive form presented in figure 9.2. In the first stage, a pioneering firm must decide whether or not to make a strategic investment commitment (e.g., in R&D or good will) that may enhance its relative competitive position in the later stage of the market. This is compared with the base-case alternative of no strategic investment. The alternative actions of the pioneering firm to make the strategic investment or not (base case) are reflected by the branches in the first stage. The dynamics of market demand (Θ) in the second stage, reflected by nature's up (u) or down (d) moves, result in a range of potential investment opportunity values over time.[17] Assuming that entry barriers are temporary and that the structure of the market will result in a duopoly, each of two firms (A and B) may invest in followup projects during the second stage. To encompass various market-structure possibilities, the second stage itself is assumed to consist of two periods (1 and 2). Given market demand moves $\Theta\{u, d\}$ in each period during the second stage,

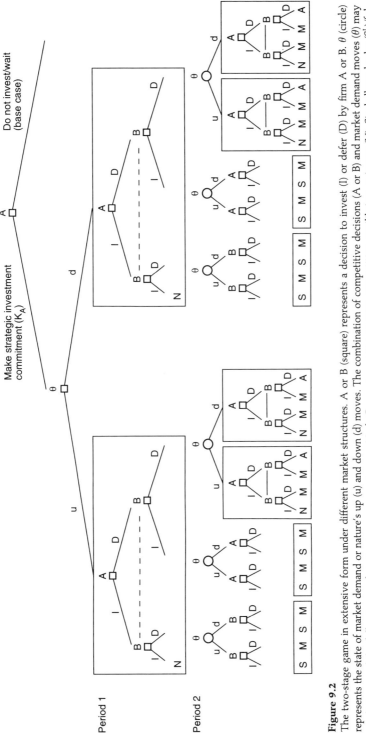

Figure 9.2
The two-stage game in extensive form under different market structures. A or B (square) represents a decision to invest (I) or defer (D) by firm A or B. θ (circle) represents the state of market demand or nature's up (u) and down (d) moves. The combination of competitive decisions (A or B) and market demand moves (θ) may result in one of the following market-structure game outcomes: Nash-Cournot quantity or price competition equilibrium outcome (N), Stackelberg leader (S^L)/follower (S^F) outcome (S), monopolist outcome (M), abandonment (0 value) (A), deferment flexibility (option value) (D).

the competitors' actions to invest (I) or to defer investment (D) in the followup project are represented by the branches A{I, D} and B{I, D}. When both firms decide to invest simultaneously in the second stage (I, I), the game ends in Nash equilibrium (N); when both firms choose to defer (D, D) under low realizations of demand, nature (Θ) moves again and the game is repeated; finally, when one firm invests first, acting as a Stackelberg leader (S^L)—or in some cases a monopolist (M)—market demand is revealed again and the competitor may then decide to invest later (as a Stackelberg follower, S^F) or to abandon (A). The competitive strategy of each firm consists of mapping the information about its competitor's actions and the development of market demand (up or down moves in Θ) to an optimal investment action by the firm. The equilibrium set of strategies can be found by backward induction, starting with the future payoffs (state net project values) of a given competitive structure and working backward using binomial risk-neutral valuation.

Suppose, for example, that project value, V_t, derives from equilibrium profits, $\pi(\Theta)$, which are a function of a market-demand parameter Θ that follows a binomial process in complete markets (spanning the profit dynamics), moving up to $\Theta^+ \equiv u\Theta$ or down to $\Theta^- \equiv d\Theta$ over the next period. In the next period, the value of a contingent claim on project value, C, will then move up (C^+) or down (C^-) in line with $V_{t+1}(\Theta^+)$ or $V_{t+1}(\Theta^-)$. As was noted in chapter 3, under risk-neutral valuation the current value of the claim can be determined from its expected future up and down state values discounted at the risk-free interest rate (r), with expectations taken over risk-neutral probabilities (p):[18]

$$C = \frac{pC^+ + (1-p)C^-}{1+r}. \tag{9.15}$$

Modeling Market-Structure Equilibrium Outcomes under Quantity Competition

Assume that firm A (the incumbent or pioneer) can make a first-stage strategic investment, K_A, which may reduce its second-stage marginal operating cost, c_A. Only firm A operates in the first stage, whereas in the second stage it competes with firm B (the entrant) in quantity. Exogenous uncertainty in future market demand is characterized by fluctuations in the demand parameter, Θ_t. In the second-stage game, assume for simplicity the linear demand function

$$P(Q, \Theta_t) = \Theta_t - (Q_A + Q_B), \tag{9.16}$$

where Θ_t is the demand-shift parameter (assumed to follow a log-normal diffusion process, or a binomial process in discrete time). Q_A and Q_B are the quantities produced by firms A and B, respectively, and $P(Q)$ is the common market price as a function of total quantity ($Q = Q_A + Q_B$). The total variable production cost for each firm i ($i = $ A or B) is

$$C(Q_i) = c_i Q_i + \tfrac{1}{2} q_i Q_i^2, \tag{9.17}$$

where c_i and q_i are the linear and quadratic cost coefficients (or the fixed and variable coefficients of the marginal cost function, $c_i + q_i Q_i$) for firm i. The value of second-stage annual operating profits for each firm i is given by

$$\pi_i(Q_i, Q_j, \Theta_t) = P\,Q_i - C(Q_i)$$
$$= [(\Theta_t - c_i) - Q_j]Q_i - (1 + \tfrac{1}{2} q_i)Q_i^2. \tag{9.18}$$

The state net present value of the followup investment for firm i, assuming perpetual operating cash flows, a required outlay I, and a constant risk-adjusted discount rate k in the last stage, can then be obtained from[19]

$$\text{NPV}_i = \frac{\pi_i}{k} - I. \tag{9.19}$$

Under contrarian quantity competition, the reaction function of each firm is downward sloping. With firm i's ($i = $ A, B) own profits maximized over its quantity, given that its competitor produces Q_j (setting $\partial \pi_i / \partial Q_i = 0$), each firm's reaction function is[20,21]

$$R_i(Q_j) = \frac{\Theta_t - c_i - Q_j}{2 + q_i}. \tag{9.20}$$

If both firms make a simultaneous investment in the second stage (I, I), a Nash Cournot-quantity equilibrium outcome will result. The equilibrium quantities, Q_A^* and Q_B^*, are obtained by equating (being at the intersection of) the reaction functions of the two firms:

$$Q_i^* = \frac{(\Theta_t - c_i)(2 + q_j) - (\Theta_t - c_j)}{(2 + q_i)(2 + q_j) - 1}. \tag{9.21}$$

In the case that firm i's early strategic investment reduces its cost (c_i) below its competitor's (c_j), then $Q_i^* > Q_j^*$. If we simplify by setting $q_i = q_j = q = 0$, this asymmetric Nash-Cournot equilibrium quantity for firm i reduces to

$$Q_j^* = \tfrac{1}{3}(\Theta_t - 2c_i + c_j).$$

For example, if firm A's early strategic investment makes $c_A = 0$,

$$Q_A^* = \tfrac{1}{3}(\Theta_t + c_B) > \tfrac{1}{3}(\Theta_t - 2c_B) = Q_B^*.$$

Substituting back into profit equation 9.18, again assuming $q_i = q_j = 0$, gives the following Nash-Cournot equilibrium profit for firm i ($i =$ A, B):

$$\pi_i^* = \frac{(\Theta_t - 2c_i + c_j)^2}{9}. \tag{9.22}$$

Note that each firm i will eventually be profitable, net of its second-stage outlay I, if demand is such that its NPV, determined from equations 9.19 and 9.22, is positive (in this case, if $\Theta_t \geq 3\sqrt{kI} + 2c_i - c_j$). If demand is very low for either firm to operate profitably, they will both wait; if $\Theta_t < 3\sqrt{kI} + 2c_j - c_i$ firm j will be unprofitable ($NPV_j < 0$) and firm i can earn monopoly profits.[22]

In case firm i invests first and firm j defers investment until the next period (I, D), the follower will set its quantity having first observed the leader's output according to its reaction function, $R_j(Q_i)$, as in equation 9.20. The Stackelberg leader i will then maximize $\pi_i(Q_i, R_j(Q_i))$ over Q_i, taking the follower's reaction function $R_j(Q_i)$ as given; this will result in the equilibrium quantity

$$Q_i = \frac{(\Theta_t - c_i)(2 + q_j) - (\Theta_t - c_j)}{(2 + q_i)(2 + q_j) - 2}. \tag{9.23}$$

If we assume for simplicity that $q_i = q_j = 0$, the Stackelberg leader's profits then become

$$\pi_i = \frac{(\Theta_t - 2c_i + c_j)^2}{8}. \tag{9.24}$$

It can be seen that the follower's equilibrium quantity and profits are lower than the leader's ($Q_j < Q_i, \pi_j < \pi_i$).[23] Further, if demand is low ($\Theta_t < 4\sqrt{kI} + 2c_j - c_i$) the Stackelberg follower will be unable to cover its investment outlay I ($NPV_j < 0$) and will not enter; the Stackelberg leader's profits can therefore improve (from those of equation 9.24) to those of a monopolist.

The equilibrium quantities (Q_i^*), profits (π_i^*, assuming $q_i = q_j = 0$), and state net project values (NPV_i^*) for the various market structures (Nash, monopolist, Stackelberg leader and follower) under contrarian quantity competition are summarized in table 9.1.

Table 9.1
Equilibrium quantities, profits, and state project values for various market structures under contrarian quantity competition in the second stage.

Action[a] (A, B)	Market structure N/M/S/A/D	Equilibrium quantity Q_i^*	Equilibrium profit[b] π_i^*	State project value[c] NPV_i	Demand state Θ_t
Second-Stage Game					
(DI, DI) (II, II)	Nash Cournot (N)	$\dfrac{(\Theta_t - c_i)(2+q_j) - (\Theta_t - c_j)}{(2+q_i)(2+q_j) - 1}$	$\dfrac{(\Theta_t - 2c_i + c_j)^2}{9}$	$\dfrac{(\Theta_t - 2c_i + c_j)^2}{9k} - I$	$\geq 3\sqrt{kI} + 2c_i - c_j$
(DI, DD) (II, DD)	Monopolist (M)	$\dfrac{\Theta_t - c_i}{2+q_i}$ $(Q_j = 0)$	$\dfrac{(\Theta_t - c_i)^2}{4}$ $(\pi_j \leq 0)$	$\dfrac{(\Theta_t - c_i)^2}{4k} - I$	$< 3\sqrt{kI} + 2c_i - c_j$
(II, DI)	Stackelberg leader (S^L)/ Monopolist (M)	$\dfrac{(\Theta_t - c_i)(2+q_j) - (\Theta_t - c_j)}{(2+q_i)(2+q_j) - 2}$	$\dfrac{(\Theta_t - 2c_i + c_j)^2}{8}$	$\dfrac{(\Theta_t - 2c_i + c_j)^2}{8k} - I'$	$\geq 4\sqrt{kI} + 2c_i - c_j$ $(< 4\sqrt{kI} + 2c_j - c_i)$
(DI, II)	Stackelberg follower (S^F)	$\dfrac{(\Theta_t - c_i)(2+q_j) - (\Theta_t - c_i)}{(2+q_i)(2+q_j)}$	$\dfrac{(\Theta_t - 2c_i + c_j)^2}{16}$	$\dfrac{(\Theta_t - 2c_i + c_j)^2}{16k} - I$	$\geq 4\sqrt{kI} + 2c_j - c_i$
(DD, DD)	abandon (A)	0	0	0	
Period 1					
(I, I)	Nash Cournot (N)	$\dfrac{(\Theta_t - c_i)(2+q_j) - (\Theta_t - c_j)}{(2+q_i)(2+q_j) - 1}$	$\dfrac{(\Theta_t - 2c_i + c_j)^2}{9}$	$\dfrac{(\Theta_t - 2c_i + c_j)^2}{9k} - I$	
(I, D)	Monopolist (M)/ Stackelberg leader (S^L)	$\dfrac{\Theta_t - c_i}{2+q_i}$	$\pi_m = \dfrac{(\Theta_t - c_i)^2}{4}$	$\dfrac{p\,NPV_u^* + (1-p)NPV_d^*}{1+r} + \pi_m$	
(D, D) (D, I)	defer (D)	0	0	$\dfrac{p\,NPV_u^* + (1-p)NPV_d^*}{1+r}$	

a. During period 1, (A, B) means that firm A took action A while competitor firm B took action B. During the entire second stage, (AA', BB') means that firm A took action A in period 1 and A' in period 2, while firm B took action B in period 1 and B' in period 2.

b. Calculated from $\pi_i = P_i Q_i - C(Q_i)$, assuming for simplicity $q_i = q_j = q = 0$.

c. Determined in the last stage from $NPV_i = \max(\pi_i/k - I, 0)$, where I is the required outlay and k is the risk-adjusted discount rate. In the first period, it may be determined from future expanded (strategic) net present values (NPV^*) in the up and down states using backward binomial risk-neutral valuation.

Numerical (R&D) Example with Different Competitive Strategies

In this section we will utilize the above competitive equilibrium model values for the different demand states in a backward binomial risk-neutral valuation tree to illustrate the different competitive strategies with a simple numerical example from research and development. Suppose pioneer firm A can enhance its competitive position to capitalize on future growth opportunities by an early R&D investment of $K_A = 110$. In the second stage, either firm A or firm B can invest an amount $I = 100$ in subsequent cash-generating projects, depending on subsequent demand (Θ) moves (where the demand parameter has initial value $\Theta_0 = 14$ and is assumed to move up or down with binomial parameters u = 1.25 and d = 0.80). If demand turns out to be favorable (i.e., Θ moves up), management will invest in followup capacity to exploit the commercial benefits of R&D; if demand turns out low, it may not invest. The risk-free interest rate (r) is assumed to be 10% (while the risk-adjusted discount rate in the last stage is estimated at $k = 13\%$). If firm A does not make the strategic R&D investment (the base case), the two firms are assumed to have symmetric second-stage operating costs of $c_A = c_B = 3$.

The competitive strategies can be derived by utilizing the state net project values of table 9.1 within the two-stage game of figure 9.2. The state project values for the base-case alternative (no strategic investment) in both periods during the last stage of the game are shown in figure 9.3.[24] Generally, two different strategies can result, as shown in figure 9.4, depending on whether the resulting benefits are proprietary or shared.[25]

Proprietary Investment: Committing and Offensive Strategy
(Positive Strategic Effect)
The top panel of figure 9.4 illustrates the first period of the two-stage R&D game for the case of proprietary investment.[26] In this case, making the strategic R&D investment commitment in the first stage results in a *proprietary* operating cost advantage for firm A when that firm is investing

Figure 9.3
The base-case two-stage game in extensive form under different market structures. A or B (square) represents a decision to invest (I) or defer (D) by firm A or B. θ (circle) represents the state of market demand or nature's up (u) and down (d) moves. The combination of competitive decisions (A or B) and market demand moves (θ) may result in one of the following market-structure game outcomes: Nash Cournot quantity or price competition equilibrium outcome (N), Stackelberg leader (S^L)/follower (S^F) outcome (S), monopolist outcome (M), abandonment (0 value) (A), deferment flexibility (option value) (D).

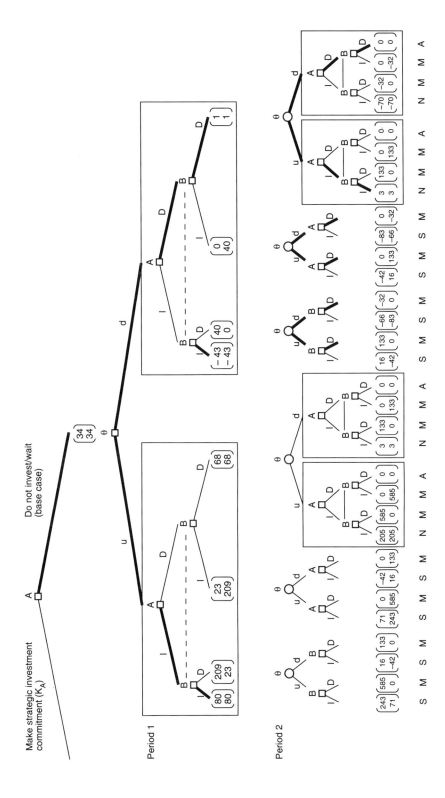

in followup capacity in the second stage. Specifically, the second-stage operating cost for firm A is reduced from 3 to 0 ($c_A = 0$) if it invests in R&D, while for firm B the second-stage operating cost remains at 3 ($c_B = 3$)—as compared to the base case, $c_A = c_B = 3$, when the firm does not invest in R&D. This up-front R&D investment commitment makes the pioneer firm tougher in the second stage, taking market share away from firm B under contrarian competitive competition. The reaction functions are illustrated in the left panel of figure 9.5, where a proprietary investment causes firm A's reaction function to shift to the right, changing the base-case Nash equilibrium outcome from N_0 to N_P. The equilibrium quantity (Q^*) and profit values (π^*) are shown in table 9.2 for the Nash, Stackelberg leader, and monopoly structures. The R&D commitment strategy in this proprietary example results in a positive strategic effect.

The top panel of figure 9.4 presents the resulting valuation of the backward binomial process, given the numbers assumed for the proprietary investment above. Consider first the subgame (in the second box) concerning investment in followup capacity, following a decision to make the strategic R&D investment and a downward market demand realization ($\Theta = d$). In this state, a followup investment action (I) by firm A dominates a deferral (D) action, since it results in a higher net value for A's followup project whether competitor firm B decides to invest (I) or to defer (D): 72 (Nash-Cournot value if both invest) > 35 (Stackelberg value if A defers and B invests); and 155 (monopolist or Stackelberg leader value, depending on whether B defers again or invests later) > 123 (option value if both defer). Knowing that firm A has a dominating strategy to invest anyway, competing firm B would choose to defer (obtaining a value of 0 rather than -77). Thus, firm A would earn monopoly profits, resulting in net present values of (155, 0) for the followup projects of firms A and B, respectively. However, if demand moves up ($\Theta = u$), as in the first box, total market demand would be sufficient for a Nash-Cournot equilibrium outcome where both firms, regardless of the other's actions, have dominant strategies to invest (I) in followup projects, resulting in values of (259, 13) for firms A and B respectively.

Using backward binomial risk-neutral valuation as in equation 9.15 results in expected growth option values of (191, 6) when firm A makes an

Figure 9.4
Competitive investment strategies in the R&D example: Proprietary versus shared strategic investment under contrarian quantity competition. Above: Proprietary investment—committing and offensive strategy (positive strategic effect). Below: Shared investment—flexible and offensive strategy (negative strategic effect).

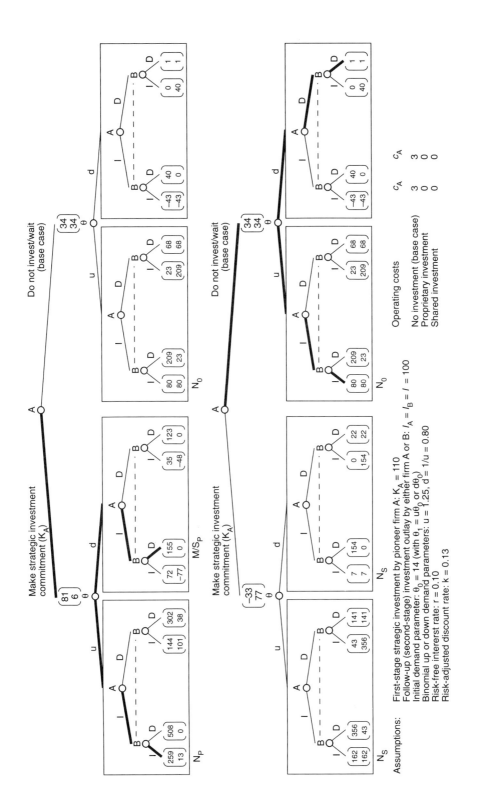

up-front strategic investment commitment.[27] Thus, after we subtract the required investment outlay of $K_A = 110$, the R&D investment for pioneer firm A results in an expanded (strategic) net present value (NPV*) of 81, as shown under the left branch in the top panel of figure 9.4. Since the base-case alternative of not making the strategic R&D investment or waiting similarly results in expected equilibrium values of $(34, 34)$, firm A would find it optimal to make the strategic R&D investment ($81 > 34$).

The heavy branches in figure 9.4 indicate the optimal actions along the equilibrium path. Pioneer firm A should invest immediately, committing to an offensive R&D strategy (i.e., invest K_A in the R&D project in stage 1). It should then make a followon commercialization investment (I) in the second stage regardless of the market demand. If market demand moves favorably ($\Theta = u$), both firms would invest resulting in a Nash Cournot-quantity equilibrium value for the pioneer (259); if market demand is unfavorable ($\Theta = d$), competitor firm B would not invest and firm A's early R&D investment can result in a monopoly profit value (155).

Shared Investment: Flexible and Offensive Strategy (Negative Strategic Effect)
Now consider the opposite case, where R&D results in a shared cost advantage (as shown in the second panels of figures 9.4 and 9.5. Here strategic R&D investment by firm A results in a more cost-effective technology that both competitors can exploit in the later stage of the market. Specifically, suppose that if firm A invests in R&D the second-stage operating costs for both firms are reduced ($c_A = c_B = 0$) relative to the base case of $c_A = c_B = 3$ when there is no strategic investment. In this case, commitment may place the pioneer firm at a strategic disadvantage by paying the cost for creating valuable investment opportunities for the competitor, particularly if it enhances the competitor's ability and incentive to respond aggressively in the later stage of the market.

The incumbent firm in this case should pursue a flexible, offensive strategy of not investing in R&D but retaining a flexible "wait and see" position in a later stage of the market (figure 9.4). If $\Theta = u$, each firm would find it dominating to invest (I) irrespective of the other's actions, which would result in a symmetric Nash-Cournot equilibrium outcome of $(80, 80)$; if $\Theta = d$, however, both firms may choose to defer and obtain $(1,1)$.[28] Backward binomial valuation thus gives symmetric initial expected values of $(34, 34)$. Given that R&D investment would result in initial equilibrium values of $(-33, 77)$, firm A would choose to wait.[29] The strategic effect in this case is negative.

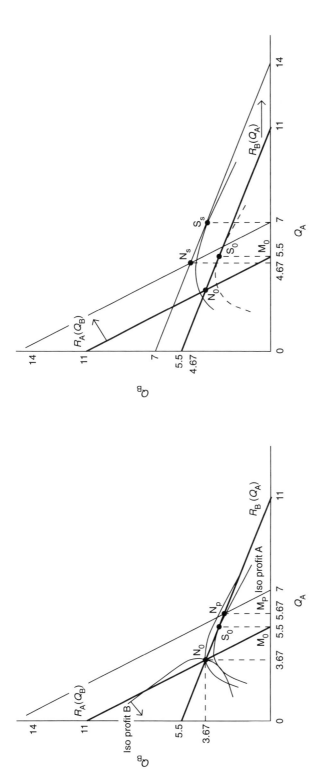

Figure 9.5
Equilibrium Nash, Stackelberg, and monopoly outcomes under the no-strategic-investment (base case), proprietary, or shared investment cases, assuming contrarian quantity competition (downward-sloping reaction curves). The demand for each firm ($i = A, B$) is of the form $P_i(Q_A, Q_B, \Theta_t) = \Theta_t - (Q_A + Q_B)$, with $\Theta_0 = 14$ ($u = 1.25$, $d = 0.8$), and the total variable production cost for firm i is of the form $c(Q_i) = c_iQ_i$. If no strategic investment: Base-case operating costs $c_A = c_B = c = 3$ (base-case Nash equilibrium at N_0). If proprietary investment/tough position: $c_A = 0$($c_B = 3$), R_A shifts to right (at $N_p Q_A^*$ ↑, Q_B^* ↓) and π_A ↑. If shared investment/accommodating position: $c_B = c_A = 0$, R_B and R_A shift to right (at $N_S Q_B^*$ ↑) and π_B ↓.

Table 9.2

Pioneer firm A	Nash Cournot outcome			Stackelberg leader			Monopoly	
	N_0	N_p	N_s	S_0	S_p	S_s	M_0	M_p
Quantity (Q_A^*)	$\frac{1}{3}(\Theta_t - c_B)$	$\frac{1}{3}(\Theta_t + c_B)$	$\frac{1}{3}\Theta_t$	$\frac{1}{2}(\Theta_t - c)$	$\frac{1}{2}(\Theta_t + c_B)$	$\frac{1}{2}\Theta_t$	$\frac{1}{2}(\Theta_t - c_A)$	$\frac{1}{2}\Theta_t$
base demand ($\Theta_0 = 14$)	3.667	5.667	4.667	5.5	8.5	7	5.5	7
up ($\Theta_1 = u\Theta_0 = 17.5$)	4.833	6.833	5.833	7.25	10.25	8.75	7.25	8.75
Profit (π_A^*)	$\frac{1}{9}(\Theta_t - c_B)^2$	$\frac{1}{9}(\Theta_t + c_B)^2$	$\frac{1}{9}\Theta_t^2$	$\frac{1}{8}(\Theta_t - c)^2$	$\frac{1}{8}(\Theta_t + c_B)^2$	$\frac{1}{8}\Theta_t^2$	$\frac{1}{4}(\Theta_t - c_A)^2$	$\frac{1}{4}\Theta_t^2$
base demand ($\Theta_0 = 14$)	13.44	32.11	21.77	15.125	36.125	24.50	30.25	49
up ($\Theta_1 = u\Theta_0 = 17.5$)	23.364	46.69	34.03	26.28	52.53	38.28	52.56	76.56

Notation: N_0, N_p, N_s are the Nash, S_0, S_p, S_s the Stackelberg equilibrium outcomes for the zero, proprietary, and shared-investment cases; M_0 and M_p are the base-case and proprietary Monopoly outcomes. $R_j(Q_i)$ is the reaction function of firm j given the quantity of firm i (Q_i), $i = A$, B. Q_i^* and π_i^* fluctuate with the state of demand Θ_t.

These examples, in which the benefits of R&D can be made proprietary or may be shared with competition, are seen to result in opposite strategic effects and different competitive strategies. If the resulting benefits are proprietary firm A should invest early, but if the investment is shared it may do better by pursuing a flexible "wait and see" strategy. The proprietary or shared nature of the benefits of the strategic investment may also determine the type of investment strategy to be pursued under recip-rocating price competition. However, reciprocating price competition can result in a reversal of the sign of the strategic effect (negative for the pro-prietary and positive for the shared investment), and in opposite invest-ment strategies, relative to the contrarian quantity competition case (see Smit and Trigeorgis 1993). Under reciprocating competition, firm A may be better off not making an immediate strategic investment if the benefits are proprietary, in order to avoid intense price competition; a hurt com-petitor can retaliate, damaging both players. Firm A should make an im-mediate strategic investment, however, if the benefits are shared and the competitor would respond positively to an accommodating pricing strat-egy that would increase profit margins for both competitors.

9.4   Implications and Conclusions

In this chapter we examined the impact of competition on investment op-portunity value using option methodology and basic game-theoretic prin-ciples. In sections 9.1 and 9.2. we focused on the optimal timing of project initiation under exogenous competitive entry. Of course, consistent with option pricing, an incumbent firm, in the absence of competition and other costs to waiting, would delay initiating a project. As is recognized in the literature, however, the presence of competition may speed up a firm's planned investment. We saw that in the case of early investment, which can preempt anticipated exogenous competitive arrivals, option valuation may enable management to determine whether (and when) to invest early for preemptive reasons or to wait despite anticipated competitive erosion. Such preemptable anticipated competitive entry was seen to be analogous to the effect of known dividends on American call options. We also saw how option-based analysis can be extended to value investment oppor-tunities with uncertain exogenous competitive arrivals modeled as Pois-son jumps. Again, random competitive arrivals could be viewed as having an impact analogous to a continuous dividend payout, depending on competitive intensity and market structure.

The last section employed basic game-theoretic principles from industrial organization to show how to endogenize competitive reactions and capture strategic effects under different market structures. Based on such a combination of real-options valuation and game-theoretic principles of industrial organization, we could distinguish various competitive investment strategies, depending on the nature of competitive reaction and whether the resulting benefits are proprietary or shared. For example, we found the following under contrarian quantity competition:

When the benefits of strategic investment are proprietary, the pioneering firm should commit to an offensive strategy. Early commitment makes the firm tougher in the second stage by creating a proprietary advantage when it is investing in followup projects. If competitive actions (quantities) are substitutes, the competitor will retreat in the later stage and the pioneering firm can become a leader as demand grows.

When the benefits of strategic investment are shared and contrarian competition would respond aggressively, the pioneering firm should not invest immediately; it should follow a flexible "wait and see" strategy. By delaying strategic investment, the pioneering firm prevents its competitor from exploiting the resulting shared benefits to grow at its expense.

However, under reciprocating price competition (see Smit and Trigeorgis 1993), the above effects can be reversed. The optimal competitive strategy may thus depend not only on the stance of the pioneering firm and the type of investment (proprietary or shared) but also on the nature of the competitor's reaction. The marriage of real-options valuation with game-theoretic principles of industrial organization may simultaneously facilitate the determination of different market-structure equilibrium outcomes in the various states of demand within a binomial valuation decision tree and a proper accounting of the interdependencies among the early strategic investment and sequential followon investment decisions in a competitive interactive setting.

Suggested Readings

Fudenberg, D., and J. Tirole. 1984. "The fat-cat effect, the puppy-dog ploy, and the lean and hungry look." *American Economic Review* 74 (May): 361–366.

Kester, W. C. 1984. "Today's options for tomorrow's growth." *Harvard Business Review* 62, no. 2: 153–160.

Kester, W. C. 1993. "Turning growth options into real assets." In *Capital Budgeting under Uncertainty*, ed. R. Aggarwal. Prentice-Hall.

McDonald, R., and D. Siegel. 1986. "The value of waiting to invest." *Quarterly Journal of Economics* 101, no. 4: 707–727.

Smit, H., and L. Ankum. 1993. "A real options and game-theoretic approach to corporate investment strategy under competition." *Financial Management* 22, no. 3: 241–250.

Smit, H., and L. Trigeorgis. 1993. Flexibility and Commitment in Strategic Investment. Working paper, Tinbergen Institute, Erasmus University, Rotterdam.

Trigeorgis, L. 1991. "Anticipated competitive entry and early preemptive investment in deferrable projects." *Journal of Economics and Business* 43, no. 2: 143–156.

10   Numerical Analysis

This chapter reviews various standard numerical procedures for solving complex option problems when analytic solutions are not available (e.g., simulation and explicit or implicit finite-difference methods) and then it describes a new, log-transformed binomial lattice approach for valuing complex capital investments with multiple interacting real options. Simulation is rather simple and flexible (e.g., in handling different stochastic processes) and allows the relevant risk-neutral probability distributions and expectations to be generated. It is generally useful in European-type options when the option payoff is complex and dependent on the history of the underlying asset, and it is more efficient when there are several underlying state variables. As a forward-moving technique, however, it is not as useful for American-type options involving early exercise or other types of intermediate (flexible) decisions or in determining optimal policies. In the latter case, finite-difference methods and lattice approaches (such as the binomial method) that follow a backward, dynamic-programming-type process are generally more appropriate.

Finite-difference methods can be used to value American as well as European options, and are more efficient when a whole set of starting (time-0) option values must be calculated. They can also handle several state variables in a multi-dimensional grid, although not very efficiently. Special care must be exercised in choosing an appropriate set of finite-difference approximations to the partial derivatives to avoid problems of stability and consistency (accuracy). If properly formulated, certain finite-difference schemes can be seen to be equivalent to dynamic programming. In general, finite-difference methods may not be readily used with history-dependent payoffs, and cannot be used at all when the partial differential equations describing the option value dynamics cannot be specified. Their implementation is more mechanical and affords less intuition than lattice approaches.

Lattice approaches are generally more intuitive, simpler, and more flexible in handling different stochastic processes, option payoffs, early exercise or other intermediate decisions, several underlying variables, etc. Their main limitation is their inability to handle more than one starting price at a time. A log-transformed binomial lattice approach is suggested here to overcome problems of consistency, stability, and efficiency encountered in other numerical methods. This method handles well real options with a series of investment outlays or exercise prices (compound options), non-proportional cash flows (dividends), exogenous jumps (e.g., competitive arrivals), and interactions among a variety of real options. Comparisons among several numerical methods regarding accuracy, consistency, stability, and efficiency are also given.

Earlier chapters presented closed-form solutions in some special real-option situations that are amenable to analytic modeling. However, in the more typical, complex real-life situations, such as those involving multiple interacting real options, analytic solutions may not exist and one may not always be able to write down a set of partial differential equations describing the underlying stochastic processes. Nevertheless, whether analytic solutions are available or not, the ability to value such complex option situations is considerably enhanced with various computational methods, most of which take advantage of risk-neutral valuation. Indeed, the key to efficient numerical computation of option values is typically the ability to use risk-neutral valuation, rather than whether analytic solutions exist or not.

In general, there are two types of numerical techniques than can be used in option valuation: those that approximate the underlying stochastic processes directly (these are generally more intuitive) and those that approximate the resulting partial differential equations. The first category includes Monte Carlo simulation as used by Boyle (1977) and various lattice approaches, such as the standard multiplicative binomial approximation of Cox, Ross, and Rubinstein (1979). Boyle (1988) shows how lattice approaches can be extended to handle two state variables, while Hull and White (1988a) suggest a control-variate technique to improve computational efficiency when a similar derivative asset with an analytic solution is available. Examples of the second category include numerical integration (Parkinson 1977) and implicit or explicit finite-difference schemes (Brennan 1979; Brennan and Schwartz 1977a, 1978; Majd and Pindyck 1987). A number of analytic approximations are also available: Geske and Johnson (1984) proposed a compound-option analytic polynomial approximation; Barone-Adesi and Whaley (1987) used a quadratic

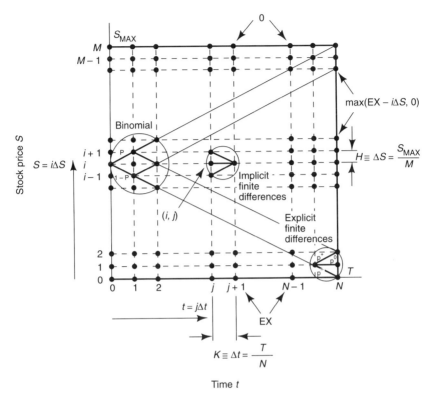

Figure 10.1
Stock price versus time for numerical approximation.

approximation (originally suggested in MacMillan 1986), and Johnson (1983), Blomeyer (1986), and others have used various problem-specific heuristic approximations. A review of some of these techniques is provided here; for other comprehensive reviews of numerical techniques, see Geske and Shastri 1985 and Hull 1993.

Approximation techniques are typically implemented in a grid of state space (e.g., stock price or asset value) versus time, such as the one shown in figure 10.1. The time until maturity, T, is usually divided into N equally spaced smaller time intervals of length $K \equiv \Delta t = T/N$, while the state (stock price) space is divided into M equally spaced subintervals of length $H \equiv \Delta S = S_{MAX}/M$, where S_{MAX} is a reasonable upper bound for the stock price (e.g., for a put option it is sufficiently high that the put is practically worthless; $S_{MIN} = 0$ by limited liability). Thus, the stock price S at time t (S_t) is given by $S = i\Delta S$ and $t = j\Delta t$, or by point (i, j) on the grid, where i is the integer index of the state variable corresponding to the net number of up steps less down steps (each of length H) and j is the integer number of time steps (each of length K). The corresponding value of an option, $F(S, t)$, at state-time point (i, j) is denoted $F_{i,j} \equiv F(i\Delta S, j\Delta t)$.

The step sizes, H and K, are small, and when considering limiting processes they are made to approach zero as the number of steps is increased. In practice, the step sizes are selected so as to ensure an accurate, stable, and computationally efficient convergence. By *accuracy* or *consistency* we mean that the discrete-time process used for computation has the same mean and variance for every time-step size as the underlying continuous process. *Numerical stability* means that the approximation errors in the computations will be dampened rather than amplified, and *efficiency* refers to the number of operations or the amount of computing time needed for a given approximation accuracy.[1] The ratio of the time step to the square of the stock-price step (the *mesh ratio*, $m \equiv K/H^2$) can be crucial for the accuracy and stability of the numeric approximation. This is the case, e.g., for the finite-difference approximation schemes whose grid is rectangular (see figure 10.1).

In a rectangular grid, in addition to the terminal condition, the option must satisfy lower and upper boundary conditions (when S reaches 0 or S_{MAX}, respectively). In the case of a put option, for example, all the nodes at the lower (horizontal) boundary (at $i = 0$) have an option value equal to the exercise price (EX), whereas the upper boundary condition (at all the nodes with $i = M$) is 0. Such boundary conditions are not necessary (i.e., the upper and lower bounds need not be reached) for the methods approximating the underlying stochastic process directly, such as for simulation or the binomial lattice approaches. These methods instead rely on a conditional starting price. In a binomial lattice, for example, only the nodes in a triangular grid conditional on the starting price, $S_0 = i\Delta S$, are used (see figure 10.1). The terminal boundary, of course, is needed for all the numerical methods. In the case of the put option, the terminal boundary values would be given by $\max(EX - i\Delta S, 0)$ at all the end nodes ($j = N$).

Among the various numerical approximation techniques used in option valuation, the binomial lattice approaches are generally more intuitive and better suited to valuing complex projects with multiple options, investment outlays, and dividend-like effects. As noted, the Cox-Ross-Rubinstein (1979) standard binomial approximation (mentioned in chapter 3 above) is not unique.[2] In fact, once the return distribution of the underlying asset is known and risk-neutral valuation is accepted, other types of numerical analysis can be employed.[3] Basically, a discrete process that appropriately approximates the assumed continuous asset dynamics over successively smaller intervals must be identified. The log-transformed method proposed here can be seen as a variation of the binomial lattice approach with improved qualities. The variation is designed and the parameters are chosen so that the valuation procedure is consistent, unconditionally stable, and computationally efficient.

10.1 Simulation in Option Valuation

The use of Monte Carlo simulation in the context of traditional capital budgeting analysis was discussed in chapter 2. Here, we build on the subsequent discussion of risk-neutral valuation and stochastic processes in chapter 3 in order to examine the use of simulation in the context of valuing European-type options involving no early exercise or other intermediate decisions. This method basically simulates the stochastic process that generates the underlying asset returns and uses risk-neutral valuation to discount the resulting simulated terminal option values at the riskless rate. Recall that the ability to create a riskless replicating portfolio if the underlying asset is traded, or to obtain a "certainty-equivalent" expected growth rate by subtracting an appropriate risk premium ($\lambda\sigma$), allows more convenient valuation in a "risk-neutral world" where the risk-neutral expectation of a future option payoff (at maturity T), F_T, can be discounted at the riskless rate, r, as follows:

$$F = e^{-r\tau}\hat{E}(F_T),\tag{10.1}$$

where $\hat{E}(\ )$ is the expectations operator in the risk-neutral world, τ is the time until maturity ($= T - t$), λ is the asset's market price of risk, and σ is the asset's volatility.

Essentially, the possible random paths (trajectories) for the underlying stochastic variable (stock price) are simulated in a risk-neutral world by using a computer to obtain the terminal asset (stock) price, S_T, and to estimate the corresponding option value, F_T (e.g., $F_T = \max(EX - S_T, 0)$ for the put option). The underlying asset value (e.g., stock price), S, is assumed to follow the standard diffusion process (or geometric Brownian motion)

$$\frac{dS}{S} = \alpha\,dt + \sigma\,dz,\tag{10.2}$$

where α is the instantaneous expected return on asset value, σ is the instantaneous standard deviation of asset value, and dz is an increment of a standard Wiener process.

Since each sample path must correspond to the stochastic process that would be followed in a risk-neutral world, the proportional growth rate of the underlying variable, α, must be replaced by $\hat{\alpha} = \alpha - \lambda\sigma$ (or, if the asset is traded, α must be replaced by $r - \delta$, where δ is a dividend yield). From chapter 3, by subdividing the option maturity T into N equal subintervals of length $K \equiv \Delta t = T/N$, the discrete-time version of the stochastic process of equation 10.2 in a risk-neutral world is

$$\frac{\Delta S}{S} = \hat{\alpha}\,\Delta t + \sigma\varepsilon\sqrt{\Delta t}, \tag{10.2$'$}$$

where ε is a random sample from a standardized normal distribution (with mean 0 and standard deviation 1). For each simulation run, N independent random samples are drawn from a standardized normal distribution ε. These can be substituted into equation 10.2$'$ to yield values for ΔS at time steps $j = 0, 1, 2, \ldots, N$ in the grid of figure 10.1, forming one simulated trajectory of S. The terminal asset price obtained in such a simulation run, S_T, is considered a random sample from the (risk-neutral) distribution of terminal stock prices. The process is repeated from 1000 to 10,000 times, each time giving a different set of terminal stock prices (S_T) and option values (F_T). The risk-neutral expectation of option values, $\hat{E}(F_T)$, can then be estimated as the average (sample mean) of the terminal option values, and can then be discounted at the riskless rate according to equation 10.1.

The accuracy of this simulation depends on the number of simulation paths used to generate the terminal stock price distribution. The standard error of the estimate of the option values, F, is given by $s/\sqrt{n}$, where s is the standard deviation of option values estimated from the simulation runs, so a large number of simulation runs is usually needed for reasonable accuracy. However, variance-reduction techniques can be used to modify the original problem to reduce s and achieve reasonable accuracy with a smaller number of runs.

One such technique, the *control-variate technique* (Hull and White 1988a), takes advantage of a similar but simpler option problem that has an analytic solution, and uses that solution to improve the accuracy of the more complex problem at hand (which has no analytic solution). Suppose we want to estimate numerically the value of an option, A, that has no analytic solution (e.g., an American put option without dividends). We can identify a similar option, B, for which an analytic solution is available (e.g., a European put without dividends). We can run two simulations in parallel, using the same ε and Δt to obtain estimates of the values of options A and B (F_A^* and F_B^*, respectively). A more accurate estimate of the value of option A is then obtained as follows:

$$F_A = F_A^* + (F_B - F_B^*). \tag{10.3}$$

The control-variate technique can also be used to improve accuracy in conjunction with finite-difference or binomial lattice approximations.

As can be seen from the above discussion, simulation may be a powerful tool for generating the relevant risk-neutral probability distributions that allow discounting of expected terminal option values at the risk-free rate. Simulation is rather simple and flexible. It can handle complex option payoffs, can be easily modified to accommodate different (even complex) underlying stochastic processes (e.g., mean reversion, jump, or mixed diffusion-jump processes), or can be used when the sample stock prices are drawn from an empirical distribution. It is particularly useful for valuing (European) path-dependent options where the option payoff depends on the history of the underlying state variable and not just its terminal value (e.g., lookback options that depend on the maximum or minimum price reached during the option's life or Asian options that depend on the average price achieved). It is more efficient than other techniques when there are several state variables, since the computer time required increases linearly with the number of variables in the case of simulation but exponentially for most other techniques. It also has the advantage that it can provide confidence limits via the standard error of the estimated value of the option.

Unfortunately, a large number of runs is needed for reasonable accuracy, so the method is generally less efficient than other computational techniques. (A variance-reduction method, such as the control-variate technique, can usually help improve accuracy.) The relative inefficiency is more pronounced when option values corresponding to different current stock prices are needed, since a simulation trial provides the option value conditional on just one specific current stock price (so many trials must be made). A major drawback of simulation is that it is basically limited to European-type options involving no early exercise or other intermediate decisions. When a simulation run has reached a given node in a path, there is no way to know if early exercise would be optimal. This is a serious constraint for the valuation of real option problems that involve multiple, interdependent discretionary decisions that essentially require a backward dynamic-programming valuation process. Simulation does not allow for the determination of optimal policies (except by trial and error) in the way that a dynamic-programming approach does. On the other hand, if several state variables are involved, it may be a more practically useful valuation approach, especially since it may allow the relevant risk-neutral probability distributions to be generated.

10.2   Finite-Difference Methods

Finite-difference methods essentially approximate the partial differential equations describing the evolution of option values by a set of difference equations, which are then solved in a backward recursive fashion. The basic idea is to replace the partial derivatives with appropriate finite differences. Here this approximation approach will be illustrated in the case of the American put option on a non-dividend-paying stock.

As was noted in chapter 3, the value of any option or contingent claim $F(S, t)$ on an underlying asset S_t must satisfy the fundamental partial differential equation

$$\tfrac{1}{2}\sigma^2 S^2 F_{SS} + (r - \delta)SF_S - F_\tau - rF + d = 0, \tag{10.4}$$

where subscripts indicate partial derivatives (i.e., $F_S \equiv \partial F/\partial S$, $F_\tau \equiv \partial F/\partial \tau = -F_t$, and $F_{SS} \equiv \partial^2 F/\partial S^2$), d is the payoff on the option or the contingent claim, and δ is a constant dividend yield on the asset or a below-equilibrium return shortfall. (Potentially, δ is 0 for a non-dividend-paying traded asset.) The above p.d.e. is subject to one terminal condition and two boundary conditions. The p.d.e. for the value of a put option on a non-dividend-paying stock is a special case of equation 10.4 with $\delta = 0$ (assuming a traded stock with no dividends) and $d = 0$ (since the option itself earns no dividends or other payoffs). Thus, as in equation 3.13, the value of a put option, $F(S, t)$, must satisfy the standard Black-Scholes p.d.e. (the same as for the corresponding call option),

$$\tfrac{1}{2}\sigma^2 S^2 F_{SS} + rSF_S + F_t - rF = 0, \tag{10.4'}$$

subject to the following set of conditions:

$F(S, T) = \max(\text{EX} - S, 0)$ (terminal condition)

$F(0, T) = \text{EX}$ (lower boundary)

$F(S, T)/S \to 0$ as $S \to \infty$ (or S_{MAX})   (upper boundary).

The objective of finite differences is to construct approximations of the partial derivatives F_S, F_{SS}, and F_t.

Implicit Finite Differences

In general, there are a variety of different ways that the partial derivatives can be approximated by finite differences. For example,

$$F_S \equiv \frac{\partial F}{\partial S} \approx (F_{i+1,j} - F_{i,j})/H \quad \text{(forward difference approximation at } j)$$

or

$$\approx (F_{i,j} - F_{i-1,j})/H \quad \text{(backward difference approximation at } j).$$

In the implicit scheme, a symmetric approximation using the average of the above is used:

$$F_S \approx (F_{i+1,j} - F_{i-1,j})/2H + O(\Delta t^2) \quad \text{(central approximation at } j).$$

The second partial derivative, F_{SS}, obtained from the difference in the backward approximations at $(i+1,j)$ and at (i,j) is given by

$$F_{SS} \equiv \frac{\partial^2 F}{\partial S^2} \approx \frac{F_{i+1,j} - 2F_{i,j} + F_{i-1,j}}{H^2} + O(H^2) \quad \text{(backward differences at } j).$$

The forward difference approximation is used for $\partial F/\partial t$, as follows:

$$F_t \equiv \frac{\partial F}{\partial t} \approx \frac{F_{i,j+1} - F_{i,j}}{K} + O(\Delta t) \quad \text{(forward approximation at } i).$$

Note that the error terms above are of a different order.

Substituting the above difference approximations for F_S, F_{SS}, and F_t (with $S = i\Delta S$) into the p.d.e. in equation 10.4' and rearranging yields the implicit finite-difference expression

$$c_i^+ F_{i+1,j} + c_i^0 F_{i,j} + c_i^- F_{i-1,j} = F_{i,j+1}, \tag{10.5}$$

where

$$c_i^+ \equiv -\tfrac{1}{2}(\sigma^2 i + r)iK,$$

$$c_i^0 \equiv 1 + (\sigma^2 i + r)K,$$

and

$$c_i^- \equiv -\tfrac{1}{2}(\sigma^2 i - r)iK,$$

with $i = 0, 1, 2, \ldots, M$ and $j = 0, 1, 2, \ldots, N$.

The above expression gives the relationship among three different (unknown) option values at time j (namely $F_{i+1,j}$, $F_{i,j}$, and $F_{i-1,j}$) and one (known) value at time $j+1$ (i.e., $F_{i,j+1}$)—where c_i^+, c_i^0, and c_i^- could be viewed as transition probabilities to jump from state i at time j to state $i+1$, i, or $i-1$ at time $j+1$, respectively. This system can be solved recursively, starting from the terminal condition (at $j = N$) and moving backward, one step at a time, to the beginning ($j = 0$). At $j = N - 1$, for example, it becomes

$$c_i^+ F_{i+1,N-1} + c_i^0 F_{i,N-1} + c_i^- F_{i-1,N-1} = F_{i,N}. \tag{10.5'}$$

The above expression can be written more generally in matrix form as

$$\mathbf{C} \mathbf{F_j} = \mathbf{F_{j+1}}, \quad \text{or} \quad \mathbf{F_j} = \mathbf{C^{-1} F_{j+1}}. \tag{10.5''}$$

The above is a system of $M - 1$ simultaneous equations (for $i = 1$, $2, \ldots, M - 1$) which must be solved simultaneously for the $M - 1$ unknowns ($F_{1,N-1}, F_{2,N-1}, \ldots, F_{M-1,N-1}$). Once obtained, these values are compared to the value of early exercise: if $EX - i\Delta S > F_{i,N-1}$, the early-exercise value $EX - i\Delta S$ replaces $F_{i,N-1}$. The above process is repeated iteratively for $j = N - 2, N - 3, \ldots, 2, 1, 0$. In the end, this iterative process yields the beginning ($j = 0$) option values, $F_{1,0}, F_{2,0}, \ldots, F_{M-1,0}$, including the desired starting value.

By taking the log transform of the Black-Scholes p.d.e. 10.4' using $X \equiv \ln S$, Brennan and Schwartz (1978) show that the transition probability matrix, $\mathbf{C}$, can become independent of state i and so its inverse in equation 10.5'' ($\mathbf{C^{-1}}$) needs to be calculated only once (and used again in each step in the iterative process).[4] The tridiagonal form of the transition matrix $\mathbf{C}$ enables us to solve the system of equations through Gaussian elimination or Gauss-Seidel iteration. In general, implicit finite-difference methods are computationally quite demanding, but are robust in that they always converge to the solution.

Explicit Finite Differences

Instead of having to solve $M - 1$ different simultaneous equations relating three different option values at time j with one option value at $j + 1$, as in the implicit method above, we can simplify the solution by expressing the difference approximations of F_S and F_{SS} at point $(i, j + 1)$ instead of at (i, j) (assuming the two are equal). Using the revised finite differences at $j + 1$ (instead of at j),

$$F_S \approx (F_{i+1,j+1} - F_{i-1,j+1})/2H \quad \text{(central approximation at } j + 1)$$

and

$$F_{SS} \approx (F_{i+1,j+1} - 2F_{i,j+1} + F_{i-1,j+1})/H^2 \quad \text{(backward differences at } j + 1)$$

$(F_t \approx (F_{i,j+1} - F_{i,j})/K$ is the same, forward difference at i) in the earlier p.d.e. (equation 10.4'), and rearranging, results in the explicit finite-difference equation

$$F_{i,j} = \frac{p_i^+ F_{i+1,j+1} + p_i^0 F_{i,j+1} + p_i^- F_{i-1,j+1}}{1 + rK}, \tag{10.6}$$

where

$$p_i^+ \equiv \tfrac{1}{2}(\sigma^2 i + r)iK = -c_i^+,$$

$$p_i^- \equiv \tfrac{1}{2}(\sigma^2 i - r)iK = -c_i^-,$$

and

$$p_i^0 \equiv 1 - \sigma^2 i^2 K = 1 - (p_i^+ + p_i^-),$$

with $i = 0, 1, 2, \ldots, M$ and $j = 0, 1, 2, \ldots, N$. Contrary to the implicit scheme, the above expression now gives the relationship between one (unknown) option value at time j (namely $F_{i,j}$) and three different (but known) option values at subsequent time $j + 1$ (namely $F_{i+1,j+1}$, $F_{i,j+1}$, and $F_{i-1,j+1}$). Since all the data are known (or have been derived) from the previous step in the backward iterative process, only one simple equation must be solved at a time, rather than a set of simultaneous equations as in the implicit scheme. In this regard, the explicit finite-difference scheme is just like the lattice approach. The coefficients p_i^+, p_i^-, and p_i^0 now are actually the (risk-neutral) probabilities that the state variable, being in state i at time j, will jump up (to state $i + 1$), jump down (to state $i - 1$), or stay in the same state (i) by next period (time $j + 1$), respectively. As probabilities they add up to unity (i.e., $p_i^+ + p_i^- + p_i^0 = 1$), and they should all be non-negative (so that $p_i^0 \equiv 1 - \sigma^2 i^2 K \geq 0$, or else instability problems may result for sufficiently large values of i).[5] Essentially, the explicit finite-difference expression in equation 10.6 simply says that the current option value is obtained from the expected future option values one period hence (using the probabilities in a trinomial lattice), discounted back one period at the riskless rate in a risk-neutral world. Equation 10.6 is again solved iteratively, starting from the terminal condition (at $j = N$) and moving backward to the beginning ($j = 0$).

A logarithmic transformation of the state variable can improve certain computational attributes of finite-difference (and other) methods, such as stability and efficiency. Brennan and Schwartz (1978) used $X \equiv \ln S$, which allowed transforming the Black-Scholes p.d.e. 10.4' into

$$\tfrac{1}{2}\sigma^2 F_{XX} + (r - \tfrac{1}{2}\sigma^2)F_X + F_t - rF = 0. \tag{10.7}$$

Unlike equation 10.4′, this transformed p.d.e. has constant (state-independent) coefficients and allows the use of an explicit difference approximation without the stability problems noted above. Substituting the same difference approximations as in the above explicit scheme (at $j + 1$) results in the same explicit finite-difference expression as in equation 10.6, and allows solving for $F_{i,j}$ in terms of $F_{i,j+1}$, except that the probabilities are now given by

$$p^+ \equiv \tfrac{1}{2}[(\sigma/H)^2 + (r - \tfrac{1}{2}\sigma^2)H]K,$$

$$p^- \equiv \tfrac{1}{2}[(\sigma/H)^2 - (r - \tfrac{1}{2}\sigma^2)H]K,$$

and   (10.8)

$$p^0 \equiv 1 - (\sigma/H)^2 K$$

(see Brennan and Schwartz 1978).Thus, in this log-transformed explicit scheme, the risk-neutral probabilities (p^+, p^-, p^0) now become independent of state i. In addition to adding up to unity, an appropriate selection of steps H and K (e.g., from p^0, $p^- \geq 0$, $K \leq H^2/\sigma^2$, and $H \leq \sigma^2/|r - \tfrac{1}{2}\sigma^2|$) can ensure that these state-independent probabilities are always non-negative and that the approximation is stable in this regard. Again, the value of an option at time j is given by its expected value at time $j + 1$, discounted at the riskless rate in a risk-neutral world, where $X \equiv \ln S$ follows a trinomial jump process (lattice) of the form

$$\Delta X = \left\langle \begin{array}{l} \nearrow p^+ \text{---} H \\ \text{---} p^0 \text{---} 0 \\ \searrow p^- \text{---} -H. \end{array} \right.$$

The mean and the variance of this jump process are given by

$$\begin{aligned} E(\Delta X) &= p^+(+H) + p^-(-H) \\ &= (p^+ - p^-)H \\ &= (r - \tfrac{1}{2}\sigma^2)K \end{aligned}$$

and   (10.9)

$$\begin{aligned} \mathrm{Var}(\Delta X) &= E(\Delta X^2) - [E(\Delta X)]^2 \\ &= [p^+(+H)^2 + p^-(-H)^2] - [E(\Delta X)]^2 \\ &= \sigma^2 K - (r - \tfrac{1}{2}\sigma^2)^2 K^2. \end{aligned}$$

Unfortunately, the above variance of the approximating (discrete) jump process is a downward-biased estimate of the variance of the continuous diffusion process, $\sigma^2 K$, by the square of the mean jump $(r - \frac{1}{2}\sigma^2)K$. In addition to accuracy (consistency) problems, stability problems may still arise if this variance can turn negative. The log-transformed binomial method described in later sections is designed to overcome these problems.

As in equation 10.6, all values of $F_{i,j}$ can again be obtained recursively from

$$F_{i,j} = \left\{ \begin{array}{l} p^+ - F_{i+1,j+1} \\ p^0 - F_{i,j+1} \\ p^- - F_{i-1,j+1}. \end{array} \right.$$

If in addition to $X \equiv \ln S$ we set $f(X,t) = e^{rt}F(S,t)$, then f satisfies the same p.d.e. as F in equation 10.7, except that rF is replaced with 0. Substituting the standard implicit finite-difference approximations (at j) from section 10.2 in this transformed p.d.e. also results in the explicit finite-difference expression in equation 10.6 with the same probabilities as in equation 10.8, again with a discrete variance biased downward by the square of the mean jump as in the Brennan-Schwartz (1978) version of equation 10.9 . That is, the explicit finite-difference approximation scheme of equation 10.6 can be obtained either by substituting the revised finite differences at $j+1$ rather than at j into the (log-transformed) Black-Scholes p.d.e., or, alternatively, by substituting the implicit finite differences into the above transformed p.d.e.

The above log-transformed explicit finite-difference method (with $X \equiv \ln S$ and $f(X,t) = e^{rt}F(S,t)$) is also similar to the numerical integration (or dynamic programming) method employed by Parkinson (1977) to approximate the American put value. In this case, the probabilities were taken from a trinomial jump process as an approximation to the normal distribution. ΔX are now normally distributed with the same mean, $E(\Delta X) = (r - \frac{1}{2}\sigma^2)K$, and an unbiased variance, $Var(\Delta X) = \sigma^2 K$, with the trinomial probabilities being a variation of the probabilities in equation 10.8:

$$p^+ \equiv \tfrac{1}{2}[(\sigma/H)^2 + (r - \tfrac{1}{2}\sigma^2)/H]K + \tfrac{1}{2}[(r - \tfrac{1}{2}\sigma^2)K/H]^2,$$

$$p^- \equiv \tfrac{1}{2}[(\sigma/H)^2 - (r - \tfrac{1}{2}\sigma^2)/H]K + \tfrac{1}{2}[(r - \tfrac{1}{2}\sigma^2)K/H]^2, \qquad (10.8')$$

$$p^0 \equiv 1 - (\sigma/H)^2 K - [(r - \tfrac{1}{2}\sigma^2)K/H]^2.$$

Again, H and K must be chosen so as to avoid negative probabilities $(p^-, p^0 \geq 0)$ and resulting stability problems $(H \leq \sigma^2/|r - \frac{1}{2}\sigma^2| + (r - \frac{1}{2}\sigma^2)K$ and $H^2 \geq \sigma^2 K + (r - \frac{1}{2}\sigma^2)^2 K^2)$. A dynamic program similar to equation 10.6 can then be solved iteratively, showing the equivalence between certain finite-difference formulations and the dynamic programming approach.

Other versions based on logarithmic transformation may have even more desirable numerical properties. McKean (1965) and Mason (1978) use the transformations

$$X \equiv \frac{\ln S + (r - \frac{1}{2}\sigma^2)\tau}{\sigma}$$

and

$$f(X, t) = e^{r\tau}F(S, t),$$

which reduce the Black-Scholes p.d.e. of equation 10.4' to a free-boundary (or an optimal stopping) problem given by the standard heat equation,

$$\tfrac{1}{2}f_{XX} + f_t = 0. \tag{10.10}$$

Substituting the (implicit) finite-difference approximations of section 10.2 into this heat equation results in the same explicit finite-difference expression (as in equation 10.6),

$$f_{i,j} = \frac{p^+ f_{i+1,j+1} + p^0 f_{i,j+1} + p^- f_{i-1,j+1}}{1 + rK}, \tag{10.6'}$$

but the risk-neutral probabilities are now given by

$$p^+ \equiv \tfrac{1}{2}K/H^2,$$

$$p^- \equiv \tfrac{1}{2}K/H^2,$$

and   (10.11)

$$p^0 \equiv 1 - K/H^2.$$

Note that these probabilities are state-independent, add up to unity, and that $p^+, p^- \geq 0$. To ensure stability, it must also be the case that $p^0 \geq 0$. This requires that the mesh ratio, $m \equiv K/H^2$, be ≤ 1, or that $p \equiv p^+ = p^- \leq \frac{1}{2}$. If the mesh ratio exceeds 1 ($m \equiv K/H^2 > 1$), the approximation may be unstable; accuracy improves as the mesh ratio becomes < 1. For example, for $p = \frac{1}{6}$ the approximation converges faster and is more accurate (i.e., it has less truncation error) than when $p = \frac{1}{2}$.

The mean and the variance of the above trinomial jump process are given by

$$E(\Delta X) = (p^+ - p^-)H = 0$$

and   (10.12)

$$\mathrm{Var}(\Delta X) = [p^+(+H)^2 + p^-(-H)^2] - [E(\Delta X)]^2$$

$$= (p^+ + p^-)H^2 = K.$$

The above variance is always non-negative and unbiased. In case $H^2 = K$ (i.e., if $m = 1$), then $p^+ = p^- = \frac{1}{2}$ and $p^0 = 0$, so this explicit finite-difference scheme reduces to a binomial lattice approximation.

Use of the backward difference approximation for f_{XX} at $j + 1$ (instead of at j) in the heat equation 10.10 would have resulted in an implicit approximation that is more computationally demanding but is always stable. The explicit scheme in equation 10.6' resulting from using the backward difference at j is simpler computationally but is stable only if the probabilities are non-negative. More generally, a weighted average of the two backward difference approximations (at j and at $j + 1$) can result in a better mix of numerical attributes. If in equation 10.10 f_{XX} is approximated with a weighted average of the backward differences

$$\frac{f_{i+1,j+1} - 2f_{i,j+1} + f_{i-1,j+1}}{H^2} \quad \text{(backward differences at } j + 1)$$

and

$$\frac{f_{i+1,j} - 2f_{i,j} + f_{i-1,j}}{H^2} \quad \text{(backward differences at } j),$$

we can obtain the more general weighted-average scheme

$$\lambda\left(\frac{f_{i+1,j+1} - 2f_{i,j+1} + f_{i-1,j+1}}{H^2}\right) + (1 - \lambda)\left(\frac{f_{i+1,j} - 2f_{i,j} + f_{i-1,j}}{H^2}\right)$$

$$= -\frac{2(f_{i,j+1} - f_{i,j})}{K}.$$ (10.13)

For $\lambda = 0$ (using the backward difference approximation at j), equation 10.13 reduces to the explicit scheme, for $\lambda = 1$ (using the backward differences at $j + 1$) it reduces to the implicit scheme, while for $\lambda = \frac{1}{2}$ it gives the Crank-Nicholson technique. The latter is generally stable, although it is more accurate for a smaller mesh ratio, m.

In general, finite-difference methods can be used to value both European and American type options and are usually computationally more efficient when an entire set of time-0 option values needs to be calculated. They can also handle several state variables in a multi-dimensional grid, although not nearly as efficiently. Of course, one must take care with the selection of the "right" set of finite-difference approximations to the partial derivatives, and one must be careful with problems of stability and consistency (accuracy), although certain logarithmic transformations can be helpful in this regard. The implicit method is computationally more demanding than the explicit, but it avoids convergence problems. If properly formulated, certain finite-difference schemes can be seen to be equivalent to dynamic programming. Finite-difference methods may not be easily used with history-dependent payoffs, and cannot be used at all when one cannot write down the partial differential equations describing the option value dynamics. Their implementation is more mechanical and affords less intuition than lattice approaches that emulate the dynamics of the underlying stochastic processes.

10.3 The Log-Transformed Binomial Lattice Approach: Theoretical Design

In the previous section I discussed the improved numerical attributes achieved via log transformation and the fact that a binomial lattice approximation can result as a special case of a log-transformed explicit finite-difference scheme.[6] Thus, in this section, instead of reviewing the traditional Cox-Ross-Rubinstein multiplicative binomial lattice method described in chapter 3 and in most standard texts, I present a log-transformed variation of the binomial method with more desirable computational attributes along the lines discussed earlier. The goal is to design a consistent, stable, and efficient binomial lattice method for valuing complex investments with potentially interacting options. The method is applicable both to the valuation of complex financial options (such as a convertible putable bond, a callable and extendable bond, or a leasing contract with multiple operating options) and to the valuing of capital budgeting projects with multiple real options. In the case of real options, the value of the underlying asset is V, the (gross) present value of the expected cash flows from immediately undertaking the real project, rather than the stock price S.[7] Let us again assume that the value of the underlying asset V follows the diffusion Wiener process

$$\frac{dV}{V} = \alpha\, dt + \sigma\, dz,$$

where α is the instantaneous expected return on the asset (project), σ is its instantaneous standard deviation, and dz is a standard Wiener process.

   In any small time interval, $K \equiv \Delta t$, $X \equiv \ln V$ then follows an arithmetic Brownian motion (or a Markov random walk in discrete time). Under risk neutrality, $\alpha = r$, so that

$$\Delta X = \ln(V_{t+\Delta t}/V_t)$$

$$= (r - \tfrac{1}{2}\sigma^2)\Delta t + \sigma\,dz,$$

where r is the risk-free rate. The increments, ΔX, are independent, identical, and normally distributed with mean $(r - \tfrac{1}{2}\sigma^2)\Delta t$ and variance $\sigma^2 \Delta t$.

If we let $k \equiv \sigma^2 \Delta t$ (transforming "time" as to be expressed in units of variance), the increments ΔX become normally distributed, with mean $E(\Delta X) = \mu k$ and variance $\mathrm{Var}(\Delta X) = k$, where $\mu \equiv r/\sigma^2 - \tfrac{1}{2}$.

The above continuous diffusion process can, of course, be approximated by an equivalent discrete-time process with the same first moments (mean and variance).[8] By subdividing the total period (project life), T, into N equal discrete subintervals of length t so that $T = N\tau$, the "time" step k can be approximated by $\sigma^2 T/N$. Within each discrete subinterval τ, X then follows a Markov random walk moving up by an amount $\Delta X = H$ with some (risk-neutral) probability, $p^+ \equiv P$, or down by the same amount $(\Delta X = -H)$ with complementary probability $p^- \equiv 1 - P$ (with $p^0 = 0$) . Note that the above discrete process is defined in a transformed "state" and "time" space (the state variable X is defined as the logarithm of V and is measured in "state space" units of length H, while time is also transformed (k) and expressed in units of variance). The mean and the variance of this discrete-time Markov process are

$$E(\Delta X) = P(+H) + (1 - P)(-H)$$

$$= 2PH - H$$

and

$$\mathrm{Var}(\Delta X) = E(\Delta X^2) - [E(\Delta X)]^2$$

$$= [P(+H)^2 + (1 - P)(-H)^2] - [2PH - H]^2$$

$$= H^2 - [E(\Delta X)]^2.$$

For this discrete-time process to be *consistent* with the above continuous diffusion Wiener process, their corresponding means and variances should be equal, i.e.,

$$2PH - H = \mu k, \quad \text{so} \quad P = \tfrac{1}{2}(1 + \mu k/H)$$

and   (10.14)

$$H^2 - (\mu k)^2 = k, \quad \text{so} \quad H = \sqrt{k + (\mu k)^2} \ (\geq \mu k).$$

The above transformations of the state and time variables were designed so as to guarantee stability as well as consistency of the discrete-time approximation to the continuous process. As noted, for any weighted average numeric scheme—such as a binomial method or the explicit finite-difference method used by Brennan and Schwartz (1978)—to be stable (i.e., for the error not to blow up) the weights must be constrained between 0 and 1 and add up to 1 (like probabilities), in turn restricting the admissible values of k and H to satisfy a certain condition. By its definition, $\text{Var}(\Delta X) \geq 0$ and, hence, $-1 \leq \mu k/H \leq 1$, which implies that $0 \leq P \leq 1$. As probabilities, P and $(1 - P)$ also add up to 1, satisfying the conditions that ensure unconditional stability with no external constraints on k and H.

10.4 Algorithm Structure with Adjustments for Cash Flows, Interacting Options, and Exogenous Jumps

The log-transformed binomial algorithm consists of four main steps: parameter value specification, preliminary sequential calculation, determination of terminal values, and backward iterative process. These are outlined in figure 10.2. First, the standard parameters affecting option values—V, r, σ^2, T, and the set of exercise prices or investment cost outlays (EX or I)—are specified, along with the desired number of subintervals (N). The greater N is chosen, the smaller the number of subintervals and the more accurate the numerical approximation, although at the expense of more computer time (and, potentially, growing approximation errors). The cash flows, CF, and their timing (if discrete), as well as the type, timing, and other characteristics of the various embedded real options must be specified as well.

The second step involves preliminary calculations needed for the rest of the algorithm. Using the values of variables calculated along the way from preceeding steps, the algorithm sequentially determines the following key variables:

time step k (from $\sigma^2 T/N$),

drift μ (from $r/\sigma^2 - \frac{1}{2}$),

$$(10.15)$$

state step H (from $\sqrt{k + (\mu k)^2}$),

probability P (from $\frac{1}{2}(1 + \mu k/H)$).

Before proceeding, it is convenient to recall our earlier notation. The index j denotes the integer number of time steps (each of length k), i is the integer index of the state variable X corresponding to the net number of

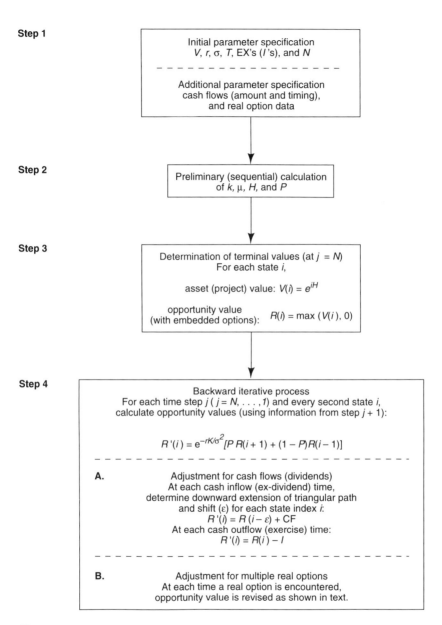

Figure 10.2
Flow chart for the log-transformed binomial algorithm.

ups less downs (i.e., $X(i) = X_0 + iH$), and $F(i) \equiv R(i)$ denotes the total investment opportunity value (i.e., the combined value for the project and its embedded real options) at state i.

The third step involves the determination of terminal boundary values (at $j = N$). For each state i, the algorithm fills in the underlying asset (project) values from $V(i) = e^{X_0 + iH}$ (since $X \equiv \ln V = X_0 + iH$); and the total investment opportunity values (or expanded NPV) from the terminal condition $R(i) = \max(V(i), 0)$.

The fourth step follows a backward iterative process, with adjustments for cash flows (dividends) and real options (and possibly exogenous competitive entry) at appropriate times. Starting from the end ($j = N$) and working backward through a triangular path (figure 10.3), the algorithm proceeds in a binomial dynamic-programming fashion. For each time step j ($j = N - 1, \ldots, 1$) and every second state i, it calculates the total invest-

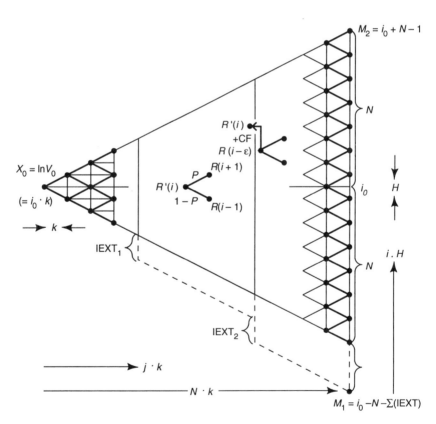

Figure 10.3
The (extended) "path triangle" for the discrete-time process.

ment opportunity values (i.e., the combined values for the project with its embedded options) using information from step $j + 1$ or earlier. That is, between any two consecutive periods, the value of the opportunity in the earlier period (j) at state i, $R'(i)$—where the prime indicates a new or revised value—is determined iteratively from its expected end-of-period values in the up and down states calculated in the previous time step ($j + 1$), discounted back one period of length $\tau = k/\sigma^2$ at the risk-free interest rate r,[9]

$$R'(i) = e^{-rk/\sigma^2}[P R(i + 1) + (1 - P)R(i - 1)]. \tag{10.16}$$

Owing to the basic binomial nature of this discrete process, the possible paths followed by the state variable X are constrained within a triangular path with vertex at the current value X_0. Note also that, for the same reason, we need only determine the values corresponding to every second state for any given time, and that the highest (M_2) and lowest (M_1) possible values of i are each shrinking by 1 at each step as we move backward in time. Taking advantage of these observations can result in significant computational savings.

Adjustments for project cash flows ("dividends"), for the various real options embedded in the project, and for exogenous competitive arrivals (jumps) must be made at appropriate times within the backward iterative process of the fourth step.

Adjusting for Cash Flows (Dividends)

Expected cash flows generated by the asset (project), whether discrete or constant proportional, just like dividend payments on a stock, require an adjustment in the valuation grid. Each time a cash inflow (CF) is expected to be received (i.e., at the "ex-dividend" time), the "cum" asset (gross project) value V ($\equiv e^{X_0 + iH}$) is reduced by CF, i.e., $V^+(i) = V^-(i) - \text{CF}$, where the superscript signs refer to values just after ($+$ or "ex") and just before ($-$ or "cum") the payment time (see figure 10.3). Since the value of the option component is unchanged, the total opportunity (asset plus option) value after payment ("ex") is

$$R'(V^+) = R(V^- - \text{CF}) + \text{CF}.$$

In terms of implementation, at each time a cash inflow is received, the "path triangle" followed by X ($\equiv \ln V$) is extended downward (see the broken line in figure 10.3) by an amount (IEXT) determined by the cash-flow drop. The revised ("ex-dividend") total value of the investment opportunity (asset plus option) at state index i, $R'(i)$, is then obtained from the opportunity value corresponding to some lower index ε nodes lower, $i - \varepsilon$ (with ε depending on the cash dividend amount CF); that is,

$$R'(i) = R(i - \varepsilon) + \text{CF}.$$

In general, with discrete nonproportional cash flows, each node in the "tree" is shifted by a different amount (ε differs for each i). Only in the special case when cash flow is a constant proportion of asset (project) value is the whole tree shifted by a constant amount. Note that the shift is done in a way that the original ("predividend") node structure is always maintained (i.e., nodes recombine). However, if the drop ε falls between two preexisting adjacent nodes when retrieving a revised opportunity value from a lower index $(i - \varepsilon)$, it may be necessary to interpolate between their opportunity (asset plus option) values so as to preserve the original node structure that would exist without "dividends". In effect, as we step backward in time, the above cash flow (dividend) adjustment shifts the whole valuation grid upward whenever a cash inflow is encountered (see figure 10.3).

On the other hand, whenever a planned investment cost outlay (a cash outflow), I, is made, the total opportunity value is revised by simply subtracting that outlay (like a negative dividend) from the current opportunity value, i.e.,

$$R'(i) = R(i) - I.$$

Adjusting for Multiple Real Options

If at any time, j, a real option is encountered as we move backward, the total opportunity value (project plus value of any other subsequent options) is revised at the indicated time to reflect the asymmetry introduced by that type of flexibility. To be more concrete, consider evaluating the complex multi-option project illustrated in figure 10.4.

Briefly, operating the project requires a series of investment outlays during the building stage (say, a first expenditure of I_1 to initiate it, to be followed by outlays of I_2 and I_3) before it is expected to generate cash inflows during the later operating stage. The project affords management the flexibility to wait up to T_1 years. Later, management may abandon early by forgoing a preplanned outlay (say, I_2), may contract the scale of operations by $c\%$, thereby saving part (I_3') of a planned outlay (I_3), or may expand production by $e\%$, if it makes an extra outlay (I_4). Finally, at any

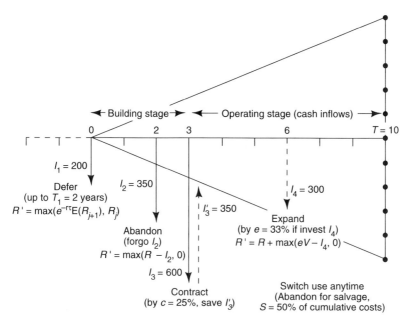

Figure 10.4
A complex R&D project with multiple options to defer, abandon, contract, expand, or switch use (abandon for salvage), with appropriate adjustments.

time, it may switch the project from the current to its best future alternative use, or may abandon for its salvage value (S).

As each of the above real options is encountered, the total opportunity value (including all subsequent options) is adjusted from R to R' for each type of flexibility, as follows:

switch use (or abandon for salvage S)[10]: $\quad R' = \max(R, S)$

expand by $e\%$ by investing additional I_4: $\quad R' = R + \max(eV - I_4, 0)$

contract by $c\%$, saving I'_3: $\quad R' = R + \max(I'_3 - cV, 0)$

abandon by defaulting on I_2: $\quad R' = \max(R - I_2, 0)$

defer until next period: $\quad R' = \max(e^{-rt}E(R_{j+1}), R_j)$.

Deferring one more period (maintaining the option) if the discounted expected opportunity value from initiating the project next period ($j + 1$) exceeds the value from exercising or investing in the current period (j) requires multiple parallel runs of the rest of the program already adjusted for other options and pairwise comparisons conditional on project initiation in successive periods as we move backward starting from the end of the deferrable period (T_1) to the present.

Adjusting for Exogenous Jumps (Competitive Entry)

The algorithm can be extended to handle exogenous competition (see chapter 9), including both anticipated arrivals of competitors that can be preempted by an early investment outlay (with an adjustment similar to the discrete cash dividends discussed in section 10.2) and random competitive arrivals.

In the case of random competitive arrivals, the underlying stochastic process would be modeled as a mixed diffusion-jump process (equation 9.13). That is, V is assumed to follow the standard diffusion Wiener process (as in equation 10.2) until a competitor arriving with instantaneous probability λ causes a jump (or a drop) in project value to $\gamma\%$ of its previous value (i.e., a market-share loss of $(1 - \gamma)\%$). As was discussed in chapter 9, the impact of such random competitive arrivals is in a way analogous to a constant "dividend" payout or "competitive opportunity cost,"

$$\delta = \lambda(\gamma - 1) - (N/\tau)\ln\gamma,$$

which can be subtracted from the drift of the original stochastic process. Thus, the drift μ in equation 10.15 would be revised (by replacing r with $(r - \delta)$) to

$$\mu' = \frac{r + \lambda(1 - \gamma)}{\sigma^2} - \frac{1}{2} + \frac{N}{k}\ln\gamma, \tag{10.15'}$$

where N denotes the number of jumps (competitors). The value of this shared opportunity with random competitive arrivals can then be calculated as a weighted sum or an expected value over a Poisson distribution with intensity parameter $(\lambda\tau)$ of the opportunity values (including all embedded options) given in equation 10.16:

$$R'(i) = \sum_{N=0}^{\infty} \left(\frac{e^{-\lambda k/\sigma^2}(\lambda k/\sigma^2)^N}{N!} \right) e^{-rk/\sigma^2}[P\,R(i+1) + (1 - P)R(i - 1)]. \tag{10.16'}$$

In terms of implementation, the program would now become computationally more involved, since parts of the original program will now have to be rerun a large (approaching infinity) number of times, each time requiring revision of μ, H, and the risk-neutral probabilities P. However, capturing the additional dimension of competitive entry is worth the extra computer time.

As can be seen from the above discussion of the log-transformed binomial lattice method, lattice approaches are generally more intuitive, simpler, and practically more flexible in handling different stochastic processes (such as the above mixed diffusion-jump process), option payoffs, intermediate decisions, or the derivation of optimal policies, and they can easily be extended to handle several underlying variables in a multi-dimensional lattice (see, e.g., Boyle 1988). If carefully designed, they can even overcome problems of consistency, stability, and efficiency encountered in other computational methods. Computational efficiency can be achieved both through log transformation and through an adjustment for nonproportional dividends that allows post-dividend nodes to recombine. The log-transformed binomial method presented here also handles well options with a series of investment outlays or exercise prices (compound options), nonproportional cash flows (dividends), exogenous jumps (e.g., competitive arrivals), and interactions among a variety of options. The main limitation of lattice methods in general is their inability to handle more than one starting price at a time, requiring multiple runs when an entire set of starting option prices is required (at a loss of computational efficiency).

10.5   Comparison of Alternative Computational Methods

This section presents numerical comparisons among several of the most important computational methods available for the valuation of options. The example of the American put option (with or without dividends), involving early optimal exercise, is used here for comparison.

Tables 10.1–10.3 present comparisons of American put values without dividends using the following methods:

Geske and Johnson's (1984) compound-option analytic polynomial approximation using three- or four-point extrapolation

Barone-Adesi and Whaley's (1987) quadratic approximation

Johnson's (1983) heuristic technique

Brennan and Schwartz's (1977a, 1978) implicit finite-difference scheme with $N = 456$ iterations

Parkinson's (1977) numerical integration

Cox, Ross, and Rubinstein's (1979) standard multiplicative binomial method with $N = 500$ iterations.

Table 10.1
American put values without dividends, calculated by Black-Scholes European (BS), compound analytic (CA), quadratic (Q), Johnson (J), finite-differences (FD), and log-transformed binomial (LTB) methods. The put option has exercise price 100.

	r^a	σ^b	T^c	V^d	Value of American put option					
					BS	CA	Q	J	FD	LTB
1	0.08	0.2	0.25	80	18.09	20.00	20.00	20.00	20.00	20.00
2	0.08	0.2	0.25	90	9.05	10.07	10.01	10.56	10.04	10.04
3	0.08	0.2	0.25	100	3.04	3.21	3.22	3.21	3.22	3.22
4	0.08	0.2	0.25	110	0.64	0.66	0.68	0.65	0.66	0.67
5	0.08	0.2	0.25	120	0.09	0.09	0.10	0.09	0.09	0.09
6	0.12	0.2	0.25	80	17.13	20.01	20.00	20.00	20.00	20.00
7	0.12	0.2	0.25	90	8.26	9.96	10.00	10.00	10.00	10.00
8	0.12	0.2	0.25	100	2.63	2.91	2.93	2.90	2.92	2.92
9	0.12	0.2	0.25	110	0.52	0.55	0.58	0.53	0.55	0.56
10	0.12	0.2	0.25	120	0.07	0.07	0.08	0.07	0.07	0.07
11	0.08	0.4	0.25	80	19.45	20.37	20.25	20.08	20.32	20.32
12	0.08	0.4	0.25	90	12.17	12.55	12.51	12.52	12.56	12.57
13	0.08	0.4	0.25	100	6.94	7.10	7.10	7.12	7.11	7.12
14	0.08	0.4	0.25	110	3.63	3.70	3.71	3.72	3.70	3.71
15	0.08	0.4	0.25	120	1.76	1.79	1.81	1.80	1.79	1.80
16	0.08	0.2	0.50	80	16.65	19.94	20.00	20.00	20.00	20.00
17	0.08	0.2	0.50	90	8.83	10.37	10.23	10.73	10.29	10.30
18	0.08	0.2	0.50	100	3.79	4.17	4.19	4.17	4.19	4.18
19	0.08	0.2	0.50	110	1.31	1.41	1.45	1.38	1.41	1.41
20	0.08	0.2	0.50	120	0.38	0.40	0.42	0.39	0.40	0.40

Source: Barone-Adesi and Whaley 1987, table IV. Implicit finite differences were computed with $N = 456$ iterations. Compound-option analytic values were computed by three-point extrapolation. In the last column we added LTB values computed with only 50 iterations, except for a few typically in-the-money observations (rows 1, 6, 7, 14, 16, 19), where $N = 456$.
a. Risk-free interest rate.
b. Instantaneous standard deviation of asset returns.
c. Option maturity.
d. Underlying asset value (e.g., stock price).

Table 10.2
American put values without dividends, calculated by Black-Scholes European (BS), numerical integration (NI), analytic polynomial (AP), Cox-Ross-Rubinstein binomial (CRR), and log-transformed binomial (LTB) methods. The put option has exercise price 100, $V = 100$, and $T = 1$.

| | r | σ | Value of American put option | | | | |
			BS	NI	AP	CRR	LTB
1	0.125	0.5	13.27	14.8	14.76	14.80	14.76
2	0.080	0.4	11.70	12.6	12.58	12.60	12.61
3	0.045	0.3	9.59	10.1	10.05	10.05	10.06
4	0.020	0.2	6.94	7.1	7.12	7.11	7.12
5	0.005	0.1	3.73	3.8	3.77	3.77	3.76
6	0.090	0.3	7.61	8.6	8.59	8.61	8.62
7	0.040	0.2	6.00	6.4	6.40	6.40	6.41
8	0.010	0.1	3.49	3.6	3.57	3.57	3.57
9	0.080	0.2	4.42	5.3	5.25	5.27	5.27
10	0.020	0.1	3.04	3.3	3.22	3.22	3.22
11	0.120	0.2	3.17	4.4	4.39	4.42	4.41
12	0.030	0.1	2.63	3.0	2.92	2.93	2.92

Sources: Geske and Johnson 1984, table I; Hull and White 1988 (CRR values with $N = 500$). We add the last column with $N = 50$ iterations.

The proposed log-transformed binomial method is presented in the last column, using $N = 50$ iterations.[11] The set of options used in the tables has been widely employed for comparing different numerical techniques— e.g., by Cox and Rubinstein (1985), Geske and Johnson (1984), Barone-Adesi and Whaley (1987), and Hull and White (1988a).

To make comparisons, we need a benchmark for accuracy. Since no method can be widely accepted as the most accurate, let us resort to an *ad hoc* measure of accuracy. Following Barone-Adesi and Whaley (1987, p. 312, n. 11; p. 316), let us assume that the finite-difference method is the most accurate, partly because of the large number of steps ($N = 456$) and partly because that method provides values closest to the median of all the methods compared in our tables (which can serve as the ad hoc benchmark for accuracy).

Table 10.1 shows that, for a variety of parameter values (r, σ, T, V), the proposed log-transformed binomial method is more accurate in valuing the American put option without dividends than the analytic, quadratic, and Johnson methods, and that it gives identical results (within penny accuracy and with less than 1% error) with finite differences with many fewer iterations ($N = 50$ vs. 456). The greatest disagreement among the

Table 10.3
American put values without dividends, calculated by Black-Scholes European (BS), analytic polynomial (AP), Cox-Ross-Rubinstein binomial (CRR), and log-transformed binomial (LTB) methods. The put option has $V = 40$ and $r = 0.0488$.

	EX[a]	σ[b]	T[c]	BS	AP	CRR	LTB
				— Value of American put option			
1	35	0.2	0.0833	0.006	0.006	0.006	0.006
2	35	0.2	0.3333	0.196	0.200	0.200	0.200
3	35	0.2	0.5833	0.417	0.432	0.433	0.434
4	40	0.2	0.0833	0.840	0.853	0.852	0.851
5	40	0.2	0.3333	1.522	1.581	1.579	1.581
6	40	0.2	0.5833	1.881	1.991	1.990	1.992
7	45	0.2	0.0833	4.840	4.999	5.000	5.000
8	45	0.2	0.3333	4.781	5.095	5.089	5.092
9	45	0.2	0.5833	4.840	5.272	5.267	5.273
10	35	0.3	0.0833	0.077	0.077	0.077	0.078
11	35	0.3	0.3333	0.687	0.697	0.698	0.705
12	35	0.3	0.5833	1.189	1.219	1.221	1.221
13	40	0.3	0.0833	1.299	1.310	1.309	1.305
14	40	0.3	0.3333	2.438	2.482	2.482	2.482
15	40	0.3	0.5833	3.064	3.173	3.169	3.174
16	45	0.3	0.0833	4.980	5.060	5.060	5.059
17	45	0.3	0.3333	5.529	5.701	5.707	5.716
18	45	0.3	0.5833	5.973	6.237	6.245	6.240
19	35	0.4	0.0833	0.246	0.247	0.246	0.246
20	35	0.4	0.3333	1.330	1.345	1.348	1.343
21	35	0.4	0.5833	2.113	2.157	2.155	2.157
22	40	0.4	0.0833	1.758	1.768	1.768	1.769
23	40	0.4	0.3333	3.334	3.363	3.387	3.385
24	40	0.4	0.5833	4.247	4.356	4.352	4.354
25	45	0.4	0.0833	5.236	5.286	5.287	5.287
26	45	0.4	0.3333	6.377	6.509	6.511	6.511
27	45	0.4	0.5833	7.166	7.383	7.385	7.387

Sources: Analytic values from Geske and Johnson 1984, table I, using four-point extrapolation. CRR binomial values with $N = 500$ from Hull and White 1988 (see also Cox and Rubinstein 1985 for $N = 150$ values). We add the last (LTB) column with $N = 50$ (except in the high-variance case, $\sigma = 0.4$, where $N = 480$).
a. Exercise price of option.
b. Instantaneous standard deviation of asset returns.
c. Option maturity.

various methods occurs when the put option is slightly in the money (rows 2, 11, 12 and 17, when $V = 90$ or 80), although the log-transformed binomial method and the finite-difference method still give the same results. In row 17, for example, the analytic method differs by +$0.07 (or +0.7%), while the quadratic method differs by −$0.07 (−0.7%) and the Johnson method by +$0.43 (+4%) from the median value ($10.30) achieved by the log-transformed binomial and finite-difference methods.

Table 10.2 compares the numerical-integration method with the analytic method and the two binomial methods for various at-the-money options (with varying r and σ). All methods agree within $0.1. The log-transformed binomial with only 50 steps seems to be as accurate as the CRR method with 500 steps: the two methods agree within $0.01 (except for row 1).[12] In most cases, the analytic method also agrees with the log-transformed binomial method within $0.01. In two instances, with low standard deviation ($\sigma = 0.1$) and low r (rows 10 and 12), numerical integration overvalues slightly relative to the analytic and the binomial methods, which are in agreement here.

Table 10.3 shows that, for a broader range of parameter values (EX, σ, and T), the log-transformed binomial (with $N = 50$) is again within $0.01 of the CRR binomial (with $N = 500$) and of the analytic approximation. In most cases, the analytic is even within $0.002 of the log-transformed binomial; however, in few (typically in-the-money) cases (rows 17, 23, and 27) it underestimates slightly relative to the two binomial approaches.

Table 10.4 compares American put values with one or two discrete cash dividends using the two binomial methods for varying parameter values (EX, σ, and T). In most instances the two methods give results within $0.01 of each other, the highest discrepancies of $0.03 occurring under high variance ($\sigma = 0.4$). The European Black-Scholes put values are included to give a measure of the early-exercise premium.[13]

Table 10.5 shows stability restrictions and consistency comparisons among implicit or explicit finite-difference schemes and their log transforms, numerical integration, the CRR standard binomial, and the log-transformed binomial methods. All but the log-transformed binomial and the log-transformed implicit finite-difference methods have specific stability constraints.[14] The log transformation eliminates the single stability restriction in the implicit finite-difference method and the binomial method and eliminates one of the two restrictions in the explicit finite-difference scheme. In terms of consistency, only the log-transformed binomial method and numerical integration are consistent for every step size. As has already been noted, explicit finite-difference methods are generally

Table 10.4
American put values with discrete cash dividends calculated by Black-Scholes European (BS), Cox-Ross-Rubinstein binomial (CRR), and log-transformed binomial (LTB) methods.[a] ($V = 40, r = 0.0488$.)

				Value of put option		
	EX	σ	T	BS	CRR	LTB
1	35	0.2	0.0833	0.01	0.01	0.01
2	35	0.2	0.3333	0.30	0.31	0.32
3	40	0.2	0.0833	1.09	1.11	1.11
4	40	0.2	0.3333	1.98	2.01	2.04
5	45	0.2	0.0833	5.33	5.41	5.41
6	45	0.2	0.3333	5.60	5.67	5.68
7	35	0.3	0.0833	0.11	0.11	0.11
8	35	0.3	0.3333	0.88	0.88	0.88
9	40	0.3	0.0833	1.55	1.56	1.56
10	40	0.3	0.3333	2.88	2.91	2.91
11	45	0.3	0.0833	5.43	5.50	5.50
12	45	0.3	0.3333	6.24	6.29	6.28
13	35	0.4	0.0833	0.30	0.31	0.31
14	35	0.4	0.3333	1.57	1.58	1.62
15	40	0.4	0.0833	2.00	2.01	2.01
16	40	0.4	0.3333	3.78	3.81	3.84
17	45	0.4	0.0833	5.65	5.70	5.70
18	45	0.4	0.3333	7.02	7.07	7.10

a. CRR binomial values are from Cox and Rubinstein 1985. European put values are obtained from the Black-Scholes model adjusted by reducing the stock price by the present value of the scheduled (escrowed) dividends. A \$0.50 discrete cash dividend is scheduled in $\frac{1}{2}$ month and in $3\frac{1}{2}$ months, so that 1- and 4-month puts ($T = 0.0833$ and 0.3333) have one and two scheduled dividends, respectively.

unstable, and the variance of the approximating discrete process can be a downward-biased (versus upward-biased in the implicit finite-difference scheme) estimate of the diffusion process.

The CRR multiplicative binomial model may also be unstable in that the error can blow up when $N < [(r - \frac{1}{2}\sigma^2)/\sigma]^2 T$. This may occur for certain parameter values because the risk-neutral probability P and the discrete process variance can become negative (see section B of the appendix to this chapter). Moreover, the CRR approximation is consistent only in the limit (as $\tau \to 0$). In contrast, if we take the logarithm of V as the state variable (X) that follows an arithmetic process and express time in units of variance, the log-transformed binomial approach is stable under any conditions and is consistent for any step size, not only in the limit.

Table 10.5
Stability restrictions and consistency comparisons between implicit or explicit finite differences (and their log transforms), numerical integration, Cox-Ross-Rubinstein multiplicative
binomial, and log-transformed binomial methods, where $m = r - \frac{1}{2}\sigma^2 (\equiv \mu\sigma^2)$, $K = $ time step
$(= \tau$; note $k = \sigma^2 K)$, and $H = $ state step $(= \Delta X)$.

Method	Stability restrictions	Consistency
Implicit finite differences	$H \leq \sigma^2/\|m\|$ [a]	Variance biased upward[h] by mean^2
Log-transformed implicit finite differences	None [b]	
Explicit finite differences	$H \leq \sigma^2/\|m\|$; $K \leq H^2/\sigma^2$ [c]	Variance biased downward[h] by mean^2
Log-transformed explicit finite differences	$K \leq H^2/\sigma^2$ [d]	
Numerical integration	$H^2 \geq \sigma^2 K + m^2 K^2$; $H \leq \sigma^2/\|m\| + mK$ [e]	Yes
CRR multiplicative binomial	$K \leq \sigma^2/m^2$ [f]	Consistent only in the limit[i] (variance biased downward by mean$^2/N$)
Log-transformed binomial	None [g]	Yes

a. See Brennan and Schwartz 1978, p. 470, equation 48.
b. That logarithmic transformation can eliminate the stability restriction in the implicit finite-
difference scheme is well known in numerical analysis.
c. See Brennan and Schwartz 1978, p. 464, equation 9; Mason 1978, p. 21, equation 4.4.
d. That logarithmic transformation in the explicit finite-difference scheme can eliminate one
of the two stability restrictions is shown in Mason 1978 (p. 20, equation 4.2).
e. See Mason 1978, p. 21, equation 4.3.
f. See section B of the appendix to this chapter for derivation.
g. The condition for consistency, $H^2 = \sigma^2 K + m^2 K^2 \geq (mK)^2$, also implies $0 \leq P \equiv$
$\frac{1}{2}(1 + mK/H) \leq 1$, which guarantees unconditional stability.
h. See Brennan and Schwartz 1978.
i. See, e.g., Cox, Ross, and Rubinstein 1979; Jarrow and Rudd 1983; Omberg 1987.

The log-transformed binomial method compares favorably in terms of computational efficiency, in part as a result of the log transformation. Geske and Shastri (1985) also note that when finite differences are log transformed they become computationally more efficient, the explicit scheme becoming the most efficient. They also find that standard binomial approximation—which was seen to be a special case of explicit finite differences with a conditional starting point allowing for improved efficiency—is still the most efficient method for evaluating one or a small number of options. Further, the log-transformed binomial method has the significant computational advantage over finite-difference schemes that only every second node in a triangular path must be calculated, instead of every node in a rectangular path. Computational efficiency is further enhanced by handling nonproportional dividends (using interpolation) such that post-dividend nodes recombine within the preexisting node structure.

10.6   Conclusions and Summary of Guidelines

Many complex option-related problems (e.g., those involving complex payoffs or multiple interacting options) cannot be modeled analytically. Numerical analysis of such problems is often an invaluable tool for the practitioner. This chapter has described various computational methods, such as simulation, finite-difference methods, and a binomial lattice approach, that are suitable for the valuation of such complex problems. In general, the method to be used in practice depends on the features of the problem at hand and on the desired accuracy and efficiency.

Simulation is relatively simple and flexible, and it allows the relevant risk-neutral probability distributions and expectations to be generated. It is useful with European-type options when the option payoff is complex, and it is more efficient when there are several underlying state variables. It is not as useful with American-type options involving early exercise or other types of intermediate decisions, or in determining optimal policies. In the latter case, finite-difference methods and lattice approaches are generally more appropriate.

Finite-difference methods can be used to value American as well as European options and are more efficient when a whole menu of starting (time-0) option values is desired. They can also handle several state variables in a multi-dimensional grid, although not as efficiently. Special care must be exercised in choosing an appropriate set of finite-difference approximations to the partial derivatives to avoid problems of stability and consistency (accuracy), although certain logarithmic transformations can be helpful. If properly formulated, certain finite-difference schemes can be seen to be equivalent to dynamic programming and other known formulations. In general, finite-difference methods may not be readily used with history-dependent payoffs, and they cannot be used at all when the partial differential equations describing the option-value dynamics cannot be specified. In comparison with lattice approaches their implementation is more mechanical and affords less intuition, although they can be more powerful when crunching a large number of different option values.

Lattice approaches emulate the dynamics of the underlying stochastic processes and are generally simpler, more intuitive, and practically more flexible in handling different stochastic processes (e.g., diffusion, jump or mixed, mean reversion), option payoffs, early exercise or other intermediate decisions and optimal policies, several underlying variables, etc. The log-transformed binomial lattice approach presented here is also designed to be favorable in terms of accuracy, consistency, unconditional stability, and computational efficiency. The latter is achieved both through log transformation and through a different adjustment for nonproportional dividends that allows post-dividend nodes to recombine. More important, the binomial lattice approach can handle easily a variety of possibly interacting options, a series of investment outlays or exercise prices (compound options), nonproportional cash flows (dividends), exogenous jumps (competitive arrivals), and other complications. The main limitation of lattice approaches is their inability to handle more than one starting price at a time, resulting in a relative loss of power when a large number of starting option values involving multiple runs are required. However, this is not a limitation in the case of valuing real options, since they typically involve one (or a few) estimates of initial values.

Suggested Readings

Boyle, P. 1977. "Options: A Monte Carlo approach." *Journal of Financial Economics* 4, no. 3: 323–338.

Brennan, M. 1979. "The pricing of contingent claims in discrete time models." *Journal of Finance* 34, no. 1: 53–68.

Brennan, M., and E. Schwartz. 1977. "The valuation of American put options." *Journal of Finance* 32, no. 2: 449–462.

Brennan, M., and E. Schwartz. 1978. "Finite difference methods and jump processes arising in the pricing of contingent claims: A synthesis." *Journal of Financial and Quantitative Analysis* 13, no. 3: 461–474.

Cox, J., S. Ross, and M. Rubinstein. 1979. "Option pricing: A simplified approach." *Journal of Financial Economics* 7, no. 3: 229–263.

Geske, R., and K. Shastri. 1985."Valuation by approximation: A comparison of alternative option valuation techniques." *Journal of Financial and Quantitative Analysis* 20, no. 1: 45–71.

Hull, J. 1993. *Options, Futures, and Other Derivative Securities.* Second edition. Prentice-Hall.

Mason, S. P. 1978. The Numerical Analysis of Certain Free Boundary Problems Arising in Financial Economics. Working paper 78-52, Harvard Business School.

Trigeorgis, L. 1991. "A log-transformed binomial numerical analysis method for valuing complex multi-option investments." *Journal of Financial and Quantitative Analysis* 26, no. 3: 309–326.

Appendix

A

This section shows that the risk-neutral probability in the log-transformed binomial model, P, converges (as $N \to \infty$) to that of the Cox-Ross-Rubinstein binomial model, q.

Let $m \equiv r - \frac{1}{2}\sigma^2 (= \mu\sigma^2)$. In the limit as $N \to \infty$, k^2 is negligible relative to k (as $k \equiv \sigma^2 T/N \to 0$), so that

$$H (= \sqrt{k + (\mu k)^2}) \to \sqrt{k}$$

(whereas in the CRR binomial model $H \equiv \ln u = \sqrt{k}$), and

$$k/H \to \sqrt{k};$$

thus,

$$P = \tfrac{1}{2}(1 + \mu k/H) \to \tfrac{1}{2}[1 + (m/\sigma^2)\sigma\sqrt{\tau}]$$
$$= \tfrac{1}{2} + \tfrac{1}{2}(m/\sigma)\sqrt{\tau} \ (= q).$$

B

This section derives the stability restriction for the Cox-Ross-Rubinstein multiplicative binomial method.

As with any weighted-average numerical scheme, the probabilities (weights) q and $1 - q$ must be constrained between 0 and 1. The condition

$$q \ (\equiv \tfrac{1}{2} + \tfrac{1}{2}(m/\sigma)\sqrt{\tau}) \geq 0$$

implies that $\sqrt{\tau} \geq -\sigma/m$, while $q \leq 1$ implies $\sqrt{\tau} \leq \sigma/m$. Both conditions together require that $\tau \leq (\sigma/m)^2$ or, alternatively (since $\tau \equiv T/N$), that $N \geq (m/\sigma)^2 T$. (Conditions on $1 - q$ lead to identical results.) If the number of iterations used is less than $[(r - \frac{1}{2}\sigma^2)/\sigma]^2 T$, the approximation errors may grow and the process may blow up. For example, if $r = 0.10$, $\sigma = 0.05$, and $T = 10$ years, the CRR binomial approximation may be unstable if $N \leq 40$. (The critical number of iterations below which stability problems may occur is higher for higher r and lower σ.)

Alternatively, if N does not satisfy the above condition, the variance of the approximating discrete process, which is a downward-biased estimate of the continuous diffusion variance, would become *negative*, leading to stability problems. From Cox, Ross, and Rubinstein 1979 (p. 249) or Cox and Rubinstein 1985 (p. 200),

Var(discrete process) = Var(continuous process) $-$ mean$^2/N$.

Note that the downward bias, mean$^2/N$, disappears and the approximation becomes consistent only in the limit, as $N \to \infty$. In practice, with N finite, to prevent the discrete-process variance from becoming negative and the process from blowing up, N must satisfy

$$N \geq \frac{\text{mean}^2}{\text{Var(continuous)}} = \frac{(mT)^2}{\sigma^2 T} = \left(\frac{m}{\sigma}\right)^2 T,$$

as above. In fact, any such method with a downward-biased variance (e.g., explicit finite differences, of which the CRR binomial method is a special case) may suffer from such stability problems. In contrast, methods guaranteeing a non-negative discrete-process variance, such as the proposed log-transformed binomial method (with variance positive by consistency design) or the log-transformed implicit finite-difference scheme (with variance positive because of upward bias), may achieve weights between 0 and 1 and, hence, require no external stability restrictions.

11   Applications

Parallel to these theoretical developments, real-options applications are now gradually receiving increased attention among major U.S. and international corporations and in the academic literature. Real-options valuation is being applied in a variety of contexts, including research and development, new ventures, natural-resource investments, land development, leasing, flexible manufacturing, government subsidies and regulation, corporate acquisitions and divestitures, foreign investment, and strategy.

11.1   Introduction

In research and development, many high-technology companies invest heavily in technologies that may result in a wide range of possible outcomes and new potential markets, but with a high probability of technical or market failure. In the pharmaceutical industry, for example, on average it costs $360 million and takes a decade to bring a new drug to market. Only one explored chemical in 10,000 becomes a prescription drug, and once a drug reaches the market it faces a 70% chance of failing to earn the cost of invested capital. Such investments are hard to sell to top management on financial grounds; their benefits are remote and hard to quantify, even though intuitively their growth potential seems promising.[1] Instead of ignoring these technologies, a company can make a capital commitment in stages, effectively taking a call option on the underlying technology (or future applications). The initial outlay is not made so much for its own cash flows as for its growth-option value.

In 1984 the W.R. Grace Corporation made an investment in a new technology for automotive catalytic converters. Although the technology proved uncompetitive on price in the automotive marker, new applications arose in cogeneration plants and in utility emission control as a result of the U.S. Clean Air Act. In the early 1980s, General Electric at first ignored the emerging magnetic resonance imaging (MRI) technology for medical diagnosis. The market at the time was unproven, and the project did not seem justified on the basis of DCF analysis; besides, the new technology would have competed with GE's existing x-ray-based CT diagnostic machine. Nevertheless, top management eventually overruled NPV analysis on strategic grounds and saw the project through to success. Walter Robb, GE's director of R&D, was quoted as having said that "the challenge is to find 30 projects a year that will pay off not by NPV but by the seat of our pants."

U.S. West, a telecommunications company adopting the options approach, has made investments in technologies intended to make its cellular phones and paging devices more user friendly (which otherwise would not be justified). "Our company doesn't have the maturity and experience to act on gut feelings," said David Sena, a U.S. West strategic planner.

In the late 1980s, the Digital Equipment Corporation used options analysis to value a proposal to build a semiconductor fabrication facility. The strategic planning and analysis group identified and valued several inherent strategic options that made the project's strategic (expanded) NPV more than twice the traditional NPV estimate of $20 million. Technology impact options, giving management the ability to consolidate the traditional manufacturing activities of two plants into one as a result of increased system functionality designed into the new silicon chips to be fabricated, were valued at $8 million. In addition, strategic technology options (providing flexibility to equip a facility to quickly "ramp up" a new manufacturing process technology if called for by the competitive environment) and options to expand capacity were estimated at an additional $13.6 million.

Merck and Co. recently embarked on extensive automation, starting with a drug packaging and distribution plant, even though technical success was uncertain and projected labor savings did not seem to justify the investment. "It was a tricky thing to convince the management. But options valuation allowed engineers to articulate the whole range of outcomes and their benefits," said Judy Lewent, Merck's chief financial officer. After management was convinced to take an option on automating the plant and promising results were achieved, it was willing to expand automation to its other operations.

In their R&D activities, pharmaceutical companies like Merck often enter into collaborative agreements with smaller biotechnology companies or universities in order to gain access to early-stage research projects.

(Several Japanese companies recently attracted media attention by developing such relationships with American universities.) Because of the small chances of making it to market and the long development horizons, cash flows are remote and highly uncertain (a 40–60% standard deviation for biotechnology stocks is not uncommon). To control risk and preserve its abandonment options, financing by the larger pharmaceutical company is often staged as a series of contingent progress "installments," with an early payment giving the right to make further investments (e.g., in clinical trials or commercialization). Merck was recently examining a project, known as Project Gamma, involving the acquisition of new technologies from a small biotech firm (for product development, scaling up of the manufacturing process, and product commercialization), that would position Merck to enter a desirable new market. Merck's Financial Evaluation and Analysis Group knew it could not rely on traditional DCF approaches and chose to use option analysis. The option value Merck arrived at was significantly higher than the required up-front investment of $2 million (a small amount relative to Merck's $1 billion annual research budget). On a different occasion, Merck used options thinking to justify a $6 billion acquisition of Medco, a company that managed prescription-drug benefits for over 30 million Americans through various employer-sponsored plans. Consistent with its strategy of getting closer to its ultimate customers, Merck saw the acquisition as an option to gain access to Medco's detailed records on more than 30 million patients. In commenting on Merck's experiences with options analysis, CFO Judy Lewent said: "When you make an initial investment in a research project, you are paying an entry fee for a right.... To me, all kinds of business decisions are options." Indeed, building and using options-based planning models was viewed as having created a valuable new capability for Merck.[2]

Many other companies have not been as perceptive as Merck in recognizing the strategic value of proving a new technology or of preserving corporate capabilities as an infrastructure for the creation, preservation, and exercise of corporate real options. In 1986 the Ford Motor Company conceded the development of small cars for the U.S. market to Mazda, and along with it allowed the erosion of invaluable technological expertise and capabilities that could be applied elsewhere. Similarly, RCA conceded to the Japanese the development of VCR technology, from which later sprang CD players, video cameras, and a range of other applications. Erosion of in-house technological expertise resulting from "passive" management has also affected Boeing and many other U.S. companies.

Even without quantitative analysis, conceptual options and strategic thinking could have helped many of these companies.

In its issues of August 12 and September 30, 1989, *The Economist* noted that options-based methods were being used or seriously considered in many practical industrial applications, and that management consulting firms were working to develop these methods further. Indeed, real-options valuation has been recently considered or adopted by a host of companies in a range of industries, including British Petroleum and Shell Oil in the oil business, the RTZ Corporation and the Newmont Mining Corporation in the natural-resources industries, the Digital Equipment Corporation and Cray Research in the computer business, and the Ford Motor Company and several Japanese competitors in the automobile industry.

11.2 Valuing a Pioneer Venture (a Growth Option)

Consider a pioneer venture (such as Project Gamma, which Merck Pharmaceuticals considered developing itself or acquiring from a small biotech firm). This type of high-tech project involves high initial costs and often insufficient projected cash inflows. Figure 11.1 represents such a project with an investment outlay of $I_0 = \$500$ million and expected cash inflows over 4 years of $C_1 = \$100$ million, $C_2 = \$200$ million, $C_3 = \$300$ million, and $C_4 = \$100$ million. Management intuitively feels a need to prove the new technology in order to enhance the company's market position if that market (or a spinoff product) should develop. Even if the pioneer venture itself does not currently appear profitable, valuable expertise and opportunity to enter a potential growth market may be lost to competitors if the investment is not made. Investing in the pioneer venture derives strategic value from the generation of growth opportunities to invest in future commercial projects. If the technology is proven, commercial production can be many times the size of the pioneer venture. The followup commercial project represented in figure 11.1 would become available in year 4 and is assumed to be 3 times the size of the pioneer venture (i.e., $I_4 = \$1.5$ billion, with 3 times the cash inflows in subsequent years).

The present value of the cash inflows expected from the pioneer venture, discounted at an opportunity cost of capital $k = 20\%$, is $V_0 = \$444$ million. Thus, the NPV is $V_0 - I_0 = 444 - 500 = -\$56$ million. The expected cash flows therefore make the venture unattractive by itself. The followup commercial project, which is 3 times the size of the pioneer venture, does not look any better. It requires an outlay of $I_4 = \$1.5$ bil-

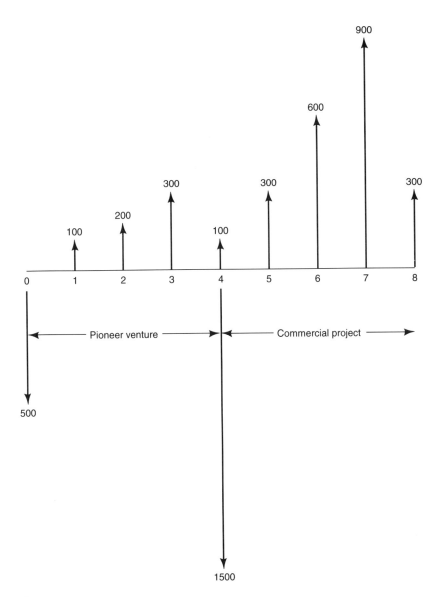

Figure 11.1
Capital outlays (↓) and expected cash inflows (↑) for the pioneer venture to prove a new technology, and potential followon commercial project (triple in size) to be acquired if the market develops.

lion as of year 4, only to generate a discounted value of subsequent cash inflows at that time of $V_4 = \$1.332$ billion. Its year-4 NPV is $-\$168$ million (3 times that of the pioneer venture), giving a time-0 NPV of $-\$81$ million after discounting for 4 years at 20%. Thus, if the firm were to commit to both projects (or "stages") right now, the total expected *loss* in net value would amount to $56 million + $81 million = $127 million.

However, management realizes that it will invest in the commercial project in year 4 only if the market is proven by that time and the project then appears profitable. Thus, investing in the negative-NPV pioneer venture is like incurring a cost to buy the option, giving the firm the right (with no obligation) to acquire the benefits of the followup commercial venture. That option will be exercised in year 4 (i.e., the exercise cost $E = I_4 = \$1.5$ billion will be incurred) only if the then value of subsequent cash inflows is sufficiently high. The $-\$56$ million NPV of the pioneer venture is the price that must be paid to acquire the growth option in the commercial project. The more uncertain the technology or the future market demand, the higher the value of this option will be. Is the value of this option worth that cost?

The growth option represented by the right to invest in the commercial venture is like a European call option with time to maturity $\tau = 4$ years and exercise price $E = \$1.5$ billion. The underlying asset value is the current (time 0) value of a claim on the commercial project's expected future cash inflows. This can be obtained by discounting the time-4 value of the cash inflows ($1.332 billion) back to the present at the 20% discount rate, i.e.,

$$V_0 = V_4 e^{-k\tau} = 1332 e^{-0.20 \times 4} = 598.5 \text{ million.}$$

Suppose the technology to be tested is quite uncertain, represented by a standard deviation $\sigma = 0.35$, while the risk-free rate, r, is 10%. Given this information, we can now follow the short-cut, practical procedure to obtaining Black-Scholes option values described in chapter 3:

$$\sigma\sqrt{\tau} = 0.35\sqrt{4} = 0.7,$$

$$\frac{V_0}{Ee^{-r\tau}} = \frac{598.5}{1500e^{-0.10 \times 4}} = 0.6.$$

From table A.1 in the appendix to this volume, the tabulated value at the intersection of 0.7 and 0.6 is 0.1185, or 11.85% of V_0. Thus, the value of the growth option to acquire the commercial project in year 4 if the market is proven by that time is currently worth $0.1185 \times 598.5 = \$71$

million. Therefore, the total strategic (or expanded) NPV of the pioneer venture is $-56 + 71 = \$15$ million. Management's intuition that it must invest in the pioneer venture for the strategic value of proving the new technology and positioning itself to take advantage of a future growth option is justified in this case, despite the negative NPV of its own direct cash flows.

11.3   Valuing the Opportunity to Develop Vacant Land

The following example provides a simple application of the basic binomial option-pricing principles to the valuation of vacant urban land, seen as an option to choose at a future date among different types of building construction. For example, Titman (1985) considers the choice between constructing a six-unit condominium apartment building or a nine-unit one, either in this period or in the next period. This framework can provide a rationale for maintaining valuable land vacant, even in the midst of a thriving real-estate market.

The optimal type (or size) of a building to be constructed in the next period is currently unknown; it will be determined by future real-estate prices that are now uncertain. Committing to either a six-unit or a nine-unit building today may be suboptimal relative to waiting one more period and making the decision after additional information about market conditions has been revealed.

Following an example similar to that of Titman (1985), suppose that the real-estate price for a one-unit condominium, P, is currently \$100,000, and that in the next period it will (with equal probability) either rise to $P^+ = \$150,000$ (if the market moves favorably) or decline to $P^- = \$90,000$ (if the market moves unfavorably). The construction cost (both now and next year) is \$80,000 per unit for a six-unit building (amounting to an exercise price of $6 \times 80,000 = 480,000$ for the entire building) and \$90,000 per unit (or \$810,000 total) for a nine-unit building. The current risk-free interest rate is $r = 0.10$. For simplicity, a rented condominium unit is assumed to just break even (i.e., the rent just covers operating expenses).

The value of the vacant land is an option on the maximum of the values from the alternative building types, developed either now or next year. Consider first the alternative that the land is developed immediately. The net present value of the future cash flows from immediate (time 0) development would be $\text{NPV}_0 = nP - C$, where n is the number of units in the building, P the current market price of a unit, and C the total cost of construction. If a six-unit building is selected (i.e., $n = 6$), the net present value

of constructing the building immediately will be $6 \times \$100,000-$
$\$480,000 = \$120,000$, whereas the construction of a nine-unit $(n = 9)$
building will be worth $9 \times \$100,000 - \$810,000 = \$90,000$. The land
will thus be worth the maximum of these two values (i.e., \$120,000) if
construction (of a six-unit building, in this case) begins immediately.

If construction is delayed until next year, the net present value (as of
period 1) of constructing a six-unit building in the next period will be

$$NPV_1^+ = 6 \times \$150,000 - \$480,000 = \$420,000$$

if market conditions are favorable and

$$NPV_1^- = 6 \times \$90,000 - \$480,000 = \$60,000$$

if market conditions are unfavorable. Similarly, for a nine-unit building the
net present value at time 1 will be

$$9 \times \$150,000 - \$810,000 = \$540,000$$

if the market moves up and

$$9 \times \$90,000 - \$810,000 = 0$$

if it moves down. Since the vacant land provides the option to choose the
building type next period (rather than immediately), after we learn which
building type is more appropriate given the market developments, we will
select the highest and best use at that time. That is, we will choose to
build a nine-unit building worth $C^+ = \$540,000$ if the market is up or a
six-unit building worth $C^- = \$60,000$ if the market is down.

Under risk-neutral valuation, the prevailing probabilities will be

$$p = \frac{(1+r)P - P^-}{P^+ - P^-} = \frac{1.10 \times 100 - 90}{150 - 90} = \frac{1}{3}$$

if the marker moves up and

$$1 - p = \frac{2}{3}$$

if it moves down. The current value of vacant land seen as an option must
then be

$$C = \frac{pC^+ + (1-p)C^-}{1+r} = \frac{\frac{1}{3}(540) + \frac{2}{3}(60)}{1.10} = \$200,000.[3]$$

If the price of vacant land were different, arbitrage profit opportunities
would arise. For example, if the land sells for only \$120,000 (the value of

immediate construction), investors can realize a risk-free profit of $80,000 with no initial investment by buying the land, selling short

$$N = \frac{C^+ - C^-}{P^+ - P^-} = \frac{540 - 60}{150 - 90} = 8$$

condominium units at the current price ($P = \$100,000$), and investing the net proceeds at the 10% risk-free rate. In fact, buying the land is equivalent to buying $N = 8$ condominium units and borrowing an amount

$$B = \frac{N P^- - C^-}{1 + r} = \frac{8 \times 90 - 60}{1.10} = 600,$$

or $600,000, at the 10% riskless rate. Thus, to avoid risk-free arbitrage profits, the current value of the vacant land must be

$$C = N P - B = 8 \times 100 - 600 = 200,$$

or $200,000.

11.4 Valuing Operating Lease Options

This section deals with the valuation of leasing contracts with a variety of embedded (possibly interacting) operating options. A leasing application with the options to cancel the lease early, extend its life, and purchase the leased asset is presented.

Much of the finance literature has concentrated on the analysis of leasing contracts, particularly pure financial leases affording no flexibility to the lessee to adjust the terms of the lease during its life. The Myers-Dill-Bautista (1976) framework of analysis, which determines the value of the displaced debt capacity simultaneously with the value of the lease, is now accepted as the standard in lease valuation. However, since that model is based on DCF, it is inadequate for valuing the various operating options written into many leasing contracts.

A few authors have attempted to use option pricing to value a particular type of option embedded in operating leases in isolation. Copeland and Weston (1982), for example, value the option to cancel a lease early, while Lee, Martin, and Senchack (1982) propose valuing options on the salvage value of the leased asset. The most comprehensive attempt to value a variety of operating options is that of McConnel and Schallheim (1983), who use a complex compound option-pricing model.

Unfortunately, even the most sophisticated of the existing theoretical models is of limited use in practical situations when more than one type of operating option is present simultaneously in a given lease, since the values of the options determined separately are often nonadditive owing to various kinds of interaction. Suppose, for example, that a leasing contract offers the lessee the options to cancel the lease early, to purchase the leased asset at a set price (either at or before maturity), and to renew the lease or extend its life. From the above discussion, it should be obvious that early exercise of the option to purchase the leased asset or cancel it early would end the lease, precluding exercise of any subsequent options (e.g., to renew or to purchase later). These later options would be less valuable, when following such prior "killing" options, than their independent valuation as stand-alone options. Moreover, in the presence of other options, a prior option to cancel early (seen as a put) would be less valuable—whereas a prior option to buy the leased asset (a call) would be more valuable—than if valued separately.

Thus, combinations of these operating lease options should be valued collectively by means of an options-based numerical analysis such as that described in chapter 10 (with appropriate adjustments). Before proceeding further, however, let us review traditional lease valuation.

Traditional Lease Valuation

Traditional lease valuation has mainly concentrated on pure financial leases, involving no cancellation or other operating options, and has been based on standard DCF analysis (e.g., NPV or IRR), with most of the controversy focusing on determining the appropriate rate(s) for discounting the various lease cash flows. Recognizing that leasing is a substitute for borrowing that displaces debt capacity, one would discount the after-tax lease cash flows (including lost depreciation and interest tax shields) at the before-tax cost of borrowing. By setting up an "equivalent loan" such that leasing generates identical cash flows in each future period as the buy-and-borrow alternative, Myers, Dill, and Bautista demonstrate that one can equivalently account for the interest tax shield on the debt displaced by leasing by adjusting the discount rate, using the *after-tax* borrowing rate.

The various component (after-tax) cash flows under the lease and under the buy-and-borrow alternative are summarized in figure 11.2. The net advantage to leasing (relative to buying and borrowing) or the NPV to the lessee—seen from the difference between the cash flows of the two alternatives in figure 11.2—can thus be expressed as follows (assuming ITC = 0):

$$NPV = V_0 - \sum_{t=0}^{N} \frac{I_t}{(1+r^*)^t} \equiv V_0 - I \qquad (11.1)$$

Buy (own) and borrow		**Lease financing**	
(Net) asset cost (own)	$-(V_0 - ITC)$	Lease payments	$-L_t$
Depreciation tax shield (own)	$+D_t T$	Lease tax shield	$+L_t T$
Net operating expenses (own)	$-O_t$		
Interest tax shield (borrow)	$+(rB_t)T$		
Expected salvage value (own)	$+E(S_N)$		

On the right: $\left.\begin{array}{c} -L_t \\ +L_t T \end{array}\right\} -L_t(1-T)$

Figure 11.2
Cash flows for lease financing versus the buy-borrow alternative. The difference between the (discounted) lease financing and buy-borrow cash flows gives an NPV (to the lessee) equal to

$$(V_0 - ITC) - \sum_{t=0}^{N} \frac{L_t(1-T) + D_t T}{(1+r^*)^t} + \sum_{t=0}^{N} \frac{O_t}{(1+k)^t} - \frac{E(S_N)}{(1+k)^N},$$

where $V_0 =$ current value (cost) of the leased asset; $ITC =$ investment tax credit; $L_t =$ lease rental payment at time t; $D_t =$ depreciation expense at time t; $T =$ lessee's effective corporate tax rate; $r_B =$ before-tax cost of borrowing; $r^* \equiv r_B(1-T)$; $B_t =$ amount outstanding at time t after principal repayments ($B_0 =$ amount borrowed at $t = 0$); $k =$ asset's risk-adjusted opportunity cost of capital; $N =$ life (maturity) of the lease; $O_t =$ net operating expenses; and $E(S_N) =$ expected salvage value.

with

$$I_t \equiv L_t(1-T) + D_t T$$

and

$$r^* \equiv r_B(1-T),$$

where V_0 is the current value (cost) of the leased asset,[1] L_t is the lease rental payment at time t, D_t is the depreciation expense at time t, T is the lessee's effective corporate tax rate, r_B is the before-tax cost of borrowing, and N is the life (maturity) of the lease.

Note that equation 11.1, with appropriate definition of variables, is presented in a standard NPV format. Of course, with nonzero ITC, net (after-tax) operating (maintenance, insurance, or other) costs covered under the lease (O_t), and with salvage value (S_N) accruing to the lessor, the net advantage of leasing to the lessee (or the adjusted present value) would be generally given by

$$APV = (V_0 - ITC) - \sum_{t=0}^{N} \frac{I_t}{(1+r^*)^t} + \sum_{t=0}^{N} \frac{O_t}{(1+k)^t} - \frac{E(S_N)}{(1+k)^N}, \qquad (11.2)$$

where k is the asset's risk-adjusted opportunity cost of capital and $E(S_N)$ is the currently expected salvage value.

The above DCF-based valuation, however, is not appropriate for the valuation of the various operating options written in typical operating leasing contracts. Ignoring or mispricing these options can significantly misvalue such contracts, since they allow the lessee valuable flexibility to adjust his or her future operations contingent on uncertain future developments in a way that maximizes benefits or minimizes losses. This again requires expanded-NPV or contingent-claims analysis. Application of CCA to operating lease options can be justified here by realizing that leasing is basically equivalent to a buy-and-borrow alternative, and therefore the payoff to a lease contract can be replicated in principle by buying the leased asset and borrowing a particular amount.

Examples of Operating Lease Options with Valuation Adjustments

Consider the generic example of a lease contract with several embedded operating options illustrated in figure 11.3. The lease calls for two ($N = 2$) prepaid rental payments (L_0, L_1) in exchange for the right to use the leased asset over the two specified periods. At the option of the lessee, the lease may be cancelled early (in year 1) after incurring a certain penalty (PEN).[4] Provided a specified additional rental payment (L_2) is made at expiration, the lessee may choose to renew the lease by extending its maturity for another period. At the end of the (initial or extended) lease term, the lessee has the option to purchase the leased asset by paying a specified percentage of its fair market value (e.g., its expected salvage value) as an exercise price (EX).

The end goal, of course, is to determine the value of the lease contract at the time of the initial decision whether to lease or to buy and borrow (C_0). To achieve this goal, a process of backward binomial risk-neutral valuation such as that described in chapter 10 can be employed, during which the value of the lease contract with embedded operating options (C_t) would be adjusted to C'_t each time an operating option was encountered, as described below.[5]

Option to Buy
The option to buy the leased asset at time t can be seen as a call option on the then salvage or replacement value of the asset, S_t,[6] worth $\max(S_t - EX_t, 0)$, and so the value of the lease contract is then increased accordingly:

$$C'_t = C_t + \max(S_t - EX_t, 0). \tag{11.3}$$

At maturity, of course, $t = N$ (here 2, or 3), and $C_N = \max(V_N, 0)$.[7]

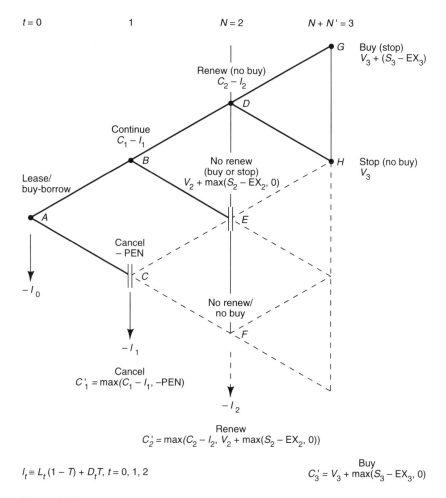

Figure 11.3
Contingency "tree" with valuation adjustments for a generic lease contract with options to cancel early, renew the lease, and buy the leased asset.

Option to Cancel
The lessee may terminate a cancellable operating lease early, just before a rental payment is due, if at that time its value from continued operation C_t (here $t = 1$), net of the lease "costs" $I_t(\equiv L_t(1 - T) + D_t T)$ then necessary for continuing, is less than the cancellation penalty (PEN) incurred:[8]

$$C'_t = \max(C_t - I_t, -\text{PEN}),\tag{11.4}$$

where $\text{PEN} \geq 0$.

Option to Renew (Extend Lease)
The option to renew the lease gives the lessee the flexibility to extend the maturity of the contract for another N' periods (here $N' = 1$), if extended operation is deemed beneficial, or else to maintain the original maturity (N). Actually, a lease contract with original maturity N with the option to renew until maturity $N + N'$ by incurring additional rental payments is equivalent to a lease with initial maturity $N + N'$ with an option to cancel early (without penalty) at N. Thus, the backward-moving binomial valuation process would start at the end of the extended maturity, $N + N'$, and when it arrives at the initial term, N, an adjustment similar to that in equation 11.4 would be made (with $\text{PEN} = 0$), i.e.,

$$C'_N = \max(C_N - I_N, 0).\tag{11.4'}$$

If the lessee can either buy the asset at the initial maturity (N) or renew the lease (without the option to buy later)—mutually exclusive options—then an adjustment combining equations 11.3 and 11.4' is sufficient, namely

$$C'_N = \max(C_N - I_N, V_N + \max(S_N - \text{EX}_N, 0)).\tag{11.5}$$

However, if the lessee also has a later option to purchase the asset at the end of the extended maturity ($N + N'$) after potential renewal, the required adjustments can become more complex. In general, during the backward binomial valuation process described in chapter 10 we would make appropriate adjustments for the operating lease options (as in equation 11.3, 11.4, 11.4', or 11.5), or subtract the required lease costs at the indicated times.

A Leasing Example

To illustrate the value of interacting operating options often written in leasing contracts, consider the known leasing example first presented in

Brealey and Myers 1984 (pp. 543, 555). This example will serve to set up the base case with no options, which will then be extended by the addition of the various operating options.

A trucking company with a 46% marginal tax rate ($T = 0.46$) was faced with the decision of whether to lease an asset (a bus) having current cost of $V_0 = 100$ (in thousands of dollars) or to buy and borrow. The lease called for six ($N = 6$) equal annual rental payments of $L = 18$, payable at the beginning of each period. The owner of the asset could depreciate it over 5 years using accelerated depreciation (ACRS) and was entitled (under the pre-1986 tax code) to a 10% investment tax credit (ITC = 10). The leased asset could be financed at a before-tax borrowing rate of 10% (giving $r^* = 0.054$). The asset's risk-adjusted opportunity cost of capital was estimated to be $k = 0.12$. Additionally, assume that the asset's expected rate of economic depreciation was $B = 15\%$ per year, the variance of leased asset value was 20%, and the risk-free interest rate was 7% ($r = 0.07$).

Without any operating lease options, the base-case lease NPV is about zero, suggesting indifference between lease financing and the buy-and-borrow alternative. This result, given in Brealey and Myers 1984, is also obtained under the CCA-based numerical analysis valuation (using 200 iterations),which, in the absence of options, reduces to a risk-neutral variation of the traditional (DCF-based) Myers-Dill-Bautista valuation as described in equation 11.1.

Consider next several extensions of the same leasing problem, first by introducing in the leasing contract, in turn, only one kind of operating option in isolation, and then by valuing certain interacting leasing options in combination.

If the lessee has an American put option to cancel the lease at any time without penalty, valued by making an adjustment in the backward binomial process similar to equation 11.4 (with PEN = 0), the value of the lease contract when it is cancellable increases to about 7, so that the value of the cancellation option itself amounts to 7% of leased asset value.[9] If a noncancellation provision during the first 3 years is added, the value of the leasing contract is reduced to about 5, so the cost of this provision to the lessee is about $(7 - 5 =) 2\%$ of V.

If the contract instead contains just an option entitling the lessee to extend the maturity of the lease for another 3 years (i.e., $N + N' = 9$), its value is increased by about 0.1. Finally, a European call option to purchase the leased asset at the initial maturity ($N = 6$) with an exercise price of

EX = 40 (equal to the expected salvage value in year 6) is worth about 6.8% of V.[10]

Consider now, for purposes of illustration, the options to renew the lease (for 3 more years) *and* purchase the leased asset present in the leasing contract in combination. Several possibilities are open here. If the lessee can both renew the lease and purchase the asset only at the initial maturity (year 6), the combined option value is 6.9. This is simply the sum of the two mutually exclusive options (6.8 + 0.1), since exercising the initial option to buy kills the option to renew the lease, and vice versa. If, instead, the asset can be purchased only at the extended maturity (year 9), with the exercise price roughly the then expected salvage (EX = 30), the combined value is about 12% of V, so that separating their exercise times adds a positive interaction among these options of about 5%. Finally, if the lessee is allowed to renew the lease and purchase the asset at either the end of the initial term in year 6 (with EX = 40) or the end of the extended term in year 9 (with EX = 30), the combined option value is increased to about 30%, indicating substantial positive interaction in this compound-call situation.

11.5   Valuing a Natural-Resource Project

The following example illustrates an actual application of options-based binomial valuation in the case of a natural-resource investment opportunity that was recently being considered by a major multinational oil company.[11] The company's executives felt that their traditional valuation techniques did not fully capture all of the opportunity's value. Despite a negative NPV of forecasted cash flows, they felt that the project's inherent flexibility and "strategic" potential might justify its undertaking. The "hard numbers" could not justify such a decision, however, and so the executives looked for alternative valuation frameworks that would help them understand better the value tradeoffs and to eventually decide whether the flexibility or strategic worth was sufficiently large to make up for the negative value of the direct cash flows.

The following analysis was a response intended to help the oil-company executives gain a better understanding of the relative importances to the project's value of various elements of operating flexibility. In the case of this mineral project, flexibility consisted of options to cancel during construction, expand production, abandon early for salvage value, or even defer project initiation. As these real options were interacting in the presence of one another, standard option formulas calculating the separate option values and adding the results were inadequate, necessitating the use of options-based numerical analysis. Sensitivity results provided an indication of the degrees to which various factors would influence the value of flexibility, reinforcing the degree of management's confidence in making judgments about their relative importances in the valuation of the project.

The project to be analyzed was a natural-resource investment producing a certain mineral. The base-scale project consisted of two main phases. The "construction phase" started with the commitment of the first outlay (in year 0) and would end when capacity came on line with the last planned capital outlay (in year 4). Overall, a series of five annual capital outlays needed to be incurred until construction was completed ($15 million in year 0, $32 million in year 1, $148 million in year 2, $176 million in year 3, and $132 million in year 4). This capital investment would result in a production capacity of 400,000 tons of the mineral annually for the base-scale project, after year 4. However, several years were required to penetrate the domestic market, resulting in a gradual buildup of sales; thus, production was not expected to reach full capacity until after year 10.[12] The mineral could be sold in the domestic market at a price of $330 per ton. In view of the selling price, sales projections, and the known costs of maintenance and operating,[13] the expected cash inflows during the project's "operating phase" from year 4 onward were estimated as shown in figure 11.4. The real risk-adjusted discount rate for the last stage of the project was estimated at 10%.

Although at the moment it was uncertain and remote, the executives felt that an export potential could be developed by year 6. At that time (year 6), they could consider adding stage II to expand the base-scale project. An additional $123 million capital investment in plant and equipment in year 6 (spread over 2 years) would increase the mine's capacity by 50%, producing an additional 200,000 tons per year that could be fully absorbed by the export market from year 8 onward. At the lower export price of $168 per ton, this capacity expansion translated into a 22% increase in the "gross" value of the base-scale project (i.e., the present value of its expected cash inflows).[14,15]

The executives could identify four types of operating flexibility embedded in this mineral project:

Cancellation during construction   In case mineral prices turned particularly unfavorable, construction could be cancelled and the developer could walk away from any subsequent planned capital outlays with no cancellation

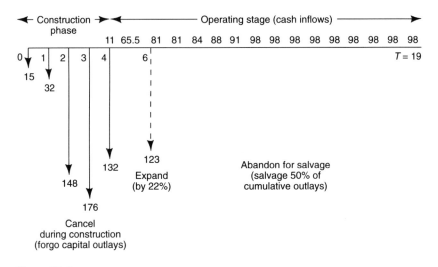

Figure 11.4
An actual minerals project with indicated capital outlays during the construction phase and expected cash inflows during the operating phase (in millions of dollars).

penalty. This option might be exercised at any time during the five-year construction phase.

Expansion At a given time (year 6), management could decide to add stage II, expanding production capacity by 50%, as discussed above. If sold at export prices, this implied an expansion of about 22% in the project's value. (The dollar value of expansion was estimated at 50% if the mineral could instead be sold at higher prices in the domestic market.)

Abandonment for salvage At any time, the project could be abandoned for its salvage value (with the machinery repositioned into alternative uses). In case of abandonment, salvage value was estimated at 50% of accumulated capital outlays, net of 10% annual depreciation.[16]

Deferral Initiation of the project could be delayed up to 2 years without any adverse competitive consequences.

The values of these real options and the operating rules that would guide managerial decisions as to when to exercise each of these elements of flexibility are implicit in the options analysis.

Base-Case Analysis

In addition to the project characteristics described above, the subsequent analysis is based on a number of facts and base-case assumptions. The

project's life was expected to be 20 years, assuming no early abandonment. The real risk-free interest rate was estimated at about 2%. The annual standard deviation of the project's gross value (or of the present
value of expected cash inflows) was estimated at 20% (i.e., the variance is
0.04).[17] Capital outlays and maintainance and operating (M&O) costs
were assumed to be known with relative certainty. (All figures are in real
terms.)

Before presenting the valuation results that capture the value of flexibility, we first determine the base-scale project's traditional discounted-
cash-flow (DCF) value, with no flexibility, as a benchmark to enable a
better appreciation of the relative importance of operating flexibility.
The discounted value of expected cash inflows from the base-scale project during the operating phase, using the risk-adjusted rate of 10%, resulted in a gross project value of $V = \$465.6$ million. The present value
of planned capital outlays during the construction phase, discounted at the
riskless 2% rate, was determined to be $I = \$476.2$ million. The difference
resulted in a negative NPV for the base-scale project:

NPV (no options) $= V - I = 456.6 - 476.2 = -10.6.$

This confirmed management's reluctance to justify the project using traditional DCF measures. To this value, however, should be added the values
imparted by operating flexibility. The value of each component of flexibility determined separately (using standard option pricing) is as follows:

cancellation during construction (valued as a compound call option on
project value with exercise prices the series of capital outlays): $41.4
million

expansion (valued as a European call on part of the project—here 22% of
V—with an exercise price the additional investment outlay of $123 mil-
lion in year 6): $17.4 million

abandonment for salvage (valued as an American dividend-paying put on
current project value, V, with exercise price the salvage value): $85.1 mil-
lion.[18]

The above separate option values are, of course, not additive, owing to
various interactions. If the project is cancelled during construction, it cannot later be expanded. If the base-scale project were in fact expanded, that
would alter the underlying asset (project scale) and the value of the later
option to abandon for salvage. Furthermore, the mere presence of the
later options to abandon for salvage or to expand would increase the

effective underlying asset for the earlier options. When our numerical analysis method was used to capture the interactions among these options, the combined value of all three options was determined to be $98.5 million (about 21% of the $476.2 million total capital outlays needed), increasing the total value of the project (from the no-flexibility NPV of −10.6) to $87.9 million.[19]

In addition to the value of flexibility, the options-based analysis simultaneously helped impute a set of operating schedules or rules that could serve as the basis for an optimal operating policy—for example, "Expand capacity if the mineral's price goes above $400 per ton at the time of decision (year 6)" or "Abandon if the price falls below $X in year t, $Y in year $t + 1$, etc."[20] These operating rules underscore the need to actively manage investment projects over time in response to future market developments, as opposed to the naive treatment depicted by a passive, mechanistic accept/reject decision at the beginning.

Sensitivity Analysis

To get a better feel for how sensitive the value of flexibility was to various factors, table 11.1 tabulates the results of our sensitivity analysis with respect to volatility of project value, estimates of salvage value, and variations in the riskless interest rate. As expected, a somewhat higher project-value uncertainty (driven mainly by the volatility in mineral prices) makes the various components of project flexibility significantly more valuable. For example, a 50% increase in the standard deviation (from 0.2 to 0.3) brings about a 40% increase in the combined flexibility value (from 98.5 to 137.3). Similarly, a 50% reduction (from 0.2 to 0.1) results in a 35% decline in flexibility value (from 98.5 to 64.6).

The value of flexibility was also quite sensitive to the percentage of capital investment that could be salvaged in case of abandonment. For example, as shown in table 11.1, a 40% decline in this percentage (from 50% to 30%) would result in a 20% reduction in the combined flexibility value (from 98.5 to 78.4). The results were not very sensitive to variation in the riskless interest rate, however. A 2% increase in the riskless rate (from 2% to 4%) would result in an increase in flexibility value of about 11% (from 98.5 to 109.7).

Finally, if the output from potential expansion (stage II) could be fully absorbed at the higher domestic price rather than sold at the export price, the expansion option would surpass in significance the ability to abandon,

Table 11.1
Sensitivity tests of combined flexibility value to variations in project volatility (standard deviation), salvage value, and riskless interest rate.

Standard deviation	Combined flexibility value ($ million)
0.1	64.6
0.15	80.7
0.2[a]	98.5
0.3	137.3
Salvage value (%)	
10	62.2
30	78.4
50[a]	98.5
70	123.0
Real riskless interest rate (%)	
0	89.5
1	93.7
2	98.5
3	103.9
4	109.7

a. Base-case assumptions.

becoming the most valuable component of flexibility (alone rising in value from $17.4 million to $125.7 million). The value of all three elements of flexibility taken together would then rise from $98.5 million to $170.4 million (about 36% of capital outlays). If the option to defer the project up to 2 years were also included, the combined value of all four options would increase further to $210.4 million (or 44% of capital outlays). Figures 11.5, 11.6, and 11.7 show how the total project value (expanded NPV) varies with project volatility, salvage value, and gross project value (V), respectively.

The above analysis again verified that the combined value of flexibility imparted by these real options amounts to a substantial percentage of the total value of capital outlays. It also emphasized once again that special care must be taken to account for possible interactions among these options. The combined value of flexibility justified going ahead with the mineral project, despite its negative NPV of expected cash flows. Options-based analysis was able not only to reverse the traditional DCF-based decision but also to underscore the importance of active management of the project over time, while providing guidelines for its optimal operation.[21]

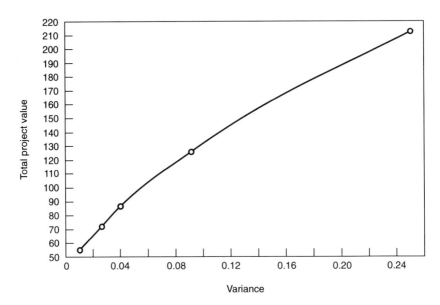

Figure 11.5
Total project value (expanded NPV) versus project variance.

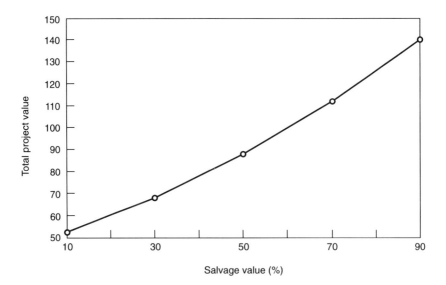

Figure 11.6
Total project value (expanded NPV) versus salvage value. (Salvage value is given as a percentage of project value.)

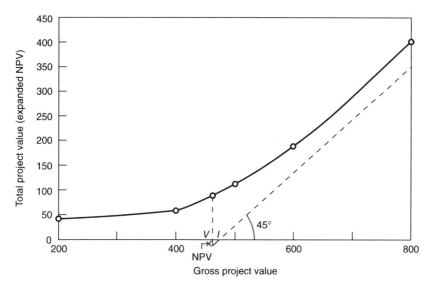

Figure 11.7
Total project value (expanded NPV) versus gross project value V.

11.6   Other Applications in the Literature

A variety of other real-options applications have appeared recently in the literature. Early applications naturally arose in the area of natural-resource investments, owing to the availability of traded resource or commodity prices, the high volatilities, and the long durations, which could result in higher and better option-value estimates.

Brennan and Schwartz (1985a) were the first to use the convenience yield derived from futures and spot prices of a commodity to value the options to shut down or abandon a mine. Paddock, Siegel, and Smith (1988) valued options embedded in undeveloped oil reserves and provided the first empirical evidence that option values are better than actual DCF-based bids in valuing offshore oil leases. As was described in the preceding section, Trigeorgis (1990a) valued an actual mineral project considered by a major multinational company. Bjerksund and Ekern (1990) valued a Norwegian oil field with options to defer and abandon. Kemna (1993) described actual cases involving the timing of developing an offshore oil field, the valuation of a growth option in a manufacturing venture and the abandonment decision of a refining production unit. Morck, Schwartz, and Stangeland (1989) valued forestry resources under stochastic inventories and prices. Stensland and Tjostheim (1990) also discussed some applications of dynamic programming to natural-resource exploration. Laughton and Jacoby (1993) studied biases in the valuation of certain commodity projects of different duration characterized by a mean-reverting price process rather than the standard random-walk assumption.

Titman (1985), Williams (1991), Capozza and Sick (1994), Capozza and Li (1994), and Quigg (1995) showed that the value of vacant urban land should reflect not only its best immediate use but also its option value if development is delayed and the land is converted to its best alternative use in the future. Quigg (1993) reported empirical results indicating that option-based land valuations are better approximations of market prices than intrinsic valuations that ignore the option to wait. In a different context, McLaughlin and Taggart (1992) viewed the opportunity cost of using excess capacity as the change in the value of the firm's options caused by diverting capacity to an alternative use. Copeland and Weston (1982), Lee, Martin, and Senchack (1982), McConnel and Schallheim (1983), Capozza and Sick (1991), and Trigeorgis (1995b) valued various operating options embedded in leasing contracts.

The flexibility provided by flexible manufacturing systems, flexible production technology, or other machinery having multiple uses was analyzed from an options perspective by Kulatilaka (1988, 1993, 1995a), Triantis and Hodder (1990), Aggarwal (1991), and Kulatilaka and Trigeorgis (1994), among others. For example, Kulatilaka (1993) valued the flexibility of a dual-fuel industrial steam boiler relative to a rigid alternative. Kamrad and Ernst (1995) valued the flexibility embedded in multi-product manufacturing agreements involving uncertainties in input price and in output yield. Baldwin and Clark (1993) studied the flexibility created by modular design that connects components of a larger system through standard interfaces.

Mason and Baldwin (1988) valued government subsidies to large-scale energy projects as put options. Teisberg (1994) performed an option-valuation analysis of investment choices by a regulated firm. Kolbe, Morris, and Teisberg (1991) discussed option elements embedded in R&D projects. Option elements involved in the staging of startup ventures were discussed by Sahlman (1988) and Trigeorgis (1993b). Willner (1995) suggested a jump-process formulation of the discovery nature of startup ventures seen as multi-stage growth options.

Strategic acquisitions of companies also often involve a number of growth options, divestiture options, and other flexibility options (Smith and Triantis 1995). Other applications of options in the strategy area were discussed in chapter 1 of the present volume. On the empirical side, Kester (1984) estimated the value of a firm's growth options at more than half the market value of equity for many firms, and at 70–80% for more volatile industries. Similarly, Pindyck (1988) suggested that growth options represent more than half of a firm's value if demand volatility exceeds 0.2.

Baldwin (1987) discussed various location, timing, and staging options that are present when firms scan the global marketplace. Bell (1995) and Kogut and Kulatilaka (1994) examined entry, capacity, and switching options for firms with multinational operations under exchange-rate volatility. Hiraki (1995) suggested that Japan's bank-oriented corporate governance system has enabled Japanese companies to jointly develop corporate real options. Various other option applications are found in areas ranging from the valuing of mean-reverting cash flows in shipping (Bjerksund and Ekern 1995) to global warming (Hendricks 1991) and to options for compliance with anti-pollution regulations (Edleson and Reinhardt 1995). The potential for future applications is not unlike a growth option.

Suggested Readings

Bjerksund, P., and S. Ekern. 1990. "Managing investment opportunities under price uncertainty: From 'last chance' to 'wait and see' strategies." *Financial Management* 19, no. 3: 65–83.

Brennan, M., and E. Schwartz. 1985. "A new approach to evaluating natural resource investments." *Midland Corporate Finance Journal* 3, no. 1: 37–47.

Edleson, M., and F. Reinhardt. 1995. "Investment in pollution compliance options: The case of Georgia Power." In *Real Options in Capital Investment: Models, Strategies, and Applications,* ed. L. Trigeorgis. Praeger.

Kemna, A. 1993. "Case studies on real options." *Financial Management* 22, no. 3: 259–270.

Kulatilaka, N. 1993. "The value of flexibility: The case of a dual-fuel industrial steam boiler." *Financial Management* 22, no. 3: 271–279.

Nichols, N. 1994. "Scientific management at Merck: An interview with CFO Judy Lewent." *Harvard Business Review* 72, no. 1: 89–99.

Titman, S. 1985. "Urban land prices under uncertainty." *American Economic Review* 75, no. 3: 505–514.

Siegel, D., J. Smith, and J. Paddock. 1987. "Valuing offshore oil properties with option pricing models." *Midland Corporate Finance Journal* 5, no. 1: 22–30.

Trigeorgis, L. 1990. "A real options application in natural resource investments." *Advances in Futures and Options Research* 4: 153–164.

Trigeorgis, L. 1995b. "Evaluating leases with complex operating options." *European Journal of Operational Research* 75 (forthcoming).

12   Conclusions and Implications

12.1   Review of Major Results

Motivated by the observed discrepancy between finance theory and corporate practice, chapter 1 explained the importance of active managerial flexibility in adapting to an uncertain and changing world marketplace and provided an overview of different types of flexibility seen as real options.

In reviewing traditional capital budgeting in chapter 2, we saw that conventional DCF approaches that either ignore real options and strategic considerations altogether or attempt to value real investment opportunities with asymmetrical claims by using a constant risk-adjusted discount rate can lead to significant errors in valuation, since asymmetric claims on an asset do not generally have the same discount rate as the asset itself (here, the value of the project).

In chapter 3, reviewing option pricing and contingent-claims analysis (with applications to financial options), we saw that any contingent claim on an asset can be valued in a world of risk neutrality by means of "certainty-equivalent" or risk-neutral expectations of future payoffs that permit discounting at the risk-free rate. However, if a nontraded real asset has a below-equilibrium return shortfall, a dividend-like adjustment may be necessary (the same holds for intermediate project cash flows or exogenous competitive entry).

Chapter 4 explained that management's flexibility to actively adapt its future actions contingent on uncertain future developments implicit in real options introduces asymmetry or skewedness in the probability distribution of net present value. This asymmetry expands the investment opportunity's true value (relative to static or passive NPV) by improving its upside potential while limiting downside losses. We thus called for an "expanded (or strategic) NPV" criterion to encompass both sources of an investment opportunity's value: the passive NPV of its expected cash flows, and an "option premium" for the value of operating flexibility and strategic interactions embedded in capital investments in a competitive environment.

Chapter 4 also presented a general conceptual framework for decision making in capital budgeting (consistent with an "expanded NPV" analysis) able to integrate the important operating-flexibility options (e.g., to defer or to abandon) with the strategic aspects of competitive interaction and project interdependencies (compoundness). We considered using a new scheme to classify projects and a set of strategic questions to help managers uncover the relationship between their implicit operating strategy and the option components of an opportunity's value, providing a practical guide in the process of capital budgeting.

In chapter 5 we considered how the options-based technique of contingent-claims analysis (CCA) can be seen operationally as a special economically corrected version of decision-tree analysis that recognizes open market opportunities to trade and borrow, and how it can be used in principle to practically quantify various kinds of managerial operating flexibility in capital budgeting. We also extended the analysis to examine the improvement in equityholders' value that results from financial flexibility, noting interactions between operating and financial flexibility. Also discussed in this chapter were a general framework based on the generic option to switch operating "modes," interproject interactions, and other extensions.

Chapter 6 presented some useful analytic results for quantifying managerial flexibility and developed various basic continuous-time relationships that are useful in quantifying the values of various types of complex options.

In chapter 7 we considered the nature of option interactions and the valuation of projects involving multiple real options. We saw that an earlier option is written not on the base-scale project as the underlying asset but on an "extended" asset that includes the value of subsequent real options. Further, exercise of an earlier option (e.g., to expand or contract project scale) may alter the scale of the project or the effective underlying asset for subsequent real options. Thus, interactions among real options present in combination may generally make their individual values non-additive, so that evaluating each option separately (using standard formulas) and adding the individual results may lead to gross overvaluation of their combined worth. The degree of interaction generally depends on the type, the separation, the degree of being "in the money," and the order of the options involved. All these parameters were seen to depend on the cumulative probability of joint option exercise.

The magnitudes and the nature of interactions among the options to defer, to abandon by defaulting on a planned investment outlay, to contract, to expand, and to switch use (or abandon for salvage value) were illustrated by means of a realistic generic example. We saw that the combined value of these real options can be of the same order of magnitude as that of expected measurable cash flows, so that ignoring them may result in significant undervaluation. On the other hand, possible negative interactions suggest that the incremental value of an additional option may be declining, and so valuation errors from ignoring particular options may be small. Sensitivity-analysis results of the impact of various factors on these types of flexibility were found to be consistent with option-theory predictions.

Chapter 8 described an options-based framework of strategic planning and control. We discussed how to integrate various strategic sources of value, such as the synergy among groups of parallel projects and interdependencies among projects over time, and provided a rationale for the use of control targets.

Chapter 9 illustrated how important competitive and strategic situations can be quantified. We examined explicit, closed-form analytic solutions capturing the impact of exogenous competitive arrivals and other factors on the total value (expanded NPV) of shared investment opportunities. Both in situations of anticipated competitive arrivals that can be preempted by an early investment and in cases of uncertain competitive arrivals, we saw that it is insightful to think of the impact of competition on the value of a real option as analogous to the impact of dividends on the value of a stock call option.

In the case of early investments that can preempt anticipated competitive arrivals, we used option-based valuation to obtain formulas that enable management to determine whether and when it would be optimal to wait (i.e., hold the real option unexercised) despite anticipated damage from competitive entry, or instead to exercise early (specifically, "just before" such an anticipated competitive arrival) for preemptive reasons. We also showed how option-based analysis can be extended to value investment opportunities with random exogenous competitive arrivals modeled as Poisson jumps. We noted that in equilibrium in a risk-neutral competitive-jump world a project must earn an expected rate of return given by $\alpha^* = r + \lambda(1 - k)$, and that competitive arrivals can be thought of as analogous to a continuous dividend payout (depending on competitive intensity and market structure). The analytical formulas suggest that the higher the intensity of competitive arrivals, other things remaining constant (as may be the case with "storable" growth opportunities with no intermediate cash flows), the more valuable the shared real option becomes if the project is to earn an expected return consistent with competitive-jump equilibrium. This suggests the seemingly counterintuitive result that a real investment opportunity on such a project in equilibrium amidst random competitive arrivals is more valuable, other things being constant, than an identical opportunity on a project without such competition. When the project has a below-equilibrium return shortfall and is expected to earn intermediate cash flows, however, a higher competitive intensity would tend to increase the "opportunity cost" of holding an option on the project (and deferring exercise) rather than acquiring the project itself, and would thus reduce the total value of the real option.

We also ventured into strategy, employing basic game-theoretic principles from industrial organization to show how to endogenize competitive reactions and capture strategic effects under different market structures. Based on a combination of game-theoretic principles of industrial organization and the binomial option-valuation tree (process), we were able to develop various competitive investment strategies, depending on the nature of competitive reaction (contrarian or reciprocating) and on whether the resulting benefits are proprietary or shared.

In chapter 10, after reviewing various standard computational methods (such as simulation and finite differences), we developed a log-transformed binomial approach, extending our ability to value complex investment projects with many real options that may interact. The proposed numerical approach provides a more intuitive framework for the analysis of real options than alternative techniques. It can easily handle a series of investment outlays or exercise prices (compoundness), discrete cash flows (or "dividends"), exogenous competitive arrivals (jumps), and a multiplicity of interacting real options. It also has improved technical qualities: it is consistent, unconditionally stable, and computationally efficient.

Chapter 11 presented various applications, including a pioneer venture, natural-resource investment, land development, and leasing options. This is an area of future growth that should gradually reduce the existing gap between theory and corporate practice.

12.2 Implications for Capital Budgeting

Viewing real investment opportunities as collections of options on real assets provides new insight into capital-investment decision making and enables managers to draw several important implications for capital budgeting, some of which may directly challenge popular conventional beliefs.[1]

Management should broaden its valuation horizon by moving toward an "expanded or strategic NPV" criterion in order to capture the flexibility of operating strategies it may implement as well as capturing other strategic interactions.[2] Under this expanded framework, the total economic desirability of an investment opportunity is explicitly seen as the sum of its static (or passive) NPV of directly measurable expected cash flows and the option premium reflecting the value of managerial operating flexibility and various strategic interactions. The incremental contribution of (and any interactions among) these additional sources of value (e.g., "deferrability value," "abandonment value," "commitment value," or "competitive loss") constituting the "option premium" should be added to the static NPV, so that an investment opportunity would now be desirable if

Expanded (strategic) NPV

= Static (passive) NPV + Option premium > 0.

By looking at real investment opportunities through this expanded conceptual lens of options valuation, managers can now better appreciate the following:

As various critics have suggested, traditional (passive) NPV may indeed undervalue projects by suppressing the "option premium" or the adaptability and strategic component of total value.

It may be justified to accept projects with negative (static) NPV if the value of managerial flexibility (i.e., the option premium) exceeds the negative (static) NPV of the project's direct expected cash flows.[3]

The value of managerial flexibility and the extent to which managers should make investment outlays in excess of what is dictated by traditional standards can now be quantified through options-based valuation.

The options framework also indicates that, other things remaining the same, the value of managerial adaptability ("option premium")

(a) is higher in more uncertain environments (again a direct consequence of the asymmetry it introduces),[4]

(b) may be higher during periods of high real interest rates,[5] and

(c) may be higher for investment opportunities that have longer duration or can be delayed longer (since more time before management has to commit capital makes an option more valuable).[6]

The beneficial effect of risk on real-option value cited in point a implies that, in more uncertain environments, real compound options (such as expansion or growth options that have a higher option-premium component) are more valuable than, say, simple deferrable investment opportunities, which in turn are more valuable than simple expiring projects. During the periods of high interest rates referred to in point b, compound options are again more valuable than simple options.

Point c implies that in the special case of a proprietary real option without any form of "dividends" (such as competitive arrivals or intermediate cash flows) management may find it optimal to wait until close to maturity before deciding whether to exercise the real option.[7] The value implicit in having control over the timing of exercising such a proprietary real option may help explain why many firms strive to achieve a dominant competitive position in their industry.

Contrary to conventional popular belief, higher uncertainty, greater interest rates, or more time before undertaking a project (though implying delayed receipt of the cash flows) does not necessarily make an investment opportunity less valuable. Although, as is traditionally recognized, each of these factors certainly damages an investment opportunity's static-NPV cash-flow component (this is indicated by down-pointing arrows in figure 12.1), they may nevertheless substantially enhance managerial flexibility and have the opposite effect on the "option premium" or adaptability/strategic component of value (upward-pointing arrows). Thus, the overall impact of these factors is not clear cut a priori, although it may prove beneficial for the total value of an investment opportunity or "expanded NPV" if it increases managerial adaptability or the "option premium" more than it reduces the "static NPV" component of value.

The presence of competitive interactions in shared options presents an interesting complication, since it may justify earlier exercise.[8] Since competitive actions may cause erosion in a real option's value that a firm may not be able to avoid by simply selling the option to others (since most real options may not be tradable), an early preemptive investment may at times be the only available way to prevent such undesirable competitive value losses. As was discussed in chapter 9, the effect of such competitive erosions on the value of a real option in a preemptive setting may be

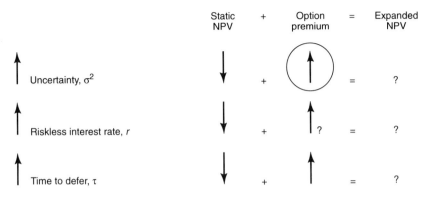

Figure 12.1
Impacts of various factors on investment-opportunity value components.

thought of as analogous to the effect of dividends on the value of a call option in justifying early exercise.

A firm with relatively little market power that is facing frequent competitive entries may find it reasonable for preemptive purposes to exercise its option to invest quite early—perhaps immediately if competitive entry is uncertain, or "just before" an anticipated entry. If no such preemptive ability exists in a reciprocating competitive environment, then exercise by one competitor may induce others to follow suit, leading to similar early exercise—especially if the first mover is likely to have a learning-curve advantage with respect to future operating costs.

In a reciprocating oligopoly situation where a common understanding that early exercise by one firm will trigger the "killing" of every firm's real options, competitors may find it preferable to defer exercising. (If mistrust develops, however, a "prisoners' dilemma" situation resulting in premature exercise is also possible.)[9]

A dominant firm exerting great market power and facing weak or infrequent competition may afford to postpone exercise until after competitors enter. Such a dominant firm may even benefit from competitive entry if weaker competitors can "prove" the market without taking significant market share away from it. In situations like this, it may make sense that the higher the frequency of competitive entries (which may cause only small damage to the firm's own project value) the faster the resolution of uncertainty in the market or the more valuable the insurance protection from waiting, and hence the more valuable the dominant firm's own real option, other things being the same.

In general, under exogenous competitive entry, management may find it justifiable to exercise relatively early (a) when its real option is shared with competitors and the anticipated loss in project value due to competitive entry is large and can be preempted, (b) when competitive pressure is intense, (c) when project uncertainty and, generally, interest rates are low, or (d) when the "competitive loss" preempted or the strategic benefit gained exceeds the "deferrability value" sacrificed by early exercise, or more generally when the value of managerial adaptability and strategic interactions (or option premium) is low relative to the (static or direct) NPV of the project's expected cash flows.

Under endogenous competitive reaction in oligopolistic markets, an early strategic investment commitment may not only affect the direct future cash flows (the direct NPV); it may also affect value indirectly by influencing the competitor's reaction and the resulting competitive equilibrium. The type of investment (proprietary or shared) and the nature of competition in the industry (contrarian or reciprocating) may thus critically influence the optimal investment strategy. In some cases, an early investment commitment may actually result in a strategic disadvantage if it reduces the firm's ability to respond to aggressive competitors who can exploit shared benefits from the strategic investment, or if it provokes a retaliatory response and intense rivalry when competitive reactions are reciprocating.

Thus, although an early strategic investment would necessarily reduce the option or flexibility value, other things constant, it may have a high or a low (even negative) "commitment" value, depending on the strategic effect. The strategic effect may be positive or negative, depending on whether the investment benefits are proprietary or shared, and may be opposite for reciprocating (e.g., price) competition than for contrarian (e.g., Cournot quantity) competition. How to quantify some of these competitive interaction and strategic effects was discussed in chapter 9.

The value of a particular type of real option may interact with other options embedded in a project. Since the combined value of several options may differ significantly from the sum of the values of the separate options, the project with all its options should be valued as a package. In complex real-life situations where analytic solutions may not be easily arrived at, binomial options-based numerical analysis can help management understand the nature and quantify the extent of interaction among multiple real options.

Capital budgeting should be seen as an active, ongoing process requiring continual monitoring and reassessment of new developments as they deviate from initial expectations, and requiring adaptation of management's implicit operating strategy in response to these developments. The larger the collection of real options or the greater the managerial flexibility attached to a project, and the more competitive and uncertain the market environment, the greater the need to determine the optimal timing of exercising these options (which will be influenced by the presence of other options) and the more valuable such active management will be. In the day-to-day management of this process, it is useful to give lower-level managers adaptable control targets that are contingent on the exercise of major future options. Because such an active strategy involves constantly monitoring the business environment for competitive moves and future investment opportunities, exercising existing options or creating new ones, capital budgeting is unavoidably intertwined with strategic planning and control.

12.3   Future Research Directions

Future research can be directed toward applying and extending these results in several new directions. Here is a list of the ten most important practical and theoretical potential contributions:

• Analyzing more actual case applications, and tackling real-life implementation issues and problems in more practical detail.

• Developing generic options-based user-friendly software packages with simulation capabilities that can handle multiple real options as a practical aid to corporate planners.

• Doing more field, survey, or empirical studies to test the conformity of theoretical real-option valuation and its implications with management's intuition and experience, as well as with actual market data when available.

• Using real options to explain empirical phenomena that are amenable to observation or statistical testing, such as examining empirically whether managements of firms that are targets for acquisition may sometimes turn down tender offers in part because of the option to wait in anticipation of receiving better future offers.

• Applying real options to the valuation of flexibility in other related areas —e.g., competitive bidding, information technology or other platform investments, energy and R&D problems, or international finance options.

• Focusing more on investments (such as in R&D, pilot or market tests, or excavations) that can generate information and learning (e.g., about the project's prospects) by extending and/or adjusting option pricing and risk-neutral valuation with Bayesian analysis or alternative (e.g., jump) processes.

• Exploring in more depth endogenous competitive counteractions and a variety of competitive/market structure and strategic issues, using a combination of game-theoretic industrial organization and option-valuation tools.

• Modeling more rigorously the various growth and strategic options— e.g., synergies between projects taken together or interactions across time.

• Extending real options in an agency context recognizing that the potential (theoretical) value of real options may not be realized in practice if managers, in pursuing their own agenda (e.g., expansion or growth, rather than maximization of the firm's value), misuse their discretion and do not follow the optimal exercise policies implicit in option valuation. This raises the need to design proper corrective incentive contracts by the firm (also taking into account asymmetric information).

• Recognizing better that real options may interact not only among themselves but also with financial-flexibility options, and understanding the resulting implications for the combined, interdependent corporate investment and financing decisions.

12.4   Conclusion

The goal of this book was to develop a systematic framework for analyzing capital-investment opportunities seen as options on real assets, with special emphases on operating flexibility and on the strategic and competitive dimensions (which are often left out of conventional discounted-cash-flow analyses). The powerful ability to quantify the thus far elusive elements of managerial flexibility and strategic interactions that the real-options paradigm brings is being recognized by an increasing number of sophisticated corporations around the world, in industries ranging from natural resources, to pharmaceuticals, to automobiles. With these powerful concepts and tools, we have entered a new stage in the evolution of capital budgeting.

Options valuation promises to offer an expanded and unifying evaluation framework for all real investment decisions by integrating capital budgeting and strategic planning under the single roof of long-term value maximization. Based on (arbitrage-free) market equilibrium, the options approach is internally consistent (unlike alternative approaches) and is well suited to the analysis of complex planning situations. Moreover, since the same consistent methodology has been used already in the valuation of most financial securities, options-based contingent-claims analysis has the potential not only to integrate all real investment decisions ("strategic" and "normal") but also to marry the real with the financing decisions under a common valuation paradigm. The potential to be able to evaluate all real projects (normal or strategic) and all financial investments (equity, debt, convertibles, etc.) through a single, consistent options-based methodology is not only fascinating; it may also have a far-reaching impact on the field of corporate finance as a whole.

Appendix

Table A.1

Value of call option relative to asset price. Rows: asset price divided by present value of exercise price. Columns: product of standard deviation and square root of time. *: zero (to four decimal places).

	0.05	0.10	0.15	0.20	0.25	0.30	0.35	0.40	0.45	0.50	0.55	0.60	0.65	0.70	0.75	0.80	0.85	0.90	0.95	1.00
0.50	*	*	*	*	0.0003	0.0015	0.0044	0.0094	0.0167	0.0261	0.0375	0.0506	0.0651	0.0808	0.0976	0.1151	0.1333	0.1520	0.1712	0.1906
0.60	*	*	*	0.0004	0.0024	0.0070	0.0144	0.0243	0.0366	0.0506	0.0661	0.0827	0.1003	0.1185	0.1373	0.1565	0.1761	0.1958	0.2157	0.2356
0.70	*	*	0.0005	0.0035	0.0103	0.0204	0.0333	0.0482	0.0645	0.0820	0.1003	0.1191	0.1384	0.1580	0.1778	0.1977	0.2176	0.2376	0.2575	0.2773
0.75	*	0.0001	0.0018	0.0077	0.0178	0.0310	0.0463	0.0632	0.0810	0.0997	0.1188	0.1383	0.1580	0.1779	0.1978	0.2178	0.2377	0.2575	0.2772	0.2968
0.80	*	0.0005	0.0050	0.0148	0.0283	0.0442	0.0615	0.0799	0.0989	0.1183	0.1380	0.1578	0.1777	0.1977	0.2176	0.2374	0.2572	0.2768	0.2963	0.3156
0.82	*	0.0010	0.0072	0.0186	0.0334	0.0502	0.0682	0.0870	0.1063	0.1259	0.1457	0.1657	0.1856	0.2055	0.2254	0.2452	0.2648	0.2843	0.3037	0.3228
0.84	*	0.0018	0.0099	0.0230	0.0390	0.0566	0.0752	0.0943	0.1139	0.1337	0.1536	0.1735	0.1935	0.2133	0.2331	0.2528	0.2724	0.2918	0.3110	0.3300
0.86	*	0.0031	0.0133	0.0280	0.0450	0.0633	0.0824	0.1019	0.1216	0.1415	0.1614	0.1814	0.2013	0.2211	0.2408	0.2604	0.2798	0.2991	0.3181	0.3370
0.88	0.0001	0.0051	0.0175	0.0336	0.0516	0.0705	0.0899	0.1096	0.1295	0.1494	0.1693	0.1892	0.2091	0.2288	0.2484	0.2679	0.2872	0.3063	0.3252	0.3439
0.90	0.0003	0.0079	0.0225	0.0399	0.0586	0.0779	0.0976	0.1175	0.1374	0.1573	0.1772	0.1971	0.2168	0.2364	0.2559	0.2752	0.2944	0.3134	0.3321	0.3507
0.92	0.0010	0.0118	0.0283	0.0467	0.0660	0.0857	0.1055	0.1255	0.1454	0.1653	0.1852	0.2049	0.2245	0.2440	0.2634	0.2825	0.3016	0.3204	0.3390	0.3574
0.94	0.0027	0.0169	0.0349	0.0542	0.0738	0.0937	0.1136	0.1336	0.1535	0.1733	0.1931	0.2127	0.2322	0.2515	0.2707	0.2898	0.3086	0.3272	0.3457	0.3639
0.96	0.0060	0.0232	0.0424	0.0622	0.0821	0.1020	0.1219	0.1418	0.1616	0.1813	0.2010	0.2204	0.2398	0.2590	0.2780	0.2969	0.3156	0.3340	0.3523	0.3704
0.98	0.0116	0.0309	0.0507	0.0707	0.0906	0.1105	0.1304	0.1501	0.1698	0.1894	0.2088	0.2282	0.2473	0.2664	0.2852	0.3039	0.3224	0.3407	0.3588	0.3767
1.00	0.0199	0.0399	0.0598	0.0797	0.0995	0.1192	0.1389	0.1585	0.1780	0.1974	0.2167	0.2358	0.2548	0.2737	0.2923	0.3108	0.3292	0.3473	0.3652	0.3829
1.02	0.0311	0.0501	0.0695	0.0891	0.1086	0.1281	0.1476	0.1670	0.1862	0.2054	0.2245	0.2434	0.2622	0.2809	0.2994	0.3177	0.3358	0.3538	0.3715	0.3890
1.04	0.0445	0.0613	0.0799	0.0988	0.1180	0.1372	0.1563	0.1754	0.1945	0.2134	0.2323	0.2510	0.2696	0.2880	0.3063	0.3244	0.3424	0.3601	0.3777	0.3951
1.06	0.0595	0.0734	0.0907	0.1090	0.1276	0.1463	0.1651	0.1839	0.2027	0.2214	0.2400	0.2585	0.2769	0.2951	0.3132	0.3311	0.3489	0.3664	0.3838	0.4010
1.08	0.0754	0.0863	0.1020	0.1193	0.1373	0.1556	0.1740	0.1925	0.2109	0.2293	0.2477	0.2659	0.2841	0.3021	0.3200	0.3377	0.3552	0.3726	0.3898	0.4068
1.10	0.0914	0.0996	0.1136	0.1299	0.1472	0.1649	0.1829	0.2010	0.2191	0.2372	0.2553	0.2733	0.2912	0.3090	0.3267	0.3442	0.3615	0.3787	0.3957	0.4125
1.12	0.1073	0.1132	0.1255	0.1407	0.1572	0.1743	0.1918	0.2095	0.2273	0.2451	0.2629	0.2806	0.2983	0.3158	0.3333	0.3506	0.3677	0.3847	0.4015	0.4181
1.14	0.1229	0.1270	0.1376	0.1516	0.1672	0.1837	0.2007	0.2180	0.2354	0.2529	0.2704	0.2878	0.3052	0.3226	0.3398	0.3569	0.3738	0.3906	0.4072	0.4236
1.16	0.1380	0.1407	0.1497	0.1626	0.1773	0.1932	0.2096	0.2264	0.2435	0.2606	0.2778	0.2950	0.3121	0.3292	0.3462	0.3631	0.3798	0.3964	0.4128	0.4291
1.18	0.1525	0.1544	0.1619	0.1736	0.1874	0.2026	0.2185	0.2349	0.2515	0.2683	0.2852	0.3021	0.3190	0.3358	0.3525	0.3692	0.3857	0.4021	0.4184	0.4344
1.20	0.1667	0.1679	0.1741	0.1846	0.1975	0.2120	0.2273	0.2432	0.2595	0.2759	0.2925	0.3091	0.3257	0.3423	0.3588	0.3752	0.3916	0.4077	0.4238	0.4397
1.25	0.2000	0.2004	0.2040	0.2119	0.2227	0.2353	0.2492	0.2639	0.2791	0.2946	0.3104	0.3262	0.3422	0.3581	0.3741	0.3900	0.4058	0.4214	0.4370	0.4524
1.30	0.2308	0.2309	0.2329	0.2385	0.2473	0.2583	0.2707	0.2842	0.2983	0.3129	0.3278	0.3429	0.3582	0.3735	0.3888	0.4042	0.4194	0.4346	0.4497	0.4647
1.35	0.2593	0.2593	0.2604	0.2643	0.2713	0.2806	0.2916	0.3039	0.3169	0.3306	0.3447	0.3591	0.3736	0.3883	0.4031	0.4178	0.4326	0.4473	0.4619	0.4765
1.40	0.2857	0.2857	0.2863	0.2889	0.2944	0.3023	0.3120	0.3230	0.3351	0.3478	0.3611	0.3747	0.3886	0.4026	0.4168	0.4310	0.4453	0.4595	0.4737	0.4878
1.45	0.3103	0.3103	0.3106	0.3124	0.3166	0.3232	0.3316	0.3416	0.3526	0.3645	0.3769	0.3898	0.4030	0.4165	0.4301	0.4438	0.4575	0.4713	0.4851	0.4987
1.50	0.3333	0.3333	0.3335	0.3346	0.3378	0.3432	0.3506	0.3595	0.3696	0.3806	0.3923	0.4044	0.4170	0.4298	0.4429	0.4561	0.4693	0.4826	0.4959	0.5092
1.75	0.4286	0.4286	0.4286	0.4287	0.4294	0.4313	0.4347	0.4395	0.4457	0.4530	0.4613	0.4703	0.4799	0.4900	0.5005	0.5112	0.5222	0.5334	0.5447	0.5560
2.00	0.5000	0.5000	0.5000	0.5000	0.5001	0.5007	0.5022	0.5047	0.5083	0.5131	0.5188	0.5253	0.5326	0.5404	0.5488	0.5575	0.5666	0.5760	0.5856	0.5953
2.50	0.6000	0.6000	0.6000	0.6000	0.6000	0.6001	0.6003	0.6009	0.6021	0.6041	0.6067	0.6101	0.6142	0.6190	0.6243	0.6301	0.6363	0.6430	0.6499	0.6571

	1.05	1.10	1.15	1.20	1.25	1.30	1.35	1.40	1.45	1.50	1.75	2.00	2.25	2.50	2.75	3.00	3.50	4.00	4.50	5.00
0.50	0.2103	0.2301	0.2500	0.2700	0.2899	0.3098	0.3295	0.3491	0.3686	0.3878	0.4803	0.5651	0.6412	0.7080	0.7655	0.8143	0.8883	0.9364	0.9657	0.9826
0.60	0.2555	0.2754	0.2953	0.3150	0.3346	0.3540	0.3731	0.3921	0.4109	0.4293	0.5174	0.5973	0.6684	0.7306	0.7840	0.8291	0.8973	0.9416	0.9686	0.9840
0.70	0.2964	0.3165	0.3358	0.3550	0.3739	0.3926	0.4111	0.4293	0.4472	0.4649	0.5485	0.6239	0.6907	0.7490	0.7989	0.8410	0.9046	0.9458	0.9708	0.9852
0.75	0.3162	0.3355	0.3545	0.3733	0.3919	0.4102	0.4283	0.4461	0.4636	0.4808	0.5623	0.6356	0.7005	0.7570	0.8054	0.8462	0.9077	0.9467	0.9718	0.9857
0.80	0.3347	0.3535	0.3722	0.3906	0.4088	0.4268	0.4444	0.4618	0.4789	0.4957	0.5751	0.6464	0.7095	0.7643	0.8113	0.8509	0.9106	0.9492	0.9727	0.9861
0.82	0.3418	0.3605	0.3790	0.3973	0.4153	0.4331	0.4506	0.4678	0.4847	0.5014	0.5799	0.6505	0.7129	0.7671	0.8135	0.8527	0.9116	0.9498	0.9730	0.9863
0.84	0.3488	0.3674	0.3857	0.4039	0.4217	0.4393	0.4566	0.4737	0.4904	0.5069	0.5847	0.6545	0.7162	0.7698	0.8157	0.8544	0.9127	0.9504	0.9733	0.9865
0.86	0.3557	0.3741	0.3923	0.4103	0.4279	0.4454	0.4625	0.4794	0.4960	0.5123	0.5893	0.6583	0.7194	0.7724	0.8178	0.8560	0.9137	0.9510	0.9736	0.9866
0.88	0.3624	0.3807	0.3987	0.4165	0.4340	0.4513	0.4683	0.4850	0.5014	0.5176	0.5938	0.6621	0.7225	0.7749	0.8198	0.8577	0.9146	0.9515	0.9739	0.9868
0.90	0.3690	0.3872	0.4050	0.4226	0.4400	0.4571	0.4739	0.4905	0.5068	0.5227	0.5981	0.6658	0.7255	0.7774	0.8218	0.8592	0.9156	0.9521	0.9742	0.9869
0.92	0.3755	0.3935	0.4112	0.4287	0.4459	0.4628	0.4795	0.4958	0.5119	0.5278	0.6024	0.6693	0.7284	0.7798	0.8237	0.8607	0.9165	0.9526	0.9745	0.9871
0.94	0.3819	0.3997	0.4172	0.4345	0.4516	0.4683	0.4848	0.5011	0.5170	0.5327	0.6066	0.6728	0.7313	0.7821	0.8256	0.8622	0.9174	0.9531	0.9748	0.9872
0.96	0.3882	0.4058	0.4232	0.4403	0.4572	0.4738	0.4901	0.5062	0.5220	0.5375	0.6106	0.6762	0.7341	0.7844	0.8274	0.8636	0.9182	0.9536	0.9750	0.9873
0.98	0.3944	0.4118	0.4290	0.4460	0.4627	0.4791	0.4953	0.5112	0.5268	0.5422	0.6146	0.6795	0.7368	0.7866	0.8292	0.8650	0.9191	0.9540	0.9753	0.9875
1.00	0.4004	0.4177	0.4347	0.4515	0.4680	0.4843	0.5003	0.5161	0.5315	0.5467	0.6184	0.6827	0.7394	0.7887	0.8309	0.8664	0.9199	0.9545	0.9756	0.9876
1.02	0.4064	0.4234	0.4403	0.4569	0.4733	0.4894	0.5053	0.5209	0.5362	0.5512	0.6222	0.6858	0.7420	0.7908	0.8325	0.8677	0.9207	0.9549	0.9758	0.9877
1.04	0.4122	0.4291	0.4458	0.4623	0.4785	0.4944	0.5101	0.5255	0.5407	0.5556	0.6259	0.6889	0.7445	0.7928	0.8342	0.8690	0.9214	0.9554	0.9760	0.9878
1.06	0.4179	0.4347	0.4512	0.4675	0.4835	0.4993	0.5149	0.5301	0.5452	0.5599	0.6295	0.6919	0.7469	0.7948	0.8357	0.8702	0.9222	0.9558	0.9763	0.9879
1.08	0.4236	0.4401	0.4565	0.4726	0.4885	0.5041	0.5195	0.5346	0.5495	0.5641	0.6330	0.6948	0.7493	0.7967	0.8373	0.8715	0.9229	0.9562	0.9765	0.9881
1.10	0.4291	0.4455	0.4617	0.4776	0.4933	0.5088	0.5241	0.5390	0.5538	0.5682	0.6364	0.6976	0.7517	0.7986	0.8388	0.8726	0.9236	0.9566	0.9767	0.9882
1.12	0.4345	0.4508	0.4668	0.4826	0.4981	0.5134	0.5285	0.5434	0.5579	0.5722	0.6398	0.7004	0.7539	0.8005	0.8403	0.8738	0.9243	0.9570	0.9769	0.9883
1.14	0.4399	0.4559	0.4718	0.4874	0.5028	0.5180	0.5329	0.5476	0.5620	0.5762	0.6431	0.7031	0.7562	0.8023	0.8417	0.8749	0.9250	0.9574	0.9771	0.9884
1.16	0.4451	0.4610	0.4767	0.4922	0.5074	0.5224	0.5372	0.5517	0.5660	0.5801	0.6463	0.7058	0.7583	0.8040	0.8431	0.8760	0.9257	0.9578	0.9773	0.9885
1.18	0.4503	0.4660	0.4815	0.4968	0.5119	0.5268	0.5414	0.5558	0.5699	0.5838	0.6495	0.7084	0.7605	0.8057	0.8445	0.8771	0.9263	0.9581	0.9775	0.9886
1.20	0.4554	0.4709	0.4863	0.5014	0.5163	0.5310	0.5455	0.5598	0.5738	0.5876	0.6526	0.7110	0.7626	0.8074	0.8458	0.8782	0.9269	0.9585	0.9777	0.9887
1.25	0.4677	0.4828	0.4978	0.5125	0.5271	0.5414	0.5555	0.5694	0.5831	0.5965	0.6600	0.7171	0.7676	0.8115	0.8490	0.8807	0.9284	0.9594	0.9782	0.9889
1.30	0.4796	0.4943	0.5088	0.5231	0.5373	0.5513	0.5651	0.5786	0.5920	0.6051	0.6671	0.7230	0.7723	0.8153	0.8521	0.8831	0.9299	0.9602	0.9786	0.9891
1.35	0.4909	0.5052	0.5193	0.5333	0.5471	0.5608	0.5742	0.5874	0.6005	0.6133	0.6739	0.7285	0.7768	0.8189	0.8550	0.8854	0.9312	0.9609	0.9790	0.9893
1.40	0.5018	0.5157	0.5295	0.5431	0.5565	0.5698	0.5829	0.5958	0.6086	0.6211	0.6804	0.7338	0.7811	0.8224	0.8577	0.8875	0.9325	0.9616	0.9794	0.9895
1.45	0.5123	0.5258	0.5392	0.5524	0.5656	0.5785	0.5913	0.6039	0.6163	0.6286	0.6865	0.7389	0.7852	0.8257	0.8603	0.8896	0.9337	0.9623	0.9798	0.9897
1.50	0.5224	0.5355	0.5485	0.5614	0.5742	0.5869	0.5993	0.6116	0.6238	0.6357	0.6924	0.7437	0.7892	0.8288	0.8628	0.8916	0.9349	0.9630	0.9801	0.9899
1.75	0.5674	0.5788	0.5902	0.6015	0.6128	0.6240	0.6350	0.6460	0.6568	0.6675	0.7186	0.7650	0.8064	0.8426	0.8738	0.9001	0.9400	0.9659	0.9816	0.9907
2.00	0.6051	0.6151	0.6250	0.6350	0.6450	0.6549	0.6648	0.6746	0.6843	0.6939	0.7402	0.7826	0.8206	0.8540	0.8828	0.9072	0.9441	0.9682	0.9829	0.9913
2.50	0.6645	0.6721	0.6798	0.6877	0.6956	0.7035	0.7115	0.7195	0.7274	0.7354	0.7740	0.8100	0.8427	0.8716	0.8967	0.9180	0.9505	0.9718	0.9848	0.9923

Table A.2
Value of put option relative to asset price. Rows: asset price divided by present value of exercise price. Columns: product of standard deviation and square root of time. *: zero (to four decimal places).

	0.05	0.10	0.15	0.20	0.25	0.30	0.35	0.40	0.45	0.50	0.55	0.60	0.65	0.70	0.75	0.80	0.85	0.90	0.95	1.00
0.50	1.0000	1.0000	1.0000	1.0000	1.0003	1.0015	1.0044	1.0094	1.0167	1.0261	1.0375	1.0506	1.0651	1.0808	1.0976	1.1151	1.1333	1.1520	1.1712	1.1906
0.60	0.6667	0.6667	0.6667	0.6671	0.6691	0.6736	0.6810	0.6910	0.7032	0.7172	0.7327	0.7494	0.7669	0.7852	0.8040	0.8332	0.8427	0.8625	0.8823	0.9023
0.70	0.4286	0.4286	0.4291	0.4321	0.4388	0.4490	0.4618	0.4767	0.4931	0.5106	0.5289	0.5477	0.5670	0.5866	0.6064	0.6263	0.6462	0.6661	0.6860	0.7058
0.75	0.3333	0.3334	0.3352	0.3411	0.3511	0.3643	0.3796	0.3965	0.4144	0.4330	0.4522	0.4716	0.4915	0.5112	0.5312	0.5511	0.5710	0.5908	0.6106	0.6301
0.80	0.2500	0.2505	0.2550	0.2648	0.2783	0.2942	0.3115	0.3299	0.3489	0.3683	0.3880	0.4078	0.4277	0.4477	0.4676	0.4874	0.5072	0.5268	0.5463	0.5656
0.82	0.2195	0.2205	0.2267	0.2381	0.2529	0.2697	0.2877	0.3065	0.3258	0.3454	0.3653	0.3852	0.4051	0.4250	0.4449	0.4647	0.4843	0.5038	0.5232	0.5423
0.84	0.1905	0.1923	0.2004	0.2135	0.2295	0.2471	0.2656	0.2848	0.3044	0.3242	0.3441	0.3640	0.3839	0.4038	0.4236	0.4433	0.4628	0.4822	0.5014	0.5205
0.86	0.1628	0.1659	0.1761	0.1908	0.2078	0.2261	0.2452	0.2647	0.2844	0.3043	0.3242	0.3442	0.3641	0.3839	0.4036	0.4232	0.4426	0.4619	0.4809	0.4998
0.88	0.1365	0.1414	0.1538	0.1700	0.1879	0.2068	0.2262	0.2460	0.2658	0.2858	0.3057	0.3256	0.3454	0.3652	0.3848	0.4042	0.4235	0.4426	0.4616	0.4803
0.90	0.1114	0.1190	0.1336	0.1510	0.1697	0.1890	0.2087	0.2286	0.2485	0.2684	0.2884	0.3082	0.3279	0.3476	0.3670	0.3864	0.4055	0.4245	0.4433	0.4618
0.92	0.0880	0.0988	0.1152	0.1337	0.1530	0.1726	0.1925	0.2124	0.2324	0.2523	0.2721	0.2919	0.3115	0.3310	0.3503	0.3695	0.3885	0.4073	0.4259	0.4443
0.94	0.0665	0.0807	0.0988	0.1180	0.1377	0.1575	0.1775	0.1974	0.2173	0.2372	0.2569	0.2765	0.2960	0.3154	0.3346	0.3536	0.3724	0.3911	0.4095	0.4278
0.96	0.0476	0.0649	0.0841	0.1038	0.1237	0.1437	0.1636	0.1835	0.2033	0.2230	0.2426	0.2621	0.2815	0.3007	0.3197	0.3385	0.3572	0.3757	0.3940	0.4120
0.98	0.0320	0.0513	0.0711	0.0911	0.1110	0.1309	0.1508	0.1705	0.1902	0.2098	0.2292	0.2486	0.2677	0.2868	0.3056	0.3243	0.3428	0.3611	0.3792	0.3971
1.00	0.0199	0.0399	0.0598	0.0797	0.0995	0.1192	0.1389	0.1585	0.1780	0.1974	0.2167	0.2358	0.2548	0.2737	0.2923	0.3108	0.3292	0.3473	0.3652	0.3829
1.02	0.0115	0.0305	0.0499	0.0695	0.0890	0.1085	0.1280	0.1474	0.1666	0.1858	0.2049	0.2238	0.2426	0.2613	0.2798	0.2981	0.3162	0.3342	0.3519	0.3694
1.04	0.0061	0.0228	0.0414	0.0604	0.0795	0.0987	0.1179	0.1370	0.1560	0.1750	0.1938	0.2125	0.2311	0.2496	0.2679	0.2860	0.3039	0.3217	0.3392	0.3566
1.06	0.0029	0.0168	0.0341	0.0523	0.0710	0.0897	0.1085	0.1273	0.1461	0.1648	0.1834	0.2019	0.2203	0.2385	0.2566	0.2745	0.2923	0.3098	0.3272	0.3444
1.08	0.0013	0.0122	0.0279	0.0453	0.0632	0.0815	0.0999	0.1184	0.1368	0.1553	0.1736	0.1919	0.2100	0.2280	0.2459	0.2636	0.2812	0.2985	0.3157	0.3327
1.10	0.0005	0.0087	0.0227	0.0390	0.0563	0.0740	0.0920	0.1101	0.1282	0.1463	0.1644	0.1824	0.2003	0.2181	0.2357	0.2533	0.2706	0.2878	0.3048	0.3216
1.12	0.0002	0.0061	0.0184	0.0336	0.0500	0.0672	0.0847	0.1024	0.1201	0.1379	0.1557	0.1735	0.1911	0.2087	0.2261	0.2434	0.2606	0.2775	0.2944	0.3110
1.14	0.0001	0.0042	0.0148	0.0288	0.0444	0.0609	0.0779	0.0952	0.1126	0.1301	0.1476	0.1650	0.1824	0.1998	0.2170	0.2340	0.2510	0.2678	0.2844	0.3008
1.16	*	0.0028	0.0118	0.0246	0.0394	0.0552	0.0717	0.0885	0.1055	0.1227	0.1399	0.1571	0.1742	0.1913	0.2083	0.2251	0.2419	0.2585	0.2749	0.2911
1.18	*	0.0019	0.0094	0.0210	0.0349	0.0501	0.0660	0.0823	0.0990	0.1158	0.1326	0.1495	0.1664	0.1832	0.2000	0.2167	0.2332	0.2496	0.2658	0.2819
1.20	*	0.0012	0.0074	0.0179	0.0309	0.0453	0.0607	0.0766	0.0928	0.1092	0.1258	0.1424	0.1590	0.1756	0.1921	0.2086	0.2249	0.2411	0.2571	0.2730
1.25	*	0.0004	0.0040	0.0119	0.0227	0.0353	0.0492	0.0639	0.0791	0.0946	0.1104	0.1262	0.1422	0.1581	0.1741	0.1900	0.2058	0.2214	0.2370	0.2524
1.30	*	0.0001	0.0021	0.0078	0.0165	0.0275	0.0399	0.0534	0.0675	0.0821	0.0970	0.1121	0.1274	0.1427	0.1581	0.1734	0.1887	0.2039	0.2190	0.2339
1.35	*	*	0.0011	0.0050	0.0120	0.0213	0.0324	0.0446	0.0577	0.0714	0.0854	0.0998	0.1144	0.1291	0.1438	0.1586	0.1733	0.1881	0.2027	0.2172
1.40	*	*	0.0005	0.0032	0.0087	0.0165	0.0263	0.0373	0.0494	0.0621	0.0754	0.0890	0.1029	0.1169	0.1311	0.1453	0.1596	0.1738	0.1880	0.2021
1.45	*	*	0.0003	0.0020	0.0062	0.0128	0.0212	0.0312	0.0423	0.0541	0.0666	0.0795	0.0927	0.1061	0.1197	0.1334	0.1472	0.1609	0.1747	0.1883
1.50	*	*	0.0001	0.0013	0.0045	0.0099	0.0173	0.0262	0.0363	0.0473	0.0589	0.0711	0.0837	0.0965	0.1096	0.1227	0.1360	0.1493	0.1626	0.1758
1.75	*	*	*	0.0001	0.0008	0.0027	0.0061	0.0110	0.0171	0.0245	0.0327	0.0417	0.0513	0.0614	0.0719	0.0827	0.0937	0.1048	0.1161	0.1275
2.00	*	*	*	*	0.0001	0.0007	0.0022	0.0047	0.0083	0.0131	0.0188	0.0253	0.0326	0.0404	0.0488	0.0575	0.0666	0.0760	0.0856	0.0953
2.50	*	*	*	*	*	0.0001	0.0003	0.0009	0.0021	0.0041	0.0067	0.0101	0.0142	0.0190	0.0243	0.0301	0.0363	0.0430	0.0499	0.0571

	1.05	1.10	1.15	1.20	1.25	1.30	1.35	1.40	1.45	1.50	1.75	2.00	2.25	2.50	2.75	3.00	3.50	4.00	4.50	5.00
0.50	1.2103	1.2301	1.2500	1.2700	1.2899	1.3098	1.3295	1.3491	1.3686	1.3878	1.4803	1.5651	1.6412	1.7080	1.7655	1.8143	1.8882	1.9364	1.9657	1.9826
0.60	0.9222	0.9421	0.9619	0.9817	1.0012	1.0206	1.0398	1.0588	1.0775	1.0960	1.1840	1.2640	1.3351	1.3973	1.4507	1.4958	1.5640	1.6083	1.6953	1.6507
0.70	0.7255	0.7450	0.7644	0.7835	0.8025	0.8212	0.8397	0.8579	0.8758	0.8934	0.9770	1.0525	1.1193	1.1776	1.2275	1.2696	1.3332	1.3744	1.3994	1.4138
0.75	0.6496	0.6688	0.6878	0.7066	0.7252	0.7435	0.7616	0.7794	0.7969	0.8141	0.8956	0.9689	1.0338	1.0903	1.1387	1.1795	1.2410	1.2809	1.3052	1.3190
0.80	0.5847	0.6035	0.6222	0.6406	0.6588	0.6768	0.6944	0.7118	0.7289	0.7457	0.8251	0.8964	0.9595	1.0143	1.0613	1.1009	1.1606	1.1992	1.2227	1.2361
0.82	0.5613	0.5800	0.5986	0.6168	0.6349	0.6526	0.6701	0.6873	0.7042	0.7209	0.7994	0.8700	0.9324	0.9866	1.0330	1.0722	1.1311	1.1693	1.1925	1.2058
0.84	0.5392	0.5579	0.5762	0.5943	0.6122	0.6298	0.6471	0.6642	0.6809	0.6974	0.7751	0.8450	0.9066	0.9603	1.0062	1.0448	1.1031	1.1409	1.1638	1.1769
0.86	0.5185	0.5369	0.5551	0.5730	0.5907	0.6082	0.6253	0.6422	0.6588	0.6751	0.7521	0.8211	0.8821	0.9352	0.9806	1.0188	1.0764	1.1138	1.1362	1.1494
0.88	0.4988	0.5171	0.5351	0.5529	0.5704	0.5877	0.6047	0.6214	0.6378	0.6540	0.7301	0.7985	0.8588	0.9113	0.9562	0.9940	1.0510	1.0879	1.1103	1.1231
0.90	0.4802	0.4983	0.5161	0.5338	0.5511	0.5682	0.5851	0.6016	0.6179	0.6339	0.7092	0.7769	0.8366	0.8885	0.9329	0.9703	1.0267	1.0632	1.0854	1.0980
0.92	0.4625	0.4805	0.4982	0.5156	0.5328	0.5497	0.5664	0.5828	0.5989	0.6147	0.6894	0.7563	0.8154	0.8667	0.9107	0.9477	1.0034	1.0395	1.0615	1.0740
0.94	0.4458	0.4635	0.4811	0.4984	0.5154	0.5322	0.5487	0.5649	0.5808	0.5965	0.6704	0.7366	0.7951	0.8459	0.8894	0.9260	0.9812	1.0169	1.0386	1.0510
0.96	0.4299	0.4475	0.4648	0.4820	0.4988	0.5154	0.5318	0.5478	0.5636	0.5791	0.6523	0.7178	0.7757	0.8260	0.8691	0.9053	0.9599	0.9952	1.0167	1.0290
0.98	0.4148	0.4322	0.4494	0.4664	0.4831	0.4995	0.5157	0.5316	0.5472	0.5626	0.6350	0.6999	0.7572	0.8070	0.8496	0.8854	0.9395	0.9744	0.9957	1.0079
1.00	0.4004	0.4177	0.4347	0.4515	0.4680	0.4843	0.5003	0.5161	0.5315	0.5467	0.6184	0.6827	0.7394	0.7887	0.8309	0.8664	0.9199	0.9545	0.9756	0.9876
1.02	0.3868	0.4038	0.4207	0.4373	0.4537	0.4698	0.4857	0.5013	0.5166	0.5316	0.6026	0.6662	0.7224	0.7712	0.8129	0.8481	0.9011	0.9353	0.9562	0.9681
1.04	0.3737	0.3907	0.4073	0.4238	0.4400	0.4560	0.4716	0.4871	0.5023	0.5172	0.5874	0.6504	0.7060	0.7544	0.7957	0.8305	0.8830	0.9169	0.9376	0.9494
1.06	0.3613	0.3781	0.3946	0.4109	0.4269	0.4427	0.4582	0.4754	0.4886	0.5033	0.5729	0.6353	0.6903	0.7382	0.7791	0.8136	0.8656	0.8992	0.9197	0.9313
1.08	0.3495	0.3661	0.3824	0.3985	0.4144	0.4300	0.4454	0.4606	0.4754	0.4900	0.5589	0.6207	0.6753	0.7227	0.7632	0.7974	0.8488	0.8821	0.9024	0.9140
1.10	0.3382	0.3546	0.3708	0.3867	0.4024	0.4179	0.4331	0.4481	0.4628	0.4773	0.5455	0.6067	0.6608	0.7077	0.7479	0.7817	0.8327	0.8657	0.8858	0.8973
1.12	0.3274	0.3436	0.3596	0.3754	0.3910	0.4063	0.4214	0.4362	0.4508	0.4651	0.5327	0.5933	0.6468	0.6933	0.7331	0.7667	0.8172	0.8499	0.8698	0.8811
1.14	0.3171	0.3331	0.3490	0.3646	0.3800	0.3952	0.4101	0.4248	0.4392	0.4534	0.5203	0.5803	0.6334	0.6795	0.7189	0.7521	0.8022	0.8346	0.8543	0.8656
1.16	0.3072	0.3231	0.3388	0.3542	0.3695	0.3845	0.3993	0.4138	0.4281	0.4421	0.5084	0.5679	0.6204	0.6661	0.7052	0.7381	0.7877	0.8198	0.8394	0.8505
1.18	0.2978	0.3135	0.3290	0.3443	0.3594	0.3742	0.3889	0.4033	0.4174	0.4313	0.4969	0.5559	0.6079	0.6532	0.6919	0.7246	0.7738	0.8056	0.8250	0.8360
1.20	0.2887	0.3043	0.3196	0.3347	0.3497	0.3644	0.3789	0.3931	0.4071	0.4209	0.4859	0.5443	0.5959	0.6408	0.6792	0.7115	0.7603	0.7918	0.8110	0.8220
1.25	0.2677	0.2828	0.2978	0.3125	0.3271	0.3414	0.3555	0.3694	0.3831	0.3965	0.4600	0.5171	0.5676	0.6115	0.6490	0.6807	0.7284	0.7594	0.7782	0.7889
1.30	0.2488	0.2635	0.2780	0.2924	0.3065	0.3205	0.3343	0.3479	0.3612	0.3743	0.4364	0.4922	0.5416	0.5845	0.6213	0.6523	0.6991	0.7294	0.7478	0.7584
1.35	0.2316	0.2459	0.2601	0.2741	0.2879	0.3015	0.3149	0.3282	0.3412	0.3540	0.4147	0.4693	0.5176	0.5597	0.5957	0.6261	0.6720	0.7017	0.7197	0.7301
1.40	0.2161	0.2300	0.2438	0.2574	0.2708	0.2841	0.2972	0.3101	0.3229	0.3354	0.3947	0.4481	0.4954	0.5367	0.5720	0.6018	0.6468	0.6759	0.6937	0.7038
1.45	0.2019	0.2155	0.2288	0.2421	0.2552	0.2682	0.2810	0.2936	0.3060	0.3182	0.3762	0.4285	0.4749	0.5153	0.5500	0.5792	0.6234	0.6520	0.6694	0.6794
1.50	0.1890	0.2022	0.2152	0.2281	0.2409	0.2535	0.2660	0.2783	0.2904	0.3024	0.3591	0.4104	0.4558	0.4955	0.5295	0.5582	0.6016	0.6297	0.6468	0.6566
1.75	0.1389	0.1503	0.1616	0.1730	0.1842	0.1954	0.2065	0.2174	0.2283	0.2389	0.2900	0.3364	0.3778	0.4141	0.4452	0.4716	0.5114	0.5373	0.5531	0.5621
2.00	0.1051	0.1151	0.1250	0.1350	0.1450	0.1549	0.1648	0.1746	0.1843	0.1939	0.2402	0.2826	0.3206	0.3540	0.3828	0.4072	0.4441	0.4682	0.4829	0.4913
2.50	0.0645	0.0721	0.0798	0.0877	0.0956	0.1035	0.1115	0.1195	0.1274	0.1354	0.1740	0.2100	0.2427	0.2716	0.2967	0.3180	0.3505	0.3718	0.3848	0.3923

Table A.3
Univariate cumulative normal distribution function.

d	$N(d)$	d	$N(d)$	d	$N(d)$
		−1.00	0.1587	1.00	0.8413
−2.95	0.0016	−0.95	0.1711	1.05	0.8531
−2.90	0.0019	−0.90	0.1841	1.10	0.8643
−2.85	0.0022	−0.85	0.1977	1.15	0.8749
−2.80	0.0026	−0.80	0.2119	1.20	0.8849
−2.75	0.0030	−0.75	0.2266	1.25	0.8944
−2.70	0.0035	−0.70	0.2420	1.30	0.9032
−2.65	0.0040	−0.65	0.2578	1.35	0.9115
−2.60	0.0047	−0.60	0.2743	1.40	0.9192
−2.55	0.0054	−0.55	0.2912	1.45	0.9265
−2.50	0.0062	−0.50	0.3085	1.50	0.9332
−2.45	0.0071	−0.45	0.3264	1.55	0.9394
−2.40	0.0082	−0.40	0.3446	1.60	0.9452
−2.35	0.0094	−0.35	0.3632	1.65	0.9505
−2.30	0.0107	−0.30	0.3821	1.70	0.9554
−2.25	0.0122	−0.25	0.4013	1.75	0.9599
−2.20	0.0139	−0.20	0.4207	1.80	0.9641
−2.15	0.0158	−0.15	0.4404	1.85	0.9678
−2.10	0.0179	−0.10	0.4602	1.90	0.9713
−2.05	0.0202	−0.05	0.4801	1.95	0.9744
−2.00	0.0228	0.00	0.5000	2.00	0.9773
−1.95	0.0256	0.05	0.5199	2.05	0.9798
−1.90	0.0287	0.10	0.5398	2.10	0.9821
−1.85	0.0322	0.15	0.5596	2.15	0.9842
−1.80	0.0359	0.20	0.5793	2.20	0.9861
−1.75	0.0401	0.25	0.5987	2.25	0.9878
−1.70	0.0446	0.30	0.6179	2.30	0.9893
−1.65	0.0495	0.35	0.6368	2.35	0.9906
−1.60	0.0548	0.40	0.6554	2.40	0.9918
−1.55	0.0606	0.45	0.6736	2.45	0.9929
−1.50	0.0668	0.50	0.6915	2.50	0.9938
−1.45	0.0735	0.55	0.7088	2.55	0.9946
−1.40	0.0808	0.60	0.7257	2.60	0.9953
−1.35	0.0885	0.65	0.7422	2.65	0.9960
−1.30	0.0968	0.70	0.7580	2.70	0.9965
−1.25	0.1057	0.75	0.7734	2.75	0.9970
−1.20	0.1151	0.80	0.7881	2.80	0.9974
−1.15	0.1251	0.85	0.8023	2.85	0.9978
−1.10	0.1357	0.90	0.8159	2.90	0.9981
−1.05	0.1469	0.95	0.8289	2.95	0.9984

Table A.4
Values of bivariate cumulative normal distribution $B(d^*, 0; \rho)$: interaction for opposite-type (negatively correlated) options.

	Correlation ($\rho = \sqrt{\tau_1/\tau_2}$)										
d^*	−1.0	−0.9	−0.8	−0.7	−0.6	−0.5	−0.4	−0.3	−0.2	−0.1	0.0
−1.00	0.0000	0.0007	0.0056	0.0132	0.0220	0.0313	0.0408	0.0504	0.0600	0.0697	0.0793
−0.95	0.0000	0.0010	0.0068	0.0153	0.0248	0.0348	0.0449	0.0551	0.0652	0.0754	0.0855
−0.90	0.0000	0.0013	0.0082	0.0177	0.0280	0.0387	0.0494	0.0601	0.0708	0.0814	0.0920
−0.85	0.0000	0.0018	0.0098	0.0203	0.0315	0.0428	0.0542	0.0654	0.0766	0.0877	0.0988
−0.80	0.0000	0.0025	0.0118	0.0233	0.0353	0.0473	0.0593	0.0711	0.0828	0.0944	0.1059
−0.75	0.0000	0.0033	0.0140	0.0266	0.0394	0.0522	0.0647	0.0770	0.0892	0.0101	0.1133
−0.70	0.0000	0.0043	0.0166	0.0303	0.0439	0.0574	0.0705	0.0833	0.0960	0.1085	0.1210
−0.65	0.0000	0.0056	0.0195	0.0343	0.0488	0.0629	0.0766	0.0899	0.1031	0.1160	0.1289
−0.60	0.0000	0.0072	0.1228	0.0387	0.0541	0.0688	0.0830	0.0969	0.1104	0.1238	0.1371
−0.55	0.0000	0.0092	0.0265	0.0436	0.0567	0.0750	0.0898	0.1041	0.1181	0.1319	0.1456
−0.50	0.0000	0.0116	0.0308	0.0488	0.0657	0.0818	0.0969	0.1116	0.1260	0.1402	0.1543
−0.45	0.0000	0.0145	0.0354	0.0546	0.0721	0.0886	0.1044	0.1195	0.1343	0.1488	0.1632
−0.40	0.0000	0.0180	0.0407	0.0607	0.0790	0.0960	0.1121	0.1276	0.1427	0.1576	0.1723
−0.35	0.0000	0.0221	0.0464	0.0674	0.0862	0.1037	0.1202	0.1361	0.1515	0.1666	0.1816
−0.30	0.0000	0.0268	0.0527	0.0745	0.0939	0.1117	0.1286	0.1448	0.1604	0.1758	0.1910
−0.25	0.0000	0.0323	0.0595	0.0820	0.1019	0.1201	0.1373	0.1537	0.1696	0.1852	0.2006
−0.20	0.0000	0.0386	0.0670	0.0900	0.1103	0.1289	0.1463	0.1629	0.1790	0.1947	0.2104
−0.15	0.0000	0.0456	0.0750	0.0985	0.1191	0.1379	0.1555	0.1722	0.1885	0.2044	0.2202
−0.10	0.0000	0.0535	0.0836	0.1075	0.1283	0.1472	0.1649	0.1818	0.1982	0.2142	0.2301
−0.05	0.0000	0.0622	0.0927	0.1168	0.1378	0.1568	0.1746	0.1916	0.2080	0.2241	0.2400
0.00	0.0000	0.0718	0.1024	0.1266	0.1476	0.1667	0.1845	0.2015	0.2180	0.2341	0.2500

Table A.4 (continued)

d^*	Correlation ($\rho = \sqrt{\tau_1/\tau_2}$)										
	−1.0	−0.9	−0.8	−0.7	−0.6	−0.5	−0.4	−0.3	−0.2	−0.1	0.0
0.05	0.0199	0.0822	0.1127	0.1368	0.1577	0.1768	0.1946	0.2115	0.2280	0.2440	0.2600
0.10	0.0398	0.0933	0.1234	0.1473	0.1681	0.1870	0.2048	0.2217	0.2380	0.2511	0.2699
0.15	0.0596	0.1052	0.1346	0.1581	0.1787	0.1975	0.2151	0.2319	0.2481	0.2640	0.2798
0.20	0.0793	0.1178	0.1462	0.1693	0.1896	0.2081	0.2255	0.2421	0.2582	0.2740	0.2896
0.25	0.0987	0.1310	0.1582	0.1807	0.2006	0.2188	0.2360	0.2524	0.2683	0.2839	0.2994
0.30	0.1179	0.1448	0.1706	0.1924	0.2118	0.2297	0.2465	0.2627	0.2783	0.2937	0.3090
0.35	0.1368	0.1589	0.1832	0.2042	0.2231	0.2405	0.2570	0.2729	0.2883	0.3034	0.3184
0.40	0.1554	0.1734	0.1961	0.2161	0.2344	0.2514	0.2675	0.2831	0.2982	0.3130	0.3277
0.45	0.1736	0.1882	0.2091	0.2282	0.2458	0.2622	0.2780	0.2931	0.3079	0.3224	0.3368
0.50	0.1915	0.2031	0.2222	0.2403	0.2572	0.2731	0.2884	0.3031	0.3175	0.3317	0.3457
0.55	0.2088	0.2180	0.2354	0.2524	0.2685	0.2839	0.2986	0.3129	0.3269	0.3407	0.3544
0.60	0.2257	0.2330	0.2485	0.2645	0.2798	0.2945	0.3088	0.3226	0.3362	0.3496	0.3639
0.65	0.2422	0.2478	0.2616	0.2764	0.2910	0.3050	0.3187	0.3321	0.3452	0.3582	0.3711
0.70	0.2580	0.2623	0.2746	0.2883	0.3020	0.3154	0.3285	0.3414	0.3540	0.3668	0.3790
0.75	0.2734	0.2766	0.2874	0.3000	0.3128	0.3256	0.3381	0.3504	0.3626	0.3747	0.3867
0.80	0.2881	0.2906	0.2999	0.3114	0.3234	0.3355	0.3474	0.3592	0.3709	0.3825	0.3941
0.85	0.3023	0.3042	0.3122	0.3227	0.3338	0.3452	0.3565	0.3678	0.3789	0.3901	0.4012
0.90	0.3159	0.3173	0.3241	0.3336	0.3440	0.3546	0.3653	0.3760	0.3867	0.3974	0.4080
0.95	0.3289	0.3299	0.3357	0.3442	0.3538	0.3638	0.3739	0.3840	0.3942	0.4043	0.4145
1.00	0.3413	0.3420	0.3469	0.3545	0.3633	0.3726	0.3821	0.3917	0.4014	0.4110	0.4207

Table A.5
Values of bivariate cumulative normal distribution $B(d^*, 0; \rho)$: interaction for similar-type (positively correlated) options.

d^*	Correlation ($\rho = \sqrt{\tau_1/\tau_2}$)										$N(d^*)$
	0.1	0.2	0.3	0.4	0.5	0.6	0.7	0.8	0.9	1.0	
−1.00	0.0890	0.0986	0.1083	0.1179	0.1274	0.1367	0.1455	0.1531	0.1580	0.1587	0.1587
−0.95	0.0957	0.1058	0.1160	0.1261	0.1362	0.1462	0.1558	0.1643	0.1701	0.1711	0.1711
−0.90	0.1026	0.1133	0.1240	0.1347	0.1454	0.1560	0.1664	0.1759	0.1827	0.1841	0.1841
−0.85	0.1099	0.1211	0.1322	0.1435	0.1548	0.1662	0.1773	0.1878	0.1958	0.1977	0.1977
−0.80	0.1175	0.1291	0.1408	0.1526	0.1645	0.1766	0.1886	0.2001	0.2094	0.2119	0.2119
−0.75	0.1253	0.1374	0.1496	0.1619	0.1744	0.1872	0.2000	0.2126	0.2234	0.2266	0.2266
−0.70	0.1335	0.1460	0.1586	0.1715	0.1846	0.1980	0.2117	0.2254	0.2377	0.2420	0.2420
−0.65	0.1418	0.1548	0.1679	0.1813	0.1950	0.2090	0.2236	0.2384	0.2522	0.2578	0.2578
−0.60	0.1504	0.1638	0.1774	0.1912	0.2055	0.2202	0.2355	0.2515	0.2670	0.2743	0.2743
−0.55	0.1593	0.1731	0.1871	0.2014	0.2161	0.2315	0.2476	0.2646	0.2820	0.2912	0.2912
−0.50	0.1683	0.1825	0.1969	0.2116	0.2269	0.2428	0.2587	0.2778	0.2969	0.3085	0.3085
−0.45	0.1776	0.1921	0.2069	0.2220	0.2377	0.2542	0.2718	0.2909	0.3118	0.3264	0.3264
−0.40	0.1870	0.2018	0.2169	0.2325	0.2485	0.2656	0.2839	0.3039	0.3266	0.3446	0.3446
−0.35	0.1966	0.2117	0.2271	0.2430	0.2595	0.2769	0.2958	0.3168	0.3411	0.3632	0.3632
−0.30	0.2063	0.2217	0.2373	0.2535	0.2703	0.2882	0.3076	0.3294	0.3552	0.3821	0.3821
−0.25	0.2161	0.2317	0.2476	0.2640	0.2812	0.2994	0.3193	0.3418	0.3690	0.4013	0.4013
−0.20	0.2260	0.2417	0.2579	0.2745	0.2919	0.3104	0.3307	0.3538	0.3822	0.4207	0.4207
−0.15	0.2360	0.2519	0.2681	0.2849	0.3025	0.3213	0.3419	0.3654	0.3948	0.4404	0.4404
−0.10	0.2459	0.2620	0.2783	0.2952	0.3130	0.3319	0.3537	0.3766	0.4067	0.4602	0.4602
−0.05	0.2560	0.2720	0.2885	0.3054	0.3232	0.3423	0.3632	0.3873	0.4178	0.4801	0.4801
0.00	0.2659	0.2820	0.2985	0.3155	0.3333	0.3524	0.3734	0.3976	0.4282	0.5000	0.5000

Table A.5 (*Continued*)

d^*	Correlation ($\rho = \sqrt{\tau_1/\tau_2}$)										$N(d^*)$
	0.1	0.2	0.3	0.4	0.5	0.6	0.7	0.8	0.9	1.0	
0.05	0.2759	0.2920	0.3084	0.3254	0.3432	0.3622	0.3832	0.4073	0.4378	0.5000	0.5199
0.10	0.2858	0.3018	0.3182	0.3351	0.3528	0.3717	0.3925	0.4164	0.4465	0.5000	0.5398
0.15	0.2956	0.3115	0.3277	0.3445	0.3621	0.3809	0.4015	0.4250	0.4544	0.5000	0.5596
0.20	0.3053	0.3210	0.3371	0.3538	0.3711	0.3897	0.4100	0.4330	0.4614	0.5000	0.5793
0.25	0.3148	0.3304	0.3463	0.3627	0.3798	0.3981	0.4180	0.4405	0.4677	0.5000	0.5987
0.30	0.3242	0.3396	0.3552	0.3714	0.3883	0.4061	0.4255	0.4473	0.4732	0.5000	0.6179
0.35	0.3334	0.3485	0.3639	0.3798	0.3963	0.4138	0.4326	0.4536	0.4779	0.5000	0.6368
0.40	0.3424	0.3573	0.3724	0.3879	0.4040	0.4200	0.4393	0.4594	0.4820	0.5000	0.6554
0.45	0.3512	0.3657	0.3805	0.3958	0.4114	0.4279	0.4454	0.4646	0.4855	0.5000	0.6736
0.50	0.3598	0.3740	0.3884	0.4031	0.4183	0.4343	0.4512	0.4692	0.4884	0.5000	0.6915
0.55	0.3681	0.3819	0.3959	0.4102	0.4250	0.4403	0.4564	0.4735	0.4908	0.5000	0.7088
0.60	0.3762	0.3896	0.4031	0.4170	0.4312	0.4459	0.4613	0.4772	0.4928	0.5000	0.7277
0.65	0.3840	0.3969	0.4101	0.4234	0.4371	0.4512	0.4657	0.4805	0.4944	0.5000	0.7422
0.70	0.3915	0.4040	0.4167	0.4295	0.4426	0.4561	0.4697	0.4834	0.4957	0.5000	0.7580
0.75	0.4899	0.4108	0.4230	0.4353	0.4478	0.4606	0.4734	0.4860	0.4967	0.5000	0.7734
0.80	0.4056	0.4172	0.4289	0.4407	0.4527	0.4647	0.4767	0.4882	0.4975	0.5000	0.7881
0.85	0.4123	0.4234	0.4346	0.4458	0.4572	0.4685	0.4797	0.4902	0.4982	0.5000	0.8023
0.90	0.4186	0.4292	0.4399	0.4506	0.4613	0.4720	0.4823	0.4918	0.4987	0.5000	0.8159
0.95	0.4246	0.4348	0.4449	0.4551	0.4652	0.4732	0.4847	0.4932	0.4990	0.5000	0.8289
1.00	0.4303	0.4400	0.4496	0.4592	0.4687	0.4780	0.4868	0.4944	0.4993	0.5000	0.7413

Notes

Chapter 1

1. At maturity, a call option to pay the exercise price, I, in order to acquire the underlying asset, V, but only if profitable, is worth $\max(V - I, 0)$. A put option to exchange V for I is similarly worth $\max(I - V, 0)$ at maturity.

2. This section relies on Baldwin and Trigeorgis 1993.

3. As discussed in chapters 3 and 5 below, options can be valued in a risk-neutral world where all assets are expected to earn the risk-free rate, r. In such a world, the project's expected return is

$$E(R) = p(0.80) + (1 - p)(-0.40) = 0.08.$$

Thus, $p = 0.4$.

4. For classic treatments of resource allocation see Dean 1951 and Bower 1970.

5. See, for example, the well-founded criticisms of Hayes and Abernathy (1980), Hayes and Garvin (1982), Kester (1984), and Myers (1987).

6. An *American* (call or put) option may be exercised at any time up to the specified maturity. In contrast, a *European* option may be exercised only at maturity.

7. Lai and Trigeorgis (1995) review the process of capital budgeting from an organizational perspective. Teisberg (1995) discusses cash-flow analysis, decision analysis, and option valuation from a practical perspective. Mauer and Triantis (1992) examine interactions between corporate financing and investment decisions.

Chapter 2

1. It can be argued that the firm should be concerned not only with the welfare of its direct owners (i.e., its stockholders) but also with that of its creditors, its employees, the local community, or even the government and the society at large. Other critics suggest that managers in practice are also concerned with other goals, such as the survival and perpetuation of the firm and reasonable growth (pointing out that managers are actually satisficers rather than maximizers), or that they often are preoccupied with their own personal welfare (salaries, perquisites, status, power, etc.); these goals, however, suffer from a lack of a measurable criterion against which to evaluate performance or alternative courses of action.

2. In finance it is customary to adopt the position that the single overriding objective of the firm is to maximize the economic welfare of its residual owners for the following reasons:

We are interested in a normative model of how managers should behave, as opposed to attempting to describe their actual behavior (which may well be suboptimal).

Top management's incentives (stock options, pensions, etc.) are tied to the welfare of the firm's owners to whom top management is eventually responsible. Management maintains some degree of discretion in deviating from that objective, but it serves under the threat of being replaced or being taken over by another firm if it repeatedly neglects the welfare of its owners.

Within certain constraints guaranteeing a stable competitive equilibrium, the pursuit of self-interest by firms in a free-market economy tends to enhance the general economic welfare.

Pursuing the welfare of other concerned publics (its broader owners, if you will) can serve in many cases as a means consistent with the goal of maximizing the residual owners' welfare in the long term.

Even if it were agreed that the firm should be concerned with other goals (as in a socialist society), it would still be useful and necessary to determine the opportunity cost of pursuing these other goals rather than maximizing the owners' welfare.

3. Maximizing the market price of a firm's stock does not always necessarily lead to maximization of the shareholders' wealth. For this to hold it is necessary to assume perfectly competitive markets in which the market price of the shares of one firm is independent of the actions of other firms; otherwise management might improve its owners' wealth by acting suboptimally if that were to substantially increase the value of their other holdings (such as shares of stock in a competing firm).

Other measures for owners' welfare have also been proposed. Profits and earnings per share are accounting measures that invariably depend on the particular income-reporting conventions that each firm may happen to use at the time, so they are clearly not appropriate as universal yardsticks of performance for all firms. Return-on-investment measures, such as return on assets or return on owners' equity, not only suffer from the same problem of reliance on accounting numbers but furthermore, as fractions, suffer from the danger of deliberate manipulation of the numerator or denominator of the ratio—to be strict, maximizing return on investment might be achieved by cutting down investment until only the most profitable project remains.

4. The present section derives from the theory developed by Fischer (1930), Hirshleifer (1958), and Brealey and Myers (1991).

5. The maximization of expected utility on the basis of two measures alone, the mean and the variance of returns, can be justified if the utility of income is assumed quadratic (which is not actually true, since it inappropriately implies increasing risk aversion to wealth) or if investment returns are normally (or lognormally) distributed.

6. The models of Fama (1977) and Myers and Turnbull (1977) assume multiplicative cash flows and are rather restrictive. More general certainty-equivalent capital-budgeting models (both multiplicative and additive) using cash-flow betas are discussed by Sick (1986). However, the assumption of additive cash flows may fail to hold when there are real options to expand, contract, or abandon.

7. The plant may later be expanded.

8. This is roughly the same as the discounted value (as of year 5) of the unconditional expected cash flows of $0.5 million in years 5–15 and the $1 million expected salvage value in year 15.

9. As is known from option-pricing theory, if the expected rate of return or discount rate for an asset is constant, then that for an option on the asset will not generally be constant; it will fluctuate with asset price movements and with time, among other factors.

Chapter 3

1. For a more general proof see Merton 1973, theorem 13. Intuitively, the reason why an American call option without dividends would not be exercised early but a put option would, lies in the fact that a call would become more valuable if the stock price rises further (which has no maximum ceiling), whereas a put is more valuable when the stock price drops (which does have a minimum floor at 0).

2. An early form of the binomial model can also be found in William Sharp's textbook *Investments*, and perhaps the basic idea dates back to Paul Cootner.

3. The Cox-Ross-Rubinstein (1979) assignment of parameters u and p has certain problems. These are discussed in chapter 10, where better assignments for these parameters are given.

4. This is not true for put options, however.

5. In the calculation of the option values for the intermediate exercise times, the exercise price may also need to be reduced by the present value of the dividends from the time of exercise until the option maturity (see Jarrow and Rudd 1983).

6. Adjustment for discrete dividends in a log-transformed binomial lattice approach is described in chapter 10.

7. That is, the actual growth rate, α, can be replaced with a "certainty-equivalent" drift $r - D$ (as in a risk-neutral world), allowing risk-free discounting to be applied in valuing the option.

8. We will later make adjustments if underlying asset V_i pays a constant continuous dividend yield, D_i, and when the contingent claim F itself pays a dividend payout d. The expected growth rate or drift in asset value V_i, α_i, would then represent its total return, μ_i, net of dividends (i.e., $\alpha_i = \mu_i - D_i$).

9. In the $n + 1$ securities can be included the contingent claim itself, and potentially the risk-free rate r.

10. The portfolio weights w_j must, of course, be adjusted over time (as variables V_i fluctuate) for the portfolio to remain riskless.

11. See, for example, Hull and White 1988b.

12. As noted, in a risk-neutral world, $\alpha - \lambda\sigma = (\mu - D) - \lambda\sigma$ becomes $(r - D) - 0 = r - D$. Thus, the value of a traded security in our actual world is the same as that in a risk-neutral world, since investor preferences do not matter.

13. In contrast with equation 3.29, in equation 3.26 λ_r (or D_r) was assumed to be zero.

14. Following Hull (1993), "traded" security here refers to a financial asset in limited supply traded in the market for investment purposes by a large number of investors, such as stock, bonds, and a few particular commodities (gold and silver). Many capital investment projects, interest rates, and most reproducible commodities (e.g., oil in the ground) that involve a convenience yield, are not considered "traded" assets for our purposes and there is no reason why their growth rate should be the same as that of a comparable traded financial security in market equilibrium. The current price of a contingent claim is determined *relative* to the

current price of the underlying asset when it is a *traded* financial security, irrespective of its expected growth rate (α) and investor risk attitudes. For a nontraded variable, however, these factors become relevant to derivative valuation via the dependence of the fundamental pricing equation 3.24 on λ_i and α_i, which are generally dependent on risk preferences. These parameters are independent of risk preferences only in special cases, such as: (1) when all assets V_i are traded securities without dividends; (2) when they are traded securities paying dividends at a constant rate D; (3) when their market price of risk is zero ($\lambda_i = 0$); (4) combinations of the above.

15. As will be discussed below, δ may represent any proportional cash-flow (dividend-like) payout on an operating capital project, or the net convenience yield in the case of a commodity. If futures prices are available (i.e., if the commodity is traded in futures markets), this dividend-like return shortfall can be easily derived from the prices of varying-maturity futures contracts (see also Brennan and Schwartz 1985a). In other cases, however, estimating this return shortfall may require use of a market-equilibrium model (see McDonald and Siegel 1985).

16. In a risk-neutral world, the expected growth rate of V is $\alpha = r - \delta$ (so that the total return with dividends is r) while $\lambda = 0$ (since market risk would be unpriced), so that again $a - \lambda\sigma = (r - \delta) - 0 = r - \delta$. Thus, the same answer is obtained in our actual risk-averse economy if we replace α with $\hat\alpha = \alpha - \lambda\sigma$, as in a risk-neutral world, and so we can adopt the latter for convenience.

17. Since one can move from the actual (risk-averse) world to the risk-neutral world simply by lowering the asset's growth rate by RP $= \lambda\sigma$, if α is deterministic and $\lambda\sigma$ is constant then $\hat E(V_T) = E(V_T)e^{-\lambda\sigma\tau}$ with E denoting the expectations operator in the actual world.

18. If the interest rate itself is stochastic, it could be treated as one of the underlying variables V_i, requiring similar adjustment. That is, the growth rate in r would be lowered by the market price of risk times the volatility associated with r ($\lambda_r\sigma_r$) for the purpose of forming risk-neutral expectations. The risk-neutral expectations of the claim's future payoffs *conditional* on each path realization would be discounted using the average value of r on each path, and then would be averaged over the probability distribution of the possible paths (see Hull 1993).

19. For our purposes, we treat a futures contract and a forward contract the same.

20. From equation 3.21 with $n = 1$, the expected return (discount rate) for a contingent claim (μ) is a complex function of the expected growth rate (discount rate) for the underlying asset (α):

$$\mu \approx \left(\frac{V}{F}\frac{\partial F}{\partial V}\right)\alpha.$$

Thus, even if α is fairly stable, μ may fluctuate with V_t and other factors.

21. This section borrows, in part, from Mason and Merton 1985 and Smith 1979.

22. Note that this notation differs somewhat from that in section 3.8, where α was used to denote just the expected growth rate or capital appreciation component of the total return. Although we could have used a different notation for the total return, it doesn't really matter since in the risk-neutral valuation that is employed it is replaced with r.

23. Merton (1977b) first derived a dynamic portfolio strategy consisting of positions in the firm and riskless borrowing whose payoff exactly replicates the payoff to any corporate liability of the firm. The continuous application of this no-arbitrage replication strategy results in a fundamental p.d.e. identical to that derived in equation 3.28.

Chapter 4

1. The "investment outlay" does not have to be a single one-time investment; it may actually be a series of investment "installments." In this case the "investment outlay" is typically interpreted as the present value of the expected investment installments. It would be more appropriate, however, to treat such projects as compound options, an earlier investment "installment" being the exercise price required for acquiring a subsequent option due to expire when the next "installment" comes due (and so on). The two approaches would generally give somewhat different results, since compoundness generally violates the additivity of option values.

2. As was noted in chapter 3, the value of a call option on a stock is higher, other things being constant, the greater the stock price and the lower the required exercise price, the greater the volatility of stock returns (since it increases the upside profit potential while the downside risk is limited due to the option asymmetry), the higher the risk-free interest rate (since it lowers the present value of the future exercise cost), and the longer the time to maturity (both through a higher total uncertainty of stock returns and through a lower present value of the exercise cost).

3. Although the analogy between stock call options and real options is a close one, it is not exact. Some of the main differences that will later be incorporated in our framework are the following: Stock call options are proprietary (exclusively owned), whereas real options may often be shared with competitors. Unlike stock call options, real options are generally not tradable (which may motivate early exercise to preempt competitors). Real options may often be interdependent (compound options).

4. As will be explained in chapter 7, the simultaneous presence of several such real options may give rise to (typically negative) interaction effects (such as between the options to expand and abandon), necessitating the use of options-based numerical analysis techniques for solving the more complex problems. (See chapter 10 for the numerical analysis of projects with multiple interacting real options.)

5. If such substitutes do not exist so that the project's uniqueness would expand the investor's opportunity set, then using either option pricing or NPV analysis would give equally inadequate results.

6. The distinction between "shared" and "proprietary" options may not always be so clear cut. For example, if one of the collective owners of a "shared" option faces substantially lower investment costs than the others (perhaps due to a steeper experience curve effect, other economies of scale, better name recognition, etc.), the "shared" option might be treated effectively as proprietary.

7. As has already been noted, the fact that real projects may not be traded does not present any conceptual problems in valuing real options. The possibility that the option to take a project may not be tradable, however, may necessitate dividend-like adjustments and justify preemptive investments, thus indirectly affecting the timing of exercise and the value of a real option.

8. There are, of course, examples of compound options in traded financial securities as well, such as callable convertible bonds.

9. Equation 4.3 implies that the investment will be deferred indefinitely in the absence of dividends. With a constant dividend yield, δ, equation 4.3' is obtained instead.

10. "Salvage value" or value in the best alternative use may come from the value of expected cash flows from switching use (inputs or outputs), a market price for which the project
may sell on a second-hand market or, in situations where subsequent expenditures are due,
the value of subsequent cost savings from discontinuing the project.

11. The initial strategic investment (e.g., in R&D) may influence the competitive position of
the pioneering firm in a later stage of the market. In a proprietary investment the firm is better able to appropriate the benefits of its strategic investment so as to hurt its competitor
$(d\pi_B/dK_A < 0)$. An example would be a first-mover proprietary cost advantage in the form
of lower relative production costs in the later operating stage. The position of a pioneering
firm is more accommodating if the resulting benefits are shared and benefit its competitor
$(d\pi_B/dK_A > 0)$. That may be the case if the benefits of testing, opening up the market, or developing a more cost-efficient technology are diffused to all firms in the industry. In this case,
both firms can have lower costs—a shared cost advantage.

12. Depending on whether firms compete in prices or in quantity, a reaction function assigns
to every price or output level of one firm the value-maximizing price or output for the other.

13. The state-payoff values at the end of the second stage are the outcomes of different
market-structure games, depending on the state of demand, each firm's actions (invest, do not
invest or defer) and their timing (simultaneous or lagged, at $t = 1$ or 2).

14. As Tirole (1990) notes, the reaction functions in such a simultaneous game are no more
than an illustrative device since the firms have no possibility of reacting; only the final Nash-
equilibrium outcome at the intersection of the two reaction functions is observed. The Nash
equilibrium is stable if the adjustment process converges to the equilibrium outcome from
any starting position.

15. In contrarian quantity competition, an aggressive firm that invests early acting as a
Stackelberg leader can acquire a larger share of the market. Under retaliating price competition, a Stackelberg price leader would choose a price on the competitor's reaction function
that maximizes its profit. Given the prior action of the Stackelberg leader, the Stackelberg
follower would then maximize its own profit, $\pi_j(\alpha_i, \alpha_j)$, taking the action of the leader, α_i, as
given. In the case of an accommodating price leader there need not be a first-mover advan-
tage, as both firms can "collude" setting higher prices compared to the situation that they
invest at the same time.

16. Under contrarian competition where the quantities produced are substitutes, the firm has
an incentive to invest in a strategic project if its benefits are proprietary or if it increases its
ability to preempt a larger share of the market. However, in reciprocating competition where
price settings are complements a strategic investment may result in lower prices via intensified rivalry. In such cases it may be appropriate to invest in strategic projects creating
shared opportunities to "soften" competitive reaction in the later stage of the market.

17. To simplify the exposition, we will ignore for the rest of this chapter the option (not) to
operate, the options to expand or contract the scale of operation, and various other options.

18. As was pointed out earlier, shared options can be differentiated further depending on
whether the impact of competition is taken as exogenous or whether it causes endogenous
strategic counteractions. The latter can be further differentiated depending on the nature of
competitive reaction (contrarian or reciprocating).

19. Normally, "competitive loss" has a negative value (i.e., it is a loss), especially if competitors enter after the firm has undertaken the project. In some cases, however, it may
actually be a gain (i.e., a negative "loss"). One example is an R&D investment that develops

a new technology that competitors can easily imitate, resulting in lower production costs and higher profits for all competitors. Another example is when a competitor's investment, such as advertising expenditures, promotes the whole product category and not just the competitor's particular brand (e.g., "Buy liquid soap" rather than "Jergens' liquid soap is the best"), thus increasing the total "market pie" for all, or reducing the need for advertising expenditures by the particular firm. In this case, a competitor's investment is like a public service benefiting all (a shared investment). As a third example, consider the effect of competition on the value of the option to introduce a new product when acceptance by the market is highly uncertain. An introduction of a substitute product by a competitor may take some market share away from the firm; on the other hand, it may resolve uncertainty about the market's reception of that type of product. It is conceivable that the "learning effect" for the firm may be more valuable than the direct market share loss, so that the firm may obtain a net gain from such competitive entry.

20. There are, of course, other forms of interproject dependence. These include mutually exclusive projects (where undertaking one project precludes undertaking the other) and synergistic projects (which enhance each other's cash flows when taken together). We will ignore these interactions here, concentrating instead on compoundness. Synergistic interactions between projects will be dealt with in chapter 8.

21. The distinction between "expiring" and "deferrable" investment opportunities is one of degree. It is also in a sense related to the distinction between shared and proprietary options in that in a shared option the threat of competition may, for preemptive reasons, effectively turn a "deferrable" option into an "expiring" one—although, in this case, management still maintains a choice as to whether or not to make an immediate preemptive investment, whereas in a strictly expiring option such a choice is precluded entirely. Also, the horizon of a deferrable real option is a relative notion compared to contractual financial options. In the case of real options, it may be useful to analyze whether the expiration of the option (end of the waiting horizon) is brought about by abrupt versus incremental changes. We can treat an abrupt event, such as the termination of a patent for producing a new product or the termination of a lease for oil drilling, as an exogenously determined point in time when the deferrable option expires. On the other hand, we can treat incremental changes in value resulting from the introduction of substitute products in a shared-deferrable option as endogenous effects analogous to dividend payments in call options—although in the extreme case where the substitute product is a technological breakthrough causing an abrupt project value drop to zero, its introduction may effectively be treated as the expiration time for the horizon of the incumbent firm's real option.

22. These tradeoffs will be analyzed in chapter 9.

23. The basic form of this classification is similar to that first proposed by Kester (1984).

24. See Kester 1981 for a more detailed description of Upton.

25. Kelor Chemical Corporation is the subject of Harvard Business School case 274-108.

26. Kester (1993) provides a similar illustration.

Chapter 5

1. This section is based in part on Trigeorgis and Mason 1987 and Trigeorgis 1993b.

2. Of this amount, $18.32 million will be necessary fixed costs; the remaining $40 million will be variable costs to be divided between advertising ($33.32 million) and maintenance ($6.68 million).

3. Assume here, for simplicity, that the project's value in its current use and in its best alternative use (or its salvage value) are perfectly positively correlated. In fact, the option to switch use would be even more valuable the lower the correlation between V and A.

4. For a detailed discussion on the nature of such option interactions, see chapter 7.

5. This section is based in part on Kulatilaka and Trigeorgis 1994. I thank Nalin Kulatilaka and the publisher of the journal for permission to use parts of the article.

6. This part is similar to Kensinger's (1987) approach, which is to look at a project as an option to exchange one set of commodities for another. Margrabe (1978) more generally values an option to exchange one risky asset for another.

Chapter 6

1. The first condition simply says that at the completion of the project ($K = 0$) the firm receives payoff V. The second condition says that as V becomes very large the project will most likely be completed; however, it will take time K/k to complete, during which time V is expected to increase at the rate ($\alpha - D$), so that a \$1 increase in V leads to an increase in $F(V, K)$ equal to $e^{-DK/k}$. The last two are the (value matching and smooth pasting) conditions that F and F_V be continuous at V^*.

Chapter 7

1. This chapter is based in part on L. Trigeorgis, "The nature of option interactions and the valuation of investments with multiple real options," *Journal of Financial and Quantitative Analysis* 28 (1993), no. 1: 1–20. Permission by the journal to use parts of the article is gratefully acknowledged.

2. Notable exceptions are Brennan and Schwartz 1985a, Trigeorgis 1993a, and Kulatilaka 1995. Brennan and Schwartz utilize the convenience yield derived from futures and spot prices of a commodity to determine the combined value of the options to temporarily shut down and reopen a mine, and to abandon it for salvage, but do not address the interactions among individual option values. This chapter follows Trigeorgis 1993a, in which I focus explicitly on understanding the nature of option interactions. The impact of option interactions on the optimal exercise schedules is examined in Kulatilaka 1995.

3. The options to contract or expand in this example have a predetermined contraction or expansion rate. More generally, the firm may have the choice to decide the level of expansion or contraction at the time it decides to expand or contract. Pindyck (1988) discusses this type of option in the context of capacity choice; Capozza and Sick (1991) and Capozza and Li (1994) discuss it in the context of scale or density of (re)development. A second option to expand at a different scale and time that leads to positive interaction with the prior call option to expand will be discussed later in this chapter. (If the timing difference between exercising the two expansion options is narrowed or eliminated, this problem reduces to the choice of capacity or density of problem.

4. The investment costs ($I_1 = 10$ in year 0, $I_2 = 90$ in year 3, $I_3 = 35$ in year 5) are assumed known in advance and placed in an "escrow account" earning the riskless rate. Discounted continuously at the assumed risk-free rate of $r = 5\%$, they yield a present value of $I = 114.7$.

5. As we have seen, management's flexibility to revise its future actions, contingent on uncertain future developments, introduces an asymmetry that expands the opportunity's true

value relative to passive NPV by improving its profit potential while limiting losses. This calls for an expanded-NPV rule.

6. This will be described in chapter 10. For other numerical work on options see Brennan 1979 and Geske and Shastri 1985; for applications to real options see Myers and Majd 1990 and Majd and Pindyck 1987.

7. Although the precise numerical results may be somewhat different, the basic interaction effects would hold under alternative specifications of the underlying stochastic process (e.g., a mean-reverting process). See also Kulatilaka 1995.

8. For simplicity, we assume here that $d = 0$. In general, however, we can incorporate any opportunity cost in delaying investment (which would be subtracted from the drift of the original project stochastic process) resulting either from intermediate cash flows missed by holding an option on the project (i.e., from waiting) rather than operating it immediately or from competitive erosion (see chapter 9 below).

9. See chapter 10 below. As was noted in earlier chapters, current option values can be determined by discounting certainty-equivalent or risk-neutral expectations of future payoffs at the riskless interest rate, r. In general, any contingent claim on an asset (traded or not) can be priced in a world with systematic risk by replacing the actual growth rate, α, with a certainty-equivalent rate, $\hat{\alpha} \equiv \alpha - RP$, where RP represents an appropriate risk premium, and then behaving as if the world were risk neutral.

10. V is determined by discounting expected cash flows at the opportunity cost of capital. A proportional cash flow (e.g., 10% of current gross project value) is treated similar to a dividend payout (see Myers and Majd 1990 for a good discussion), although here we assume no dividends for simplicity.

11. This result holds unambiguously in the case of a subsequent call. If the later option is also a put, the second effect will still be negative if exercising the prior put reduces the scale of the later put proportionally. However, in cases where the exercise price of the later put is not reduced in proportion to the project's value, the second effect may be positive although the net overall interaction may still be negative.

12. If exercising the prior call (e.g., in a compound call option) can expand the underlying asset or the scale of the project (i.e., $V'' > V$), a subsequent option on that higher asset may be more valuable and interactions can be positive. The option to defer a project—a call whose exercise does not alter the "underlying asset" for subsequent options—is more complex. First, as the cash flows and future options are pushed back, allowing more time for crucial variables to change, the increased variability may make subsequent options somewhat more valuable. However, if initiation of the project is delayed (e.g., because the project is not yet good enough), a subsequent call option to expand may be less valuable and exhibit a negative interaction (though mitigated by the above positive side effect). More important, since the option to defer is written on the portfolio of gross project value plus the value of subsequent options, it would at first glance appear to be more valuable, other factors being the same. At the same time, however, the presence of subsequent options may enable management to adjust better to changing market conditions, increasing the value of early investment relative to a similar situation without such flexibility. Thus, the incremental value of the option to wait would tend to decrease relative to immediate investment. This effect typically would dominate and lead to negative overall interactions between the flexibility to defer and other subsequent real options.

13. Ironically, it is a better approximation to add up their separate values, other factors being the same, when the options are small (out of the money). To turn this around, it is least

appropriate simply to add up the separate option values precisely when it is most needed, that is, when they are most valuable (in the money).

14. The probability of joint exercise is related to the double-shaded area $A'C$.

15. The options would still be approximately additive, though less so, if one of the two European options (e.g., the put) were replaced with its American counterpart, extending the possible exercise times on the same side relative to the other European option's maturity. However, the conditional probability of joint exercise (here proxied by a double-shaded trapezoidal area), and hence the degree of interaction, would be somewhat higher. If the American put option (e.g., to switch use) extends its potential exercise times both before and after the other (European call) option's maturity, a hybrid situation is possible. That is, there may be negative interaction in the first part (where part of the put precedes the call) and positive interaction in the latter part (where the call precedes part of the put). The interactions (both of which would be small) would partially cancel each other out, leading to better additive approximation.

16. In the continuous-time analogue, of course, the conditional probability is not precisely zero. Option-value additivity will still approximately hold, however, if it is small enough.

17. This bivariate cumulative standard normal distribution function has d^* as a lower integral limit, d as an upper integral limit, and a negative correlation coefficient, which makes intuitive sense when the two options involved are of opposite types and are exercisable under negatively correlated circumstances.

18. P_F and P_L denote the marginal probabilities of exercising the first option and the later option, respectively; $P_{F,L}$ denotes the joint probability of exercise.

19. For $d^*, d, \rho > 0$,

$$B(d^*, d; \rho) = B(d^*, 0; \rho_1) + B(d, 0; \rho_2)$$

(for similar-type options) and

$$B(d^*, d; -\rho) = B(-d^*, 0; -\rho_1) + B(d, 0; -\rho_2) - 0.5$$

(for opposite-type options), where

$$\rho_1 = \frac{\rho d^* - d}{\sqrt{(d^*)^2 - 2\rho(d^*)d + d^2}}$$

and

$$\rho_2 = \frac{\rho d - d^*}{\sqrt{(d^*)^2 - 2\rho(d^*)d + d^2}}.$$

For example, if $d^* = d = \rho = 0.5$, then $\rho_1 = \rho_2 = -0.5$, so that

$$B(0.5, 0.5; 0.5) = B(0.5, 0; -0.5) + B(0.5, 0; -0.5) = 2(0.2731) = 0.5462$$

and

$$B(-0.5, 0.5; -0.5) = B(-0.5, 0; 0.5) + B(0.5, 0; 0.5) - 0.5$$

$$= 0.2269 + 0.4183 - 0.5$$

$$= 0.1452.$$

Similarly,

$$B(-0.5, 0.4; -0.8) = B(-0.5, 0; 0) + B(0.4, 0; 0.6) - 0.5$$

$$= 0.1543 + 0.4210 - 0.5$$

$$= 0.0753.$$

Other useful relationships (which also apply to table A.4 in the appendix for $d = 0$ and $N(d) = 0.5$) include the following:

$$B(-d^*, -d; \rho) = B(d^*, d; \rho) - N(d^*) - N(d) + 1$$

(e.g., $B(-0.5, -0.5; 0.5) = 0.5462 - 0.6915 - 0.6915 + 1 = 0.1632$),

$$B(d^*, -d; -\rho) = N(d^*) - B(d^*, d; \rho)$$

(e.g., $B(0.5, -0.5; -0.5) = N(0.5) - B(0.5, 0.5; 0.5) = 0.6915 - 0.5462 = 0.1453$), and

$$B(-d^*, d; -\rho) = N(d) - B(d^*, d; \rho)$$

(e.g., $B(-0.5, 0.5, -0.5) = N(0.5) - B(0.5, 0.5; 0.5) = 0.6915 - 0.5462 = 0.1453$). The following special cases are also sometimes useful:

$$B(-d^*, d; 0) = N(d^*)N(d),$$

$$B(0, 0; \rho) = 0.25 + \frac{\arcsin \rho}{2\pi}.$$

20. Figure 7.10 is similar to figure 3 in Myers and Majd 1990 and verifies their results when only the option to abandon for salvage is present, even with a series of planned investment-cost outlays.

21. The impact of correlation in figure 7.11 is determined with both project-value and salvage-value variances equal to 0.25, and under the simplifying assumption that all outlays are compressed into a single outlay of equivalent present value.

22. As noted, interaction becomes precisely zero and the two European opposite-type options are purely additive if they are exercisable at exactly the same time as well as being out of the money.

23. By design, the option to abandon construction with no recovery has no incremental value in the presence of the option to switch use.

24. If the additional option to expand is instead shifted to mature in year 4, so that it precedes the option to contract, then there is a slight positive interaction: E4 & C5 = 31.2 vs. E4 + C5 = 31.1. If the order is reversed, the options to contract in year 5 and to expand later in year 7 are still about additive, but with a slight negative interaction instead: C5 & E7 = 41.8 vs. C5 + E7 = 41.9.

25. Assuming a proportional nature for the call options to expand, the presence of the later call option increases the value of the first call option. This is clear since the first call option is written on the total project value, which increases in the presence of the second call option. Similarly, the possibility of exercising the first call option to expand the project increases the value of the second proportionate call option, leading to a double positive or super-additive effect.

26. Although in principle there can be significant positive interactions, such as when expanding more than once, for the sequence of real options dealt with in this chapter interactions are typically negative. Positive interactions are more prevalent, however, among interdependent projects such as in R&D, in investments designed to gain a positioning in a new market, and in other "strategic" investment commitments.

27. With the second option to expand in year 4 included, the joint value of all six options increases to 122, or 67% of their added separate values. Although the particular numbers

change when both expansion opportunities are considered, the net aggregate behavior of these options remains essentially the same.

28. The exact size of the error would, of course, depend on the type of neglected options (that is, whether they are puts or calls similar to the other options present) and on the extent to which they are in the money, depending on the relative size of their exercise costs. It would also depend on the overlap of their exercise regions with those of the options included.

29. A simple selection rule is to eliminate those options (usually put options) that are of similar type and are exercisable under similar circumstances as other included real options, particularly if their exercise costs are such that they are in-the-money options.

30. Total project value increases almost linearly with the riskless rate.

Chapter 8

1. This chapter relies in part on Lenos Trigeorgis and Eero Kasanen, "An integrated options-based strategic planning and control model," *Managerial Finance* 17 (1991), no. 2/3: 16–28. I would like to thank my co-author, Eero Kasanen, and the publisher of the journal for permission to use parts of the article.

2. This idea originated with R. F. Meyer and is sketched in Harvard Business School case 4-176-113 (1976), "General Meter Corporation."

3. The value for operating costs, -108, assumes that $I_C = 10$ will cut unit costs by the same percentage ($c = 10\%$) whether or not there is expansion.

4. In a deterministic world, the strategic-planning formulation and the option model give identical results. Under uncertainty (say, in V), strategic planning done in a backward dynamic-programming fashion with repeated iterations and built-in contingent decision variables is correct in principle if the right discount rate can be identified. The option approach can be seen as a transformation of this problem that overcomes the discount-rate pitfall by transforming the probabilities into risk-neutral ones so as to allow risk-free discounting.

5. Here, for simplicity, the cost is assumed to be a constant proportion (80%) of sales. However, the model can handle any deterministic cost function.

6. Under uncertainty, even if the combined NPV is negative, the strategic value of the growth option may make the strategic investment commitment worthwhile.

Chapter 9

1. Baldwin (1982) finds that optimal sequential investment may require a positive premium over direct NPV to compensate for the loss of future investment opportunities. Roberts and Weitzman (1981) find that a project is more attractive when managers have the freedom to continually review its status, especially when the uncertainty in benefits is greater. Venezia and Brenner (1979) investigate the optimal duration of stochastic growth investments and show that investment value grows with uncertainty.

2. The analysis can be extended to accommodate stochastic costs (Margrabe 1978; Carr 1988).

3. A stochastic drop in project value at anticipated times can be incorporated (Geske 1978). Random competitive arrivals with a deterministic drop are analyzed in section 9.2 below.

4. As shown by Merton (1973) and discussed in chapter 3 above, it is not optimal to exercise an American call option without dividends before its expiration date.

5. Spence (1977) argues that existing firms in an industry facing competitive threat should carry excess capacity so as to expand output and reduce prices when entry is threatened, thereby preempting competitive entry. Spence (1979) finds that constraints on growth and the timing of entry place firms in asymmetrical positions concerning investment, with the firms in the most advantageous positions preempting the market to some degree. Dasgupta and Stiglitz (1980) show that an incumbent firm can preempt potential competitors by spending excessive amounts on R&D; they also find that a monopolist would delay innovation whereas the threat of competition may induce a firm to innovate earlier. Reinganum (1983) argues that entrants stimulate innovation both through their own provocative behavior and through their provocation of incumbent firms. Pindyck (1980) notes that a monopolist will intensify exploratory activity for exhaustible resources later relative to a competitive industry.

6. Alternatively, we can view a preemptive investment as a compound option with sequential exercise prices (the prices being the values lost for not preempting a competitor, d_j). Thus, at each intermediate stage the incumbent may choose to wait, pay d_j, and retain the option to continue for the next stage (to pay a similar premium to the next competitor); or may make a preemptive investment and pay the investment cost I to obtain project value V, for a net value NPV $\equiv V - I$. Carr's (1988) model for compound exchange options might be useful in this respect, although some of his assumptions, such as the one requiring that all options in the sequence have the same delivery asset, do not exactly hold here (where the delivery asset may be either d_j or I).

7. Project value, V, consists of a risky part (V') that cannot be appropriated by competitors and a certain part (representing escrowed competitive dividends equal to $d_1 e^{-r t_1} + d_2 e^{-r t_2}$) that will be lost to competitors at the known entry times t_1 and t_2. The relevant proof would follow the arguments presented in Jarrow and Rudd 1983 (p. 125ff) and in Roll 1977.

8. Recall the analogy with an American call option with anticipated dividends whose early exercise may be optimal just before an "ex-dividend" date. In practice, a preemptive real investment may have to take place earlier than "just before" an anticipated competitive entry to allow time for a competitor to revise its entry plans.

9. Here V' represents the present value (as of time 0) of the project if implemented at a known later time (t_j), whereas V corresponds to the present value of the project if it were to be implemented immediately (as in scenario A).

10. This value actually is a lower bound, since it assumes a prior commitment to exercising only at t_1, t_2, or T. In reality, the actual value would be higher by the flexibility to exercise at other intermediate times.

11. This can be seen from the convexity of the C-versus-V curve with I held fixed, or from the C-versus-I curve with V held fixed. For example, with I held fixed,

$$C(V, T, I) - C(V', T, I) \leq V - V' = (V - I) - (V' - I) \equiv \text{NPV} - \text{NPV}';$$

with V held fixed,

$$C(V, T, I) - C(V', T, I) \leq I' - I = (V - I) - (V - I') \equiv \text{NPV} - \text{NPV}'.$$

12. This observation is also emphasized in Kester 1993.

13. For simplicity, we compare holding the option until maturity despite anticipated competitive arrivals versus an immediate ($t = 0$) preemptive exercise, ignoring for now the pos-

sibility that preemptive exercise just before t_1 may be preferable to exercise at $t = 0$. From earlier discussion we have

$$\text{NPV} - \text{NPV}' \geq C(V, T, I) - C(V', T, I).$$

But $C(V, T, I) - C(V', T, I)$ must exceed $C(V, T, I) - \text{NPV}$ to justify immediate exercise (or NPV must exceed $C(V', T, I)$). Therefore, for immediate exercise to be preferable it must hold that

$$\text{NPV} - \text{NPV}' > C(V, T, I) - \text{NPV}.$$

14. Alternatively, the $\tau = T$ curve in figure 9.1 shifts down relatively more than the $\tau = t_1$ curve, so that R_D is reduced more in value relative to R_E, or $R_C - R_E$ becomes lower relative to $R_C - R_D$.

15. The "dividend" analogy holds both in the case of uncertain competitive arrivals and in the case of anticipated competitive entry with early preemptive investment. The analogy is limited only in that for a stock option the dividend is received by the holder of the stock, whereas here the "dividend payout" is lost to the competitor. This distinction is not relevant to the valuation.

16. This section is based on Han Smit and Lenos Trigeorgis, Flexibility and Commitment in Strategic Investment, working paper, Tinbergen Institute, Erasmus University, Rotterdam, 1993. I would like to thank Han Smit for permission to use some of our joint work.

17. Constant binomial parameters, u and d, may not be a realistic representation of the project dynamics under endogenous competitive reaction. The binomial parameters may change according to the state of market demand and equilibrium profits.

18. In complete markets spanning the equilibrium profit values, the risk-neutral probabilities can be obtained from

$$p = \frac{(1 + r)\pi - \pi^-}{\pi^+ - \pi^-},$$

where π is the current profit value and where π^+ (π^-) is the next period's up (down) profit value. These risk-neutral probabilities are thus dependent on time and the state of demand, as they endogenize competitive reaction.

19. For simplicity, we assume zero taxes and depreciation so that the operating cash flows are equivalent to the operating profits. The risk-adjusted discount rate k for the last stage used to determine the gross project state value ($V_i = \pi_i / k$) can be obtained from an equilibrium model such as the CAPM.

20. The slope of this reaction function, given by

$$R_i'(Q_j) = -\frac{1}{2 + q_i},$$

is determined by the quadratic cost coefficient q_i. The downward-sloping reaction function suggested by the above negative slope (for $q_i \geq 0$) results in contrarian competition where one firm can increase its quantity (or market share) at the expense of the other, as illustrated in figure 9.5 (where $q_i = 0$). Further, the fixed marginal production cost for firm i, c_i, determines the intercept of the reaction function, $(\Theta - c_i)/(2 + q_i)$; thus, a change in this cost would cause a parallel shift in the relevant reaction function, altering the equilibrium quantities.

21. As illustrated in figure 9.5 (with $q_i = 0$), if pioneering firm A's early strategic investment (K_A) would create a first-mover cost advantage (reducing c_A below c_B, say to 0) that would

result in proprietary benefits and make the firm tougher its intercept would increase and its reaction curve would shift to the right, increasing its equilibrium quantity (Q_A^*) while reducing that of its competitor (Q_B^*)—moving from Nash equilibrium outcome N_0 to N_P. By contrast, if firm A would take an accommodating position resulting in shared benefits with its competitor (e.g., also reducing the competitor's cost c_B, say to 0), B's reaction curve would also shift to the right, increasing its equilibrium output (Q_B^*) to that of outcome N_s.

22. It can be seen from equation 9.20, with $Q_j = 0$, that the profit-maximizing quantity for a monopolist firm i (point M in figure 9.5, where $q_i = 0$) is

$$Q_i = \frac{\Theta_t - c_i}{2 + q_i} \quad \text{(with } Q_j = 0\text{)}.$$

23. Using the leader's optimal quantity from equation 9.23 in the follower's reaction function in equation 9.20 gives

$$Q_j = \frac{(\Theta_t - c_j)(2 + q_i) - (\Theta_t - c_i)}{(2 + q_i)(2 + q_j)}.$$

24. For example, in the base case of figure 9.3, when $\Theta = d$ and both firms defer (D, D) and then Θ moves up and both firms invest (I, I), the state project value in the resulting Nash equilibrium is

$$NPV_i = \frac{(\Theta_t - 2c_A + c_B)^2}{9k} - I = \frac{(14 - 2 \times 3 + 3)^2}{9(0.13)} - 100 = 3.$$

If firm A invests and B defers, A's monopoly profit value is

$$\frac{(\Theta_t - c)^2}{4k} - I = \frac{(14 - 3)^2}{4(0.13)} - 100 = 133.$$

25. An R&D investment may create either proprietary or shared benefits, depending on the diffusion of knowledge. A proprietary advantage may, for example, be based on reduced costs or may be the result of a learning process that is difficult to imitate and will not be eliminated by subsequent technological advances. If the benefits of opening up the market cannot be made proprietary to the pioneering firm, however, there is a free-rider problem: competing firms entering later can take advantage of this diffusion of knowledge and replicate the pioneer's products or processes.

26. Owing to space considerations, figure 9.4 does not show the last period of the game, which incorporates the equilibrium project values for the Nash (N), Stackelberg leader/follower (S), or monopoly (M) games (summarized in table 9.1) in the various states shown in figure 9.2. These are illustrated in detail for the base-case alternative in figure 9.3. All the numerical values shown in figure 9.4 are, nevertheless, the expected values derived from backward binomial valuation based on the entire multistage game and the equilibrium payoff values of table 9.1. For example, in the base case (figure 9.3) with $\Theta = d$, the value (1, 1) is the expected value from applying the backward binomial risk-neutral valuation of equation 9.15 using the subsequent Nash equilibrium values (3, 3) if Θ later moves up and both firms invest, and the (0, 0) abandonment values if $\Theta = d$.

27. From equation 9.15 with $p = 0.53$ (obtained from the dynamics in equilibrium-state profits), the contingent-claim (growth-option) value for firm A is

$$C_0 = \frac{0.53 \times 259 + 0.47 \times 155}{1.10} = 191,$$

so

$$NPV_0^* = C_0 - K_A = 191 - 110 = 81.$$

Similarly, for firm B,

$$\text{NPV}_0^* = \frac{0.53 \times 13 + 0.47 \times 0}{1.10} = 6.3.$$

28. Actually, there are two pure Nash equilibria, $(40, 0)$ and $(0, 40)$, if we assume that one firm invests first and the other defers. Although once found in one of these states they wouldn't move, it is not clear how they would end up in one of these states in the first place. Both firms know that if they both end up investing they will be worse off with $(-43, -43)$, so they might do better to wait and receive $(1, 1)$. The same expected outcome $(1, 1)$ also obtains if a *mixed* Nash equilibrium is used instead where each competitor chooses to appear unpredictable to the other. The equilibrium probabilities that each firm will invest (such that its expected value is independent of that probability) are $P_A^* = P_B^* = 0.476$, yielding for each firm an expected profit value of

$$0.476(0.476)(-43) + 0.476(1 - 0.476)(40) + (1 - 0.476)(0.476)0 + (1 - 0.476)^2(1) = 1.$$

29. If firm A had decided to make the R&D investment, whether Θ would move up or down each firm would have a dominating strategy to invest regardless of the other's action, resulting in symmetric Nash-equilibrium values of $(162, 162)$ if $\Theta = u$ (first box) or of $(7, 7)$ if $\Theta = d$ (second box). In the latter case, both firms would have done better to defer instead (a prisoner's dilemma). From backward risk-neutral valuation, the initial gross value for each firm is

$$\frac{0.5 \times 162 + 0.5 \times 7}{1.10} = 77$$

(with $\text{NPV}_A = 77 - 100 = -33$).

Chapter 10

1. For more formal definitions of stability (using the mesh ratio) and efficiency see Geske and Shastri 1985, pp. 53–56. See also section B of the appendix to this chapter.

2. See Jarrow and Rudd 1983 and Rendleman and Bartter 1979 for alternative choices of the binomial parameters.

3. Boyle (1988) and Omberg (1988) use trinomial processes.

4. Brennan and Schwartz (1978) show that, as the lower and upper boundaries become remote, the elements of any row of the matrix inverse $(\mathbf{C}^{-1})$ are non-negative and sum to unity, like (risk-neutral) transition probabilities (p_q) that the logarithm of price (X) will jump by qH to an infinity of possible states in a generalized jump process (or birth-and-death chain) of the form

$$F_{i,j} = \sum_{q=-\infty}^{\infty} \frac{p_q F_{i+q,j+1}}{1 + rK}.$$

The variance of this process, however, is biased upward by the square of the mean, i.e.,

$$\text{Var}(\Delta X) = \sigma^2 K - (r - \tfrac{1}{2}\sigma^2)^2 K^2.$$

5. Unlike the explicit method, which may have stability problems if a "probability" turns negative for some values of i, the implicit method does not have this problem. It always converges to the solution as the steps become smaller (a rule of thumb is to keep $H^2 \approx K$). It is, however, computationally less efficient, since a large number of simultaneous equations must be solved at each step.

6. Brennan and Schwartz (1978) previously introduced a log transformation of the Black-Scholes p.d.e. in the context of finite-difference methods in order to obtain a transformed p.d.e. with constant coefficients. In particular, the finite-difference coefficients (probabilities) of the transformed p.d.e. became state independent and remained non-negative, avoiding serious stability problems that were making the untransformed explicit finite-difference method impractical. Although it guaranteed stability, the Brennan-Schwartz (1978) explicit finite-difference scheme's estimate of the variance was biased downward (by the square of the mean) and thus was problematic with regard to accuracy and consistency. The log-transformed binomial method proposed here instead involves a log transformation of the underlying asset value (not of the p.d.e.) in a binomial lattice framework that is more intuitive and is designed to overcome various numerical difficulties encountered in other computational methods.

7. This is the gross or naked project value, not including any required investment cost outlays or any embedded real options. To the firm, V represents the market value of a claim on the future cash flows from installing the project now.

8. The approach of Hull and White (1988a), without their control-variate technique, is also a reasonable alternative that performs well. Again, we must assign the jump parameters so that the mean and the variance of the log normal process equal those of the jump process. This is similar to the approach suggested here, except that Hull and White work with the log normal process rather than transforming to the normal process (which would allow for symmetric state spacing). As will be discussed later, log transformation may improve the accuracy, stability, and efficiency of the numerical procedure.

9. To simplify the notation, subscripts j on the left side of equation 10.16 and $j+1$ on its right side are dropped from R.

10. The time sequence of "first-passage" project values for which $R = S$ is saved and determines the abandonment exercise schedule or the critical boundary below which the project should be abandoned for its salvage value.

11. In a few (typically in-the-money) cases (rows 1, 6, 7, 14, 16, and 19), $N = 456$ (as in finite differences) was used for better accuracy.

12. This efficiency comes from log transformation and from a different choice of binomial parameters. Additional efficiency also results from the different adjustment for nonproportional dividends.

13. We were also able to confirm with close accuracy the results on the American put option to abandon for salvage that Myers and Majd (1990) obtained using explicit finite differences, both with a constant cash payout under deterministic salvage (their table I) and with stochastic salvage (their table III).

14. For stability restrictions in implicit finite-difference schemes see Brennan and Schwartz 1978, p. 470, equation 48. For restrictions in explicit finite-difference schemes see their equation 9; see also Mason 1978, p. 21, equation 4.4. For restrictions in numerical integration see ibid., equation 4.3. For a derivation of the restriction in the Cox-Ross-Rubinstein (1979) binomial approach, see section B of the appendix to the present chapter.

Chapter 11

1. For a good discussion involving some of the examples that follow, see A. K. Naj, "In R&D, the next best thing to a gut feeling," *Manager's Journal, Wall Street Journal*, May 21, 1990.

2. See N. Nichols, "Scientific management at Merck: An interview with CFO Judy Lewent," *Harvard Business Review*, January–February 1994: 89–99.

3. This value differs from the value obtained from discounting the expected net future value of the building next year,

$$0.5 \times 540 + 0.5 \times 60 = 300,$$

using the risk-adjusted discount rate for a condominium. If condominiums are correctly priced in the market so that the current market price fairly reflects the discounted value of expected future cash flows, i.e.,

$$\frac{0.5 \times 150 + 0.5 \times 90}{1 + k} = 100,$$

the discount rate for a condominium would be $k = 0.20$, or 20%. This is not the proper discount rate for the vacant land (option), however. The imputed (ex post) discount rate for land that would correctly arrive at the option value,

$$\frac{0.5 \times 540 + 0.5 \times 60}{1 + k'} = 200,$$

is $k' = 0.50$, or 50%, in this case. If the 20% rate were used to discount the option payoffs, an erroneous land value of $250,000 would result.

4. The penalty may include loss of a security deposit as well as other fees (legal or otherwise) specified in the contract.

5. Equations 11.3–11.5 below represent adjustments in the value of the leasing contract at specified *future* times. Only after successive determinations of expected values with riskless backward discounting, and with proper adjustment for lease costs at indicated times, would the net *current* value of the lease contract, C_0, be obtained.

6. Unlike other options (e.g., to cancel or renew), which are treated as having the value of operating the leased asset, V_t, as the "underlying asset," the option to buy is written on the replacement cost, S_t.

7. If the lessee has the option to purchase the leased asset before maturity (an American call), the adjustment in equation 11.3 will be applied in each period as the numerical valuation proceeds backward.

8. If the option to cancel early is of the American type, the relevant adjustment from equation 11.4 would again be invoked in every period in which a rental payment is due. Of course, if a specified initial period is covered under a noncancellation provision, it is exempted from such adjustments.

9. This would also be the cost of signing a guarantee protecting against cancellation.

10. This value of the option to buy can be confirmed using standard call-option tables (see table A.1 in the appendix) as follows: For an asset paying a dividend,

$$\delta = k + B = 0.12 + 0.15 = 0.27,$$

the effective (dividend-adjusted) underlying asset is

$$S^* = S_0 e^{-\delta T} = 100 e^{-0.27 \times 6} = 20.$$

Thus, the asset value divided by the present value of the exercise price is

$$\frac{S^*}{EX e^{-rT}} = \frac{20}{40} e^{0.07 \times 6} = 0.76,$$

which specifies the table column. From the row corresponding to $\sigma\sqrt{T} = 0.447\sqrt{6} = 1.10$, the value of this call option is about 34% of S^* (= 20), or 6.8.

11. This example is based on application of the option-based valuation methodology (described above) to a mineral project of a major multinational company. I thank Henry D. Jacoby and Scott P. Mason for their help and ideas, and I thank company executives for providing data and help in formulating the application.

12. Projected sales during the operating phase were (in thousands of tons per year) 67 in year 4, 284 in year 5, 340 in years 6 and 7, 350 in year 8, 363 in year 9, 372 in year 10, and 400 (full capacity) in years 11–19.

13. For the base-scale project, fixed maintenance and operating (M&O) costs were $8 million in year 4 and $16 million per year from year 5 onward. Variable M&O costs were $44 per ton.

14. For simplicity, it is assumed that the entire output of stage II, if in fact built, would be exported, whereas the output of the base-scale project is sold in the domestic market. In reality, if export demand is not still satisfied, it might be possible to export any unused capacity (i.e., the difference between production capacity and domestic sales) from the base-scale project. Similarly, if future domestic sales were to exceed base-scale capacity, part of the stage-II output could be sold to satisfy the excess demand at home at the higher domestic prices. Ignoring these possibilities would lead to small underestimates of the option to expand and of the project's value.

15. The additional fixed M&O cost for stage II was $3 million per year from year 8 onward; the variable M&O cost was unchanged ($44 per ton).

16. The salvage value would include a portion of any additional outlays on the stage-II expansion.

17. The volatility in project value is, of course, a key determinant of the value of flexibility, and must be estimated with utmost care. The project standard deviation value of 0.2 used here is about the same as that of the average stock. For many real assets, such as commodities, oil, minerals, and other natural-resource investments, the standard deviation of *price* is between 0.2 and 0.4. It is thus reasonable to use a standard deviation of 0.2 for the present value of cash flows (that depend on price) for this mineral project in the base-case analysis. Sensitivity results are presented over the range 0.1–0.3.

18. In this case, the ability to get out of the project seems to exceed the value of the opportunity to expand its scale (so long as the stage-II output is sold at the lower export prices).

19. If the option to defer initiating the project up to 2 years is also included, the combined value of all four options could rise to $131.1 million (about 28% of the $476.2 million capital outlay), increasing the project's total value to $120.5 million.

20. The value of flexibility determined above should be viewed as an upper bound, since it will be fully realized only if the optimal operating rules are in fact followed (i.e., if the project is actually canceled, expanded, or abandoned precisely when indicated). To the extent that actual operation departs from the optimal rules, the flexibility value actually realized will be below its theoretical value as calculated above.

21. The multinational company that engaged in the preliminary exploration of options analysis because of dissatisfaction with its traditional DCF-based techniques had, in the meantime, fallen (perhaps for reasons not unrelated to those techniques) into serious financial difficulties that distracted management's attention from further exploring the potential of

options-based analysis. It soon had to sell its mineral reserves to another company that, ironically, also justified the acquisition price on the basis of the options framework. In the same light, there is evidence that the RTZ Corporation used an options framework in the valuation of the gold assets in the $3.6 billion acquisition of British Petroleum's mining properties, and went through with the deal even though gold prices had declined considerably from the $420 per ounce prevailing at the beginning of the 6-month negotiation process. (DCF values suffered accordingly.)

Chapter 12

1. Some of the following implications agree with similar observations by Kester (1982, 1993).

2. An "operating strategy" is an implied commitment on the part of management to a plan of action (such as when to start, operate, or end a project), contingent on the occurrence of uncertain future events. The "option premium" is due in part to management's flexibility to change from a preconceived plan to a more advantageous course of action when, as uncertainty clears up, circumstances turn out differently from what was originally expected.

3. As we saw in chapters 4 and 9, it may also be justifiable to defer a project with a positive NPV if the benefits of deferral would exceed the associated costs. Further, Schwab and Lusztig (1972) recommend rejecting a positive-NPV project whose value turns positive only close to the end of its expected horizon in order to maintain flexibility in light of unforeseen investment opportunities.

4. The owner of an option on an asset, unlike the owner of the asset itself, has the right to benefit from any potential increases in the asset's value, but has no symmetric obligation to exercise in case the asset's value drops. Thus, more uncertainty increases the option owner's upside potential, while that owner's downside risk remains limited.

5. As interest rates increase, ceteris paribus, the present value of the future investment outlay needed to exercise the real option is reduced and the option becomes more valuable. The validity of this result is, of course, limited to situations where other parameters remain constant and where the project pays no "dividends" (such as intermediate cash flows) and is expected to earn a rate of return commensurate with market equilibrium. If other parameters do not remain the same, a different result is possible. For example, if the project pays intermediate cash flows or has a "below-equilibrium" expected rate of return, then higher interest rates would translate into a higher required equilibrium rate of return, with the resulting shortfall between the actual and equilibrium returns acting like a continuous dividend yield with a negative impact on the value of the option. Also, if the most predominant type of flexibility is the option to abandon (a put option), then the option premium may again decrease with higher interest rates, other things being the same.

6. From basic option theory, this has two sources (in the absence of dividends): As the time to expiration increases, the total uncertainty of the asset's value will increase and the present value of the investment (exercise) cost will decrease, both leading to an increase in option value. If any form of dividends (such as competitive arrivals) is present, then the present value of "dividends" lost for the holder of a call option increases with time to expiration; the effect is to reduce option value (other things constant), making early optimal exercise possible.

7. This, of course, holds under the standard diffusion Wiener dynamics for an asset earning an equilibrium expected rate of return. Other authors using different dynamic structures have

similarly found, for example, that a monopolist would delay exercising an option to innovate or explore relative to a competitive situation (see, e.g., Dasgupta and Stiglitz 1980; Pindyck 1980). If competition is present or if a nontraded real project earns an expected return below the market equilibrium, then the resulting "dividend effect" may turn premature exercise into an optimal action.

8. The notion that competition may induce premature exercise is also supported in the economic literature. For example, Dasgupta and Stiglitz (1980) show that competitive threat may induce a firm to innovate earlier, and Reinganum (1983) finds that competitors may stimulate innovation through their provocation of incumbent firms.

9. The idea that reciprocating competition under mistrust will induce premature exercise is also supported in the R&D literature. For example, Dasgupta and Stiglitz (1980) show that competitive threat may induce a firm to innovate earlier, and Reinganum (1983) finds that competitors may stimulate innovation through their provocation of incumbent firms.

Bibliography

Abramowitz, M., and I. Stegum. 1972. *Handbook of Mathematical Functions*. Dover.

Aggarwal, R. 1991. "Justifying investments in flexible manufacturing technology." *Managerial Finance* 17, no. 2/3: 77–88.

Ang, J. S., and S. Dukas. 1991. "Capital budgeting in a competitive environment." *Managerial Finance* 17, no. 2/3: 6–15.

Baldwin, C. 1982. "Optimal sequential investment when capital is not readily reversible." *Journal of Finance* 37, no. 3: 763–782.

Baldwin, C. 1987. "Competing for capital in a global environment." *Midland Corporate Finance Journal* 5, no. 1: 43–64.

Baldwin, C., and K. Clark. 1992. "Capabilities and capital investment: New perspectives on capital budgeting." *Journal of Applied Corporate Finance* 5, no. 2: 67–87.

Baldwin, C., and K. Clark. 1993. Modularity and Real Options. Working paper, Harvard Business School.

Baldwin, C., and R. Ruback. 1986. "Inflation, uncertainty, and investment." *Journal of Finance* 41, no. 3: 657–669.

Baldwin, C., and L. Trigeorgis. 1993. Real Options, Capabilities, TQM, and Competitiveness. Working paper 93-025, Harvard Business School.

Barone-Adesi, G., and R. Whaley. 1987. "Efficient analytic approximation of American option values." *Journal of Finance* 42, no. 2: 301–320.

Bartter, B., and R. Rendleman. 1979. "Fee-based pricing of fixed-rate bank loan commitments." *Financial Management* 8, no. 1: 13–20.

Bell, G. 1995. "Volatile exchange rates and the multinational firm: Entry, exit, and capacity options." In *Real Options in Capital Investments*, ed. L. Trigeorgis. Praeger.

Bjerksund, P., and S. Ekern. 1990. "Managing investment opportunities under price uncertainty: From 'last chance' to 'wait and see' strategies." *Financial Management* 19, no. 3: 65–83.

Bjerksund, P., and S. Ekern. 1995. "Contingent claims evaluation of mean-reverting cash flows in shipping." In *Real Options in Capital Investment*, ed. L. Trigeorgis. Praeger.

Black, F., and J. Cox. 1976. "Valuing corporate securities: Some effects of bond indenture provisions." *Journal of Finance* 31, no. 2: 351–367.

Black, F., and M. Scholes. 1973. "The pricing of options and corporate liabilities." *Journal of Political Economy* 81 (May–June): 637–659.

Blomeyer, E. C. 1986. "An analytic approximation for the American put price for options on stocks with dividends." *Journal of Financial and Quantitative Analysis* 21, no. 2: 229–233.

Bower, J. 1970. *Managing Resource Allocation*. Harvard Business School Press.

Boyle, P. 1977. "Options: A Monte Carlo approach." *Journal of Financial Economics* 4, no. 3: 323–338.

Boyle, P. 1988. "A lattice framework for option pricing with two state variables." *Journal of Financial and Quantitative Analysis* 23, no. 1: 1–12.

Brealey, R., and S. C. Myers. 1991. *Principles of Corporate Finance*, fourth edition. McGraw-Hill.

Brennan, M. 1979. "The pricing of contingent claims in discrete time models." *Journal of Finance* 34, no. 1: 53–68.

Brennan, M., and E. Schwartz. 1977a. "The valuation of American put options." *Journal of Finance* 32, no. 2: 449–462.

Brennan, M., and E. Schwartz. 1977b. "Convertible bonds: valuation and optimal strategies for call and conversion." *Journal of Finance* 32, no. 5: 1699–1716.

Brennan, M., and E. Schwartz. 1978. "Finite difference methods and jump processes arising in the pricing of contingent claims: A synthesis." *Journal of Financial and Quantitative Analysis* 13, no. 3: 461–474.

Brennan, M., and E. Schwartz. 1982. "An equilibrium model of bond pricing and a test of market efficiency." *Journal of Financial and Quantitative Analysis* 17, no. 3: 301–329.

Brennan, M., and E. Schwartz. 1985a. "Evaluating natural resource investments." *Journal of Business* 58, no. 2: 135–157.

Brennan, M., and E. Schwartz. 1985b. "A new approach to evaluating natural resource investments." *Midland Corporate Finance Journal* 3, no. 1: 37–47.

Capozza, D., and G. Sick. 1991. "Valuing long-term leases: The option to redevelop." *Journal of Real Estate Finance and Economics* 4, no. 2: 209–223.

Capozza, D., and Y. Li. 1994. "The intensity and timing of investment: The case of land." *American Economic Review* 84, no. 4: 889–904.

Capozza, D., and G. Sick. 1994. "The risk structure of land markets." *Journal of Urban Economics* 35: 297–319.

Carr, P. 1988. "The valuation of sequential exchange opportunities." *Journal of Finance* 43, no. 5: 1235–1256.

Carr, P. 1995. "The valuation of American exchange options with application to real options." In *Real Options in Capital Investment*, ed. L. Trigeorgis. Praeger.

Chung, K., and C. Charoenwong. 1991. "Investment options, assets in place, and the risk of stocks." *Financial Management* 20, no. 3: 21–33.

Constantinides, G. 1978. "Market risk adjustment in project valuation." *Journal of Finance* 33, no. 2: 603–616.

Copeland T., and J. F. Weston. 1982. "A note on the evaluation of cancellable operating leases." *Financial Management* 11, no. 2: 60–67.

Cox, J., J. Ingersoll, and S. Ross. 1985a. "An intertemporal general equilibrium model of asset prices." *Econometrica* 53 (March): 363–384.

Cox, J., J. Ingersoll, and S. Ross. 1985b. "A theory of the term structure of interest rates." *Econometrica* 53 (March): 385–407.

Cox, J., and S. Ross. 1975. The Pricing of Options for Jump Processes. Working paper 2-75, University of Pennsylvania.

Cox, J., and S. Ross. 1976. "The valuation of options for alternative stochastic processes." *Journal of Financial Economics* 3, no. 1/2: 145–166.

Cox, J., S. Ross, and M. Rubinstein. 1979. "Option pricing: A simplified approach." *Journal of Financial Economics* 7, no. 3: 229–263.

Cox, J., and M. Rubinstein. 1985. *Options Markets*. Prentice-Hall.

Dasgupta, P., and J. Stiglitz. 1980. "Uncertainty, industrial structure and the speed of R&D." *Bell Journal of Economics* 11 (autumn): 1–28.

Dean, J. 1951. *Capital Budgeting*. Columbia University Press.

Dixit, A. 1979. "A model of duopoly suggesting a theory of entry barriers." *Bell Journal of Economics* 10, no. 1: 20–32.

Dixit, A. 1980. "The role of investment in entry deterrence." *Economic Journal* 90 (March): 95–106.

Dixit, A. 1989. "Entry and exit decisions under uncertainty." *Journal of Political Economy* 97 (June): 620–638.

Dixit, A., and R. S. Pindyck. 1994. *Investment under Uncertainty*. Princeton University Press.

Donaldson, G., and J. Lorsch. 1983. *Decision Making at the Top: The Shaping of Strategic Direction*. Basic Books.

Edleson, M., and F. Reinhardt. 1995. "Investment in pollution compliance options: The case of Georgia Power." In *Real Options in Capital Investment*, ed. L. Trigeorgis. Praeger.

Fama, E. 1977. "Risk-adjusted discount rates and capital budgeting under uncertainty." *Journal of Financial Economics* 5, no. 1: 3–24.

Fischer, I. 1930. *The Theory of Interest*. Macmillan.

Fischer, S. 1978. "Call option pricing when the exercise price is uncertain, and the valuation of index bonds." *Journal of Finance* 33, no. 1: 169–176.

Fudenberg, D., and J. Tirole. 1984. "The fat-cat effect, the puppy-dog ploy, and the lean and hungry look." *American Economic Review* 74 (May): 361–366.

Galai, D., and R. Masulis. 1976. "The option pricing model and the risk factor of stock." *Journal of Financial Economics* 3, no. 1/2: 53–81.

Garman, M. 1976. A General Theory of Asset Valuation under Diffusion State Processes. Working paper, University of California, Berkeley.

Geske, R. 1978. "The pricing of options with stochastic dividend yield." *Journal of Finance* 33, no. 2: 617–625.

Geske, R. 1979. "The valuation of compound options." *Journal of Financial Economics* 7, no. 1: 63–81.

Geske, R., and H. Johnson. 1984. "The American put option valued analytically." *Journal of Finance* 39, no. 5: 1511–1524.

Geske, R., and K. Shastri. 1985. "Valuation by approximation: A comparison of alternative option valuation techniques." *Journal of Financial and Quantitative Analysis* 20, no. 1: 45–71.

Harrison, J. M., and D. M. Kreps. 1979. "Martingales and arbitrage in multiperiod securities markets." *Journal of Economic Theory* 20 (June): 381–408.

Hayes, R., and W. Abernathy. 1980. "Managing our way to economic decline." *Harvard Business Review* 58, no. 4: 66–77.

Hayes, R., and D. Garvin. 1982. "Managing as if tomorrow mattered." *Harvard Business Review* 60, no. 3: 71–79.

Hendricks, D. 1991. Optimal Policy Responses to an Uncertain Threat: The Case of Global Warming. Working paper, Kennedy School of Government, Harvard University.

Hertz, D. 1964. "Risk analysis in capital investment." *Harvard Business Review* 42 (January–February): 95–106.

Hiraki, T. 1995. "Corporate governance, long-term investment orientation, and real options in Japan." In *Real Options in Capital Investment*, ed. L. Trigeorgis. Praeger.

Hirschleifer, J. 1958. "On the theory of optimal investment decisions." *Journal of Political Economy* 66 (August): 329–352.

Hodder, J. 1986. "Evaluation of manufacturing investments: A comparison of U.S. and Japanese practices." *Financial Management* 15, no. 1: 17–24.

Hodder, J., and H. Riggs. 1985. "Pitfalls in evaluating risky projects." *Harvard Business Review* 63, no. 1: 128–135.

Hull, J. 1993. *Options, Futures, and Other Derivative Securities*, second edition. Prentice-Hall.

Hull, J., and A. White. 1987. "The pricing of options on assets with stochastic volatilities." *Journal of Finance* 42, no. 2: 281–300.

Hull, J., and A. White. 1988a. "The use of the control variate technique in option pricing." *Journal of Financial and Quantitative Analysis* 23, no. 3: 237–252.

Hull, J., and A. White. 1988b. "An overview of contingent claims pricing." *Canadian Journal of Administrative Sciences* (September): 55–61.

Ingersoll, J. 1976. "A theoretical and empirical investigation of the dual purpose funds: An application of contingent-claims analysis." *Journal of Financial Economics* 3, no. 1/2: 83–123.

Ingersoll, J. 1977. "A contingent-claims valuation of convertible securities." *Journal of Financial Economics* 4, no. 3: 289–322.

Ingersoll, J., and S. Ross. 1992. "Waiting to invest: investment and uncertainty." *Journal of Business* 65, no. 1: 1–29.

Jarrow, R., and A. Rudd. 1983. *Option Pricing*. Irwin.

Johnson, H. E. 1983. "An analytic approximation for the American put price." *Journal of Financial and Quantitative Analysis* 18, no. 1: 141–148.

Johnson, H. E. 1987. "Options on the maximum or the minimum of several assets." *Journal of Financial and Quantitative Analysis* 22, no. 3: 277–284.

Jones, E. P., and S. P. Mason. 1980. "Valuation of loan guarantees." *Journal of Banking and Finance* 4, no. 1: 89–107.

Jones, E. P., S. P. Mason, and E. Rosenfeld. 1984. "Contingent claims analysis of corporate capital structures: An empirical investigation." *Journal of Finance* 39, no. 3: 611–624.

Kamrad, B., and R. Ernst. 1995. "Multiproduct manufacturing with stochastic input prices and output yield uncertainty." In *Real Options in Capital Investment*, ed. L. Trigeorgis. Praeger.

Kasanen, E. 1993. "Creating value by spawning investment opportunities." *Financial Management* 22, no. 3: 251–258.

Kasanen, E., and L. Trigeorgis. 1994. "A market utility approach to investment valuation." *European Journal of Operational Research* (Special Issue on Financial Modelling) 74, no. 2: 294–309.

Kemna, A. 1993. "Case studies on real options." *Financial Management* 22, no. 3: 259–270.

Kensinger, J. 1987. "Adding the value of active management into the capital budgeting equation." *Midland Corporate Finance Journal* 5, no. 1: 31–42.

Kester, W. C. 1982. Evaluating Growth Options: A New Approach to Strategic Capital Budgeting. Working paper 83-38, Harvard Business School.

Kester, W. C. 1984. "Today's options for tomorrow's growth." *Harvard Business Review* 62, no. 2: 153–160.

Kester, W. C. 1993. "Turning growth options into real assets." In *Capital Budgeting under Uncertainty*, ed. R. Aggarwal. Prentice-Hall.

Kogut, B., and N. Kulatilaka. 1994. "Operating flexibility, global manufacturing, and the option value of a multinational network." *Management Science* 40, no. 1: 123–139.

Kolbe, A. L., P. A. Morris, and E. O. Teisberg. 1991. "When choosing R & D projects, go with long shots." *Research-Technology Management* (January-February): 35–40.

Kulatilaka, N. 1988. "Valuing the flexibility of flexible manufacturing systems." *IEEE Transactions in Engineering Management* 35, no. 4: 250–257.

Kulatilaka, N. 1993. "The value of flexibility: The case of a dual-fuel industrial steam boiler." *Financial Management* 22, no. 3: 271–279.

Kulatilaka, N. 1995a. "The value of flexibility: A general model of real options." In *Real Options in Capital Investment*, ed. L. Trigeorgis. Praeger.

Kulatilaka, N. 1995b. "Operating flexibilities in capital budgeting: substitutability and complementarity in real options." In *Real Options in Capital Investment*, ed. L. Trigeorgis. Praeger.

Kulatilaka, N., and A. Marcus. 1988. "A general formulation of corporate real options." *Research in Finance* 7: 183–200.

Kulatilaka, N., and A. Marcus. 1992. "Project valuation under uncertainty: When does DCF fail?" *Journal of Applied Corporate Finance* 5, no. 3: 92–100.

Kulatilaka, N., and S. Marks. 1988. "The strategic value of flexibility: reducing the ability to compromise." *American Economic Review* 78, no. 3: 574–580.

Kulatilaka, N., and E. Perotti. 1992. Strategic Investment Timing under Uncertainty. Working paper, Boston University.

Kulatilaka, N., and L. Trigeorgis. 1994. "The general flexibility to switch: Real options revisited." *International Journal of Finance* 6, no. 2: 778–798.

Lai, V. S., and L. Trigeorgis. 1995. "The strategic capital budgeting process: A review of theories and practice." In *Real Options in Capital Investment*, ed. L. Trigeorgis. Praeger.

Laughton, D. G., and H. D. Jacoby. 1993. "Reversion, timing options, and long-term decision-making." *Financial Management* 22, no. 3: 225–240.

Lee, W., J. Martin, and A. Senchack. 1982. "The case for using options to evaluate salvage values in financial leases." *Financial Management* 11, no. 3: 33–41.

Lewellen, W., and M. Long. 1972. "Simulation versus single-value estimates in capital expenditure analysis." *Decision Science* (October): 19–33.

MacMillan, L. W. 1986. "Analytic approximation for the American put option." *Advances in Futures and Options Research* 1: 119–139.

Magee, J. 1964. "How to use decision trees in capital investment." *Harvard Business Review* 42 (September–October): 79–96.

Majd, S., and R. Pindyck. 1987. "Time to build, option value, and investment decisions." *Journal of Financial Economics* 18, no. 1: 7–27.

Margrabe, W. 1978. "The value of an option to exchange one asset for another." *Journal of Finance* 33, no. 1: 177–186.

Mason, S. P. 1978. The Numerical Analysis of Certain Free Boundary Problems Arising in Financial Economics. Working paper 78-52, Harvard Business School.

Mason, S. P., and C. Baldwin. 1988. "Evaluation of government subsidies to large-scale energy projects: A contingent claims approach." *Advances in Futures and Options Research* 3: 169–181.

Mason, S. P., and R. C. Merton. 1985. "The role of contingent claims analysis in corporate finance." In *Recent Advances in Corporate Finance*, ed. E. Altman and M. Subrahmanyam. Irwin.

Mauer, D., and A. Triantis. 1992. Interactions of Corporate Financing and Investment Decisions: A Dynamic Framework. Working paper, University of Wisconsin, Madison.

McConnel, J., and J. Schallheim. 1983. "Valuation of asset leasing contracts." *Journal of Financial Economics* 12, no. 2: 237–261.

McDonald, R., and D. Siegel. 1984. "Option pricing when the underlying asset earns a below-equilibrium rate of return: A note." *Journal of Finance* 39, no. 1: 261–265.

McDonald, R., and D. Siegel. 1985. "Investment and the valuation of firms when there is an option to shut down." *International Economic Review* 26, no. 2: 331–349.

McDonald, R., and D. Siegel. 1986. "The value of waiting to invest." *Quarterly Journal of Economics* 101, no. 4: 707–727.

McKean, Jr, H. P. 1965. "Appendix: A free boundary problem for the heat equation arising from a problem in mathematical economics." *Industrial Management Review* 6 (spring): 32–39.

McLaughlin, R., and R. Taggart. 1992. "The opportunity cost of using excess capacity." *Financial Management* 21, no. 2: 12–23.

Merton, R. C. 1973. "Theory of rational option pricing." *Bell Journal of Economics and Management Science* 4, no. 1: 141–183.

Merton, R. C. 1974. "On the pricing of corporate debt: The risk structure of interest rates." *Journal of Finance* 29, no. 2: 449–470.

Merton, R. C. 1977a. "An analytic derivation of the cost of deposit insurance and loan guarantees: An application of modern option pricing theory." *Journal of Banking and Finance* 1, no. 1: 3–11.

Merton, R. C. 1977b. "On the pricing of contingent claims and the Modigliani-Miller Theorem." *Journal of Financial Economics* 5, no. 2: 241–249.

Morck, R., E. Schwartz, and D. Stangeland. 1989. "The valuation of forestry resources under stochastic prices and inventories." *Journal of Financial and Quantitative Analysis* 24, no. 4: 473–487.

Myers, S. C. 1976. "Using simulation for risk analysis." In *Modern Developments in Financial Management*, ed. S. C. Myers. Praeger.

Myers, S. C. 1977. "Determinants of corporate borrowing." *Journal of Financial Economics* 5, no. 2: 147–176.

Myers, S. C. 1987. "Finance theory and financial strategy." *Midland Corporate Finance Journal* 5, no. 1: 6–13.

Myers, S. C., D. Dill, and A. Bautista. 1976. "Valuation of financial lease contracts." *Journal of Finance* 31, no. 3: 799–819.

Myers, S. C., and S. Majd. 1990. "Abandonment value and project life." *Advances in Futures and Options Research* 4: 1–21.

Myers, S. C., and S. Turnbull. 1977. "Capital budgeting and the capital asset pricing model: Good news and bad news." *Journal of Finance* 32, no. 2: 321–333.

Omberg, E. 1988. "Efficient discrete time jump process models in option pricing." *Journal of Financial and Quantitative Analysis* 23, no. 2: 161–174.

Paddock, J., D. Siegel, and J. Smith. 1988. "Option valuation of claims on physical assets: The case of offshore petroleum leases." *Quarterly Journal of Economics* 103, no. 3: 479–508.

Parkinson, M. 1977. "Option pricing: The American put." *Journal of Business* 50, no. 1: 21–36.

Pindyck, R. 1980. "Uncertainty and exhaustible resource markets." *Journal of Political Economy* 86 (December): 1203–1225.

Pindyck, R. 1988. "Irreversible investment, capacity choice, and the value of the firm." *American Economic Review* 78, no. 5: 969–985.

Pindyck, R. 1991. "Irreversibility, uncertainty, and investment." *Journal of Economic Literature* 29, no. 3: 1110–1148.

Porter, M. E. 1980. *Competitive Strategy*. Free Press.

Quigg, L. 1993. "Empirical testing of real option-pricing models." *Journal of Finance* 48, no. 2: 621–640.

Quigg, L. 1995. "Optimal land development." In *Real Options in Capital Investment*, ed. L. Trigeorgis. Praeger.

Reinganum, J. 1983. "Uncertain innovation and the persistence of monopoly." *American Economic Review* 73, no. 4: 741–748.

Rendleman, R., and B. Bartter. 1979. "Two-state option pricing." *Journal of Finance* 34, no. 5: 1093–1110.

Roberts, K., and M. Weitzman. 1981. "Funding criteria for research, development, and exploration projects." *Econometrica* 49, no. 5: 1261–1288.

Robichek, A., and S. C. Myers. 1966. "Conceptual problems in the use of risk-adjusted discount rates." *Journal of Finance* 21 (December): 727–730.

Roll, R. 1977. "An analytic valuation formula for unprotected American call options on stocks with known dividends." *Journal of Financial Economics* 5, no. 2: 251–258.

Rubinstein, M. 1976. "The valuation of uncertain income streams and the pricing of options." *Bell Journal of Economics* 7 (autumn): 407–425.

Sahlman, W. 1988. "Aspects of financial contracting in venture capital." *Journal of Applied Corporate Finance* 1: 23–36.

Schwab, B., and P. Lusztig. 1972. "A note on investment evaluations in light of uncertain future opportunities." *Journal of Finance* 27, no. 5: 1093–1100.

Shapiro, A. 1985. "Corporate strategy and the capital budgeting decision." *Midland Corporate Finance Journal* 3, no. 1: 22–36.

Sick, G. 1986. "A certainty-equivalent approach to capital budgeting." *Financial Management* 15, no. 4: 23–32.

Sick, G. 1989. Capital Budgeting with Real Options. Salomon Brothers Center, New York University.

Siegel, D., J. Smith, and J. Paddock. 1987. "Valuing offshore oil properties with option pricing models." *Midland Corporate Finance Journal* 5, no. 1: 22–30.

Smit, H.T.J., and L.A. Ankum. 1993. "A real options and game-theoretic approach to corporate investment strategy under competition." *Financial Management* 22, no. 3: 241–250.

Smit, H.T.J., and L. Trigeorgis. 1993. Flexibility and Commitment in Strategic Investment. Working paper, Tinbergen Institute, Erasmus University, Rotterdam.

Smith, C. 1976. "Option pricing: A review." *Journal of Financial Economics* 3, no. 1/2: 3–51.

Smith, C. 1977. "Alternative methods for raising capital: Rights versus underwritten offerings." *Journal of Financial Economics* 5, no. 3: 273–307.

Smith, C. 1979. "Applications of option pricing analysis." In *Handbook of Financial Economics*, ed. J. L. Bicksler. North-Holland.

Smith, K. W., and A. Triantis. 1995. "The value of options in strategic acquisitions." In *Real Options in Capital Investment*, ed. L. Trigeorgis. Praeger.

Spence, M. 1977. "Entry, capacity, investment, and oligopolistic pricing." *Bell Journal of Economics* 8, no. 2: 534–544.

Spence, M. 1979. "Investment strategy and growth in a new market." *Bell Journal of Economics* 10 (spring): 1–19.

Stensland, G., and D. Tjostheim. 1990. "Some applications of dynamic programming to natural resource exploration." In *Stochastic Models and Option Values*, ed. D. Lund and B. Oksendal. North-Holland.

Stulz, R. 1982. "Options on the minimum or the maximum of two risky assets: Analysis and applications." *Journal of Financial Economics* 10, no. 2: 161–185.

Teisberg, E. 1994. "An option valuation analysis of investment choices by a regulated firm." *Management Science* 40, no. 4: 535–548.

Teisberg, E. 1995. "Methods for evaluating capital investment decisions under uncertainty." In *Real Options in Capital Investment*, ed. L. Trigeorgis. Praeger.

Tirole, J. 1990. *The Theory of Industrial Organization*. MIT Press.

Titman, S. 1985. "Urban land prices under uncertainty." *American Economic Review* 75, no. 3: 505–514.

Tourinho, O. 1979. The Option Value of Reserves of Natural Resources. Working paper 94, University of California, Berkeley.

Triantis A., and J. Hodder. 1990. "Valuing flexibility as a complex option." *Journal of Finance* 45, no. 2: 549–565.

Trigeorgis, L. 1988. "A conceptual options framework for capital budgeting." *Advances in Futures and Options Research* 3: 145–167.

Trigeorgis, L. 1990a. "A real options application in natural resource investments." *Advances in Futures and Options Research* 4: 153–164.

Trigeorgis, L. 1990b. Valuing the Impact of Uncertain Competitive Arrivals on Deferrable Real Investment Opportunities. Working paper, Boston University.

Trigeorgis, L. 1991a. "Anticipated competitive entry and early preemptive investment in deferrable projects." *Journal of Economics and Business* 43, no. 2: 143–156.

Trigeorgis, L. 1991b. "A log-transformed binomial numerical analysis method for valuing complex multi-option investments." *Journal of Financial and Quantitative Analysis* 26, no. 3: 309–326.

Trigeorgis, L. 1993a. "The nature of option interactions and the valuation of investments with multiple real options." *Journal of Financial and Quantitative Analysis* 28, no. 1: 1–20.

Trigeorgis, L. 1993b. "Real options and interactions with financial flexibility." *Financial Management* 22, no. 3: 202–224.

Trigeorgis, L. (ed.). 1995a. *Real Options in Capital Investment: Models, Strategies, and Applications*. Praeger.

Trigeorgis, L. 1995b. "Evaluating leases with complex operating options." *European Journal of Operational Research* 75 (forthcoming).

Trigeorgis, L., and E. Kasanen. 1991. "An integrated options-based strategic planning and control model." *Managerial Finance* 17, no. 2/3: 16–28.

Trigeorgis, L., and S. P. Mason. 1987. "Valuing managerial flexibility." *Midland Corporate Finance Journal* 5, no. 1: 14–21.

Venezia, I., and M. Brenner. 1979. "The optimal duration of growth investments and search." *Journal of Business* 52, no. 3: 393–407.

Williams, J. 1991. "Real estate development as an option." *Journal of Real Estate Finance and Economics* 4, no. 2: 191–208.

Willner, R. 1995. "Valuing start-up venture growth options." In *Real Options in Capital Investment*, ed. L. Trigeorgis. Praeger.

Index

Abandonment option, 2, 4–5, 9, 12–13, 18, 140, 146, 358
applications of, 363
cost switching and, 188
decision-tree analysis of, 61–65
on dividend-paying project, 100
flexibility and, 126, 132, 143, 166–167
with multiple options, 245, 326–328
put, 5, 6, 67, 126
quantitative analysis of, 208–210
sensitivity analysis of, 242–243
timing and, 197
Abandonment value, 64–65, 143, 148–149
Acquisitions, 343–365
Active management, 193, 258, 269
Adaptive system, 190–196
After-tax borrowing rate, 350
Alteration of operating scale, 2
American call option, 69, 78–79, 94
Black-Scholes valuation of, 117
with dividends, 93, 276, 301
put-call parity and, 211
American put option, 69, 78, 82–83
Black-Scholes valuation of, 92
to cancel lease, 355
put-call parity and, 211
and switching of use, 243–246
valuation of, 329–331
without dividends, 310–311
Applications, 341–344, 363–365
Arbitrage, 73, 97, 102, 156, 215
Assets, nontraded, 101–107
Asymmetry, 367
management flexibility and, 121–124
switching costs and, 178–179
traditional valuation and, 151–152

Backward difference approximations, 319
Base-case analysis
for natural-resource projects, 358–360
in two-stage game, 294–298
Binomial distribution, 85
Binomial option pricing, 134, 370
application of, 347–349
flow chart for, 323
of natural-resource project, 356–363
process of, 84–87
risk-neutral probability and, 85, 338–339
vs. other methods, 329–336
Bivariate distribution, 212–217, 220–225, 237–239
Black-Scholes option pricing , 89–92, 346
American call, 117
dividend-adjusted, 99–100
European call, 92, 94, 109, 219, 280–281
European put, 117
exchange option, 211
finite-difference methods and, 312, 315, 318
formula for, 86–87, 131, 215, 217
log-transformation, 314
vs. other methods, 329–336
Poisson jumps and, 286
proprietary option, 287
riskless hedge portfolio and, 214
Bonds, 113–115
Brownian motion, 86–88, 230, 309, 320. *See also* Wiener process
Business strategy, 270

Call options, 1, 4, 69–71, 117
American. *See* American call option
Black-Scholes valuation of, 86–87, 91–92

Call options (cont.)
on common stock, 125, 128–129
compound, 126, 218–225, 238
compound exchange, 215–217
on dividend-paying stock, 287
European. *See* European call option
at expiration, 77
hedge ratio of, 92
perpetual, 79
risk-neutral valuation of, 75–76
value of, 73, 78, 81, 82
Cancel option, 354, 357–358
Capital
rationing of, 257
weighted average cost of, 47
Capital asset pricing model (CAPM), 40–52,
97–98, 118, 122, 127, 154
Capital budgeting, 129–145, 270, 367. *See
also* Certainty-equivalent approach;
Contingent-claims analysis; Discrete-time
analysis; Net present value; Risk-adjusted
discount rate
decision making in, 27–28, 368
failure of, 4–9
financial objective of, 23–24
implications of, 370–375
as ongoing process, 375
options in, 1–4
phases of, 259–260
strategic planning and, 7
Capital investment, 1. *See also* Capital
budgeting
Cash flows
adjustments for, 322–329 (*see also*
Dividends)
incremental, 191–196
for lease financing vs. buy-borrow, 350–
351
net, 132
Certainty-equivalent approach, 34–38, 48–
51, 57, 103, 119, 127, 309
Certainty-equivalent coefficient, 35
Commitment, 130, 134, 136–139, 296, 298
Committing and offensive strategy, 141,
294–298
Competition, 19–20, 273–302
analysis scenarios for, 277–281
contrarian, 137–142, 292–293
deferrable investment opportunity and,
276–277
dominance relationships and, 281–284

endogenous reaction in strategic
investment, 288–301
entry adjustments, 328–329
exogenous arrivals (jumps), 284–288, 328–
329
interactions, 128, 133–134, 372–373
investment opportunity value and, 301
quantity, 137–141, 290–293, 374
real options and, 19–20
reciprocating, 142
strategies, 140–142, 294–301
Competitive-jump equilibrium, 285–286
Competitive loss, 143, 149, 374
Complex options, 218–225
Compound analytic polynomial
approximation, 329–336
Compound exchange options, 215–217
Compoundness, 167, 203
cost switching and, 173, 177–184
interproject, 132–133, 196–197
intraproject, 132
Compound options, 132, 143–145, 196,
203, 213–215, 220–221, 251
Construction, 9–10. *See also* Default option;
Time-to-build option
Consumption, 25–26
Contingent-claims analysis, 95–107, 124,
152, 155–160, 169, 367–368
corporate liabilities and, 107
financial-options applications of, 115–116
fundamental pricing equation for, 95–98
nontraded assets and, 103–107
with one state variable, 101–103
with two state variables, 98–101
Continuous-time models, 203–225, 230, 237
Contract option, 9–12, 163–164
cost switching and, 187
with multiple options, 326–328
sensitivity analysis of, 242, 244
Control targets, 258–259, 265–269
Control-variate technique, 306, 310–311
Convenience yield, on nontraded assets,
103–107
Conversion process, in adaptive system,
190–196
Corporate liabilities, 107–116, 151
Cost switching, 172–188
Cournot quantity competition, 137, 374
Cox-Ross-Rubinstein binomial, 16, 308, 320,
329–339
Critical price (or value), 217

Debt
  callable coupon, 113
  convertible, 113–115
  zero-coupon, 109–111
Decision nodes, 132, 161
Decision problems, types of, 130
Decision-tree analysis, 23, 57–68, 152–161
Default option, 167–168, 197. *See also* Time-
  to-build option
Defer option, 2, 4, 9, 10, 17–18, 358
  applications, 363
  capital budgeting and, 144–145
  competition and, 140
  continuous-time analysis, 204–208
  discrete-time analysis, 158–161
  with multiple options, 245, 326–328
  sensitivity analysis, 240–242
  switching costs and, 186–187
Deferrability value, 144, 149, 159, 374
Dependence, interproject, 261
Diffusion process, 96, 107, 116, 204, 208–
  210, 215, 218, 309, 320
Discounted-cash-flow analysis, 1, 8, 127,
  132, 152, 170
  applications, 367
  bias and, 7
  decision-tree analysis and, 160–161
  in lease valuation, 350–352
  limitations, 4–9, 15
  natural-resource project, 359
  traditional, 154–155
Discounting, multiple periods, 48
Discount rates, 48, 215. *See also* Risk-
  adjusted discount rate
  with abandonment option, 4–7
  constant, 51, 67
  decision-tree analysis and, 67–68
  single or constant risk-adjusted, 161
Discrete-time analysis, 84–87, 152–201
Diversification, 41
Dividends, 79, 93–95, 102, 118, 275–277,
  287, 301, 325–326, 372
Dominance, in investment strategies, 281–
  284
Dynamic programming, 57, 179, 185, 305,
  312, 324, 337

Equity, 108–110
Euler formula, 215
European call options, 69, 93, 213
  Black-Scholes valuation of, 92, 94, 109,
  219, 280–281

compound, 213–214, 236
multiple option interactions and, 231, 235
to purchase lease, 355–356
value of, 79, 118–119
European put options, 69, 90
  Black-Scholes valuation of, 92, 117, 219
  multiple option interactions and, 231, 235,
  242
  value of, 80, 83
  without dividends, 310–311
Exchange option, 16, 210–213, 222–225
Exercise, optimal, 261
Exercise boundary, 220
Exercise price, 4, 69–70, 124, 209, 322
Expansion option. *See* Growth option
Expiration date, 69–70
Expiring options, 144–145
Extend lease option, 354

Financing decision, 28–29, 32
Finite-difference methods, 305–306, 312–
  320, 329–337
Flexibility, 8, 15, 136, 151, 227
  to abandon, 126, 132, 143, 166–167
  active management and, 367
  in adaptive firm, 192–194
  applications of, 367–368
  capital budgeting and, 121–126, 132
  to defer, 131–132
  examples of, 153–155, 158–168
  financial, 168–172
  financial-operating interaction, 168–172
  interest-rate uncertainty and, 197–200
  manufacturing/production, 364
  multiple options, 228–230
  operating, 168–172, 357–358, 368, 371
  to optimally time project initiation, 273 (*see
    also* Defer option)
  potential (unrealized), 190
  process, 13, 188–189
  product, 13, 189
  quantifying (*see* Continuous-time models;
    Discrete-time analysis)
  to switch operating modes, 171–196
Flexible manufacturing, 14, 189–190, 364
Flexible and offensive strategy, 298–301
Forward-looking techniques, 56, 185, 305.
  See also Monte Carlo simulation
Free-boundary problems, 57
Fundamental pricing equation, 95–98, 102,
  107
Futures contracts, 69–70, 103–107

Game theory, 20, 129, 301–302
Gamma distribution, 286
Government subsidies, 364
Growth options, 2, 9–15, 197, 258, 358
  applications of, 344–347, 363
  cost switching and, 187
  discrete-time analysis of, 162–163
  with multiple options, 326–328
  sensitivity analysis of, 243, 245
  strategic interactions and, 261, 264–266

Hedge ratio (delta), 74, 76, 91–92
Hedging, 72, 75, 156, 214
Hysteresis, 185–186

Incentives, 258
Infrastructure, 14–15
Interactions, 3, 18–19, 168–170, 228–256,
  258, 368–369
  interproject, 132–133, 143–144, 196–197
  intraproject, 143–144, 167
Interdependencies, 215–217
Interest-rate uncertainty, 197–200
Internal rate of return, 26, 30, 53, 54
Investment, shared, 137, 140–143, 298–
  301, 374
Investment, strategic, 4, 131–132, 140–142,
  264–266
  active project management over time, 269
  commitment, 130–131
  cost-reduction, 263
  dominance relationships, 281–284
  early, 275–277
  endogenous competitive reaction in, 288–
  301
  evaluation of, 142–143
  optimal, 26, 30, 261, 374
  shared, 298–301
  timing of, 273–274
Investment opportunity, 151, 158, 170, 207
  with abandon option, 166
  with contract option, 163
  with default option, 167
  with defer option, 158
  with expand (growth) option, 162
  expiring, 144
  with multiple real options, 227–232
  shared-simple-deferrable, 149
  with temporary shut down option, 164
  valuation, 133–134
Investment options, 124–126. See also Real
  options

Investor, diversification by, 41
Ito process, 88
Ito's lemma, 89, 90, 96

Jump processes
  mixed diffusion-jump, 286
  pure, 284–285
  trinomial, 316, 318
Jumps
  exogenous, 328–329
  Poisson, 273, 284–288, 301, 369–370

Killing options, 350, 373

Land, valuation of, 347–349, 364
Lattice approaches, 305–306, 337
Learning curve, 276
Leasing contracts, 349–356, 364
Loan guarantee value, 111–112
Log-transformed binomial, 320–329

Market-equilibrium model, 17
Market opportunity line, 27, 29
Market risk premium, 34, 103. See also Risk
  premium
Market structure, 139–140, 290–293
Markov process, 86–88, 321. See also
  Stochastic process; Wiener process
Markov random walk, 320–321
Martingale approach, 218–225
Maturity date, 69–70
Monopoly, 134, 140, 298
Multi-factor asset-pricing model, 97
Multiple options, 3, 254–256
  adjustments, 326–328
  flexibility, 229–230
  interactions, 232–239
  interdependencies and, 18–19
  investment opportunity, 227–232
  magnitude (or degree) of interaction, 234–
  239, 247
  negative interaction, 245, 249, 256
  net present value, 229–230
  nonadditivity of option values, 232–239
  positive interaction, 234, 249–252, 256
  separation vs. degree of interaction, 248
  valuation results, 240–254
  valuation with interactions, 244–254
Multiplicative binomial option pricing, 84–
  87, 329–339
Myers-Dill-Baustista lease valuation, 349,
  350, 355

Nash-Cournot equilibrium, 291–293, 296
Nash equilibrium, 134, 139, 141, 298
Natural-resource project
  sensitivity analysis of, 360–363
  valuation of, 356–363
Net present value, 1, 4, 23–25, 29, 48, 132, 200, 208
  under certainty, 25–32
  certainty-equivalent form, 47, 50–51
  correctness of, 24–52, 127
  expanded expected, 61, 66, 122–123
  expanded or strategic, 121–124, 134, 149, 152–153, 160, 200, 258, 283, 367, 371
  expected, 49, 55–56, 59–60
  interest-rate uncertainty and, 198–199
  multiple-options example, 229–230
  and natural-resource projects, 9–10, 360–363
  negative (passive or static), 19, 125, 160, 229–230, 367, 371
  positive, 197–198
  probability distribution of, 55–56, 68, 122–123, 155
  risk-adjusted-discount-rate form of, 48, 50, 59
  static, passive, or traditional, 11, 124, 126, 130–131, 134, 145, 148–150, 152, 229–230, 283, 371
  under uncertainty, 32–52
  value-maximizing, 258–259, 268
Numerical methods or techniques, 20–21, 305–337
Numerical comparisons, 329–336

Operating lease options, 349–356
Operating modes, 171–196
Operating options, 158–168. See also Real options and specific types of operating options
Operating strategy, 121–122, 147–150
Option premium, 71, 122–124, 147–149, 152, 160, 371–373
Option pricing, 349, 367, 376–377. See also Binomial option pricing; Black-Scholes model; Black-Scholes option pricing; Contingent-claims analysis; Finite-difference methods
  continuous-time, 89–92, 203–205
  corporate liabilities, 107–116
  vs. decision-tree analysis, 153–161
  discrete-time analysis of (see Discrete-time analysis)
  dividend adjustments, 93–95
  fundamental equation, 95–98, 107
  vs. futures contracts, 69–70
  numerical comparison of methods, 329–336
  numerical techniques, 20–21, 305–307
  quantitative (continuous-time), 20, 203–225
  rational properties, 77–83
  replication, with synthetic options, 72–77
  risk-neutral, 16–17, 20
  simulation, 309–312
  standard assumptions of, 83
  synthetic, 72–77
  theory of, 69–107
  valuation idea, basic, 72–77
Options. See Real options and specific options
Options analogy, 127–129
Option-value additivity, 172–177, 184, 234–237, 254
Ordinary least-squares regression analysis, 42–43
Organizational capabilities, 195–196
Ownership
  exclusiveness of, 142–143
  nonexclusiveness of, 128

Pharmaceutical industry, 341–343
Pioneer venture, 344–347
Poisson distribution, 328
Poisson jumps, 273, 284–288, 301, 369–370
Portfolio
  insurance, 72
  replicating, 72–74
  riskless hedge, 75, 97, 214
Preemption, 128–129, 136, 140, 275–277, 280
Prisoners' dilemma, 373
Product flexibility, 189
Productive-investment decision, 27–28, 32
Productive-opportunity curve, 26–30
Projects
  deferrable, 144 (see also Defer option)
  immediate accept-or-reject decisions on, 144, 269
  initiation of, in preemptive competition, 273–284
  interdependence of (see Interactions)
  investment, active management, 258, 269
  with multiple options, 9–14, 153–190, 227–229, 356–359

Projects (cont.)
  multi-stage, 38, 132 (*see also* Compound
    options)
  natural resource, 356–363
  new classification, 129–134
  parallel, synergy in, 262–264, 270
  sequential interdependencies, 264–266,
    270
  strategic interactions in sets of, 261–266
  valuation of, 257–261
Proprietary (or exclusive) options, 128, 140,
  143–148, 279, 372
Pseudo-American option, 93–94, 281
Put-call parity, 80, 92, 112, 211, 219, 222–
  225
Put options, 4–7, 12, 69–72, 126
  abandonment, 5, 6, 67, 209–210, 242–
    243
  American, 82–83, 209–210, 243
  compound, 218–225
  compound exchange, 224–225
  at expiration, 77
  government subsidies, 364
  guarantee, 4–7, 72
  hedge ratio, 76
  pricing theory, 76–77, 92, 101, 209, 225,
    243
  risk-neutral valuation and, 76–77, 219

Random walk, 83, 320–321
Real options, 1–4, 69. *See also specific real
  options*
  applications of, 341–344, 363–365
  collections of, 124–126, 227
  competition and, 19–20, 273–303
  compound, 129 (*see also* Compound
    options)
  conceptual framework of, 15–16, 121–150,
    371
  criticisms and remedies of, 14–15
  deferrable, 144 (*see also* Defer option)
  examples of, 9–14
  exercising immediately, 277–279
  foundations of, 16
  hedge ratio of, 74, 76, 91–92
  interactions of, 3, 18–19, 228–256, 258,
    368–369
  interdependencies of, 18–19 (*see also*
    Interactions)
  literature on, 3–4, 14–21, 363–365
  multiple. *See* Multiple options
  nontradability of, 128–129

preemption of, 128–129, 136, 140, 275–
  277, 280
premium, 122–124, 147–149, 152, 160,
  371–373
proprietary (*see* Proprietary options)
separate valuation of, 17–18, 240–244
shared, 128, 143–148, 374
strategy and, 19–20, 257–261, 273–284,
  288–303, 375–377
valuation of (*see* Option pricing)
Renew option, 354
Research and development, 14, 58–65, 67,
  294–301, 341–342, 364, 375–376
Research, future directions for, 375–376
Restart operations, 12, 18, 187. *See also* Shut
  down
Reward-to-variability ratio, 47, 97
Risk
  adjustment of, 16–17, 34–38
  allowance for, 32–52 (*see also* Uncertainty)
  category of, 38
  diversifiable, 43
  market, 43, 56, 98
  market price of, 47, 97, 218
  nondiversifiable, 43, 56, 98
  premium, 34, 36, 97, 103, 119, 309
  profiles, 54
  systematic, 43, 56, 98
  total, 43, 56 (*see also* Variance)
  unsystematic, 43
Risk-adjusted discount rate, 35–37, 48, 50,
  255
Risk-neutral expectations, 102, 119, 218,
  309, 367
Risk-neutral growth rate, 102, 118, 127
Risk neutrality, 98, 367
Risk-neutral probability, 75–76, 85, 102,
  157, 218–219, 265, 290, 318
  dividends and, 93
  in log-transformed binomial model, 338–
    339
Risk-neutral stochastic process, 218
Risk-neutral valuation, 16–17, 20, 57, 75–
  77, 91–94, 101–103, 199–200, 215, 218–
  225, 290, 348

Salvage value, 166, 210. *See also*
  Abandonment option
Security characteristic line, 42, 44
Security market line, 44–47
Sensitivity analysis, 52–54
  abandonment option and, 242–243

contract option and, 242, 244
defer option and, 240–242
expansion option and, 243, 245
limitations of, 53–54
of natural-resource project, 356–363
risk-adjusted discount rate and, 255
switch use option and, 243–246
Shared options, 143–145
Shortfall, 17, 102, 118, 217–218, 285, 288
Shut down (temporarily) option, 2, 12, 18, 164–166, 187, 208–209
applications of, 363
continuous-time analysis of, 208–209
Simple options, 144–145
Simulation, 336
Monte Carlo, 54–57, 155, 306, 309–312
in option valuation, 309–312
traditional techniques of, 54–57
Slack, managerial, 267
Stackelberg leader-follower game, 134, 139–140, 290–293, 296, 298
Standard diffusion process, 88, 215. See also Wiener process
Start-up venture. See Pioneer venture
Stochastic process, 87–89, 93. See also Markov process; Wiener process
Stock, common, 70, 128
Stock prices, behavior of. See also Wiener process
discrete-time, 88
stochastic process and, 87–89
Strategic investment, 258, 288, 296, 301
Strategic planning
active project management and, 269
capital budgeting and, 7
framework of, 257–261
Strategies, 137
competitive, 140–142
dominating, 281–284
real options and, 19–20, 257–261, 273–284, 288–303, 375–377
in two-stage games, 134–135, 288–290
Strike price. See Exercise price
Switching costs, 171–190
Switch use option, 3, 9, 13, 16, 126, 151, 166–167, 203, 236
compound exchange, 215–217
costs and, 177–184
flexibility, 171–196
with multiple options, 326–328
sensitivity analysis, 243–246
Synergy, 262–264, 270

Taylor-series expansion, 89
Time-preference curve, 25–26
Time-to-build option, 2, 10–11, 188, 207–208
Trinomial jump process, 316, 318
Twin security, 17, 153–156

Uncertainty
decision-tree analysis and, 57–68
net present value and, 32–52
sensitivity analysis and, 52–54
traditional simulation and, 54–57

Value components, 147–150, 373
Value-maximizing strategy, 257–271
Variance (standard deviation), 40
Ventures, 344–347. See also Pioneer venture

Wiener process, 86–90, 95–96, 107, 218, 230, 275, 286, 309, 320. See also Stochastic process